PRAIRIE CO-OPERATION — A DIARY

by Jack Trevena

Author:

Jack Trevena

Secretarial Officer
Federated Co-operatives Limited
Saskatoon, Saskatchewan

Research Consultant:

Dr. Ian MacPherson, B.A., M.A., Ph.D.,
Associate Professor, University of Winnipeg

Editor:

Elaine Kisiow
Co-operative Curriculum Project

Photographic Researcher:

Gary Moir
Co-operative Curriculum Project

Production Director:

Martin O'Connor
Director, Co-operative Curriculum Project

Published By:

Co-operative College of Canada
Saskatoon, Saskatchewan

Acknowledgements

The Co-operative College of Canada gratefully acknowledges the
contribution of Federated Co-operatives Limited and the Government of
Manitoba Co-operative Curriculum Project toward the research,
development and design of PRAIRIE CO-OPERATION—A DIARY.

ISBN 0-88817-002-5

Printed in Canada by Public Press for
Co-operative College of Canada
141-105th Street,
Saskatoon, Saskatchewan

Preface

Co-operatives are people joining together to provide some form of service for each individual member.

The story of co-operatives in Western Canada, where a high degree of **co-operative development** has taken place within the last seventy-five years, is both interesting and enlightening.

Co-operatives have played a significant role in the social and economic development of our nation, especially the prairies. Today co-operatives are an important part of the financial field taking such forms as credit unions, insurance and trust co-operatives. Primary producer and marketing co-operatives have arisen in the areas of dairy, poultry, livestock, fruit, grain, fishery and handicraft industries. Agricultural machinery co-operatives, fertilizer, lumber and petroleum co-operatives have recently become a natural part of the growth of manufacturing in Western Canada. As well, a large variety of retailing, consumer, service, housing and medical co-operatives have become a recent addition to the development of co-operative enterprise.

Federated Co-operatives Limited is pleased that a member of its staff has undertaken to research the co-operative movement in Western Canada. **PRAIRIE CO-OPERATION,** provides a chronology of co-operative development in the Western Prairie Provinces. But even more important **PRAIRIE CO-OPERATION** gives the reader an insight into the political, social and economic climate that provided the base for the Co-operative Movement in Western Canada.

Gordon M. Sinclair, President
Federated Co-operatives Limited
Saskatoon, Saskatchewan

1

CHAPTER 1
CO-OPERATION

An observant visitor to Canada's Prairie Provinces can easily see that co-operative organizations are much in evidence. For here are to be found the world's largest grain handling co-operatives; the world's first co-operatively-owned petroleum refinery; an impressive number of credit unions; and more retail Co-operatives in Saskatchewan alone than in the United States. There are insurance co-operatives, health care co-ops, housing co-ops, a co-operative college, and numerous others. If he probes a bit deeper, a visitor may discover in the Prairie Provinces another type of organization known as a 'farm organization'. Though few in number as compared to co-operatives, farm organizations have always played an important part in the development and protection of Prairie agriculture.

FARM ORGANIZATIONS

Co-operatives and farm organizations, though basically formed for different purposes as will be explained, have important features in common. Both are a means by which people, as members, practise co-operation--the art of working together for a common purpose. Democracy is an important feature of both types of organizations. The leaders, elected by the members, are responsible to the membership they serve and, through the democratic process, leaders can be replaced if the majority of the members become dissatisfied with their activities.

Farm organizations differ from co-operatives in terms of their basic function. A co-operative is usually formed for a commercial purpose such as buying or selling, or to provide a commercial service to its members. Farm organizations are not formed to undertake commercial ventures. More likely, a farm organization exists to unite farmer-members in efforts to persuade governments to adopt agricultural policies favorable to the farmers.

The distinction outlined in the last paragraph is not iron-clad, for farmer-owned co-operatives not infrequently become concerned with agricultural policies and, on occasion, farm organizations will venture into some forms of commercial activity.

Indeed, years ago, and particularly prior to 1913, when legislation enabling co-operatives to be incorporated was passed by each of the three Prairie Provinces, farm organizations of the time did much to encourage co-operative activities. At that time, members of farm organizations, when coming together for a meeting of their local chapters, would often use the occasion to club together for the purchase of necessities. They practised co-operation as they worked together to pool their needs for such goods as barb wire, fence posts, lumber, flour, apples, coal, and other necessities that could be purchased in bulk. The farmers would attempt to buy a railway carlot direct from the miller or other source of supply. When it arrived, they would come together to unload the car, each taking and paying his share, and saving the profit that would otherwise have accrued to middlemen and merchants.

Outside of the early farm organizations, co-operation was displayed by pioneer farmers in many other ways. Legendary are the building bees of early times. When a homesteader arrived to settle on a farm holding, his first need was to build a house and a barn. It was a common occurrence for his neighbors to volunteer their labour to help with the construction. In the little communities that sprang up along the railway lines, co-operation through building bees led to the construction of many of the first churches and schoolhouses of pioneer days.

It was co-operation, but even more; it was the practise of the Golden Rule: "Do unto others as you would have them do unto you." For the farmer who helped his neighbor to raise a barn without pay, knew that he could count on his neighbors to help him at time of need. Obviously then, co-operation made a most important contribution to the taming of the Prairies for it helped pioneer settlers, who seldom had wealth, to cope with conditions that were to them strange, severe, and near-insurmountable.

CO-OPERATIVES

During the nineteenth and early twentieth centuries, many people used to think that men were naturally competitive and that competition was essential for progress. Some people disagreed then and now people today disagree. One scholar, Dr. Ashley Montagu, has even argued, "Man was born for co-operation, not for conflict."

When people practise co-operation in order to work together to provide themselves with goods or services they require, they usually set up a formal organization known as a co-operative or a co-operative association, through which to carry on their activities.

DEFINITION OF A CO-OPERATIVE

A co-operative is an organization, created for the practise of co-operation. People voluntarily join a co-operative so they can own and democratically control and patronize the means of providing themselves with goods or services. Any cost savings from the

Barn Raising

activities of co-operatives are shared by the members in ratio to the patronage each member has given.

The foregoing is but a broad, generalized definition of a co-operative. It needs to be examined in more detail to be well understood. For that reason, words and phrases are elaborated upon as follows.

A Co-operative is an organization: Incorporated under either provincial or federal law; co-operatives differ from other incorporated bodies in many ways, the most important of them being:

(a) In private profit businesses, earnings are distributed to shareholders according to the number of shares each holds. In a co-operative, earnings are distributed to members according to the extent to which each member patronizes the organization.

(b) In annual meetings of private profit enterprise, the shareholders are entitled to a vote for each share they hold. In a co-operative, each member has but one vote, regardless of how many shares the member may have.

(c) Proxy voting is permitted in a private profit enterprise, which means that one shareholder may vote on behalf of other shareholders. By that means, one shareholder, or small group of shareholders, may wield great voting power to control the company. Co-operatives do not permit proxy voting, hence ensure that decisions generally reflect the will of the majority of members present.

(d) Shares of private profit businesses may be bought, sold, or exchanged for speculative purposes. From day to day, the company may not know exactly who holds its shares. On the other hand, the shares of a co-operative are not purchased by its members for speculative purposes, but as a condition of membership and a means by which members provide their co-operative with a portion of its capital requirements.

People Voluntarily Become Members: People who desire to become members of a co-operative are expected to complete an application for membership, and to invest in one or more shares of the organization. The application must be approved by the organization's board of directors to be valid. The board may reject an applicant if it appears that the reason for joining is not in the interests of the organization, or when an applicant is unable to qualify for membership. For example, a farmer-owned co-operative such as a wheat pool, would reject an application by a person who neither owned nor operated a farm because such a person could not use the services provided.

To Own: A co-operative must be owned by the members it serves. That is a fundamental requirement of a true co-operative, for if ownership were held by outside parties apart from the membership, the members could not have exclusive right to control their organization or to retain the benefits it provides.

To Democratically Control: Co-operative legislation requires that a co-operative hold an annual general membership meeting. All members must be notified in advance. At these meetings, the members receive reports on the operation of their co-operative. The members may also prepare and consider resolutions, or otherwise express their desires respecting policies and programs to be followed.

Most important, the members nominate and elect, usually from their own ranks, a board of directors to act on their behalf during the coming year. A key responsibility of the board is to appoint a general manager, and to ensure that the co-operative is operated by the manager according to the policies established by the members, through their board.

As previously noted, each member has one vote at co-op meetings, regardless of the number of shares he holds or the extent to which he patronizes the co-operative. This limitation ensures that the organization does not become dominated by a minority group that may influence policies in its own particular interest.

In a very large co-operative it may be impractical to attempt to assemble all or even a good portion of the members for a meeting. Thus, when a co-operative has a large number of members, it may divide the membership into groupings based on districts or even subdistricts. The members of each district would be invited to attend local meetings to discuss affairs of their co-operative, and to elect, from their ranks, delegates to act for them at the organization's annual meeting. Where a delegate system is employed, it is usually the delegates who elect the board of directors.

Patronize the Means of Providing Themselves With Goods and Services: Through ownership and democratic control, members assure themselves that their co-operatives will serve them as they desire to be served, and return the resulting economic advantages to them according to the patronage each member has given. It should be obvious that if the members do not patronize their own business, they prevent it from carrying out its basic purpose.

There are, of course, different types of co-operatives to serve different purposes:

(a) **Marketing Co-operatives:** These are also known as "producers' co-operatives" and, as the terms imply, are formed by producers of agricultural or other commodities for the marketing of their production. Examples include the wheat pools which operate country elevators through which farmers market their grain; co-operative dairies; honey co-ops to serve beekeepers; livestock marketing co-ops; and co-operatives for marketing fruit, vegetables, fish, handicrafts, and many other products. Marketing co-operatives may become involved in allied activities such as flour milling, fish filleting and processing, and so forth, but their basic purpose is that of assisting producers to ensure themselves the utmost of fair returns for their produce.

(b) **Retailing Co-operatives:** *Also known as consumers, supply and purchasing co-operatives. The purpose of these organizations is to supply members with various types of merchandise they require at fair, reasonable prices, with due concern for quality and ethical trading practises. Examples include the UFA Co-operative which operates a number of outlets in Alberta. Another example is The Co-operative Retailing System comprised of more than 400 retailing co-operatives in the four Western Provinces and N.W. Ontario. This system collectively owns and controls Federated Co-operatives Limited, which provides its member societies with wholesaling, manufacturing and other services. The purpose of this system is described by its Mission:*

"The Mission of The Co-operative Retailing System is to foster social justice by improving the economic position of its members through co-ordinated procurement, manufacturing and distribution of goods and/or services while providing individual members with a sense of belonging to, and participation in an organization of their own."

(c) **Financial Co-operatives:** *The term embraces a host of co-operatives providing various kinds of financial services to members. Most numerous are credit unions which offer savings, loan, and other services. There are also co-operative credit societies that serve as central organizations for the credit unions. Other financial co-operatives in Canada include insurance co-operatives; a co-operative trust company; and a co-operative superannuation society to provide retirement income for employees of co-operatives.*

(d) **Service Co-operatives:** *The term is used to describe a broad range of co-operatives formed to provide a particular type of service to members. In Alberta, for example, electrical co-ops were formed by farmers to provide service in areas not served by electrical utility companies. In many rural communities, co-*operatives have been formed to provide and operate community halls and curling rinks; some even have snowplow co-ops to clear roadways. Across the Prairies one may find seed cleaning co-ops; machinery co-ops; health care co-ops; funeral co-ops; co-operative day-care centres to help working mothers; handicraft co-operatives; and many others. The great variety indicates that co-operation and co-operatives can be adapted to serve an almost endless list of needs or purposes.

Cost Savings . . . Are Shared By Members: *One of the most distinctive features of a co-operative is that it returns to its members, the people who own and control it, whatever surpluses result from its operation after income tax and other expenses are paid.*

Members share the surpluses according to the extent to which each contributed to them by patronage of the co-operative. Thus, the term, "patronage refund" or "patronage dividend" is used to describe the return to members

A patronage refund may not be returned immediately in cash, but may be held by the co-operative in the member's name and joined with whatever sum the member deposited in shares upon joining the organization. In this way the members, as owners of the co-operative, meet their obligation to provide their organization with the capital it needs in order to provide facilities and carry on its operations. Further, the members, either directly or through the delegates or board of directors they elect, make decisions as to whether all or part of the patronage refund or accumulated patronage refunds, will be returned in cash.

Generally speaking, co-operatives aim to return all possible cash to members, for doing so is to prove that the organization is efficiently serving them. When cash repayments are made, priority is given to full repayment of equities of deceased members, and to those members who have either reached retirement age or conditions as described by the bylaws of the co-operatives, or who can no longer use the services of the co-op because they have moved away, retired from farming, etc.

Operating surpluses result mainly from the loyal patronage provided by members coupled with the co-operative's operating efficiency. The co-operative provides goods and services to its members at competitive prices, but may charge a lower price if the competitive price appears to be exhorbitant. Thus, members are assured of a fair price at the time of transacting business, and may expect a further reduction through patronage refunds. The effects of the patronage refund are twofold: (1) to eliminate the profit

3

motive from co-operatives, and (2) to reduce the final price paid by members to the bare cost of providing the goods or services.

As the late Dr. J.P. Warbasse asserted, the co-operative does not seek to create income for its members, but to reduce their outgo—their cost of marketing, of buying merchandise, of providing themselves with financial and other services.

REASONS FOR CO-OPERATIVES

A definition of co-operatives, an explanation of types, purposes, and methods of co-operatives is really not enough if one does not understand why people form and join co-operatives. True, the patronage refund and cash returns that result in provision of services "at cost" are an important attraction. But when one stops to think of the need for members to provide capital, to attend meetings, and to accept other responsibilities, and to realize that their delegates, board members, and other elected officers devote countless hours to co-operative work and often without remuneration, it begins to become obvious that the value of co-operation and co-operatives goes far beyond the patronage refund.

We need, therefore, to list some of the reasons why co-operatives were formed:

(a) Most important in the formation of early Prairie co-ops, and still of concern, was the need for people to decrease the power which others held and used against them. An outstanding example is provided by the experience of farmers before grain handling co-ops were formed. Private elevator companies operated to the disadvantage of farmers and to their own advantage, by offering low grades for grain, taking excess dockage and sometimes scaling short weights. Farmers who complained were told they could "take it or leave it," and because they had no other means of moving their grain, they could only succumb to the power of the elevator companies. Their answer eventually was to form co-operatives to provide them with elevator services.

Similarly, many of the earlier retail co-ops were born because farmers felt a need to act against the power of merchants who charged excessively high prices. Later, credit unions were formed in part, at least, to provide loans at more moderate rates of interest.

(b) Many co-operatives were formed to provide a service that other forms of enterprise were not willing to offer. The electric co-ops in Alberta are an example. In areas that power companies would not serve, farmers formed co-ops through which they got electrical services. In the Saskatchewan community of Wilkie, a movie theatre is co-operatively owned by local people and the credit union. The owner decided to sell out but could find no buyer and had decided to abandon the facility. The community and its surrounding area would have been without a theatre. It was then that co-operators acted and bought out the theatre, ensuring its continued service to the community. As a bonus, they were able to control the type of films shown, selecting those that were acceptable to most people, avoiding those regarded as trash or obscene.

(c)   In many smaller rural centres, co-operatives are needed to help keep the community alive. Since the mid-1930's, the rural population of the Prairie provinces has been declining. The effect has been felt by local businesses, and many have closed out. When that happens, people remaining in the community and its surrounding area are deprived of local services. They are further deprived because the resulting loss of taxation revenue forces the community to curtail its services. In such situations people turn to co-operatives to provide themselves with local stores and other services they need, knowing that their co-operative will remain as long as they give it the support it must have. Thus, in many communities, co-operatives are by far the largest taxpayers. Because they are there, people come to the community to shop. As they do, they also patronize other local businesses so that they too benefit. In one Alberta community local businessmen, through their Chamber of Commerce, took the lead in forming a retail co-operative to operate a food store. At the time the community had no food store, so that people went to other towns for their groceries and the local business-men suffered as a result.

(d)   Many co-operators deplore the fact that many business places in their communities, large and small, are owned by people living in far off places and whom they do not know. Profits earned by the businesses are taken away to those far off places. On the other hand, a co-operative returns its earnings to its members, thereby helping to keep that money within the community. Economists say that every dollar a co-operative returns to a community will generate at least $5 worth of business activity in that centre.

(e)   There are many people, not all of them co-op members, who are alarmed at the extent to which Canada's industries and resources are owned or controlled from outside this country. Co-operatives owned and controlled by the members they serve, are recognized as Canadian-owned.

(f)   Further afield, it is of interest to note that organizations of United Nations encourage the formation of co-operatives among people of developing nations. When introduced to co-operative techniques people of those nations learn to organize to help themselves. In so doing they learn to practise democracy. Canada has had similar experience as a result of assisting native people in the Far North to form co-operatives to operate stores and to market fish, furs, needlework, carvings and other artwork, etc. Indeed, many renowned leaders have expressed encouragement for co-operatives, the following being but a few examples:

"Leading economists of today, both in England and the United States, are pretty well one in the favor with which they view the Co-operative Movement as a movement exceptionally beneficial from the point of view of enabling the mass of the people to improve their own conditions, and from the point of view of the general betterment and welfare of the people of the country."

—W.L. Mackenzie-King
former Prime Minister of Canada

"If all nations were to approach the task of improving economic and social conditions both at home and beyond their borders in the same spirit that motivates the Co-operative Movement, a great contribution would be made to human welfare and real progress would be made towards the establishment of permanent world peace."

—Rt. Hon. Louis St. Laurent
former Prime Minister of Canada

"I would have you reflect on the security which the development of co-operative methods provides against the tyranny of trusts and combines. There is no guarantee that the power of a trust will not be used against the general well-being of both producers and consumers. The Co-operative movement provides a safeguard against this danger, of a value proportionate to its strength."

—Earl Grey, former Governor General of Canada
and donor of the Grey Cup Football Trophy

"Co-operative and mutual business has been a very important and constructive part of our free economy ever since Benjamin

Franklin organized the first mutual insurance company in Philadelphia in 1752. It is one of the finest expressions of the American spirit. Here groups of people, faced with common needs, invest their capital and organize their own co-operatives to meet those needs. This is self-help at its best."

-John F. Kennedy
former U.S. President

"By mobilizing the many co-operative organizations throughout the world to stimulate the development of co-operative movements in developing countries you will be making a greatly needed contribution to the implementation of the goals of the second United Nations development decade."

-U. Thant,
Secretary-General of United Nations

BIRTH OF A MOVEMENT

As industrialization and urbanization changed European society in the nineteenth century, many people in all European countries organized co-operatives. In time, emigrants from Europe would repeat the experiments of their fathers in Canada; in time, too, news of the European experiments brought back by reporters and visitors from Canada would provide valuable guidelines for Canadian development. The most important European precedents, however, were British, partly because of the political ties between Canada and Great Britain mostly because so many British co-operators emigrated to Canada between 1890 and 1930.

The story of how a small band of people who became known as the "Pioneers of Rochdale" formed the world's first successful co-operative has been told and retold countless times. It was on the evening of Saturday, December 21, 1844, that they opened for the first time, a tiny shop on the ground floor of a warehouse at No. 31 Toad Lane in the flannel weaving town of Rochdale, Lancashire, England.

The Pioneers were not the first to attempt co-operative enterprise. They did, however, put together a set of policies and methods, which became known as "principles", that were so wisely conceived as to ensure success of their venture. Before then, as early as 1760, workmen at Woolwich and Chatham, England, indignant over high prices charged by corn (grain) millers, organized themselves to own and operate a corn mill. In Ayrshire,

Scotland, in 1769, a co-operative store, probably the first, was begun. A similar store opened in 1795 at Oldham, England. It appears that a good number of others were formed throughout Britain before the Rochdale Pioneers opened their store. Robert Owen, for example, spoke of having visited Carlyle in 1836, where he saw "six or seven" co-operative societies.

Even in the town of Rochdale there was a predecessor to the Pioneers' store. Its stalwarts rented a house at No. 15 Toad Lane, setting up a shop in the "front" room. It was agreed that the manager, J. Read, lived in the house and opened the store for business in the evenings. It was so popular that soon it was open all day. Patrons would purchase their supplies on weekdays, and Mr. Read would make note of what they had taken expecting that, in accordance with the rules of the "Co-op Shop", payment would be made the following Saturday when the workers received their wages. Unfortunately, as the impoverished workers lost their jobs or got too far into debt, payments fell behind with the result that the Co-op Shop, strangled by credit, was closed in 1835. But it was not forgotten. It had proven that workers could organize to operate their own store, and it had shown them some of the pitfalls they must avoid in future ventures of that kind.

For more than a year before opening their store, the Pioneers met frequently to discuss their venture. They could not act with haste, for they did not have the necessary capital. Wages were low and unemployment was rampant at the time. But, in the year, they put aside pennies at a time until they had put together the hardly great sum of 28 pounds. At a meeting on August 11, 1844, the Pioneers committed themselves to open a store. They elected their officers, and two of their number, Charles Howarth and James Daly, were appointed to draw up the rules ("principles") for their organization. The two examined conditions required by the Friendly Societies Act, and considered reasons why other co-operative ventures had not met with greater success. It was Howarth who put the crowning touch to the rules when he conceived the idea of returning the profits or surpluses to members in measure to the extent by which each member helped to create them through patronizing the store. The result was a rule: "That at each quarterly general meeting the officers in their financial statement shall publish the amount of profit realized during the preceding quarter which shall be divided thus: interest at the rate of three-and-a-half per cent per annum shall be paid upon all shares paid up previous to the quarter's commencement; the remaining profits shall be paid to each member in proportion to the amount of money expended at the stores." It was Howarth, then, who was responsible for introducing the concept of a "patronage refund" or patronage dividend, to the Rochdale Society of Equitable Pioneers, as the organization was called.

Whether Howarth actually "invented" the patronage refund is argued. Brown notes that Archibald Campbell had advocated in Glasgow, in 1830, that profits be turned back to customers instead of to investors. He notes also that the patronage dividend scheme had been tried at Meltham Mills some 17 years before 1844. At any rate, the rules were drawn up and were certified, October 24, 1844, as conforming to the Friendly Societies Act. Some 250 copies were printed and sold for twopence each.

It is not greatly useful here to dwell at length on the rules of "principles", for of necessity they were, in good measure, contrived to fit the needs and conditions of the times. It was reasonable that they would be altered as social, economic, and political conditions changed in years to come. These matters will be subjects for Chapter II.

It is more important at this point to note that the Rochdale Society of Equitable Pioneers was not only highly successful, but provided an inspiring example that was quickly followed by many others. By 1863, there were sufficient co-operative societies to enable the Co-operative Wholesale Society to be formed in England; it was soon followed by the Scottish Co-operative Wholesale Society. The two amalgamated in 1973. In addition, at a congress held in London in 1869, the Co-operative Union was created to carry on educational work and, generally, to promote co-operation.

WHO WERE THE PIONEERS?

It is commonly said that the band of Pioneers responsible for the start of the Rochdale store, and the Co-operative Movement that now spans the world, consisted of 28 members. It would seem more correct to say "about 28 members", for there appears to be uncertainty as to precisely who belongs on the list.

Brown, who compiled a list from minutes of the meeting held August 11, 1844, and from other sources, gives a list of 32. However, using lists gleaned from various sources and showing different numbers. G.D.H. Cole, author of **A Century of Co-operation,** concludes that the following 28 deserve recognition:

1. James Daly, joiner.
2. Charles Howarth, warper.
3. John Bent, tailor.
4. James Tweedle, clogger.
5. James Smithies, woolsorter.
6. Joseph Smith, woolsorter.
7. William Lee, weaver.

8. John Whitehead, weaver.
9. James Holt, weaver.
10. Robert Buckley.
11. Edmund Fitton, weaver.
12. George Ashworth, weaver.
13. James Bamford, weaver.
14. Benjamin Brierley, weaver,
15. John Lomox, weaver.
16. Joe Crabtree, weaver.
17. William Taylor, weaver.
*18. Samuel Ashworth, weaver,
19. John Holt, weaver.
20. James Standring, weaver.
21. James Lord, weaver.
22. Miles Ashworth, weaver.
23. Abraham Taylor, weaver.
24. James Maden, weaver.
25. James Knowles, weaver.

26. Abraham Holt, weaver,
27. James Manock, weaver.
*28. Samuel Ashworth, warehouseman.

Samuel Tweedale, shown by Brown as attending the August 11 meeting, does not appear on Cole's list of 28 Pioneers. Since the name Samuel Ashworth appears only once on Brown's list, there is reason to suspect that Cole's number 18 and 28 should read as Samuel Ashworth and Samuel Tweedale.

Cole also lists three others who attended the August 11 meeting, but whose names did not appear on the minute book until shortly afterward. They are:

29. William Cooper, weaver.
30. Benjamin Rudman, pedlar.
31. William Mallalieau, spinner.

There are a number of other names mentioned in association with the Pioneers, including that of a woman, Ann Tweedale. But perhaps the exact names are not all that important; it is sufficient to say that it was but a small band that played a critical role in founding a movement which, by the early 1970's, could claim to serve some 285 million members through 573,000 co-operative societies (including 245,000 credit unions) spread throughout the world.

ORIGINS OF CREDIT UNIONS

A credit union is an organization of people co-operating together to provide financial services for themselves. Members deposit their savings in credit unions; they earn a flat rate of interest, and members can then borrow from the accumulated savings at a reasonable rate of interest.

Credit unions did not originate in Britain, but in Germany. Thus, for many years the co-operative movement and the credit union movement were regarded as being distinctly separate. In Canada's Prairie Provinces there is a close working relationship between credit unions and co-operatives and they are regarded as being part of the same Co-operative Movement.

Frederick William Henry Raiffeisen, mayor of the Bavarian community of Flammersfeld, is regarded as being the father of credit unions. He was, however, influenced by Victor Aime Huber who, during the late 1840's, was preaching co-operative ideas on the Continent basing some of his concepts on the experiences of the Rochdale pioneers.

A countryman of Raiffeisen, Hermann Schulze-Delitzsch, was also significant in the early development of co-operative credit societies. A judge, Schulze-Delitzsch, was greatly concerned, as was Raiffeisen, over the plight of working class people who needed credit. The people were being exploited and victimized by money lenders charging usurious rates of interest so that it was extremely difficult to get out of debt and more difficult to save for time of future need. Schulze-Delitzsch organized recreational, social, and welfare work to help needy people and, in 1850, set up the first credit association. In time, it grew into a co-operative bank, stimulating thrift by enouraging people to save, and providing fair credit to farmers and artisans.

After helping form a consumer-distribution society, Raiffeisen, with the help of some prosperous citizens, established a money-lending society in 1849, for it appeared to him that it was providing a form of charity to the needy rather than a means by which they could help themselves. He then turned his attention to assisting his people to form self-help credit societies somewhat along the lines of those fostered by Schulze. In 1869, Raiffeisen organized what is regarded as being the first true credit union or "people's bank" as it was then called. It differed from earlier efforts, such as those of Schulze-

Delizsch, by being open to more people especially those with low incomes. As well as following general concepts of co-operative societies, Raiffeisen put great stress on three policies:

1. Only members could borrow.
2. Loans were provided for only provident and productive purposes, and at low interest.
3. The most important security a man could offer for a loan was his own character.

By the time he passed away in 1883, there were 423 credit unions or "Raiffeisen banks" in Germany, and his plan was already spreading throughout Europe and other parts of the world, reaching Canada in 1900 and the U.S.A. in 1909.

CHAPTER II
THE FEUDAL MODEL

The Rochdale Society of Equitable Pioneers dealt mainly in foods during the earliest days of their venture. Brown notes that when the Rochdale store opened on December 21, 1844, the stock consisted of butter, sugar, flour, oatmeal, and candles, all costing 16 pounds, 11 shillings and 11 pence.

It is interesting to note that the first known co-operative store on the Canadian prairies, was also in the grocery trade. The Winnipeg Co-operative Association, operating in 1885, advertised tea in a Winnipeg newspaper in that year.

Most of Canada's co-operatives were inspired by, and fashioned after, the Rochdale model. A study of the matter also lends to belief that the conditions that provoked the early formation of both co-operatives and farm organizations in the Prairie Region of Canada, likewise had their origins in Britain. Before Confederation in 1867, Canada was a colony of Britain. The British North America Act, the Act of Confederation, required approval of the British Parliament. In addition, the settlers who came from Britain, both before and after Confederation, most certainly carried their culture with them, infusing Canada with a strong measure of British thought and practise respecting trade and commerce, politics, religion and, to a lesser extent perhaps, social class.

To trace the origin of the forces that were behind the start of co-operatives and farm organizations of the Prairies, we must examine developments as they took place in Britain. It will require consideration of events that took place long before the Rochdale Store was opened. Those events form a long story in themselves, so an excess of detail must be avoided. Fortunately, however, there are many excellent books easily available to offer more details, some of them being listed in the bibliography that will follow.

POWER STRUCTURE

During the early nineteenth century class divisions and heredity influenced and characterized much of British social, economic and political life. A state of democracy did not exist, although there was a form of representative government.

About democracy, Pierre Elliot Trudeau, who became Canada's 20th Prime Minister in 1968, in a book **Federalism and the French Canadians,** has written "Democracy cannot be made to work in a country where a large part of the citizens are by status condemned to a perpetual state of domination, economic or otherwise."

In feudal times, and until democracy began to slowly emerge in Britain from 1832 on, the largest proportion of the population lived in a perpetual state of class, political and economic domination imposed by the upper ruling class. In all Europe, similar conditions prevailed, provoking Jean-Jacques Rousseau to observe, in 1762, that: "Man was born free and everywhere he is in chains."

The old class system with its extremes of rich and poor tended to be self-perpetuating. Among the aristocracy, titles and the privileges of wealth, power, and rank that went with them, were passed from deceased father to eldest son. Such was generally also the case with respect to the estates of the landed gentry. In the first instance, it was likely that both titles and large holdings of land could be traced to a grant made to an ancestor for some valued service to king and country. For such a service, a man might be awarded a title, an annual stipend, or a large tract of land; perhaps even all three. The award would then continue as family property. A further perpetuation of wealth and privilege resulted by the arrangement of marriages that would unite families to greater wealth, social status, and resulting power. For the second and successive sons of the aristocracy and gentry, a respectable status and income was assured through appointment to high positions. It was largely from their ranks that officers of military forces, justices, upper civil servants, bankers, lawyers, and occasionally ranking officials of the church were drawn.

Under these conditions, Parliament, as it evolved, could not be regarded as a body devoted to the common good. More appropriately, it was devoted to the perpetuation of the privileged class, by restricting efforts of the lower classes to achieve upward mobility. Its lawmakers were greatly inclined to pursue advantage for themselves and, when necessary, to obtain advantage for those to whom they owed favor. Oligarchic, cruel, corrupt, superficial, self-satisfied, masters of intrigue, selfish and blind—these are some of the terms historians have used to describe the ruling class and the oppressive system of government. It would be wrong, however, to assume that all members of the ruling class earned such description. There were certainly those who displayed humanitarian traits. Such men are easily overlooked when one attempts to summarize a broad spectrum of historic events. It needs to be recognized too, that in the centuries before the 1800's, great changes that would influence the course of history, were gathering momentum.

MERCHANT TRADERS

Next to the ruling class in Britain were the merchant traders. The term does not mean shopkeepers, but men who were engaged in promoting foreign trade. As a class they had grown in prominence after the Crusades of between 1076 and 1272, and even more so after the discovery of America.

Historians report that the merchants, who did not have the right to vote, nevertheless did influence the policies of the voting classes. To engage in trading, or any other form of what might be regarded as a menial pursuit, was beneath the dignity of the aristocracy. Not so, however, was the matter of increasing one's wealth through trade, hence the merchants were not infrequently aided by aristocrats who financed ventures in expectation of a profit. Trade was also a means by which the income of the nation could be enhanced, especially if the trading resulted in the import of raw

materials for manufacture, and the export of finished products. It was logical to believe that through the regulation of trade and tariffs, the ruling class could reduce the burden of taxation upon themselves as well as earn a profit.

To stimulate trade, and to provide for settlement and administration of lands to which Britain laid claim in America, some large companies were formed. The Hudson's Bay Company, formed to develop the fur trade in the Canadian North-West, is but one example. A number of the states of the United States of America were originally established in a similar manner. For example: In 1606, a joint stock company was founded by "Knights, Gentlemen, Merchants and Other Adventurers of London", as the London Company of Virginia. With the help of slaves, the first of whom arrived in 1619, the company established a tobacco industry which grew rapidly in the colony. In 1609, Henry Hudson, an Englishman, sailed along the Atlantic coast of America in search of a passage to India. He gave glowing reports of land near the mouth of a river that became known as the Hudson. As a result, a troupe of Dutch merchants were inspired to obtain a charter in 1621, for the Dutch East India Company. A colony was then set up by Dutch settlers on what became known as Manhattan Island. For about $24-worth of trinkets, the island was "purchased" from the Indians. The colony was captured by the British about 1664, and the name changed from New Netherland to New York. The State of Maryland had its beginnings in 1632, when George Calvert (Lord Baltimore) was granted a Charter by King Charles I to an area of land north of the Potomac River. George Calvert died shortly after the Royal Seal was affixed to the Charter which was then inherited by his son, Cecil, the second Lord Baltimore. The colony then founded was known as Maryland. Calvert did not bother to visit his colony, but governed it through a deputy. Next in 1663, eight prominent members of the aristocracy who had been of much help in restoring Charles II to the throne of England were rewarded with the grant of an extensive area of land which they called Carolina. Then, in 1681, a large grant of land, which was to become known as Pennsylvania, was awarded to William Penn as consideration for a debt of 16,000 pounds owed by Charles II to Penn's father. The first white settlers arrived from Sweden, but their settlement and others were captured by the Dutch in 1655, then regained by the British in 1664. Soon after, Penn opened his colony as a haven for Quakers who were the object of religious persecution in England. Still later, in 1732, a number of "Gentlemen, The Trustees for Establishing the Colony of Georgia in America", received a Royal Charter. The colony, named after George II, was the last of 13 states to be founded as colonies. The founding of those colonies meant, of

course, that North American settlement was begun under feudal influences, and with the officers of the companies being charged with responsibility for maintaining law and order as well as stimulating trade with Britain. The extent by which Britain benefitted from the trade with America is questionable. No doubt profit accrued to the aristocracy who had shares in the companies. But for Britain, gains were offset by the cost of wars to defend colonies already possessed and to capture those held by other nations, particularly France and Spain.

In this context of events, it is of interest to note some observations by Willcox:

"The officer class of every European state, including Britain, was virtually synonymous with the aristocracy, and had to be as long as the old regimes survived; for only those who depended on the crown for their privileges and were tied to it by long tradition could be trusted to command the force on which the social order depended. But no country had enough aristocrats in its population to officer a mass army, any more than it had enough money in its treasury to equip and feed such an army...Campaigns were not only limited in their aims but also, for the most part, inconclusive in their results; and the principal reason was the nature of the armies involved. They were composed of soldiers who served for pay, not love of their country. Many of the small states hired out their troops to the highest bidder, and even in the national monarchies the enlisted men knew little of nationalism."

GROWTH OF INDUSTRY

On the home front, industry in Britain was changing in the 18th Century. The path toward becoming "a nation of shopkeepers" and the "workbench of the world" was being trod. Historical writers, including those concerned with the start of the Co-operative Movement, seem to follow faithfully a tradition of referring to an "Industrial Revolution." They are, however, not always consistent when suggesting when it began, and even less consistent in suggesting when it came to an end. Some say it has not yet ended, but most common are the dates from about 1770 to 1840 for start and end.

The year of 1770 as a starting date seems to be tied to the work of James Watt who, in 1769, introduced a steam engine that could be applied to manufacturing. He was not the first inventor of devices for steam power, but did invent the means of making more efficient use of ideas of earlier inventors. His work is summed up on a plaque attached to a marble statue in Westminster Abbey:

JAMES WATT
Who, directing the forces of an original genius,
Early exercised in philosophic research
to the improvement of
THE STEAM ENGINE,
enlarged the resources of his country,
increased the power of men,
and rose to an eminent place among the most
illustrious followers of science and the real
benefactors of the world.

The fact is though, that a great deal of industrial progress had already been made before Watt's steam engine came onto the scene.This will become clear as the progress of various industries is reviewed.

TEXTILE INDUSTRY

For a long period, Britons had reason to regard sheep as perhaps their most important economic asset. It grazed on land not easily cultivated, was a source of food, and finally, gave rise to an industry which, in 1785, was by far Britain's largest with an annual value of 17 million pounds. Next in line was the iron and ironwares industry with an annual value of 12 million pounds.

An English woollen industry existed as early as the 12th century. It was Edward III, however, who pointed the industry toward its future. Mills in Lancashire where the warm, moist climate provided conditions needed for spinning cotton, had greatly improved their product. In 1769, Richard Arkwright's invention of the water frame displaced the old system of hand spinning for both cotton and wool. Between 1770 and 1790, water power was first used to operate spinning mules at New Lanark, and soon even this was replaced with steam power.

Cotton, regarded as Britain's first truly urban industry, grew in importance. The weight of raw cotton imported and consumed in the United Kingdon (a term used to embrace England, Scotland, Wales and Ireland; whereas the term Britain refers to all her dependencies but Ireland) grew from 5 million pounds weight in 1781 to 124 million in 1810, and 164 million in 1818. The silk industry in Britain owes its start to two brothers, John and Sir Thomas Lombe. Sir Thomas, in 1734, smuggled out of Italy machinery for producing silk cloth. For this he was rewarded by Parliament with a grant of 14,000 pounds. The machinery was set up in a factory on an island where its secrets were carefully guarded.

Heilbroner indicates that the Lombe factory, built in 1743, was, in its time, a huge building, 500 feet in length and six storeys high, and described by Daniel Defoe as consisting of "26,586 wheels and 97,746 movements which work 73,726 yards of silk thread every time the water wheel goes round, which is three times in one minute." To this, Heilbroner adds further comment: "Equally worthy of note were the children who tended the machines round the clock for 12 or 14 hours at a turn, cooked their meals on the grimy black boilers, and were boarded in shifts in barracks where, it is said, the beds were always warm."

The linen industry does not appear to have been greatly encouraged in Britain. One likely reason is that growing flax from which linen is made, was not as practical as raising sheep which offered greater utility as food, a source of wool, and as a means of using land considered unfit for crops. However, the linen industry did flourish in Scotland in the early 1700's, even more than it did in Ireland. It was feared that if the Irish linen trade expanded, Britain's trade, particularly with Holland, would suffer. In the first half of the 18th Century, the linen industry grew in both England and Scotland, but lagged behind cotton and still farther behind wool.

It will be seen that with respect to all four textiles-wool, cotton, silk and linen-there were moves to protect the trades of Britain against foreign competitors. Even more, there were steps taken to guard British know-how, as witness the Act of 1714 to prohibit exports of "tools and utensils" used for the production of cotton textiles, and a further Act of 1780 by which the export of specifications or models of machinery for cotton production was forbidden.

COAL, IRON, AND STEAM

Britain's coal mines made possible the large-scale production of iron and steel and, in turn, the latter made possible the steam engine, and, later, steam powered transportation.

By the start of the 18th Century, coal was in general use for domestic purposes. It was mined from seams at or near the surface where it was relatively safe to work. But by 1775, coal was in strong demand in the iron industry and being taken from deeper seams. For ventilation at the lower levels, there were systems of drafts to draw in fresh air from above, all of which required the aid of numerous doors and traps for operation.

To say the least, mining underground was a dangerous occupation. In the deeper pits explosions were a constant danger, even to miners at work with the aid of a single candle. It is said that in the Tyne coalfields alone, some 415 lives were lost between

9

1801 and 1815 because of explosions. Down in a mine three groups of workers could be found. The most important, and somewhat better paid than the rest, was the miner, crouched on his knees in the small, narrow tunnel, picking away at the coal seam. Next to him were the "hurriers" who took the coal away in tubs or small trucks to the bottom of the pit or main entrance to the mine. From there it was either hoisted to the surface or else it was carried up ladders by women or boys, slung in "corves" on their backs. Small children, from 5 to 8 years of age, were also to be found in the mines. Their task was to open and close the doors as the tubs or carts passed by, in order to keep the air circulation system going.

In 1815, Sir Humphrey Davy designed a safety lamp for miners While it reduced the danger of underground explosions, miners complained that it did not provide as much light as a single candle, and they therefore avoided its use.

Waters notes that: "Owners of the collieries were chiefly aristocrats and larger landowners like Lord Londonderry, Lord Durham, and the Duke of Portland, and feudal conditions survived to a late date."

Iron was in common use in the 14th and 15th centuries, but then mainly for manufacturing weapons of war. Crude cannons were being fashioned in Sussex at about 1330 or 1340. Cannons were greatly improved when, in 1543, a method of casting them in one piece was devised. In earlier times iron smelting was done with charcoal made from wood. But in 1709, when England's forests were nearly exhausted, Abraham Darby devised a means of making coke from coal. Coke then replaced charcoal for smelting. In 1742, Huntsman's process for resmelting clay crucibles enabled hard, crucible steel to be produced, the product being suitable for making steel cutting tools, dies, and fine machinery. In 1784, Henry Corts invented the "puddling" process by which wrought iron could be produced from cast iron.

With these inventions and refinements that came soon after, plus the addition of steam power, Britain's iron and steel industry was poised along modern lines and the quantity of production grew quickly; to 700,000 tons in 1830 to 1,000,000 tons in 1835, and 2,000,000 tons by 1847.

Steam power spurred the development of both coal mining and the iron and steel industries. It is difficult to say who was the first to conceive and develop a steam engine. Hart indicates that the idea had been the object of a number of very early experimenters, even before 1543 when, it is said, a Spaniard, Blasco de Garay, astounded spectators by moving ships propelled by steam. In 1663, the second Marquis of Worcester, Edward Somerset, claimed to have "invented an admirable and forcible way to drive up water by

PHOTOGRAPH OF THIRTEEN OF THE ORIGINAL MEMBERS
OF THE
ROCHDALE EQUITABLE PIONEERS' SOCIETY.

| JAMES STANDRING. | 2. JOHN BENT. | 3. JAMES SMITHIES. | 4. CHARLES HOWARTH. | 5. DAVID BROOKS. | 6. BENJ. RUDMAN. | 7. JOHN SCO |
| 8. JAMES MANOCK. | 9. JOHN COLLIER. | 10. SAMUEL ASHWORTH. | 11. WILLIAM COOPER. | 12. JAMES TWEEDALE. | 13. JOSEPH SMITH. |

10

fire." It was Thomas Newcomen, however, who put together a steam driven pump in 1712. His pump seems to be the springboard for steam power. It proved to be most useful in drawing water from mines, a problem that had to be overcome before coal mining could be carried on at the lower depths. James Watt, in 1763-64, was asked to overhaul a model of Newcomen's engine. He quickly discovered its means of operation and soon set himself to the task of improving it. Watt's first major invention, in 1769, was an improvement to Newcomen's engine. In 1781, he obtained a patent for a steam engine that provided a rotary motion which enabled it to be used to power other forms of machinery. Thereafter, steam power was soon applied in factories and in other forms of industry.

The steam engine, of course, required the use of coal, as it also required iron and steel for its construction. Thus Britain marched forward becoming by the mid-1800's the 'workbench of the world'. At least some of those inventions that made progress possible had been made well before the dates generally ascribed to the start of the 'Industrial Revolution'.

TRANSPORTATION

In 1675, Britain's roads were in a deplorable state. Horsedrawn carriages to carry people and wagons to haul freight frequently bogged down in mud. In that year, an Act was passed authorizing construction of turnpikes or main roadways under direction of the parishes. In some parishes, little was done to improve roads, and in others the task was taken over by "turnpike trusts". In 1773, a further Act was passed requiring upkeep of the turnpike roads. On the turnpike, users were required to pay and as the number of tollgates increased, so did the cost of moving freight and of travel by coach. In 1810, Telford and McAdam developed a process for surfacing roads with rolled granite. The result was greatly improved roads and more rapid transportation; coaches that had travelled at four to five miles an hour could now move at seven to eight miles an hour, and between Liverpool and Manchester, a speed of up to 12 miles an hour was attained.

In 1755, a canal was built to Liverpool from a point 12 miles distant, and in 1761, the Bridgewater canal was built and paid for by the Duke of Bridgewater to carry coal from his mine at Worsley to the Town of Manchester. Over the next 70 years, about 4,700 miles of canals were built to carry freight.

Next came the railways. Rails of wood, and later of iron, were in fact, in use well before the steam locomotive for it was discovered that wheeled, horse-drawn carts could be moved with comparative ease on rails. This means was used to move coal and ore from mines to canals.

In 1808, Richard Trevethick demonstrated at London his first high-pressure steam locomotive. It was George Stephenson, however, who developed the first practical locomotive. Stephenson, an illiterate man, built as his first steam locomotive an engine he called "My Lord" which, in July, 1824, hauled a cargo of 30 tons up a moderate grade at 4 miles an hour. On September 27, 1825, the Stockton & Darlington railway line was officially opened. A train, pulled by a greatly improved locomotive built by George Stephenson and which he called the "Rocket", reached a speed of 12 to 16 miles an hour. The Rocket was the forerunner of the fast, efficient steam locomotives to follow. By 1843, Britain had 2,000 miles of railways carrying 23 million passengers a year. And by 1850 the mileage had increased to 6,621, and the number of passengers to 73 million.

Harrison shows in his work drawings that indicate the extent to which class distinction applied to early railways. The first class coaches, for the aristocracy were tall, roomy, and with windows fitted with curtains. For the middle class there was the second class coach, less roomy, but covered, and with glass windows. For the common man there was the third class open coach-no roof, and sides that reached only a little higher than the back of the benches.

AGRICULTURE

About 12,000 years ago, man had begun to learn how to cultivate food for himself at will. People could then begin to settle in villages; their need to be nomadic in search of food through hunting, fishing, and scavenging the land decreased in proportion to their ability to produce food. And when one person could produce more food than was needed by his or her family, it became possible for others to pursue other forms of work. In the first instance, therefore, the ability to produce food in abundant supply, made it possible for man **to turn to the arts, sciences, trades and professions.**

Nevertheless, agriculture, by modern standards, was in a primary state by the early 1700's. But it was the means by which the majority of people were able to sustain themselves. So long as they produced at least the minimum of food they required, there was no reason to attempt to produce more, for the lack of transportation was an obstacle to trading in foods. Moreover, discoveries of improved farming methods were not easily shared. However, a revolution in agriculture, as important as that which took place in industry, began about 1760, gaining in momentum as new farming methods and better means of transportation developed.

At the start of the 1700's, farming was carried on in wide, open fields, not the small fields marked off by walls or hedges that exist in Britain today. Land under cultivation was divided into strips of about one acre each, with the length being about 10 times that of the width. The strips were separated, one from the other, by an unploughed margin or 'baulk', and each was likely to belong to a different tenant farmer. A single farmer might have strips in various parts of his landlord's holdings. The strips were planted to crop according to a common agreement that required the landlord's consent. Crops were rotated; generally it was wheat one year, barley the next, and in the third year the field would be fallowed. In addition to the cropping strips, there was a common meadow where sheep and cattle were put to graze. Once the crops were taken off the strips, cattle were free to graze on the stubble. But the livestock was of poor quality. Meadows were not seeded to 'artificial' grasses to provide better fodder, and in the winter months, nourishing fodder of any kind was scarce. By 1694, however, at least some turnips were being grown as a field crop. and used to feed sheep in the winter.

As early as the 13th Century, the old system of farming began to change as a result of 'enclosures'—the dividing of open fields into many separate fields fenced off by walls or hedges. The enclosures enabled farmers to be more independent, one from the other, in their operations. For example, instead of the common pasture, each farmer provided grazing for his own herd. The chances that cattle would be infected by disease were thus much lower. The number of enclosures was small partly because of restraining laws, and partly because each landowner, in order to enclose his lands, was required to obtain authority to do so through an Act of Parliament, a costly process. In the decade 1700 to 1710, only one enclosure Act was passed. In the next decade eight were passed, and in the next, 33, so that by 1760, 271 were passed, followed by 1,859 more by 1800. The enclosures drove many small leaseholders and others off the land. A poor leaseholder, who depended on rights to use common fields, could not afford to lease the larger holdings defined by the enclosures. Many small leaseholders then sold their rights to richer neighbors and left for the growing industrial centres. For those who remained as leaseholding farmers or as their workers, agriculture soon became a more complex but improved occupation.

Thomas William Coke of Norfolk, owner of a large estate, pioneered substantial advances in farm practise. He turned his attention toward improving land that had been regarded as too light for profitable cultivation. He marled the land, fertilized with manure and bone, and selected good seed for wheat and grasses. He drilled the seed into the ground, avoiding the old way of casting it about by hand. Coke introduced oil-cake for cattle feed and the practise of stall-feeding. Coke helped his farmer-tenants to improve their land, offering them long-term leases on condition that they use the most up-to-date methods. He was generous in providing them with cottages and other buildings. The improved production that followed brought its own reward to Coke—he was able to raise the rents of his tenants from 2,200 pounds in 1776 to 20,000 pounds by 1816. In 1793, Coke together with Lord Lonsdale, the Duke of Bedford, Sir John Sinclair and Arthur Young, established a "Board of Agriculture", a body supported partly by public funds and dedicated to the encouragement of more efficient farming methods.

Robert Bakewell of Leicestershire, described as a "practical farmer and businessman", also made an important contribution. He pioneered improved breeding of cattle and sheep, changing "English sheep from the resemblance between dog and a goat, to the plumb fleece-covered animal we know today," to use the words of Plumb. Jethro Tull was another pioneer of improved farming. He lived between 1674 and 1741, and was the inventor of a horse-drawn seed drill that dropped the seed in rows. He also invented a horse-drawn 'hoe' for cultivation, believing that keeping the soil 'fine' so that air and rain could get to the roots would be as beneficial as applying manure which then meant risking the weed-carrying capacity of barnyard manure. Charles Viscount Townshend was another benefactor of farm practise. In 1730, he retired from political life to his Norfolk estate. There he marled and fertilized his poorest land, used Tull's inventions to drill and horse-hoe, and grew fine crops of turnips which were used for winter feeding of livestock. Townshend also studied crop rotation, devising

a four-year program for the planting of wheat, turnips, barley and clover, eliminating the traditional third-year fallow, and all with much success.

POPULATION

The agricultural revolution increased the supply of food and, in turn, it is believed, was responsible for an increase in Britain's population.

Plumb provides statistics that show a large gain in average weight of cattle sold at Smithfield, England, between 1710 and 1795:

	1710	1795
Oxen.........	370 lb.	800 lb.
Calves	50 lb.	150 lb.
Sheep........	38 lb.	80 lb.

The gains can be attributed to the enclosures which made it possible to protect herds against disease or to confine disease; and to the improvement of fodder. In turn, these improvements meant more and better food for human consumption. The population began to grow at an accelerated rate. In 1760, the population of England and Wales was estimated at 6,000,000. Subsequent estimates were as follows:

1781	7,400,000
1791	8,200,000
1801	9,000,000
1811	10,300,000

Britain's first official census was taken in 1801, but Scotland does not appear to have been included in the count. Earlier population figures were derived from parish records and are not likely to be more than approximately accurate; there is, in fact, doubt as to the accuracy of the census of 1801 and those of some census years which followed. It is, however, interesting to note, alongside the population figures, the statement by Toynbee in his lectures of 1884, that "one-half the land in the United Kingdom is owned by 2,512 persons". By a footnote, Toynbee explained that "the owners of properties of over 3,000 acres, and yielding a rental of at least 3,000 pounds, are 2,512 (in number)."

THE WORKING CLASS

It does not seem possible to outline briefly, in a manner that seems credible, the extent of the suffering, deprivation, and indignity imposed in the past upon the working classes and poor who, in number, comprised the majority of the population. Neither employers nor the ruling class of the 18th or 19th centuries can be wholly blamed for the conditions affecting the working class of that time. Rather, one must look to earlier times of feudalism and its structure. The feudal lords were protectors of the peasants, providing them with shelter and plots of land to cultivate in order to sustain themselves. In return, peasants were obliged to do work for their feudal lord, to give him part of what they produced and, if necessary, to be his soldiers.

Quite naturally, such a structure divided people into two groups or classes consisting of a minority of powerful "superiors" and the vast numbers of "inferiors". An extreme example of measures taken by the "superiors" to control their "inferiors" is provided by a Statute passed during the brief reign of Edward VII from 1547 to 1553:

"If any person shall bring to two justices of the peace any runagate servant, or any other which liveth idly or loiteringly by the space of three days, they shall cause that idle and loitering servant, or vagabond to be marked with a hot iron on the breast with the mark of V and adjudge him to be slave to the same person that brought him for two years after, who shall take the said slave and give him bread, water, or small drink and refuse him meat and cause him to work, by beating, chaining, or otherwise, in such work as he shall put him unto, be it never so vile: And if he shall absent himself from his said master by the space of fourteen days, then he shall be adjudged by two justices of the peace to be marked on the forehead, or the ball of the cheek, with a hot iron, with the sign of an S, and further he shall be judged to be the slave to his said master for ever."

Histories, from feudal times onward, make note, not infrequently, of an evidently sincere belief that it was "ordained by God" that some people be wealthy, privileged and powerful, while others were destined to occupy but a low station of service to their masters. By its application, the belief became a custom, reinforced by self-interest of the "superiors", and manifest in innumerable laws to subdue and control the "inferior" class and protect the authority, power and privileges of the "superiors".

This Parliamentary system was evident in Britain up to 1832 and beyond; it was evident too, in the emerging factories where, in the words of Holyoake: "The capitalist was a new feudal lord, more cruel than the king who reigned by conquest. The old feudal lord had taken some care for his vassal, and provided him with sustenance and dwelling. The new lord of capital charges himself with no duty of this kind, and does not even acknowledge the laborer's right to live. His condition is no affair of the employer. Thoughtfulness for the workman might be manifested as an act of patronage, but not as an act of duty or right."

Again, it would be unjust to assume that all of the aristocrats, landed gentry, factory owners or employers of the 17th to 19th centuries were cruel or inhuman in their treatment of workers. If such were the case, reforms that did take place might well have been impossible. It is true that in the new factories wages were atrociously low, and working conditions deplorable. But as Waters states: "It must not be thought that there were no humane or farseeing men among employers who would gladly have raised wages of workers, but they were forced, by their position, to conform to the pattern set by others, for in the competitive system the price is set by the lowest rate, and the master who underpaid his workers to the point of starvation and worked his machinery 16 or more hours a day could undersell those who would like to use more humane methods. With Parliament refusing to coerce the bad ones, the good ones were helpless."

As early as 1597, steps were taken to aid the poor. In that year an Act was passed, to become effective in 1601, charging parishes of the church with responsibility for administering charity. Each parish was to appoint four overseers for the purpose, and to levy rates (compulsory taxes) on owners of property, to build work-houses and to provide work and wages for the unemployed. This Act was the foundation of welfare legislation until well into the 19th century, but was, of course, altered from time to time. Another Act, passed in 1723, called upon every parish to build a workhouse, an atrocity of human degradation to shelter the unemployed. In most parishes the operation of the workhouse was assigned to a contractor. If he was paid a lump sum for the job, he would likely admit as few persons as possible and make their lives so utterly miserable as to induce people to starve rather than enter. On the other hand, if he was paid on a "per head" basis, he would be inclined to admit as many as he could, and to extract from each all possible work. When a man came to a poorhouse with his family they were separated, the husband to one quarter, wife to another, and children to still another, and they had no time to be together. Discipline was strict, the food sparse and at times rotten, and the place cold and without comfort.

In 1782, still another Poor Law was enacted. It permitted parishes to group themselves into unions for purposes of administering to the poor, and reserved the workhouses for the aged and infirm. It provided also, that able-bodied men be found work outside of the workhouse, or else granted relief while living at their own abodes. Thus, there were at least three systems for sustaining the unemployed. The "Roundsman System" provided that a laborer who was out of work might be leased to a farmer to work at a set price, and if that price were not enough for minimum sustenance, the difference would be provided from the poor rate. The "Labour-Rate System" provided that ratepayers (persons who paid the Poor Law tax) could employ a certain number of paupers in lieu of paying the tax. In a third system, paupers worked in gangs under a foreman and the farmers thus served paid the Poor Law overseers for services performed. In 1795, still another system came into effect. It was originated by a group of judges who were appalled by the misery of underpaid workers. Their first thought was to press for a scale of minimum wages, but after further consideration, it was decided to augment wages earned by the workers from the poor relief funds. By this means, a man's pay could be brought up to the bare subsistence level at least. But the flaw in the system was that it relieved the need for employers to pay wages compatible with the cost of living, for they knew the workers could rely on charity for the essential difference between a too-low and a living wage.

Between the foregoing lines, one gets at least a glimpse of the poverty of the times. By 1834, it was said, one out of every six inhabitants was on relief. A Royal Commission, headed by Nassau Senior, was formed to investigate matters and recommended procedures "to encourage frugality and discourage laziness by providing relief in such a manner that an individual would lose his self-respect by asking for it", to use the words of Schultz. In the changes that resulted, able-bodied men who asked for relief were required to live in the workhouses, separated from wives and children, and where heat and food were kept to a minimum. A still further report for 1844 showed that nearly one-and-a-half million people had been granted relief, either within the workhouses or outside.

Under such conditions, it is hardly unreasonable to expect that workers would be aroused to act in their own interests. Why they did not do so to a greater extent than they actually did can be explained by some Acts of Parliament. For example, in 1714, the Riot Act was passed. It provided that if 12 or more persons **unlawfully, riotously, and tumultuously assembled together to the** disturbance of public peace, failed to disperse upon being ordered to do so by a Justice of the Peace, and remained for one hour, the offence was a felony punishable by death. In 1795, the Seditious Meetings & Assemblies Act provided that a meeting, attended by more than 50 persons for the purpose of discussing grievances respecting the church or state, was illegal unless five days' prior notice was given in newspapers to state the purpose for which the meeting was held. In 1799, a general Combinations Act was passed. It forbade workers to form a combination (union) to demand better wages and working conditions, and replaced some 40 similar acts of the past. For an offence under the new act, a worker could be sentenced to imprisonment for three months, by a single magistrate who could, in some instances, be his employer. In 1800, the Act was amended to provide that trial be before two magistrates, neither of whom were associated with the trade of the accused.

In 1817, a peaceful meeting was held at St. Peter's Fields, Manchester, to petition Parliament for reform. But it was broken up violently by yeomen with several hundred people injured and eleven fatalities. Thereafter, in 1819, the Seditious Meetings Act was passed requiring that six days' notice of political meetings be given to a justice who was empowered to alter the time and place of the proposed assembly. The Act declared illegal any meeting for the purpose of exciting people to hatred or contempt of the Government, and provided that houses or places for public lectures or debates be licensed. At the same time, the Blasphemous and Seditious Libels Act was passed to make it an offence, to print or publish anything that might tend to make the Government an object of contempt or hatred. Still a further Act, the Stamp Duty on Newspapers Act, was designed to prevent the publication and sale of newspapers at a price of less than sixpence, exclusive of duty. It was obviously a move to raise the price of newspapers above that which most workers could afford, ensuring that the papers would not be a means of agitation.

There were also other types of oppressive legislation. In 1719, an Act was passed to protect British industry from the prospect of foreign competition by prohibiting the migration of skilled artificers (craftsmen). Some skilled iron workers had gone to Russia at the invitation of Peter the Great, and some clockmakers had gone to France. In 1750, a further Act prohibiting emigration of skilled workers also made it an offence to export tools and utensils used in industries.

There were also laws to protect the game which aristocrats enjoyed hunting from being poached by the poor. In 1770, a law provided that for killing game at night, a sentence of from three to six months would be imposed, and for a second offence, 12 months plus a whipping. The Game Law of 1800, even more severe, provided that hard labor be the punishment for two persons found with a gun or other evidence of intent to poach. A second offence meant two years plus a whipping, or service in the Royal Navy. Five years later, in 1805, a person needed, according to another Act, only to be found with the implements needed for poaching by night to be liable to seven year's 'transportation', i.e., to exile to one of the colonies.

CHILD LABOUR

It was said by members of the ruling class that the problem of the poor was that "there are so many of them." Ridiculous though it sounds it was, in essence, true, but mainly because of the low wage level. The lowest wages were paid to children, but women received not much more. The highest wage went to men, but since it was not enough to keep a family, both women and children were forced to 'earn their keep'. The employers, of course, with an eye to keeping costs low, often tended to hire children and women, even for what could be classed as "man's work". Through the operation of the Poor Laws, a supply of orphan children or other wards of the parishes was assured. Cheyney notes that as late as 1812, a government official, proposing to Parliament a bill for training boys for service in the Royal Navy, said he could readily secure 90,000 boys of the proper age from the poorhouses of the country.

In 1788 an Act to relieve hardships of apprenticed chimney sweeps was passed. Waters notes that the apprentices were put to work at an age of four or five years and were paupers or children people wanted to get rid of. Their inhumane task was to climb up inside chimneys to remove the soot and, sometimes, to extinguish a chimney fire. The Act was not effective, for it was rarely applied against an offending master. There were, however, a few convictions such as the case recorded in The Liverpool Mercury, July 19, 1816, of a man sentenced to two years imprisonment after causing "by brutal treatment", the death of his apprentice chimney sweep, "a child of five or six years of age."

In 1802, a Factory Act, known as the Health & Morals act, was passed. It was intended to protect pauper children in cotton and woollen mills only, and provided that no child under the age of nine could be apprenticed; hours of work were to be limited to 12 per day with no night work for children; factories were to be ventilated and whitewashed; and apprentices were to be properly clothed, educated, and sent to church once a month. This Act too became a "dead letter", meaning that it was not observed. In 1816, an Act provided that children were not to be apprenticed at places of work more than 40 miles from their homes, and again it was stated that no children under nine years were to be apprenticed. An Act of 1819, pertaining to cotton mills, was another "dead letter." In 1815, still another Act was passed, providing for specified meal times at factories, and a quarter holiday on Saturday. This was followed by still another Act of 1831 to limit hours of work to 12 hours per day for all persons under 21, and to prohibit night work for persons under that age. Also in 1831 was the Truck Act, yet another "dead letter", but intended to oblige employers to pay workers in the "coin of the realm". Some employers had set up 'company shops' from which the workers were required to purchase their provisions rather than be paid their wages in money. By this means, the employer got back a part of the wages paid through profit on goods "sold" to workers.

In the session of 1831-32, Michael Sadler introduced a "Ten Hours Bill" to Parliament. It was directed to a Select Committee, of which he was a member, for study. Sadler, however, lost his seat in the election of 1832, and his place on the Committee was taken by Lord Ashley (later to become Earl of Shaftsbury). The Committee, known as the Sadler Committee, went to work, examining child labor conditions in the factories, and questioning a number of witnesses. Testimony given to the Committee appears in Parliamentary Papers of 1831-32, and includes the following:

Witness: Mr. Matthew Crabtree, called in, and examined:

What age are you?
Twenty-two.

What is your occupation?
A blanket manufacturer.

Have you ever been employed in a factory?
Yes.

At what age did you first go to work in one?
Eight.

How long did you continue in that occupation?
Four years.

Will you state the hours of labor at the period when you first went to the factory, in ordinary times?
From 6 in the morning to 8 at night.

Fourteen hours?
Yes.

With what intervals for refreshment and rest?
An hour at noon.

When trade was brisk what were your hours?
From 5 in the morning to 9 in the evening.

Sixteen hours?
Yes.

With what intervals for dinner?
An hour.

How far did you live from the mill?
About two miles.

Was there any time allowed for you to get your breakfast at the mill?
No.

Did you take it before you left your home?
Generally.

During those long hours of labor could you be punctual; how did you awake?
I seldom did awake spontaneously; I was most generally awoke or lifted out of bed, sometimes asleep, by my parents.

Were you always in time?
No.

What was the consequence if you had been too late?
I was most commonly beaten.

Severely?
Very severely, I thought.

In those mills is chastisement towards the latter part of the day going on perpetually?
Yes, perpetually.

So that you can hardly be in a mill without hearing constant crying?
Never an hour, I believe.

Do you think that if the overlooker were naturally a human person it would still be found necessary for him to beat the children, in order to keep up their attention and vigilance at the termination of those extraordinary days of labor?
Yes, the machine turns out a regular quantity of cardings, and of course they must keep as regularly to their work the whole of the day; they must keep with the machine, and therefore however human the slubber may be, as he must keep up with the machine or be found fault with, he spurs children to keep up also by various means; but that which he commonly resorts to is to strap them when they become drowsy.

At the time when you were beaten for not keeping up with your work, were you anxious to have done it if you possibly could?
Yes; the dread of being beaten if we could not keep up with our work was a sufficient impulse to keep us to it if we could.

When you got home at night after this labor, did your feel much fatigued?
Very much so.

Had you any time to be with your parents, and to receive instructions from them?
No.

What did you do?
All that we did when we got home was to get the little bit of supper that was provided for us and to go to bed immediately. If the supper had not been ready directly, we should have gone to sleep while it was preparing.

Did you not, as a child, feel it a very grievous hardship to be roused so soon in the morning?
I did.

Were the rest of the children similarly circumstanced?
Yes, all of them; but they were not all of them so far from their work as I was.

And if you had been too late you were under the apprehension of being cruelly beaten?
I generally was beaten when I happened to be too late, and when I got up in the morning the apprehension of that was so great, that I used to run, and cry all the way as I went to the mill.

Witness: Peter Smart, called in, and examined:

You say you were locked up night and day?
Yes.

Do the children ever attempt to run away?
Very often.

Were they pursued and brought back again?
Yes, the overseer pursued them and brought them back.

Did you ever attempt to run away?
Yes, I ran away twice

And were you brought back?
Yes, and I was sent up to the master's loft, and thrashed with a whip for running away.

Were you bound to this man?
Yes, for six years.

By whom were you bound?
My mother got 15 shillings for six years.

Do you know whether the children were, in fact, compelled to stop (stay) during the whole time for which they were engaged?
Yes, they were.

By law?
I cannot say by law; but they were compelled by the master. I never saw any law used there but the law of their own hands.

To what mill did you next go?
To Mr. Webster's, at Battus Den, within 11 miles of Dundee.

In what situation did you act there?
I acted as an overseer.

At 17 years of age?
Yes.

Did you inflict the same punishment that you yourself had experienced?
I went as an overseer; not as a slave, but as a slave-driver.

What were the hours of labor in that mill?
My master told me that I had to produce a certain quantity of yarn. The hours were at that time fourteen; I said that I was not able to produce the quantity of yarn that was required, I told him that if he took the timepiece out of the mill I would produce that quantity, and after that time I found no difficulty in producing the quantity.

How long have you worked per day in order to produce the quantity your master required?
I have wrought nineteen hours.

Was this a water-mill?
Yes, water and steam both.

To what time have you worked?
I have seen the mill going till it was past 12 o'clock on Saturday night.

So that the mill was still working on the Sabbath morning?
Yes.

Were the workmen paid by the piece or by the day?
No, all had stated wages.

Did that not almost compel you to use great severity to the hands then under you?
Yes, I was compelled often to beat them in order to get them to attend to their work, from their being overwrought.

Did you keep the hands locked up in the same way in that mill?
Yes, we locked up the mill; but we did not lock the bothy (on a farm, the bunkhouse).

Did you find that the children were unable to pursue their labor properly to that extent?
Yes, they have been brought to such condition that I have gone and fetched up the doctor to them, to see what was the matter with them, and to know whether they were able to rise or not able to rise; they were not at all able to rise; we have had great difficulty in getting them up.

When that was the case, how long had they been in bed, generally speaking?
Perhaps not above four or five hours.

In 1834, the House of Commons, subdued by the horrors of the testimonies provided by the Commission's report, passed a Factory Act to prohibit employment of children under the age of nine years. Children from nine to 13 years were to work not more than nine hours per day and 48 hours per week, and were to attend school two hours per day and be excluded from night work. For persons 13 to 18 years of age, the work-day was set at 12 hours and the weekly limit at 69, with no night work. Medical inspection and holidays for child workers were provided, and factory inspectors appointed to ensure that the act was carried out.

From industrialists, however, came a reaction. A petition was circulated by the Master Spinners and Manufactures of Oldham, in February, 1836, and sent to members of Parliament. Its wordings included the following:

"that the eighth section of the said Act enacted 'That after the expiration of thirty months from the passing of such Act it will not be law or for any person whatsoever to employ, keep, or allow to remain, in any factory or mill for a longer period than forty-eight hours in any one week, any child who shall not have completed his or her thirteenth year of age .

"That the said Act has prohibited the employment of children under twelve years of age for more than nine hours in any one day since the first day of March one thousand eight hundred and thirty five, and such prohibition has tended greatly to injure the interests both of your Memorialists (petitioners) and the parents of such children, without any advantage resulting to the children themselves.

"That your Memorialists are looking forward with great anxiety and alarm to the situation in which they will be placed on the first day of March next, by the working of children under thirteen

years of age being restricted to forty-eight hours in one week, for that such restriction will have the effect of throwing all children under thirteen years of age wholly out of employment, and will render it impossible for your Memorialists to work their respective mills with advantage...

"That your Memorialists are far from a total repeal of the provisions of the said Factory Act, but humbly submit that it is absolutely necessary to the carrying on of the cotton trade with advantage, to allow the employment of children of eleven years of age for sixty-nine hours a week..."

John Fielden, M.P. for Oldham, himself an owner of large cotton mills, was blunt in his letter of reply to the 72 mill owners behind the petition:

"The prayer of the Memorialists, that young children between eleven and thirteen years of age should be allowed to work in factories sixty-nine hours in the week instead of forty-eight hours a week, which the law now prescribes, is so revolting to my feelings, and so opposed to my views of the protection such children are entitled to, that I must decline supporting the prayer of the Memorialists."

In 1847, Fielden presented another Factory Act to limit working hours for women and young children to ten per day, or 10½ hours per day with a Saturday half-holiday. This Act, which was passed, also limited the hours for men since factories could not operate without the women and children at their posts.

CHAPTER III
VOICES OF FREEDOM

The Factory Act of 1834 was most significant for its moderation of the plight of working children; it was also significant because it represented a rebuff against the inhuman, selfish arrogance of the industrialists, denoting a new insight into the oppression of the workers. Such a change had to come, but it came neither quickly nor willingly, as witness that it took 47 years from the passage of legislation in 1788 on behalf of chimney sweeps, to get a reasonably effective Act on child labor. For this, the blame can be traced to the inept Parliament perpetuated by a relatively small number of the aristocracy and landed gentry whose first consid-

eration was generally their own interests. Votes could be bought, and voting controlled by the most prominent persons in each district for the secret ballot was not used. According to Cheyney: "The statement in the House of Commons...in 1793, that out of the whole 513 members, 300 owed their appointment to only 162 electors...has never yet been controverted."

It is obvious that from the clumsy, unjustifiable structure there arose a great disparity in terms of both wealth and political power. In the absence of reliable, workable statistics, an accurate table showing the disparity is impossible. On the basis of an estimated population of 14,000,000 for Great Britain in 1814, and national income in the order of 297 million pounds, the following rough caculations are made:

Group or Class	% of Population	% of Income
Workers, including tradesmen, factory and shop workers and farm labourers	66.8	32.7
Landed gentry, not including aristocracy; farmers and freeholders	21.3	25.8
Merchant traders, factory employers, etc. ..	5.3	12.4
Professional persons and civil servants	3.5	6.1
Innkeepers and publicans	1.6	3.0
Aristocracy	1.5	20.2

A structure so one-sided in its allocation of political power, wealth, freedom and justice, and so lacking of human consideration, could not last. Change was inevitable. It came, but not all from within Britain, being motivated from three sources:

1. The thinking of economic philosophers who advocated freedom.
2. The American Revolution.
3. The French Revolution.

THE ECONOMIC PHILOSOPHERS

There were a good number of men who, during the period from about 1760 to 1850, proposed economic or political reform, or other means of improving society.

ADAM SMITH, who had been a professor at the University of Glasgow, published in 1776, a very lengthy book, "An Inquiry Into

The Nature and Causes of the Wealth of Nations." *This book is still given much attention today, but its title is generally abbreviated to* "Wealth of Nations." *Adam Smith was probably the most important of the early economic philosophers, but by no means the first. In his book he names at least a hundred others who had in some way helped to stimulate his thoughts. Smith, and others who* followed, promoted the 'laissez-faire' concept of economic activity— *a concept based on a theory that governments should not interfere but allow business freedom to set its own course. Freed from government restraints, Smith believed that businessmen would be regulated by their own self-interest and by competition with one another. Production levels would be regulated by the law of supply and demand—an economic law which holds that when goods in high demand become scarce, prices will rise. Higher prices, Smith reasoned, would encourage more production, causing prices to decline. By the same means, the income or the profits of the manufacturers would be regulated. Likewise, labor would shift to those industries where demand was greatest since wages would likely be higher. Smith was a strong advocate of "division of labor," that is, having workers specialize in tasks at which they could become skilled. He used as an example a pin factory where, he said, "One man draws out the wire, another straights it, a third cuts it, a fourth points it, a fifth grinds it at the top for receiving the head; to make the head requires two or three distinct operations....Those ten persons could make among them upwards of forty-eight thousand pins in a day, but if they had all wrought separately and independently...they certainly could not each make twenty..." Such a division of labor had, of course, already existed in the textile* industry as it did in clockmaking and other pursuits. Adam Smith's 'Wealth of Nations' *was frankly critical of the low wages and impoverished conditions of workers. In this regard he contradicted persons in high places of both industry and Parliament who held the view that workers must be kept poor, otherwise they would not feel need to work hard and be productive.*

Smith's views were also contrary to many other laws and practises of the time. The laws that required a seven-year apprenticeship, and those that prevented workers from moving from one parish to another (as did the Poor Laws), prevented free movement of workers from one area to another, hence from one industry to another. Smith was critical too, of the monopolies granted by Parliament to the great mercantile companies set up to exploit the colonies, and of those towns within Britain that refused to allow industries to establish. For Smith's concepts to work, government restraint of industry must be overcome. Smith's writing, though greatly admired, was apparently of not great

influence on Parliament at first, for as we have seen, many more restrictive laws were passed in the late 1700's and early 1800's. However, industrialists ignoring the criticism of themselves that it provided, found in the 'Wealth of Nations' *arguments they used in opposing Factory Acts and other legislation favoring the workers. Thus, Adam Smith's writing, and the doctrines of laissez-faire, became a dominating influence upon industry and Parliament, especially after 1832.*

Perhaps some idea of the exuberance with which laissez-faire was pursued is provided by a lecture entitled 'Acres of Diamonds,' delivered by a Boston minister, Rev. Russel H. Conwell, who declared: "Money is power! Every good man and woman should strive for power. Tens of thousands of men and women get rich honestly. But they are often accused by an envious, lazy crowd of unsuccessful persons of being dishonest and oppressive. I say: Get rich! Get rich!"

JEREMY BENTHAM, who lived from 1748 to 1832, is not as well remembered as Adam Smith. Yet, according to one historian, "Jeremy Bentham probably did more than any single man to change the climate of opinion in England during the 19th Century with respect to politics and law." He was the son of a wealthy solicitor, and thus was able to become familiar with the laws and legal system at an early age. Bentham became convinced that the oppressive laws needed to be changed. By chance, he found in a pamphlet a phrase, 'the greatest happiness to the greatest number.' The phrase captivated him; it became the basis of his reasoning that happiness is the aim of life, and every man is best able to judge that which brings him happiness.

Bentham produced a book, "The Theory of Legislation," *in 1776, in which, like Adam Smith's book, he attacked laws restraining freedom of religion or expression of political opinions, and he advocated removal of laws for the purpose of protecting privileges of the ruling class. He proposed that trade unions be made legal, that punishments provided by the criminal laws be less severe, and that there be a drastic reform of Parliament with the right to vote being greatly extended.*

Jeremy Bentham did not live to see all his proposed reforms enacted. But he attracted a good many followers, known as 'Benthamites', who carried on his work. The Factory Act of 1834, the legalizing of trade unions through repeal of the Combination Law of 1824, and a further Bill of 1825, were undoubtedly a result of the influence of Benthamites. Bentham's philosophies tended to provide the rulers with a 'social conscience,' and, when coupled to those of Adam Smith, helped to foster the era of laissez-faire.

THOMAS MALTHUS, is noted for a writing he produced in 1789, entitled, "An Essay on the Principle of Population as it Affects the Future Improvement of Society." In this essay, Malthus declared that the human population tends to grow at a faster rate than does the supply of food. Thus where other philosophers envisioned a future world of peace, freedom and plenty, Malthus saw a future scarcity of food that would bring about quite the opposite result. He looked upon 'vice and misery, famine, disease and war' as having value in providing checks on the growth of population, and implied to some at least that, in the long run, the lot of the poor masses could not be improved. His theories were used from time to time in argument against the provision of doles(relief) for the poor, and to support the segregation of sexes in the workhouses, all to discourage the poor from having families. Otherwise, Malthus' essay was not taken seriously at the time, even though Britain's population was increasing, and by 1800, home-grown food was insufficient to meet the nation's need. At that time, however, the potential for food production in America and in British colonies such as Australia and Canada, appeared to be enormous; enough to dowse Malthus' gloomy predictions. In addition, trade policies assured Britain of a food supply, for food was obtained from the colonies in exchange for Britain's manufactured goods. The predictions by Malthus would, however, be brought back to mind in the latter part of the 20th Century, and have implications for agriculture in Western Canada.

ROBERT OWEN was not among the Pioneers of Rochdale, yet he is regarded as one who did much to bring about the start of the Co-operative Movement. He was also an advocate of factory reform and trade unions. In 1800, when he was 29 years of age, Owen bought a set of textile mills at New Lanark, a somewhat remote village in the mountains of Scotland. He was, according to one historian, "the first owner to realize the disastrous human results of laissez-faire, to condemn the selfish spirit of competitive capitalism, and to advocate unrestrained co-operation for every purpose of social life."

Owen paid his workers well and he limited their hours of work. He provided good housing at a reasonable cost. The streets of the village were clean and tidy. There was a school for the young children, and he did not permit those of young years to be employed. Owen did not believe in punishing his workers, but used a system by which the sections of his factory that did a good job were given recognition. Likewise, those that did a poor job were identified, and so the workers, as a matter of self-respect, did their best to do a good job. The venture was a great success, for Owen himself made a fortune while his workers enjoyed a standard of living and working conditions much superior to those of workers in other factories. By 1815, New Lanark was regarded as an outstanding example that attracted world-wide attention. It is said that between 1815 and 1825, some 20,000 visitors came to learn about Owen's techniques. But Owen was not satisified. He believed that working people should form villages of co-operation where they could produce goods and pursue happiness. In 1817, he left New Lanark and tried in vain to interest members of the aristocracy in his plan.

Owen then journeyed to the United States. He bought 30 acres of land in Indiana on which to set up a village of co-operation called New Harmony. The colony, begun in 1825, attracted a good number, but the people who came did not have a common bond of interest or desire, so that it was impossible to find agreement on plans or goals. Within two years, the venture failed, costing Owen the bulk of his fortune. Returning to England where trade unions were now permitted, Owen attempted to organize the many small unions that had emerged into a Grand National Consolidated Trades Union. It is said that by 1833-34, a million workers had become affiliated with this organization. But it fell apart because employers took action against leaders of some small unions that had resorted to strikes for better wages or working conditions. The employers found an old law prohibiting secret oaths, and charged that the oaths, taken by workers on joining a union, fell into that category. Six laborers were tried for administering the oaths, and sentenced to 7 years' transport (i.e., exile to a colony).

It should not be assumed that New Lanark was Owen's only success. He did, by his New Lanark example, provide a strong agrument in favor of improved factory conditions; by providing that both workers and employers could benefit. He pioneered education for children, and he promoted the idea of both producers' and consumers' co-operatives.

AMERICAN REVOLUTION

From 1756 to 1763, Britain was at war with France. The Seven Years' War, ended by the Treaty of Paris, left Britain in possession of the French Colonies in North America.

In America, the French presence had not been the only problem. Indians were hostile to the colonists so that it was necessary for the legislative assemblies of the colonies to assess taxes for defence. In 1757, the Pennsylvania assembly sent one of its elected members,

Benjamin Franklin, to London in effort to bring pressure upon the heirs of William Penn, the chief 'landlords' of the colony, to pay taxes to assist the colony to protect itself. Franklin remained in London, except for a return to America from 1762 to 1764, until 1775. In that time he worked, largely in vain, to persuade Parliament that colonists have rights.

King George III, who was crowned in 1761, was determined to restore to the monarchy much of the power held by the aristocracy. He was opposed, of course, and as a result parliament became a 'divided house'. Of George III, Pares wrote: "His idea of firmness was extremely simple; a flat refusal particularly to resist any threat to established institutions, enforcement of law, or the general principle of 'subordination'."

Parliament began to enforce the Navigation Acts, a matter which affected the colonies of America by restricting trade. The Act required that goods moving between Britain and the colonies be carried in British vessels. The colonies were not permitted to export to other countries, materials required by Britain, nor to export directly to any other country; all goods were to be shipped to Britain, where any applicable taxes or duties were applied, then re-shipped to their final destination. Similarly, imports by the colonies were restricted to those produced by British manufacturers. Navigation Acts had been passed as early as 1651 but had, to some extent, been evaded by the American colonies which had developed an illegal trade with the West Indies.

Next, in 1765, Parliament passed the Stamp Act, a means of raising revenue from the colonies of America, to pay the cost of keeping a permanent military force to deal with hostile Indians. The Stamp Act provided for a tax on newspapers, pamphlets, deeds, mortgages, and a number of other legal documents. The tax was bitterly opposed by the colonists who denied that parliament, in which they were not represented, had the right to impose taxes upon them. In October 1765, delegates from nine colonies met, preparing a petition of their grievances to be sent to the king and to parliament. At the same time, merchants of the colonies united in agreement not to handle British goods so long as the Stamp Act remained. Their boycott was so effective that trade between Britain and America came to a halt, causing merchants in Britain to call for an end to the tax. The Stamp Act was repealed, but the bill for repeal carried as a rider, a declaration proclaiming the right of Parliament to impose direct taxes on the colonies-a denial of the colonies' claim that there should be no taxation without representation.

Parliament acted to exercise its claimed right by imposing, in 1767, heavy duties on tea, glass and lead, coupled with tight controls and inspection of warehouses, stores, and other places to ensure that the tax was not evaded by smuggling goods.

Massachusetts, and especially Boston, was aroused in anger and called for a further boycott of British goods. King George III and his ministers then ordered two batallions of infantrymen to be sent from Halifax to Boston, expecting that the presence of troops would be enough to cause submission. But in March, 1770, rioting broke out between Boston people and the troops. The troops fired, killing five colonists. The event caused great resentment in the colony, and in Britain where the slogan of "no taxation without representation" had caused demands for reform of Parliament and the extension of the franchise, a civil war seemed near at hand. It was, however, averted, and Parliament then repealed the duties imposed in 1767, all but a token tax on tea that was left to symbolize Britain's 'right' to tax the colonies.

Britain made a further concession by enabling the East India Company to sell tea to America at a price lower than that of duty-free smuggled tea, the reduction in price being at least enough to cover the token tax. But, by standing by their principles, colonists in New York and Philadelphia stopped the unloading of tea from British **ships, and in Boston, in 1772, a group of colonists, dressed as** Indians, swarmed aboard British ships to dump their cargoes of tea into the harbour. Britain retaliated in 1774, closing the port of Boston until payment for the destroyed tea had been made. Town meetings were forbidden, and British troops took over the public buildings. At this point, Virginia called for a meeting of representatives of all 13 colonies and Canada, to consider the stubborn intrusion of Britain into their affairs. The meeting, or Congress of the Colonies, took place at Philadelphia in September 1774, but without representatives from Canada or Georgia. The Congress did not call for a separation from Britain, but in a petition, asked George III to protect the rights of the colonies against further violations. It was agreed that the Congress should meet again next May 1775, but, by April, war between the colonies and Britain had begun.

Benjamin Franklin returned from London in 1775, and almost immediately was asked to go to Paris to enlist French aid against the British. In Paris, Franklin's mission became well known, and he was regarded by the French, themselves longing for freedom, as a symbol of liberty. Members of the French aristocracy, seeing an opportunity to repay defeats suffered at the hands of Britain, undertook to send supplies to America. Then, after American successes in late 1777, France openly went to war with Britain, soon to be followed by Spain. The war dragged on until 1783, when Britain, weary of fighting, officially recognized that her former colonies were independent and united as the United States of America. The colonies had, by adoption of the Declaration of Independence on July 4, 1776, united themselves to "solemnly publish and declare, That these United States are, and of Right out to be Free and Independent States; that they are Absolved from all Allegiance to the British Crown..."

FRENCH REVOLUTION

The French Revolution is generally said to have begun in 1789, and is best remembered for its violence. The fact is, however, that important steps toward freedom from feudal tyranny began somewhat earlier than 1789, and might have led to a peaceful transition to freedom were it not for the stubborn resistance of the king and aristocracy.

Conditions in France at the time were even more incredibly oppressive and feudalistic by far, than in Britain. France, which had the largest population of any country in Europe, consisted of three classes known as 'estates' or 'orders', with the king as the ruling head with supreme power. The first estate consisted of the clergymen of high office, and the second of the aristocracy. All others, from wealthiest merchants to humblest peasants, were of the third estate. Most of the land was owned by the first two estates. The only body to resemble a national parliament was called the Estates-General, but it had not been called into session since 1614. Government was through decrees issued by the king. There were also, in the provinces, local parlements, of which the parlement of Paris was the most influential, but all were dominated by the first and second orders.

France, without a national assembly, had no national budget but did indeed have a great national debt built up through years of wars of past decades and including the help given to the American colonies in their War of Independence. Since the first and second estates had largely exempted themselves from taxes, the tax burden generally fell upon the third estate. Taxation fell especially heavily on the poorer peasant class for as well as paying taxes imposed by the privileged orders, the poor also paid rents and **feudal dues to their aristocratic landlords, plus tithes imposed by** the church. Peasants were further burdened when compelled by their landlords, to use the lords' mills for grinding corn, their ovens for baking bread, or wine-presses for crushing grapes. In contrast, the noblemen of higher station had a life of idle luxury, sustained by the income received from the peasants and by drawing large pensions. While the king held enough power to do so, he did nothing to reform the ancient, unjust system, and would have met with stern opposition from the first and second orders if he had tried.

Between 1774 and 1786, three successive comptrollers-general (national treasurers) warned the king of the desperate financial condition of his country. One of them Charles Calonne, showed that annual deficits of as much as 70,000,000 livres had existed for many years. Each of the three comptrollers-general urged the king to reform taxation and end exemptions granted to the privileged orders. But each was dismissed, being forced out of office by an aristocracy determined to retain its position of wealth and status. The next comptroller-general, Lomenie de Brienne, hoped that an Assembly of the Notables would agree to the need and logic of his reform proposals. At his urging the king called the Assembly of Notables into session, the first since 1626. This body, consisting of nobles, bishops and magistrates was hostile to reform. So was the Paris parlement. Disturbed by the proposals that seemed to have the support of the king, the parlement, in 1788, published a document denouncing royal authority and declaring that it was parlement that was the true defender of the people and guardian of the laws. The king responded by surrounding parlement with troops and arresting two members while depriving all others of some of their rights.

A number of disturbances, inspired by the nobles and fueled by resentment over the high price of bread, broke out in many parts of France. The king then agreed to consult the people by calling into session the Estates-General. The session was to be held in May, 1789, a matter for which an election was required.

In the months that followed, a national movement emerged, working on behalf of the third estate. In Paris, a "Patriot Party" was formed, its ranks including some liberal-minded nobles and a number of important men of the third estate. Among them was the Marquis de Lafayette, who had been an officer in the French forces in the American War of Independence. The Patriots and others demanded reform, drew courage from their knowledge of the American Revolution. On this point, Lefayette wrote: "Men believed that they saw in the American Revolution the pattern of all revolutions; there lay the example of a free society which, with seeming else, had shaped itself by virtue of abstract principles. ... Layfayette sincerely believed that France could imitate America without serious disturbances. The Paris parlement, however, was not prepared to consider reform. On September 25, 1788, it declared that the coming Estates-General session must be constituted in the same manner as it had when last convened 174 years earlier. This meant that each of the three bodies estates would be represented, but each would meet separately to consider matters brought before the Estates-General, and each estate would cast one vote.

Obviously, the votes cast by the first and second estates would defeat the third estate. The King, however, countered by granting the third estate a double vote. When the Estates-General met on May 5, 1789, a dispute immediately began over voting procedures. The third estate demanded that voting be through a simple majority with each member casting his individual vote. The first and second estates argued for the old system. When the assembly was directed to go to the separate rooms for each estate, the members of the third estate refused to comply, determined that all business and voting should be done in a general assembly of all orders. The insurgent third estate continued to occupy the assembly hall and finally, on June 17, proclaimed itself as the National Assembly with the sole right to legislate taxation. The king deprived the National Assembly of the right to use the assembly hall, and for that reason, the Assembly met, on June 20 on a tennis court, taking oath that it would not dissolve until it had successfully adopted a proper constitution for France. A number of the clergy and aristocracy then joined the Assembly but the king, under pressure of the first and second estates, ordered several foreign regiments to Paris and Versailles. The king also agreed to call a 'royal session' of the three estates on June 23, to settle problems of procedure and to propose reforms. He did, in fact, suggest some reforms to the session, but also made it clear that he did not intend to give up any royal privileges. He then called for the orders to go to their separate rooms, but again, the third estate, now known as the 'commons,' refused to leave the assembly hall where they were joined by most of the clergy and by more aristocrats. On June 27, the king directed all other members of the Estates-General to join the assembly, and thereby, the National Assembly replaced the Estates-General. It was indeed a victory for the third estate.

However, on July 12, rioting began. The Bastille, a Paris prison, was stormed and its inmates released. The electors of the third estate formed a militia to subdue the violence of the poor and to guard against plots by the aristocracy. Lafayette was named as its commander. By August 26, a Declaration of the Rights of Man was drawn up by the National Assembly and approved by the king. Its opening words were similar to those of the American Declaration: "All men are born and remain free and equal in rights." The next step was to draw up a Constitution of France, a statement of the methods by which the aims of the Declaration would be carried out.

By August, 1789, it appeared as though a revolution had been accomplished, without great violence. But King Louis XVI was plotting behind the scenes, calling for Austrians and others to send armies to restore the old regime. At the same time, the successful revolutionaries had dreams of liberating all Europe from feudal regimes. On April 20, 1792, war against Austria was declared. On February 1, 1793, war was declared against Britain and Holland, and on March 1, against Spain. These wars were to last until 1815 when the Duke of Wellington defeated Bonaparte Napleon at the Battle of Waterloo. It was between 1792 and 1794 that France had its reign of terror in which King Louis XVI, Queen Marie Antoinette, and so many others were executed. In the end, the violence had far exceeded anything expected by Layfayette.

REFORM BILL OF 1832

Except for a lull between 1802 and 1805, Britain was at war with France from 1793 to 1815, quelling the aim of French revolutionaries to assist other people to overthrow their rulers. Even when the war began in 1793, demand for reform was strong within Britain. In that year, parliament, by vote of 282 to 41, agreed that petitions on reform would not even be accepted. The old ruling class remained in control. As Evans explains. "It was the smallness of the electorate which made control by the Government and the great landowners so easy, especially as the ballot was unknown, so that a vote cast against the great man's nominee might have grave consequences for the voter. In 1829, when his choice was defeated at Newark, the Duke of Newcastle checked over the votes and expelled every one of his tenants who had voted the wrong way."

The French Revolution, however, made an impression in Britain. Among the ruling class, it created fear and the realization that if the French experience was to be avoided, some concessions by way of reform were imperative. There were also some members of the aristocracy and gentry who favored reform on its own merits.

The rally at St. Peter's Fields in 1817, which was broken up by yeomen, was but one of many evidences of demand for reform. This rally, also known as the "Peterloo Massacre", was attended by a huge number of people—one writer says 50,000, another 80,000. Demand for reform of parliament and for extension of the right to vote to all men, had become a widespread, popular theme. But it required three attempts by the Whig (Liberal) government to get through Parliament, a bill providing for only a modest extension of the franchise.

The first attempt began March 31, 1831, when Lord John Russell placed a reform bill before the House of Commons. It provided for an increase in the number eligible to vote, and also for a redistribution of seats, the latter having been unchanged since 1688. The bill was given first reading and after debate of seven days, passed second reading with a majority of but one. The Prime Minister, Earl Grey, was convinced that unless the reform bill passed there would be a revolution. He saw little hope that it would pass third reading in Commons, and less still for survival in the House of Lords. So, he asked for dissolution of parliament so that a general election could be held.

Reform was, of course, the key issue of the general election held in May by which the Whigs were returned with some 90 more seats. On June 27, 1831, the reform bill was put before the new House of Commons where it was passed, September 22, by a clear majority of 109. It then passed to the House of Lords, where it was rejected on October 7, by a majority of 41. Rioting in protest of the blocking of reform broke out in several places, including Bristol where an uprising lasted for three days. Thomas Attwood, leader of "The Political Union of the Middle and Lower Classes," vowed he would assemble a million men on Hampstead Heath to protest the blocking of reform. But not all working men favored the reform bill. It was designed to benefit only their employers, the group held responsible for poor wages and working conditions.

After a fall recess, the House of Commons again assembled. In March, Lord Russell, put the bill before Commons for the third time. With some minor amendment, it passed on March 26, 1832, and was sent to the House of Lords. In April, the Lords passed the bill; by a majority of 9, then began debate on amendments of their own that would all but destroy it. The Prime Minister, Earl Grey, resigned in protest. The Duke of Wellington, an opponent of reform, consented to form a government that would bring about a more modest reform, but he failed in his attempt, and Grey was asked to return. Grey returned on May 15, but only after he had been promised by the king that 50 or 60 new Whig peers would be appointed if necessary, to overcome the Tory majority in the House of Lords. The promise was threat enough; the House of Lords reluctantly passed the Reform Bill which became law in June, 1832. The Bill gave voting rights to all men living in boroughs (incorporated towns) who paid annual rents of ten pounds. In the counties (rural areas) leaseholders paying an annual rent of 50 pounds, copyholders "to the value of 10 pounds per annum," and freeholders "to the value of 40 shillings," were enfranchised.

The new voters were of the wealthier middle class only, including men of professional status—factory owners, successful merchants and other employers, but no women. The monetary qualifications excluded the working class. The 10 pounds qualification in the boroughs was equal to about 3 months' wages for an average man working in a Leeds spinning mill in 1831. The 50 pounds qualification for leaseholders was equal to at least 100 weeks' wages for an agricultural worker.

Reference to numerous writings indicates that there is a great deal of uncertainty as to the number eligible to vote before and after the Reform Bill. The numbers given vary widely. After an examination of evidence from many sources it was assumed that figures provided by the Encyclopedia Britannica are reasonably accurate. This source shows 438,000 voters in a population of 10,207,000 in 1831 and 720,784 in 1832, for an increase of about 283,000. Thus, after the Reform Bill only 7.1% of the population over the age of 20 had voting rights.

This voting structure, an alliance of aristocracy, landed gentry, and the more powerful members of the business class, remained unchanged for the next 35 years. Not until mid-August 1867, some weeks after Confederation in Canada, was there further extension of the franchise. So far as the texture of parliament was concerned, a number of authors seem to support the view of Encyclopedia Americana which says:

"The famous Reform Act (of 1832), far from undermining aristocratic power, actually enhanced it in some ways, for it removed glaring anachronisms without seriously hurting landed interests. The reformed House of Commons showed almost as much aristocratic control as the old. The changes made by the act in individual qualification for the vote had even less effect, increasing the total electorate by roughly 50% to about 800,000, or 1 in 30 of the population. The big landowners more than held their own against traders and industrialists until at least the 1880's." By no means did the Reform Bill of 1832 bring about a state of democracy. But it did, at least, break up the old traditional and self-perpetuating style of parliamentary control.

OTHER REFORM MEASURES

Besides the Factory Act of 1834 and repeal of the Combinations Acts which led to the legalizing of trade unions, there were other reforms to increase civil liberties. These reforms were unquestionably the result of a strong religious revival that had been ascending since the latter part of the 18th Century to inspire demand for a more rational, brotherly society.

Between 1823 and 1827, Robert Peel, Britain's Home Secretary, succeeded in revising laws respecting crime. Before then the statute books had accumulated a list of over 200 offences, including petty theft, for which the death penalty was imposed, and there were more than twice as many offences for which transportation to convict settlements in Australia was listed as punishment. Peel eliminated the death penalty for over 180 offences and also reduced the number for which transportation was provided. In 1810 and in 1813 there had been attempts to ease the punishments for crime, but both had been quashed by the House of Lords. In 1813, two brothers, ages 10 and 12, were transported for seven years for stealing some linens while in 1814, a lad of 14 years was hanged for petty theft. How sorely more humane laws were needed!

Another reform of note was that of abolishing slavery in the British colonies by a bill passed in 1833. The slave trade, carried on by British vessels, had been abolished in 1807, but not without opposition from the owners of vessels who, by transporting as many as 100,000 Negro slaves a year in some 200 vessels, had a profitable trade, particularly with the West Indies since 1709.

THE CHARTISTS

Their exclusion from the franchise while the Reform Bill of 1832 gave political power to their employers caused great resentment among associations of working men. From this discontent emerged a movement known as 'Chartism', so named because its leaders developed a Charter calling for political reforms.

As Rees explained: "The suspicion that a Parliament elected on the principles of 1832 would act in the interests of the employers was confirmed. Consequently, it seemed that the only way to escape was to reopen the question of political democracy and to demand that the suffrage should be so extended that such class legislation would be impossible."

The Chartists were not a single body or organization, but a conglomerate of many smaller bodies, and since these did not adhere to a uniform code of procedures or aims, the movement was never without division in its ranks. The Charter was drafted by William Lovett with the assistance of Francis Place, both of the Working Men's Association founded in London in 1836. Lovett had earlier been influenced by Robert Owen and was a secretary for Owen's Association for Promoting Co-operative Knowledge.

That demands listed in the People's Charter were reasonable, it is obvious since all have since been adopted:

(a) The right to vote for all men.
(b) Voting by secret ballot.
(c) Equal electoral districts.
(d) Removal of the property qualifications for parliamentary candidates.
(e) Payment of members of Parliament.
(f) Parliament to meet at least annually.

In addition to that of the Working Men's Association of London, another large faction of the Chartists developed at Birmingham through the revival, in 1837, of the Birmingham Political Union of which Thomas Attwood was a leading figure. An Assembly of 200,000 workers took place at Birmingham in August 1838, and called for supporters of the Charter from throughout the country to appoint delegates to attend a convention to be held in London. Mass meetings throughout Britain followed, and the convention met at London, February 4, 1839. Its purpose was to prepare a National Petition to convey demands of the Charter, to Parliament. The Petition was completed and supported by 1,200,000 signatures. It was carried to Parliament and on July 12, 1839, there was a motion put forth that members meet as a Committee of the Whole House to consider it. Benjamin Disraeli, future prime minister, used the debate on the motion to argue for a return to the pre-1832 status of parliament. He blamed conditions on the Reform Bill that had given political power to the middle class which, he said, was lacking in any sense of duty towards the lower orders. Before the Reform Bill, Disraeli claimed, power was entrusted to those who exercised it with public spirit and sympathy! The motion to debate the Chartists' Petition was defeated, 235 to 46. The Chartists next proposed a general strike in order to impress Parliament. The threat of such action led to an intervention by the authorities who acted with the blessings of Parliament. Lovett was arrested and imprisoned for 12 months on a charge of seditious libel. Henry Vincent of the Working Men's Association was also sent to prison. At Newport, from 2,000 to 3,000 miners rallied under leadership of John Frost, former mayor of that town, with aims of releasing Vincent. However, the authorities had placed a regiment in a local hotel. The soldiers fired on the Chartists, slaying 14 and wounding about 50 more. Scores of others were arrested. Thus, the original Chartist movement was stalled.

During its time, the original movement had issued a good many pamphlets in support of reform and democracy. One, published in 1836, calculated that out of 6,000,000 males of voting age, only 840,000 had the right to vote, with but one-fifth of the 840,000 electing a majority to the House of Commons, meaning that one-fortieth of the population had the power to make laws binding upon the rest. Between 1840 and 1842, a revival of the Chartists' agitation was attempted through a new organization, The National Charter Association. It obtained 2,000,000 signatures to a petition calling for the release of John Frost from prison, and 3,000,000 signatures for a further petition on Parliamentary reform. But the Chartists' strength was now waning, for interest had turned to a new body, The Anti-Corn Law League.

11

THE CORN LAWS

Farmers of Western Canada and elsewhere are often bitter in denouncing what is referred to as a 'cheap food' policy. To farmers, it is an irony that they must sell produce at prices set on world markets by the law of supply and demand but at the same time must purchase necessities at prices often protected by tariffs and dumping duties that assist domestic manufacturers. The 'cheap food' policy that affects agriculture of Western Canada can be traced to the repeal of the Corn Laws in Britain, in 1846.

In Britain, the word 'corn' was used rather than the word 'grain', hence in Canada, the Corn Laws might have been called Grain Laws. Corn Laws were enacted in Britain as early as 1534, but were amended many times in order to adjust the effect. The Corn Laws

were, in essence, a protection for British agriculture. When the price fell below a fixed level as it might in a year of a bumper crop, a duty was imposed on imports of grain to keep the price from falling too low, and at the same time, exports of surplus grain were encouraged. If, however, the price in Britain rose beyond a fixed amount, imports were encouraged to moderate British prices. The prices were set on the basis of so much per "quarter" or "qtr"; a quarter of grain being 504 pounds, of barley 445 pounds, and of oats, 336 pounds.

In operation, the Corn Laws were meant to give some stability to grain prices which always tend to vary widely from time to time simply because weather conditions generally determine whether the outcome of a crop will be a scarcity or surplus. Price stability had important implications, not only to landowners, tenant farmers and agricultural workers, but to the nation itself, for the burden of poor relief fell greatly upon the landowners. In times of a poor crop, or low prices, it would be difficult to bear the burden of taxes for poor relief and other purposes including the cost of wars. Following the war against France, which ended in 1815, conditions in Britain worsened. The harvest of 1816 was a failure, and the crops of the next two years were also poor. The price of corn rose, but farmers had little to sell. Many farm laborers were thrown out of work, while the high price of bread aroused low-paid workers, with the result that a good number of demonstrations took place throughout the country.

Factory owners, in answer to demands for a living wage, increasingly blamed the protection afforded by the Corn Laws, for causing the workers' problem. In September, 1838, at Manchester, an Anti-Corn Law Association was begun by a group seeking repeal of the Corn Laws. The Association developed into the Anti-Corn Law League with two cotton mill owners, John Bright of Rochdale and Richard Cobden of Manchester, as leading figures. Both became members of Parliament.

The Anti-Corn Law League put forth a strenous effort with the aid of assessments upon factory owners and others who regarded repeal of the Corn Laws to reduce the price of bread as being more favorable to themselves than the payment of higher wages. At the time, Britain was enveloped in an economic depression. Factory owners blamed the Corn Laws, asserting that they prevented countries desiring to purchase British manufactured goods from doing so because those countries could not pay for the goods with food products.

The League circulated hundreds of thousands of pamphlets, staged rallies, published newspapers and bought newspaper space, circulated petitions, and made numerous representations to Parliament. It succeeded in convincing many of the working class that it was the protection afforded to landowners that kept workers at the starvation level. A contrary opinion was expressed by a Mr. Ferrant, a Member of Parliament, speaking on the Corn Laws in the Commons on February 14, 1842:

"Sir, I made inquiries into the truth of their assertions that the Corn Laws were the cause of the depression of trade, and of the misery and starvation of the working classes; and I found that during the operation of the Corn Laws in the last twenty years, the Messrs. Marshall, flax-spinners of Leeds, have accumulated two millions' in money, and have purchased immense landed estates; but this firm were not satisfied with this enormous wealth; they must carry out by themselves the principle of free trade, and set up mills in Belgium, where there are no Corn Laws, and where labour is at a starvation price....I will add a few more instances of the injurious effects of the Corn Laws on the Anti-Corn Law League manufacturers....The Hon. Member for Stockport (Mr. Cobden) had during these last twelve years accumulated half-a-million of money, when night after night during the last session, he asserted that the Corn Laws had ruined his trade in Lancashire, he was actually, at the very time, running his mill both day and night."

The Chartists too, opposed the repeal of the Corn Law. According to Cole & Postgate: "Chartists workers had not denied that repeal of the Corn Laws would benefit momentarily the town working class. But they said, with great truth, that the Anti-Corn Law Leaguers and their supporters were precisely the manufacturers whose greed and cruelty made their lives intolerable."

Debates on the Corn Law divided the House of Commons. But, fate intervened. In August of 1845, a blight destroyed the potato crop in Ireland so that, in 1846, countless numbers of Irish were starving, for of the Irish population of 8,200,000, over half were peasants engaged in subsistence farming and dependent upon the potato crop. The Irish had to be fed with wheat, but the English and European wheat crops were a failure so that grain had to be brought from elsewhere. If the wheat was to serve its purpose amid the Irish distress and poverty, it had to be imported without the tariff of the Corn Law, and this was done.

Sir Robert Peel, prime minister, though at first opposed to repeal of the Corn Laws, now reversed his stand. With a majority of 98 in a vote by 556 members, a bill for repeal of the Corn Law passed through the House of Commons. It was passed by the House of Lords and given Royal Assent on June 26, 1846, to be fully effective in February of 1849. As one writer notes, it was nothing but common sense to expect that by the time the bill became effective, the Irish potato blight problem could be expected to have disappeared, a matter which seemed to escape consideration. Its work accomplished, the Anti-Corn Law League met to dissolve on July 2, 1846. Its advocates, greatly pleased with the result, took up a collection for the leaders, providing a purse of 80,000 pounds for Cobden and a valuable library for Bright.

Without doubt, the Anti-Corn Law League did permanent injury to agriculture. It created a division between agricultural and nonagricultural interests, or between rural and urban people. The League's success in furthering the aims of the industrialists destroyed the status of agriculture, creating within industries a form of class system in which manufacturers and merchant traders assumed predominant strength while agriculture was relegated to a subordinated serving-class role. This condition, with its inequality of status, was most certainly transplanted to Canada.

ROCHDALE SOCIETY OF EQUITABLE PIONEERS

It was amid the decline of Chartism and the upsurge of the Anti-Corn Law League that the Rochdale Pioneers opened their store in 1844. Rochdale was a centre of strong agitation by both movements. It was there that the Chartists packed a large Anti-Corn Law rally to pass, against the opposition of John Bright, a resolution favoring extension of the right to vote to all men. Now, as Chartism waned while the mill owners enthusiastically backed the cause of the Anti-Corn Law League, the Pioneers turned quietly to the development of their own plan. It must have been clear to them that the economic plight of the working people would not greatly improve so long as they were forced to depend on a system by which they were dominated both politically and economically by that sector with the right to vote and control parliament. The answer had been advocated by Robert Owen—the formation of co-operative societies in which the people served kept ownership and control to themselves and thereby avoided domination by any outside group. And since the most pressing need of the moment was to reduce the cost of food, it was logical that the Pioneers should direct their effort toward the opening of a store.

The Pioneers were wise in their choice of policies or 'principles' for their society. They provided for 'open membership' to all who could use the services. They provided that each member should have one vote only, ensuring that no minority could outvote the majority and that all the members would enjoy equal rights. The Pioneers provided for the return of surplus earnings to the members as patronage refunds on their purchases, and for limited interest on capital, both provisions ensuring that the organization would not be used for speculative purposes. Cash trading was adopted as a principle for several reasons. One reason was to safeguard the interests of the membership as a whole, for under laws of the time, the Society did not have limited liability. In the event of financial difficulty, all members would be liable for the Society's indebtedness. Another reason for cash trading was to encourage the members to avoid the use of credit. Many workers were in the bondage of merchants who extended credit, often at high interest. They could hardly complain if served with shoddy or adulterated goods, for the laws provided for imprisonment of those who failed to pay their debts. In addition, the Pioneers vowed that "none but the purest of goods shall be sold", and "there shall be fair weights and honest measurers". Both policies were ruling against

common practices of merchants as well as manufacturers. There were now laws to protect consumers against shoddy goods or against adulteration of foods. The Pioneers also stressed the need for the Society to provide for the education of its members. Education in the Society's aims was a part of the program. But it went further, for it was intended that members be assisted in the matter of understanding the social and technical changes taking place, and have opportunity to learn skills by which to earn a living.

There was no law under which the Pioneers could incorporate the Society to obtain limited liability. For that reason, it was registered under the Friendly Societies Act. The Friendly Societies Act, however, was not designed for trading societies. A new Friendly Societies Act passed in 1846 made some provision for trading societies, but empowered them only to trade with members, a matter which made producers' co-operatives uncertain of their status.

In 1852, R.A. Slaney and John Bright (the Bright of the Anti-Corn Law League) persuaded parliament to pass an Industrial and Provident Societies Act providing for the needs of both consumers' and producers' co-operative societies. Further improvement was provided by a second Industrial and Provident Societies Act of 1862 which provided for limited liability and enabled co-operative societies to form a wholesale and to engage in manufacturing. This was done by making it legal for one society to hold shares in another; i.e., for co-operative stores to be shareholders of a wholesale society. Thus, in 1863, the Co-operative Wholesale Society was formed by 48 retailing co-operatives. It was followed in 1868 by the Scottish Co-operative Wholesale Society. Wholesale societies had, by then, become a necessity, for private retailers were aligning against co-operative societies and refusing to deal with wholesalers who served the co-operatives. Brown outlines an example of shopkeepers' tactics: 'By 1859, the Pioneers' Society reached a six figure turnover, the sales totalling 104,102 pounds. There were 2,703 members, with an average shareholding of 10 pounds and average weekly purchases of 14 shillings per member. Having regard to the slender incomes, 14 shillings weekly expended at their own shop showed the loyalty of the co-operators was established. Rival shopkeepers were alarmed. Parliament had been dissolved, and John Bright commended Richard Cobden to the electors of his native town (Rochdale). Thereupon the walls of Rochdale were plastered with bills issued by 'A shopkeeper', urging the tradesmen to remember that 'the chief supporters of the Bright-and-Cobden faction are also the leading supporters of the Co-operative Stores. (They) are aiders and abettors of this iniquitous system. Will the shopkeepers still go on aiding the men who are fostering the system which is destined at no distant period to snatch their daily bread from their jaw?"

This, of course, was an example of behaviour on the part of shopkeepers similar to that of the factory owners who petitioned against easing of conditions of child labor; or of the shipowners who objected to an end to the slave trade. It could not be justified except as a matter of selfish interest.

INCOME TAX

In 1799, Britain imposed an income tax for the first time, to help finance the war against France. Being most unpopular, the tax was withdrawn once the war came to an end. In 1842 there was a general revision of duties and tariffs and, apparently, a miscalculation as to the effect on government revenues. An income tax was again imposed, purportedly as a temporary measure but it has remained ever since.

The Friendly Societies Act of 1842 under which the Rochdale Society was registered contained a clause exempting such societies from tax on income earned from government bonds. This Act, which was not designed for trading societies, made no mention of the liability for tax on income from trading. Likewise, the Industrial and Provident Societies Act of 1852 neglected to define the income tax status of co-operative societies. The Rochdale Society, at the insistence of government officials who were acting without specific guidance from the Act, paid an income tax but did so under protest since it was obvious that individual members of the Society did not earn enough to become liable for the tax. In 1853, the Friendly Societies were declared to be exempt of income tax on earnings from government bonds or from tax on earnings derived from trading. This ruling further strengthened the argument of the co-operatives, but the matter remained unsettled until 1862 when the new Industrial and Provident Societies Act became law. It contained a clause according to co-operatives the same exemptions as provided to Friendly Societies. By 1879, however, private dealers complained that co-operatives were evading tax and that a number of stores which were operating the Industrial and Provident Societies Act, were really not co-operatives and yet were avoiding tax. The latter, according to Cole, were such institutions as civil service stores, army stores, navy stores and the like, begun on a co-operative basis by middle-and upper-class people, but which were subsequently turned into ordinary profit-making concerns by refusing entry on equal terms to new members and appropriating all profits for the benefit of existing members.

The whole matter was fully examined by a Parliamentary Committee. In 1880, to use Cole's words: "It was laid down that exemption from income tax should be restricted to Societies which placed no limitation on the entry of new members, and it was in addition specified that the exemption should not extend to the profits of trade with non-members. The trade with non-members was small in amount, for it usually pays those who trade with real Co-operative Societies to become members, and the Co-operative Movement naturally welcomed a provision which excluded bodies which were not really Co-operative from the scope of exemption. It should, however, be understood that Co-operators were not by any means completely exempted. Co-operative Societies remained liable to income tax under Schedules A and B, income from ownership or occupation of land, and individual Co-operators whose incomes were above the exemption limit were taxable on the interest occurring to them from share or loan capital in Co-operative Societies. What did become established was that 'dividend on purchases,' as distinct from interest on shares or loans, was not taxable income, because the Co-operative trading 'surplus' could not be correctly regarded as a 'profit'."

OTHER REFORM BILLS

The Act which united Canada in Confederation at July 1, 1867, was actually passed through the British House of Commons and given Royal Assent by Queen Victoria on March 29, 1867. Since there had been no broadening of the franchise since the Reform Bill of 1832, Britain's Parliament at the time of Canada's Confederation was still controlled by the aristocrat-gentry-industrial alliance. In 1866, however, the Whigs introduced a bill proposing some extension of the franchise. It was strongly opposed from within the Whig ranks as well as by the Tories, forcing the Whigs to resign. The Tories, with Benjamin Disraeli as house leader within the Commons, assumed office. But before the next session of Parliament was called, mammoth rallies demanding the right to vote for all working men took place throughout the country. John Bright addressed many of those rallies in support of reform. At Leeds, a rally was attended from 100,000 to 200,000; at Birmingham, it was said that the crowd was more than 200,000; and at Manchester, between 100,000 and 200,000 rallied amid torrents of rain. At the Manchester rally, two resolutions were passed:

"That this meeting protests against the perpetuation of class government to the exclusion of the great majority of the people from the franchise; refuses to allow itself to be made an instrument to further the means of contending parties or the selfish interests of any class; and pledges itself to adopt all means of organizing and agitating for the only just basis of representation—registered residential manhood suffrage and the ballot."

"That this meeting, while recording its indignation at the results offered in Parliament and by the Press to the working classes and their advocates, calls on the people of this country to allow themselves no longer to be trifled with by an oligarchic few, and to rally round those men who have upheld their cause."

Prior to the opening of the new Parliament, Queen Victoria spoke to the Tory leaders to express her desire for reform. The speech from the throne, read by the Queen but prepared by the Tories, promised that the government, "without unduly disturbing the balance of political power, shall freely extend the franchise." The ensuing reform bill proposed the granting of the right to vote to about 400,000 who had a certain level of education plus 50 pounds in savings, and a dual vote to every direct taxpayer. The Whigs attacked the proposals so vigorously as to cause the Tories to make drastic amendments. The amended bill passed third reading in the Commons on July 15, 1867, and was given Royal Assent on August 15. It added about one million men to the voters' list, the majority being of the towns or boroughs. It tended to widen the gap between rural and urban people caused by the repeal of the Corn Laws, for the Reform Bill of 1867 did not extend the vote to agricultural workers or to miners of the rural villages.

In 1872, the Ballot Act provided for use of the secret ballot, a matter which the Chartists had demanded. The secret ballot ensured that new voters enfranchised in 1867, were not intimidated by their landlords or by employers. A third reform bill passed in 1884 enfranchised agricultural laborers so that by now, 4 out of 5 men had the right to vote. Still another Act of 1885 redistributed parliamentary seats on the basis of population—another reform that had been demanded by the Chartists.

But for women, there was still no right to vote. On May 20, 1867, John Stuart Mill proposed in the House of Commons that women be given the right to vote. He had in his hands a petition bearing 1,500 signatures, directed to him by a group of middle class women. The petition pointed out that men who owned property had voting rights, but, if a woman inherited such property, she would not inherit the right to vote. Mill's proposal was promptly defeated, but from then on there was increasing demand for women for the right to vote. In 1918, women of 30 years of age were given the franchise, and in 1928, the age was reduced to 21 years. In 1931, nearly 97% of the men and women over the age of 20 years were eligible to vote. A state of political democracy had finally arrived.

The last two chapters have given a glimpse of conditions and events in Britain during the period from about 1750 to 1867. For one who is not too familiar with the past, some of the content of those two chapters may seem incredible. All, however, can easily be confirmed by the reading of the history of the 18th and 19th centuries.

We saw, in those two chapters, how a small but powerful body of men controlled the social and economic affairs of Britain to their own benefit, and kept her people in a bondage of misery through cruel, oppressive laws. It was an hypocritical age, not only in Britain but in France and other European countries, for the men whose inhumane use of power created the tyranny under which the masses lived, were at the same time members of the genteel class among which good breeding, refined manners and leadership were marks of distinction. This class of aristocrats and landed gentry, with their wealth, luxury, and high social status, provided a model to be followed by a new middle class that was rising to prominence through the Industrial Revolution—the factory owners, wealthier merchants, financiers, and other commercial men.

More than one historian has noted that a common ambition among the new middle class was to obtain the wealth necessary for the purchase of an estate in order to live in the style of the landed gentry. It would be surprising if this were not the case, particularly since there was no other model to follow, except that of the aristocrats and gentry. Here we must be reminded of the findings of sociologists who declare that all human behaviour is learned; that individuals acquire a pattern of behaviour by observing that which is acceptable to other people.

Since, as the sociologists point out, man has a drive for 'upward mobility', meaning to move up the social ladder, it would be only natural for the new middle class to expect that their upward mobility required them to adopt, so far as possible, the attitudes style, and social norms of the superior class.

As we have seen, the upper class was, until 1832, in full control of Parliament and used that privilege as a means of serving itself. During the Industrial Revolution, great changes came about in manufacturing, and simultaneously agriculture was vastly improved. Until 1832, change had taken place in every quarter except government. Then, in 1832, the new industrial class was *given what must be regarded as a form of recognition and importance, by being extended the right to vote— an opportunity to become part of the ruling class.*

Now, in Chapter IV, we return to Canada, to the era prior to Confederation of 1867, to find the merchant class very active indeed, and without the restraint of strong upper classes such as aristocrats and gentry.

CHAPTER BIBLIOGRAPHIES
Chapters I, II and III

ALLEN, AGNES *The Co-operative Story,* Manchester: Co-operative Union Limited, 1953

BRIGGS, ASA. *The Nineteenth Century.* Toronto: London, Thames and Hudson, 1970.

BRIGGS, ASA. *Victorian People.* Harmondsworth, Middlesex, England: 1970.

BRYANT, ARTHUR. *English Saga 1840-1940.* London: Fontana Books,1953.

BROWN, W. HENRY. *The Rochdale Pioneer.* Manchester, England: The Co-operative Wholesale Society Ltd., circa 1945.

CHEYNEY, EDWARD P. *Modern English Reform.* New York: A.S. Barnes and Company, Inc., 1962.

CLARK, G. KITSON, *The Making of Victorian England.* Edinburgh: T.A. Constable Ltd., 1970.

COLE, G.D.H. *A Century of Co-operation.* Manchester: Holyoake House, 1944.

COLE, G.D.H. and POSTGATE, RAYMOND. *The Common People,* London: Methuen and Company Ltd., 1966.

EDWARDS, A.C.W. *Peace and Reform 1815-1837.* London: G. Bell and Sons Ltd., 1920.

EVANS, R.J. *The Victorian Age 1815-1914.* London: Edward Arnold, Publishers Ltd., 1962.

GRETTON, R.H. *Commercial Politics 1837-1856.* London: G. Bell and Sons Ltd., 1930.

HALEVY, ELIE. *Victorian Years 1841-1895.* New York: Barnes and Noble Ind. 1961.

HALL, ALICE J. "Benjamin Franklin." *National Geographic,* (July, 1975).

HARDING, EWING. *From Palmerston to Disraeli 1856 to 1876.* London: G. Bell and Sons Ltd., 1920.

HARRISON, J.F.C. *The Early Victorians 1832-1851.* St. Albans: Panther Books Ltd., 1973.

HART, IVOR B. *James Watt and the History of Steam Power.* Cambridge, Ontario: Collier Books Division, 1961.

HEILBRONER, ROBERT L. *The Wordly Philosophers.* New York: Simon and Shuster Inc., 1966.

HOWARD, BRETT. "Boston, The Athens of America." *Mankind Magazine,* IV, Number III, 1973.

HURWITZ, HOWARD L. *An Encyclopedic Dictionary of American History.* New York: Pocket Books, Simon and Shuster Inc., 1974.

LEFLER, HUGH T. *History of the United States.* Cleveland, Ohio: The World Publishing Company, 1970.

MAURIOS, ANDRE. *A History of France.* New York: Farrar, Straus and Cudahy, 1956.

PARES, RICHARD. *King George III and the Politicians,* London: Oxford University Press, 1967.

PLUMB, J.H. *England in the Eighteenth Century 1714-1815.* Harmondsworth, Middlesex, England: Penguin Books Ltd., 1959.

PRATT, N.S. *The French Revolution.* New York: The John Day Company, 1970.

REES, J.F.R. *A Social and Industrial History of England.* London: Methuen and Company Limited, 1920.

ROUSSEAU, JEAN—JACQUES. *The Social Contract and Discourse on the Origin of Inequality.* New York: Pocket Books, Washington Square Press, 1971.

RUDDOCK, J.W. *An Epitome of English Social History.* London: Blackie and Son Ltd., 1950.

SCHULTZ, HAROLD J. *History of England.* New York: Barnes and Noble Ind., 1968.

SOMERVELL, D.G. *English Thought in the Nineteenth Century.* London: Metheun and Company Ltd., 1936.

TOYNBEE, ARNOLD. *The Industrial Revolution.* Boston: The Beacon Press, 1957.

TREMAIN,ROSE. *The Fight for Freedom for Women.* New York: Ballantine Books Inc., 1973.

WARBASSE, JAMES PETER. *Co-operative Democracy.* New York: Harper and Brothers Publisher, 1942.

WATERS, CHARLOTTE M. *An Economic History of England.* London: Oxford University Press, 1928.

WATT, FRANCIS. *The Life and Opinions of the Right Honourable John Bright.* London: Ward, Lock and Company, Circa 1895.

WILLCOX, WILLIAM B. *The Age of Aristocracy.* Toronto: D.C. Heath and Company. 1966.

A DIARY
1541—1974

1541

CHAPTER IV
CANADA BEFORE CONFEDERATION

1. Feudal Land System: In 1541, King Francis I of France, ordered that the feudal system of land holding be introduced to New France. His aim was to encourage settlement of the French claims along the St. Lawrence River by encouraging some of the lower nobility of old France to accept a higher status in New France. Under the feudal system, a tract of land was awarded to a 'gentleman' or noble, the size of the tract depending upon the rank of the recipient. The person to whom the award was made, a seigneur, could hold the land in perpetuity for himself and heirs, and under certain conditions, could sell it. The seigneur was expected to sub-divide his holding into farmsteads for tenant farmers who paid him annual rents and performed such other services as required. Among the other services required of tenants was the building of a mansion or manor house for the seigneur, and a mill where the tenants, on paying a fee to the seigneur, could grind their grain to flour. In New France, holdings were usually beside a river with the farmsteads in long, narrow strips that gave each tenant access to the water. Though decreed in 1541, the seigneurial system developed but slowly, for the new settlers came in small numbers.

1606

2. First Wheat: The first wheat growing of which there is record in Canada, was at Port Royal (now Annapolis, Nova Scotia), where Samuel de Champlain and Baron de Poutrincourt founded a small colony. The fertile land was cultivated and a plot sown to wheat. Poutrincourt wrote: "It grew under the snow and in the following midsummer it was harvested."

1663

3. French Administration: Before 1663, France had hoped to colonize New France through the chartering of companies which, while engaged in the fur trade, would be required to encourage settlement, provide administration, and defend the colony. Most notable was the "Company of One Hundred Associates", chartered in 1627 by the king of France. The charter was awarded to a group of nobility, government officials, and wealthier merchants. It provided the Company with a monopoly on both the fur trade in New France and fur markets in old France. The Company did not comply with its obligations, but devoted its interest to the profits of fur trading. Thus, in 1663, King Louis XIV of France, by an order of April 28, set up a Sovereign Council to administer affairs in New France. Reflecting the social order of old France, the Council consisted of a Governor representing the king, followed in order of rank by a Bishop, and Interdant (administrator), and 5 councillors. The Council was empowered to make laws governing New France, but the king held final right to approve or reject such laws.

1670

4. Hudson's Bay Company: Two disgruntled French fur traders, Pierre Radisson and Medart Chouart des Groselliers, were responsible for the start of a British fur trading company which was granted a Royal Charter in 1670 by King Charles II of England. The

13

1670

two traders had earlier left Trois Rivieres on an expedition towards Hudson's Bay. They did not have the permission of the Governor of New France, hence on their return, a valuable stock of furs they had obtained was confiscated, and in addition, the two were fined. Nevertheless, the two traders asked the Governor to charter a company for fur trading in the Hudson's Bay area, but he refused. Radisson and Groselliers then journeyed to England where they obtained a more interested hearing. As a result, the king provided a charter to "The Governor and Company of Adventurers of England Trading Into the Hudson's Bay", otherwise known as the Hudson's Bay Company. Shareholders of the Company included Prince Rupert who was its first Governor, the Dukes of York and Albernarle, the Earls of Shaftsbury, Craven and Arlington, plus other aristocrats and several wealthy London merchants. The charter provided the Company with rights as "true and absolute lords and proprietors" of all lands drained by rivers entering into the Hudson's Bay. The area, which became known as Rupert's Land after Prince Rupert, was vast indeed. It included that part of the Prairies which later became the Provinces of Manitoba, Saskatchewan, Alberta, as well as lands later included in the states of Minnesota, North Dakota, and Montana and all lands to the north of what are now the Prairie Provinces. The Company, engaged in fur trading, was also responsible for administration, law and order within its holdings. It developed into a very large fur trading concern with many trading posts. Its officers and employees were organized along military lines, with levels of rank the head of a trading post, or Factor, having status of a commanding officer.

1678

5. Brandy Trading: In 1678, King Louis of France ordered a group of prominent New France colonists to propose a policy on the sale or trade of liquor to Indians. The clergy had objected to the provision of spirits to Indians. Fur traders, who knew that liquor was a means of striking advantageous bargains with Indians, declared that they, not the clergy, should decide on matters of commerce. The French traders further argued that their sale and trade of liquor was necessary; if they ceased to supply liquor to the Indians it would provide a competitive advantage to the British fur traders.

1754

6. Wheat In Rupert's Land: At a place by the Saskatchewan River in the Carrot River Valley, north of the present town of Melfort, Saskatchewan, grain was grown as early as 1754. A French explorer and fur trader, Chevalier Louis de la Corne had seeded a plot in the previous spring. He was paid a visit by an English trader, Anthony Hendry, who wrote in a report:

" Certainly no other man save this resourceful officer would ever have thought of trying to grow grain in this wild, unknown land.

Of a surety, the meal is fine flavored and what he does not use will make him rich in skins from the Indians."

Arthur Bennett, in a booklet, "Chevalier de la Corne and the Carrot River Valley of Saskatchewan", has written:

" When Chevalier de la Corne returned to Canada and exhibited samples of the grain he had grown in the mysterious northwest, there was a great amount of almost incredulous interest manifested by the Frenchmen who had never before dreamed of anything but valuable furs coming out of the vast unknown."

1756 to 1763

7. Seven Years' War: The Seven Years' War between France and Britain began in 1756. It was a war over trade and colonies and fought in many corners of the globe. It had, however, particular effect in North America where strife between the French and British colonies had been vigorous for a good number of years. Both French and English had brought Indians to their side so that in areas of hostility, life was in constant danger. In 1758, British forces captured Louisbourg, a strong French fortress and settlement of about 4,000, on Cape Breton Island. In 1759, British forces under General George Wolfe defeated the French under command of General Montcalm in a battle of about twenty minutes' duration on the Plains of Abraham, to capture Quebec. In the following year, 1860, Montreal surrendered to the British who then placed New France under military rule until 1763 when the Treaty of Paris confirmed Britain to be in possession of Canada.

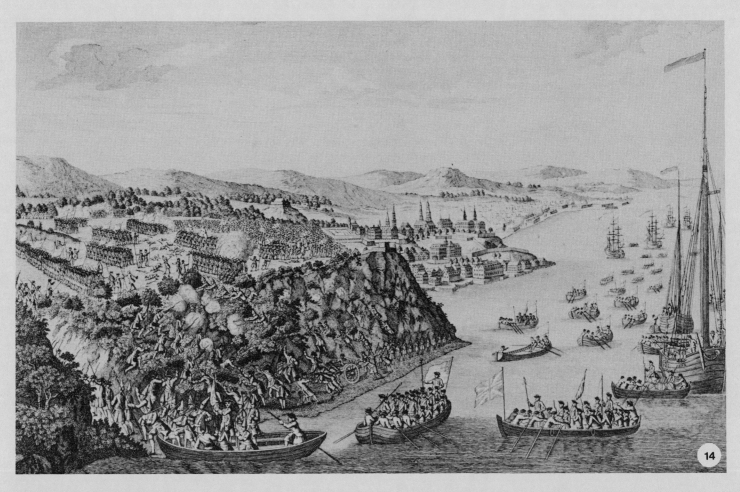

1756 to 1763

8. British Merchants: After the fall of New France, inhabitants were offered an opportunity to return to their homeland. Many did so, most of them being of the wealthier class of merchants, traders, and government officials. English merchants, perhaps about 500, many from Boston, quickly moved into Montreal and Quebec to assume charge of the wholesale trade and other forms of commerce. Almost immediately, this group began to agitate for a responsible government, obviously expecting that it would enable them, through political power, to enhance their commercial interests.

1768

9. Trade and Manufacturers: Sir Guy Carleton, appointed by Britain to govern her Canadian colony, reported to his superiors in the homeland that the decline in trade during the Seven Years' War had made it necessary for the colonists to become more self-reliant. Thus, they had begun manufacturing some linen, and linen and wool textiles, some pottery, and some tanned leather. In reply, the Governor was advised that care must be taken to ensure that the colonists do not engage themselves in manufacturing that would compete with British goods. The Navigation Act applied to Canada as it did to other British colonies in America.

1771

10. Grain Exported: In 1771, Canada's first exports of grain took place when some 200,000 bushels of Quebec origin were shipped to Britain.

1774

11. Quebec Act: By 1773, the defiant attitude of American colonies toward Britain was clearly evident. Britain then moved to reduce possibilities that the French people of Canada would side with the Americans. The Quebec Act of 1774 was passed to guarantee religious freedom to the French Roman Catholics, and the application of French civil law to such matters as marriage, landowning, leasing of lands, and seignioral dues. Against the wishes of the English merchants, the Act provided for the governing of Quebec by an appointed Governor who was assisted by an appointed council. By a separate Act passed in 1774, Britain permitted Quebec to levy duties on imports in order to provide revenue for the government of the colony.

1774 to 1783

12. American Independence: In 1774, the thirteen colonies in America invited Canada to be represented at a congress to discuss relations with Britain. The invitation was declined. Early in 1775 the War of Independence began. French-speaking Canadians, fairly well satisfied by terms of the Quebec Act, particularly with the guarantee of religious freedom it provided, showed no interest in joining the American cause. The English merchants also desired to remain at peace. It was seen that if American trade with Britain declined, it would mean greater opportunity for the Canadian merchants.

15

13. United Empire Loyalists: In the latter stages of the American War of Independence, those people of the American colonies who remained loyal to Britain were subject to harassment. Some had all their possessions confiscated or were driven off; others left voluntarily, so that in all, about 50,000 Loyalists moved to Canada. A majority of them settled in Nova Scotia, New Brunswick and Prince Edward Island. About 5,000, however, moved to Quebec and to the upper St. Lawrence and Niagara Peninsula, laying foundations for a new English colony. The Loyalists who desired to take up farming were given grants of land and other necessities with which to become established.

1784

14. North-West Company: At Montreal, a number of English-speaking merchants of the fur trade joined their forces to operate under the name of the North-West Company. This Company employed many French-speaking whites and Metis. For that reason it has often been regarded as a French organization. Its control, however, rested in the hands of Scottish and English merchants of Montreal. Associated with the North-West Company are such names as Alexander Mackenzie, Simon Fraser, David Thompson, Simon McTavish, and others who left their mark on Canadian history. This new Company is said to have been the largest commercial enterprise in North America at the time. It was an aggressive organization; its aim was to invade the Canadian west in competition with the Hudson's Bay Company. The North-West Company set up a central outpost at Fort William (Thunder Bay), where furs were brought from the many trading posts that were set up, and assembled for shipment to Montreal.

1784

16

1791 to 1792

15. Constitutional Act: Britain recognized that a change to the method of governing her colonies was needed. A lesson had been learned from the American Declaration of Independence. And the entry of 50,000 Loyalists into Canada was a further consideration. Thus, in 1791, the British parliament passed a Constitutional Act for Canada. It provided for a division of Quebec into two segments, Upper Canada and Lower Canada. Lower Canada, predominantly French, was to the east of English-speaking Upper Canada. A Governor-General, appointed by the Crown and responsible to Britain, was to serve both sectors. In addition, both Upper and Lower Canada were each to have:

* A Lieutenant-Governor appointed by the Crown, and subordinate to the Governor-General.
* An Executive Council, the members of which were appointed for life. The Executive Council was to advise the Governor-General, and its members were also to serve as professional administrators in the manner of cabinet ministers of today.
* A Legislative Council, of which members were appointed for life. This Legislative Council had power to make laws but approval of the Governor-General was needed before a law could be put into effect.
* An Elected Assembly which shared with the Legislative Council the right to make laws. The Assembly had power to levy taxes, but all its decisions were subject to approval of the Legislative Council and the Governor-General. Persons owning property or paying rents of a specified value were eligible for election to the Assembly which was required to meet at least annually. Elections were to be held every four years.

It is evident that this form of administration did not satisfy English-speaking merchants of Lower Canada for the subordinated Elected Assembly was not a body which the merchants could either control or influence to their advantage.

1812

16. Selkirk Settlers: Thomas Douglas, the wealthy Earl of Selkirk, had conceived a plan by which he might simultaneously aid many poor people of Britain while helping to develop colonies of the British Empire. He had already brought, at his own expense, groups of Britons to establish colonies in Prince Edward Island and Upper Canada. And in 1811, he had purchased a controlling interest in the Hudson's Bay Company. As a result, the Company which, by its Charter was expected to encourage settlement on its holdings, gave Selkirk the right to use some of 116,000 square miles of its holdings in the Prairie region. In 1812, a group of Scottish settlers, sponsored by Selkirk, reached "the place where the Red and Assiniboine rivers meet" (now Winnipeg) to set up homestead farms. They had journeyed via Hudson's Bay, following the route traditionally used by the Hudson's Bay Company. At their new settlement, the Selkirk Settlers as they were called, attempted to grow cereals and garden produce. The seed they had brought from

1812

the Old Country was not suitable for the severe prairie climate. For one or two years at least, the Settlers were often near starvation. At first, some friendly Metis helped the Settlers by providing food and supplies. Also, some Settlers were able to buy, at high prices, some provisions from the North-West Company. These sources of help were not long lasting.

17. British-American War: In 1812, while Britain was at war with France, the United States of America declared war on Britain. Behind this declaration of war was a belief that Canada, and Lower Canada in particular, could easily be persuaded to join the United States. The belief proved to be false. In the war that followed, several battles were fought in both Canada and the northern part of the U.S.A. In 1814, Britain sent a strong naval force against America which merely prolonged the war.

1815 to 1817

18. Selkirk Settlers: The aggressive North-West company was openly competing with the Hudson's Bay Company within the territory on which the latter, by its Charter, had a monopoly. The North-West Company had strong objection to the Selkirk Settlement, for settlement of any extent would obviously injure the fur trade. In June, 1816, a party of Indians and Metis involved in the fur trade, confronted a group of Settlers. Gunfire broke out, leaving 21 Selkirk Settlers dead. Lord Selkirk, absent at the time, received news of the tragedy. He hired a body of Swiss soldiers who were involved in the war of 1812-14, and attacked the North-West Company's outpost at Thunder Bay, capturing the post and arresting some Company officials. Selkirk then returned to his colony where a further group of Settlers had arrived, and commenced to rebuild the settlement. Selkirk, in failing health, returned to Britain in 1817.

1821

19. Merger of Fur Trading Companies: In 1821, the North-West Company merged with the Hudson's Bay Company, creating a larger organization operating under the Hudson's Bay Company's name and Charter. The long supply line to Montreal was costly to the North-West Company, while competition had been expensive to both organizations. The competition caused both to extend the number of trading posts and number of traders. In proportion to costs, the number of pelts obtained was decreasing. With the merger, the Montreal merchants behind the North-West Company were given a fair settlement. The capital thus obtained was then used to launch new ventures at Montreal, such as banking and other forms of commerce. The result was to enhance Montreal's already established status as the financial and commercial capital of Canada.

1832

20. Successful Grain Crops: The Selkirk Settlers, after years of trial by which acclimatized seed was produced, were rewarded with bountiful grain crops. It was then predicted that the vast Prairies would eventually become the 'breadbasket of the British Empire'. The prediction could not, however, be fulfilled until there was a means of transporting grain to seaports and markets abroad.

21. Rebellion In Lower Canada: The government system provided by the Constitutional Act of 1791 was a failure in an important respect: control of the Executive and Legislative councils which had power over the Elected Assemblies, was vested in persons of power

1837

and wealth who were not hesitant about using their positions on the Councils to their own advantage. The government thus tended to be an oligarchy like that of the aristocracy and gentry of Britain.

In Upper Canada the controlling clique was referred to as the 'Family Compact'. Its counterpart in Lower Canada was called the 'Chateau Clique'. Members of the Compact and Clique held for speculative gain large tracts of land, were owners of the chartered banks and other financial institutions, and generally dominated all profitable avenues of commerce and transportation. Their positions thus gave them power over the farming population which comprised a majority in both Upper and Lower Canada.

An agitation for reform had been mounting over several years, particularly among the farming class who desired that it be easier to obtain grants of land for cultivation as well as roads and schools. Reforms or improvements proposed by members of the Elected Assemblies were ineffective, for the members of the Compact or Cliques who sat on the Legislative or Executive councils had power to reject decisions of the Assembly. Several petitions were sent to Britain without result. Most petitions called for a more responsible form of government. But, in 1837, the British Parliament responded by adopting a set of Ten Resolutions which clearly stated that the colonies in Canada were to have neither self-government nor an elected legislature.

In Lower Canada, Louis Papineau was a leader in the agitation. He was a member of the Elected Assembly. He had been chosen by that body as its Speaker, but the Governor overruled the Assembly on the matter. When it became known that Britain had denied responsible government, followers of Papineau organized themselves for more aggressive action. English-speaking residents of Lower Canada likewise organized themselves to counter the French, with the result that riots broke out in several places, developing to a rebellion after an order was issued for Papineau's arrest.

In Upper Canada a similar but smaller revolt was begun but suppressed by troops. Two rebels were hanged, several others imprisoned.

1838 to 1839

22. Lord Durham's Report: At Queen Victoria's personal request, John George Lambton, the Earl of Durham, was appointed as Governor-General for all Canada. He arrived in 1838, bringing with him a company of able men to make a thorough study of conditions in Canada. From their studies, in which Durham took very keen interest, he prepared a lengthy report which was put before the British House of Commons in 1839.

"I expected to find a contest between a government and a people,"

Durham wrote. "I found two nations warring in the bosom of a single state; I found a struggle, not of principles, but of races; and I perceived that it would be idle to attempt any amelioration of laws or institutions until we could first succeed in terminating the deadly animosity that now separates the inhabitants of Lower Canada into the hostile divisions of French and English."

Durham confirmed the existence of the Compact and Clique: "Successive Governors have submitted or yielded to this well

1838 to 1839

organized party the real conduct of affairs. The bench, the magistracy, the high offices of the Episcopal Church, and a great part of the legal profession, are filled by adherents to this party: by grant or purchase, they have acquired nearly the whole of the waste lands of the Province; they are all powerful in the chartered banks..."

Referring to the revolts of 1837, Durham wrote: "If Colonial Legislatures (elected assemblies) have frequently stopped supplies (allocation of government funds), if they have harassed public servants by unjust or harsh impeachments, it is because the removal of an unpopular administration could not be effected in the Colonies by those milder indications of a want of confidence which have always sufficed to attain the end in the mother country."

Durham considered the difference between the governments of Upper and Lower Canada and that of the United States neighbors: "No large community of free and intelligent men will long feel contented with a political system which places them, because it places their country, in a position of inferiority to their neighbors."

The fact that a numerically small English-speaking faction had gained a disproportionate amount of economic control in Lower Canada did not escape Durham's attention: "The ascendency which an unjust favouritism had contributed to gave to the English race in the government and the legal profession, their own superior energy, skill and capital secured to them in every branch of industry. They have developed the resources of the country; they have constructed or improved its means of communication; they have created its internal and foreign commerce. The entire wholesale and a large portion of the retail trade of the province, with the most profitable and flourishing farms, are now in the hands of this numerical minority of the population."

Most important in terms of what followed, was Durham's recommendation for elected, responsible government for Canada. He argued: "If the colonists make bad laws, and select improper persons to conduct their affairs, they will generally be the only, always the greatest, sufferers; and, like the people of other countries, they must bear the ills which they bring on themselves, until they choose to apply the remedy. But it surely cannot be the duty or the interest of Great Britain to keep a most expensive military possession of these Colonies, in order that a Governor or Secretary of State may be able to confer Colonial appointments on one rather than another set of persons in the Colonies."

19

1840

23. Red River Settlement: While affairs of Upper and Lower Canada were the focus of attention, the population of the Red River settlement, i.e. lands in the general area of Winnipeg, was rising. By 1840, it was estimated to number 4,000 who were mainly established along the river banks. In 1821, there had been about 419 immigrants. The numbers do not include native Indians and Metis. In part, the rise of population represented an influx of French people from Lower Canada, who settled in a good many predominantly French villages with the Church as their central institution.

1841

24. Union of Upper and Lower Canada: As a result of Lord Durham's report, the British Parliament, in 1840, passed an Act of Union which took effect February 1, 1841. This Act provided for a union of Upper and Lower Canada under one government, with Upper Canada to be known as Canada West and Lower Canada as Canada East.

The governing body consisted of a Governor-General appointed by the Crown; a Legislative Council, the members of which were appointed for life; and a Legislative Assembly of elected members, with an equal number from both provinces. At the time, the population of Canada East was 600,000, including 150,000 English-speaking inhabitants. The population of Canada West, was 400,000. Since both East and West had equal representation in the Legislative Assembly, it was obvious that representation was not based upon population. Representation by population had been recommended by Lord Durham even though he was aware that for a time at least, the French-speaking population would exceed the English-speaking. Thus, the adoption of equal representation was obviously intended to ensure British supremacy.

When the plan was proposed to Upper Canada, the Family Compact found it objectionable. Obviously it would make it difficult for Compact members to retain their privileged positions. In Lower Canada the only prior approval sought was from a Special Committee which was not representative of French opinion. Thus, both Upper and Lower Canada were discontented from the start. Nevertheless, Britain had passed the Act of Union and it was now

law. The election of members to the new Legislative Assembly followed, marked by numerous incidents of riotious behaviour, particularly in Canada East.

1843

25. Diversion of Prairie Fur Trade: On the Prairies, the monopoly of the Hudson's Bay Company was being challenged by the growth of ox-cart transportation. From Pembina, in North Dakota near the U.S.-Canada border, a regular transport service to St. Paul was being carried on. St. Paul, a busy metropolis even at that time, is on the banks of the Mississippi River. Thus, goods were easily transported from the Eastern U.S. seaboard. In Canada, Indians and Metis had discovered that American traders offered better prices

1843

for furs, and better merchandise in exchange. For that reason, trade with Americans grew. The Hudson's Bay Company, with its monopoly on both incoming and outgoing trade, attempted to stop what it regarded as illicit trading. The traders ignored the Company's rules, avoiding interception by travelling off the main trails. So, the cart service grew, employing 600 carts by 1858 and about, 2,500 by 1869.

1844

26. Rochdale Pioneers: It was at this stage of Canada's history that the Pioneers of Rochdale opened their store on Toad Lane.

27. Native Co-operation: In Rupert's Land, far removed from Rochdale, a most interesting display of co-operation and democracy was being provided by native Indians and Metis of Canada's prairies. The display could be seen at the great buffalo hunts of this era.

For ages, Indians had hunted the buffalo for food, a practise that had no apparent effect on the buffalo population. The size of the great herds that roamed the prairies is almost beyond imagination. One party of whites travelling through the Qu'Appelle Valley spoke of having heard sounds of an approaching herd. The party ran for a safe vantage point where the herd could be seen crossing a stream, several hundred a minute, for nearly 24 hours. It was believed that more than a million buffalo thundered by.

It was white settlers who caused the great herds to vanish. They regarded buffalo tongues and other tid-bits as delicacies and encouraged the slaughter of the animals by Indians and Metis.

The great buffalo hunts were organized in an evident spirit of democracy and co-operation. Before a hunt took place, the Indians and Metis, and perhaps the whites who were to take part, came together in an encampment. In the centre of the camp, and for two or three days, the hunters met to formally elect the leaders of the hunt, and to democratically decide upon the rules to be followed. Ten captains were chosen by vote, one being selected as the chief of the hunt. Each captain was responsible for directing those hunters, about 10 in number, who were to assist him to maintain order and enforce the rules. A typical set of rules is listed as follows:

* No buffalo run on the Sabbath day.
* No party to fork off, lag, or go before, without permission.
* No person or party to run buffalo before the general order.

* Every captain with his men in turn to patrol camp and keep guard.
* For first trespass against these laws, offender to have saddle and bridle cut.
* For second offense, offender to have coat taken off and cut up.

1844

* For third offense, offender to be flogged.
* Any person convicted of theft, even to the value of a sinew, to be brought to the middle of the camp and the crier to call out his or her name, adding the word, 'Thief!' each time.

1845

28. Diversion of Prairie Fur Trade: The trading done via ox-cart trains to St. Paul was now definitely affecting the Hudson's Bay Company. The Company imposed new taxes on both imports and exports, and for persons caught carrying furs to U.S. traders, penalties that included a public flogging were provided. Efforts to restrict illicit trade also required that senders of letters from Red River show their name on the envelope so that any suspected to be connected with illicit trade might be identified. The new regulations were not respected; trading with the St. Paul merchants became more and more common. Eventually, it is said, even the Hudson's Bay Company began to direct its own trade through the St. Paul route.

29. Grain and Flour Exports: In the emergency caused by the Irish potato crop failure, Britain suspended the Corn Laws and immediately called for shipments of wheat and flour from her colony of Canada in preference to other sources. Business interests quickly invested large sums to set up flour mills at Montreal and other ports along the St. Lawrence to take advantage of this new trade. Some grain was bought by the millers from U.S. sources. Thus, flour milling became an important part of the economy of Canada East where its control was mainly in the hands of the English-speaking merchant class.

1849

30. British Trading Policies: The repeal of the Corn Laws by Britain in 1846 now had an effect on Canada's trade with Britain, for it was in 1849 that the last of Britain's tariffs on imported grain were removed. Further, in 1849, Britain repealed her Navigation Acts. Those Acts, which had required the use of British vessels for trade between the colonies and Britain while prohibiting the colonies from trading with other than Britain, had ensured Canada of a market for raw materials. But with these Acts repealed, the assured market vanished; Canada was no longer given British preference, but obliged to compete with other countries in foreign trade. In this matter, the United States had a distinct advantage. Canadian merchants were alarmed as their trade diminished.

31. Annexation Manifesto: At Montreal, a group of leading merchants (one writer says 350 but another puts the figures at 1,000) expressed their discontent at Britain's free trade policies by adopting a manifesto. This document, known as the "Annexation Manifesto" and published in a Montreal newspaper, advocated "friendly and peaceful separation from the British connection and a union upon equitable terms with the great North American confederacy of sovereign states." The merchants expressed their discontent with Britain, saying: "The reversal of the ancient policy of Great Britain, whereby she withdrew from the colonies their wonted protection in her markets, has produced the most disastrous effects upon Canada—unprosperous agriculture, real estate scarcely saleable upon any terms, rivers and canals unused, no manufacturing, few railways and so on. Our country stands before the world in humiliating contrast with its immediate neighbor, exhibiting every symptom of a nation fast sinking to decay." The manifesto does not appear to have gained support of any extent outside of the Montreal business interests who, it should be noted, were predominantly English-speaking.

32. Land Rights in Red River: In the north-west, around the Red River, immigrants were arriving in small numbers so that by 1849, the settlers among the river banks numbered 5,000. Though they were setting up homestead farms, they were warned that they had no rights to ownership of the land for it all belonged to the Hudson's Bay Company. A seed of discontent over land tenure began to grow.

1854

33. Reciprocity With U.S.: Alarmed by the insistence of Montreal merchants for annexation (see 31), Lord Elgin, Governor-General,

1854

sought a compromise through reciprocal free trade between Canada and the United States. The latter had imposed some tariff barriers to protect U.S. industries against foreign trade. At first the Americans felt that reciprocal trade would be of more benefit to Canada than to themselves. Elgin bargained, however, offering as an inducement, fishing rights for the Americans along Canadian coasts (i.e. in Maritime waters) and free navigation for United States' vessels on the St. Lawrence with Canada to have navigation rights on Lake Michigan. The Americans accepted, agreeing to a ten year Reciprocity Treaty. As a result commercial trade with the United States developed to offset the loss of trade with Britain. The condition of the Montreal merchants improved so that they soon forgot their Annexation Manifesto. Maritimes fisheries had, however been to some extent, sacrificed on the altar of industrial commerce. The Treaty, when it expired ten years hence, was not renewed by the Americans.

1854 to 1860

34. Annexation of North-West Proposed: In Toronto, which had become well established as the commercial capital of Canada West, George Brown, editor of the Toronto **Globe,** had become leader of a Reform party. Brown had noted that in 1851, the English-speaking population had surpassed that of the French. Thereupon he called for reform of the system of representation by which Canada East and Canada West had equal representation. Equal representation had been provided by the Act of Union of Upper and Lower Canada when the French population exceeded British numbers in Canada. Now Brown called for representation according to population. His slogan, "rep by pop" became a much-used cliche.

Brown was also convinced that the best means of enlarging trade and commerce was not reciprocity, but expansion of Canada to include the territories to the West. He proposed annexation of the lands held by the Hudson's Bay Company saying, in a **Globe** editorial: "If Canada acquires this territory, it will rise in a few years from a position of a small and weak province to be the **greatest colony** any country has ever possessed." He also proposed a union of all British colonies in Canada, suggesting that it would "draw the teeth and cut the claws of Lower Canada." Brown was an influential man. What he said or wrote became the feelings of many.

23

35. Gold in British Columbia: In 1858, gold was discovered on the Fraser River. Thousands of American prospectors flocked to the area to stake claims. The situation gave rise to fears that the United States would act to annex the area, while at the same time the presence of gold aroused among business interests in Canada further interest in extending Canada to include the western lands.

**1854
to
1860**

36. Ottawa Chosen As Capital: Ever since the Union of Upper and Lower Canada, there had been debate as to where the centre of government should be placed. Canada East argued for Montreal or Quebec, but in Canada West, Toronto and Kingston were preferred. In frustration, the matter was referred to Queen Victoria who chose Ottawa as the site for the capital. The failure of the two Canadas to agree on a site for the capital is indicative of governmental problems of the decade. Election after election took place, but no party could muster a clear majority in the Elected Assembly. In 1858, a coalition party was in power, led by John A. Macdonald of Canada West and Georges Etienne Cartier of Canada East. At their request, A.T. Galt, a railway entrepreneur, agreed to join the government as minister of finance but on condition that a federation of all British colonies in North America be given prompt and serious consideration.

**1857
to
1859**

37. Hudson's Bay Company Rights: In 1857, two years before the trading license of the Hudson's Bay Company was due for renewal, the British House of Commons was pondering the future of the North-West. The Company's desire for renewal, the threat of U.S. annexation, and the interest of Canada in acquiring lands to the West ensured that the matter was of more than routine concern. Accordingly, the House of Commons formed a special Committee to determine whether the lands controlled by the Company had a potential for other than fur trading. The Governor of the Hudson's Bay Company, Sir George Simpson, testified before the Committee, saying that the land was not fit for settlement and for that reason the Company's monopoly on trade ought to be renewed. Some other witnesses, however, expressed views contrary to those of Simpson. To confirm matters one way or the other, Britain directed Captain George Palliser to explore the region to determine its value for agricultural or other purposes. Meanwhile, Canada sought its own answer to the question as to value of the Hudson's Bay lands, appointing Henry Hind and S.J. Dawson to make an assessment.

38. Annexation Proposed: Within the United States were some who advocated annexation to the U.S. of lands held by the Hudson's Bay Company. The U.S. Treasury Department went so far as to appoint James W. Taylor as a special agent to investigate conditions in the North-West. Taylor reported, soon after, that he believed conditions of the area were "ripe for annexation". It should be noted that the government of Canada East and Canada

**1857
to
1859**

West had no jurisdiction over Rupert's Land. However, the trade being done by the relatively small number of inhabitants of the Red River area with St. Paul traders was jealousy eyed by Montreal merchants.

39. Value of Colonies in Doubt: In Britain's House of Commons, some speakers expressed doubt as to the value of retaining the colonies. Before Britain had begun to so zealously follow the laissez-faire doctrines of free trade, her colonies had been of great value as a means of providing raw materials to the mother country and as a market for her manufactured goods. Now, however, free trade policies and efforts of colonies to achieve self-determination, created an entirely new outlook toward colonies. Moreover, Britain had become the "workbench of the World", the leading trader in manufactured goods, and leading source of investment capital. The colonies, when in need of capital, sought to obtain it from the mother country, calling on the Government of Britain to guarantee loans for constructing railways, canals and other public works, and to provide grants for defense purposes. Increasingly, Britain's House of Commons resented such demands from the colonies and took the view that, instead of adding to the burden of British taxpayers, the colonies ought to be more self-reliant and accept responsibility for their own defense and internal development.

40. American Civil War: In April, 1861, civil war broke out between the northern states of the U.S. which desired to abolish slavery, and the southern states that aimed to defend it. This conflict lasted for four years, with the north being victorious.

1864

41. Prelude to Confederation: A coalition government for Canadas East and West, led by John A. Macdonald, Georges Etienne Cartier and George Brown, and including A.T. Galt, E.P. Tache, William McDougal, Thomas D'Arcy McGee and other notables, arranged a meeting with politicians of the Maritime colonies. At this meeting held in Charlottetown in September, a confederation of British colonies in Canada was proposed. In October, a further meeting held in Quebec, lasting two weeks, adopted a set of 72 resolutions which became the basis for confederation. A sense of urgency prevailed at these meetings for it was seen that the Civil War in the U.S. was nearing its end. It appeared possible that the northern states would next turn their

Land for the abode of a civilised race in place

SOR H. Y. HIND, GEOLOGIST TO THE EXPLOR

mobilized armies to the north to conquer the British colonies in Canada. D'Arcy McGee was among those most concerned over possibilities of an invasion from the U.S. He warned: "They coveted Florida, and seized it; they coveted Louisiana, and purchased it, they coveted Texas and stole it; and they picked a quarrel with Mexico which ended by their getting California. Had we not the strong arm of England over us, we would not now have a separate existence..."

1865

42. No Appeal To Electorate: The terms for confederation of the colonies had been decided at the October meeting in Quebec, but not all agreed that such a union should take place, at least not without first putting the matter before the electorates of the colonies. In March, 1865, A.A. Dorion, speaking in debate in Canada East, declared: "Everywhere this scheme has been protested against and an appeal to the people demanded; and yet we are about to give them a constitution. I shall oppose this scheme...and insist that...it shall be submitted to the people before its final adoption." There was, however, no opportunity provided to the electorates of the colonies. Instead, George Brown was sent off to Britain in 1865, to begin the process of winning acceptance for the confederation plan.

43. Fenian Raids: Beginning in 1865, and continuing into 1866, was a series of armed raids into Canada by the Fenians, a group of Irish Americans aiming to stir up a war between Britain and the United States as part of a scheme to free Ireland from British rule. About 2,000 Canadian troops were stationed along the U.S. border to intercept the raiders.

27

1866

44. Annexation Bill Proposed: A bill introduced to the U.S. House of Representatives proposed "admission of the states of Nova Scotia, New Brunswick, Canada Selkirk, Saskatchewan and Columbia, into the United States." The bill was not given serious consideration by the U.S. House, but it did add to fears already present in Canada.

45. Westminster Conference: In December, 1866, what is known as the Westminster Conference was held in London, to draft for consideration by the British House of Commons, final terms for confederation of British colonies in Canada. The terms were based on the 72 resolutions from the Quebec meeting of 1864.

46. British North America Act: On March 15, 1867, Britain's Parliament passed, with minimal debate, the British North America Act, otherwise known as the Act of Confederation. The Act was given Royal Assent by Queen Victoria on March 27, and became effective July 1, 1867. Terms of the Act provided that each of the provinces joined in confederation would continue to have its own legislature while the Dominion Parliament would "make Laws for the Peace, Order and Good Goverment of Canada, in relation to all Matters not coming within the Classes of Subjects by this Act assigned exclusively to the Legislatures of the Provinces."

The structure for the Dominion Parliament provided for:

* A Governor General, appointed by the reigning monarch to carry on "the Government of Canada on behalf and in the Name of the Queen."
* A Privy Council to be chosen by the Governor-General.
* A Senate, a body comparable to the House of Lords in Britain, to which members were appointed for life by the Governor-General.
* A House of Commons to "consist of One Hundred and Eighty-Five Members, of whom Eighty-Two shall be elected for Ontario, Sixty-five for Quebec, Nineteen for Nova Scotia, and Fifteen for New Brunswick." The number of seats for Quebec was permanently fixed at 65, with seats of the other provinces being determined on the basis of their population as related to that of Quebec.

47. First Dominion Government: In the election which followed passage of the B.N.A. Act, the Conservative Party won by a modest majority:

PROVINCE	CONS.	LIB.	TOTAL
Ontario	46	36	82
Quebec	45	20	65
Nova Scotia	3	16	19
New Brunswick	7	8	15
Total	101	80	181

In this instance, both Ontario and Quebec favored the Conservatives, while the Maritime Provinces gave their strongest support to the Liberals. The Maritime Provinces had, in 1854, seen their coveted fishing ground used by Canada East and Canada West, as a bargaining tool for reciprocity which mainly benefitted the two Canadas. Now, with only 10 members in the House of Commons as compared to 147 seats held by Ontario and Quebec, the Maritimes were obviously not in a position to exert great influence within Confederation.

48. Other Partners To Confederation: As a matter of interest, the following is provided to show when the various provinces of Canada joined Confederation:

1867 New Brunswick	1871 British Columbia
Nova Scotia	1873 Prince Edward Island
Ontario	1905 Alberta
Quebec	Saskatchewan
1870 Manitoba	1948 Newfoundland

1867

49. The National Grange: In the United States, The National Grange of the Patrons of Husbandry, was formed. It was destined to become an important farm organization, and was concerned with the social and cultural uplift of farmers until 1873 when the Grange began a crusade for reform along political and economic lines. The founder, Oliver Hudson Kelley, viewed co-operative enterprise as a means of improving the economic condition of farmers. In 1869, he advised locals of the Grange "to have flouring mills, flour their own wheat and keep the bran and shorts for feed, and not send any raw material into the eastern market but instead appoint a business agent at St. Paul who should receive the flour and sell it on commission." In 1874, pressure for co-operatives had become great, and the principle of co-operative enterprise was adopted in a declaration of the Grange which proposed "buying together, selling together, and in general, acting for mutual protection..." It also proposed "to bring producers and consumers, farmers and manufacturers, into the most direct and friendly relations possible." The Grange then became active in forming co-operative stores, grain elevators, livestock shipping associations and cheese factories. There were attempts to manufacture farm implements, sewing machines, wagons, and other needs, on a co-operative basis. Most of those ventures had failed by 1880 but the concept of farmer-owned co-operative enterprise became firmly established.

50. United States Purchases Alaska: In 1867, the United States purchased Alaska from Russia for $7,200,000. It was believed that this was a prelude to annexation of the North-West so that all territories between the United States and Alaska, would become part of the U.S.A.

51. American Railways: In 1867, the extent to which railways were being built in the United States could not escape notice in Canada. By this time, the Union Pacific Railway was under construction. It was completed on May 10, 1869, as America's first transcontinental railway. Meanwhile, the Northern Pacific Railway, in 1867, began construction of a line from Duluth, at the head of Lake Superior, to Puget Sound on the Pacific coast. This line, just south of the U.S.-Canada Border, was financed by Jay Cooke, probably the wealthiest financier in the U.S. following the civil war, who hoped that his line would serve the Canadian west and discourage any plans for construction of a Canadian transcontinental line.

CHAPTER V
RUPERT'S LAND 1868 to 1896

1868 to 1896

52. In Chapter IV it was seen that commercial interests were well established, first at Montreal then at Toronto, well before Confederation. They had, without question, provided an influence which, coupled with fears of American annexation, given impetus to both the Canadian and British governments in the matter of placing the fertile areas of the North-West under Canada's jurisdiction. The electorate of the Confederated provinces was not consulted in the question of absorbing the North-West into Canada. Nor were the people of the Red River area who, for many years, had been concerned because they did not have title to the lands they occupied.

Louis Riel, the chosen leader of the rebellions of 1869 and 1885, deserves, in all fairness, to be regarded as the West's first prominent farm leader. In both rebellions, land tenure for the settlers was a major issue second only to demand for responsible and representative government, and representation in the House of Commons at Ottawa. In both of the rebellions the initial agitation was begun, not by the Metis led by Riel, but by immigrant whites. It was, however, the Metis who became the aggressors.

At Red River, James Wickes Taylor was an active spectator if not contributor to the agitation. It is possible that his presence, and fears that insurrection would lead to U.S. annexation, was the deciding reason why troops were sent to the North-West. Aside from this, however, one must also consider the low position of

**1868
to
1896**

Metis in respect to the British social structure or class system. In this, the order of ranking had been defined by the sequence in which Britons were recorded the right to vote—agricultural workers who did not own property being among the very last men to be enfranchised. Thus, it was an affront to the highest men of Canada that Riel and his followers, who neither owned land nor could boast of British blood, should make demands upon them.

At this time, the Government of Canada was actively promoting immigration of the West, and took steps to set up experimental farms to help establish agriculture on the plains. Coincident with these developments, business interests of Eastern Canada chose Winnipeg as their Western outpost. In 1887, the Winnipeg Grain Exchange was begun.

Co-operatives and farm organizations began to appear, and in 1887 an Act providing for incorporation of co-operative associations was passed by the Manitoba legislature only to become a 'dead letter' soon afterward.

53. Transfer of Hudson's Bay Lands Negotiated: In 1868, the Canadian government requested Britain to arrange for the transfer to Canada of lands held by the Hudson's Bay Company. After a favorable reply, a delegation of Canadian officials went to London for further negotiations. The Canadian government carried out its intention without consulting its own electorate in confederated Canada. Nor was there any consultation with the people of the Western plains. Yet, even before the Canadian delegation went to London, the Canadian government sent a party of surveyors to Rupert's Land. This act, together with the government's neglect to inform the people of the West of its plans, gave rise to rumours, discontent, and further concern over land tenure.

54. Another Call For Annexation: The St. Paul Chamber of Commerce, aware that annexation of the West to Canada would end the Red River trade at that centre, issued a demand that the United States annex British North-West America. It was proposed that the Hudson's Bay Company be offered ten million dollars for its land.

1869

55. Transfer of Rupert's Land: On December 1, 1869, Rupert's Land was officially transferred to the custody of Canada. In return, the Hudson's Bay Company was to receive about $1,500,000 in cash, plus the privilege of retaining about 45,000 acres of lands on which its trading posts were located, and 1/20th of the lands in each township opened for settlement. The Government of Canada did not await Royal Assent of the Act providing for transfer, but carried on with the surveying of the Red River area. The already established farmsteads of the Red River were, for the most part, laid out in narrow fields extending back from rivers for as much as two miles, and most of the fields were unfenced. It was obvious that the method of surveying being imposed would not have regard for these cultivated lands to which neither Metis nor white immigrant settlers had title.

56. Provisional Government: The settlers of Red River were greatly agitated by the presence of surveyors, especially since the Government of Canada had not consulted them in any way with regard to its intentions. Amid the growing unrest, the Metis who had been encouraged to regard themselves as a 'new nation',

1869

chose Louis Riel as their leader. Riel had been trained, but not ordained, for the priesthood. He had been born at Red River but educated in Eastern Canada. Riel established a 'provisional government' at Red River, so that the people of the area could be represented in negotiations with the Government of Canada. There

was, at this time, no other formal channel since the Hudson's Bay Company's jurisdiction had ended, but the Government at Ottawa had done nothing to provide for administration or representation of the Red River.

57. World's First Department Store—Zion's Co-operative Mercantile Institute: On March 1, 1869, the world's first department store opened for business at Salt Lake City, Utah. It was a co-operative store, owned by members of the Mormon Sect who had founded Salt Lake City. Brigham Young, second president of the Mormon Church who was Mormon leader at the time, deplored the fact that so many able-bodied men of the Sect were engaged in shopkeeping—operating numerous small shops, each specializing in a particular line of merchandise, and some 'general' stores. In his opinion, "Two-thirds of them ought to be out in the field preaching."

Brigham Young conceived a plan for bringing together a number of the individual stores under one roof, forming an emporium in which various types of commodities were segregated into 'departments'. "This will enable us to save time and money for the purchasers," he declared. "Buyers should be no more wasteful of their time than sellers." Thus, Zion's Co-operative Mercantile Institute, organized October 16,1868, was opened for business on March 1, 1869, in a sturdy-looking two-storey building. Its name was derived from the Mormon aim of building Zion, a perfect community for the Godly. A few months later, in 1870, the organization was incorporated.

People outside the Mormon Church at first ridiculed Brigham Young's venture. But after the world's first department store opened for business, ridicule turned to admiration. Zion's Co-operative Mercantile Institute soon gained such a volume of trade as to become one of the very largest retailers in the United States. Visitors came to see for themselves, marvelling at the store's convenience and efficiency. By 1896, giant department stores set up along the lines of Brigham Young's venture could be found in all big cities of the United States, particularly in the Eastern states. Before the nineteenth century came to an end, the department store concept had crossed the Atlantic and begun to take root in Europe and in Britain from whence had come the idea of co-operative stores.

By 1901, Zion's Co-operative Mercantile Institute had long out-grown its original premises. In that year a much larger and impressive, modern, three-storey department store building was built and occupied. The Mormon settlers of Salt Lake City who gave birth to the world's first department store are known to have formed co-operatives to serve a number of purposes, including co-operative irrigation projects to serve their farms.

1870

58. Province of Manitoba: Riel's provisional government prepared and submitted to Ottawa, a 'Bill of Rights' embodying demands of the people of the Red River settlements, both Metis and immigrant settlers. The demands were not unreasonable, but included:

* Representation in the Government of Canada.
* The right of people of the Red River settlements to elect members to their own legislature.
* Acknowledgement of the settlers' claims to lands they occupied.
* A railway to connect Winnipeg with the nearest railroad (then in the U.S.A.).
* Official status for both French and English languages in the courts and in the legislature.
* Appropriation of public lands for the building of schools, roads, and other public works.

The Government of Canada responded by creating the Province of Manitoba by an Act of Parliament, May 12, 1870, and providing for a legislature in the new province. The name, Manitoba, was chosen by Riel who was then sentenced to five years' exile from Canada for his part in the uprising. At this time, the new Province had a population of about 12,000—558 Indians, 5,757 Metis, 4,083 English half-breeds, and 1,565 'whites'. Manitoba was given all the rights enjoyed by other provinces except control of natural resources which was retained by the Dominion Government. The Act provided for official use of both English and French, and for the continuation of the educational rights of various dominations.

The Province of Manitoba, as established by the Manitoba Act of 1870, was of "postage stamp" size as compared to the province of today; it consisted of only 14,000 square miles.

1872

59. Dominion Lands Act: To encourage settlement of the Prairies, the Dominion Government passed the Dominion Lands Act of 1872 (also known as the 'Homestead Act'). It provided for a free homestead of 160 acres to incoming settlers to be granted by the Dominion Government. Settlers were required to agree to remain on their free lands for at least three years, and to pay a fee of $10 to register their holdings. If they so chose, settlers could also purchase from the government, a quarter-section adjoining their free holdings. This Act applied to the North-West Territories and to the Province of Manitoba, for in creating that province, the Dominion Government had not relinquished its ownership of Manitoba lands.

60. Canadian Pacific Railway: In 1872, the Government of Canada enacted legislation to provide for construction of a railway to join British Columbia, a Province formed in 1871, with Eastern Canada. The railway, to link Canada from sea to sea, was vitally important to settlement of the Prairies. An important feature of the legislation was the policy by which agricultural lands would be used as a means of paying for railway construction. The 1872 Act, however, limited the amount of land to be used for this purpose to 50 million acres. The story of the building of the Canadian Pacific Railway has been ably told by Pierre Berton in his books, "The Last Spike" and "National Dream", both of which are recommended for further references.

61. Dominion Election: In the election of 1872, the Conservative Party was returned to power but with a reduced majority. In this election, the Provinces of British Columbia and Manitoba were involved:

PROVINCE	CONS.	LIB.	TOTAL
Ontario	38	50	88
Quebec	38	27	65
Nova Scotia	11	10	21
New Brunswick	7	9	16
Manitoba	3	1	4
British Columbia	6	—	6
	103	97	200

1873

62. Territorial Council: On May 23, 1873, the Dominion Government provided the necessary legislation to enable a Territorial Council to be established, with representation from the Districts and an assembly headed by a Lieutenant Governor appointed by the Dominion Government. That the apparent beginnings of self-government in the Territories was less than satisfactory to the inhabitants is made evident by a writing of John Hawkes in **Saskatchewan and Its People.** He wrote:

" One looked over the audience (of settlers) and found all kinds of faces except the weak face. And these were people who, for years after they obtained representation on the Council, found that they were begging in vain for what they considered to be the elementary rights of free born citizens. Their elected members were without power. The Lieutenant Governor presided over their deliberations, and the position was not that the representatives of the people made the laws, but that the Lieutenant Governor was the law-maker, and the popular representatives were graciously permitted to 'aid' him. The Lieutenant Governor spent the money as he pleased, for whatever views the elected members might express, they had no power of enforcing them. The Lieutenant Governor in his relations to the people through their chosen members was an autocrat... An exasperating feature of the situation was that this autocratic governor whom the people's men were only allowed to 'aid' and serve, was himself only a servant of the chief autocrat at Ottawa, via: the Minister of Interior; and this put the parody of popular government in a peculiarly humiliating light; and a greater part of the 'fight for freedom' was for freedom from the galling domination of a mere appointed official who represented not the Crown, but the Minister of the Interior."

1874

63. The Grange: by 1874, The Grange of the Patrons of Husbandry, a farmers' organization which originated in the U.S.A. in 1867, had become established in Ontario. On June 2, 1974, there was a meeting between officials of the National Grange of the U.S.A. and the Canadian organization. The purpose of the meeting was to lay plans that would allay possibilities of any conflict of

1874 jurisdiction arising between the U.S. and Canadian organizations. It was decided at this meeting, that a Dominion Grange should be formed to serve Canada's farmers.

64. Grange In Manitoba: The first local of the Grange to appear in the West was formed at Winnipeg in 1874. An evident purpose was to call the attention of governments to existing farm problems.

65. Grange in the North-West Territories: Although information is sparse, it is evident that at least two lodges of the Grange were formed in the North-West between 1872 and 1900. Both of them were in that area which was in 1905, to become the Province of Alberta. It is said that no locals of the Grange existed in that part of the Territories which became the Province of Saskatchewan.

66. Election of 1874: Because of what is called the "Pacific Scandal", the Conservative Government of Sir John A. Macdonald was forced to resign. It had been charged in the House of Commons that the Conservatives had accepted $325,000 for the 1872 election campaign from persons seeking favorable contracts for the building of the railway. In the election of 1874, the Liberals were victors with a strong majority:

PROVINCE	LIBS.	CONS.	TOTAL
Ontario	64	24	88
Quebec	33	32	65
Nova Scotia	17	4	21
New Brunswick	11	5	16
Prince Edward Island	6	—	6
Manitoba	2	2	4
British Columbia	—	6	6
	133	73	206

67. Dominion Grange Incorporated: The Dominion Grange of the Patrons of Husbandry, which had origins in the United States, was showing rapid growth among Canadian farmers. In 1875, it had 247 lodges in Canada, and in December, 1879, was said to have 766 lodges with a total membership estimated at $31,000. In 1877, the Dominion Grange was granted incorporation by the Government of Canada.

1878 **68. Grange In Manitoba:** Two more locals of the Grange were formed near Winnipeg, one at Headingly, and the other at High Bluff, "in protest against high prices charged by merchants of Winnipeg". Other locals were soon formed at Carberry, Gladstone, Arden and Eden in Manitoba.

1878

69. Election of 1878: During its term of office, the Liberal Government under Alexander Mackenzie favored the building of short railway links to waterways or other means of transport, rather than the major task of a single transcontinental railway. Thus, as Riel had asked, a line was built from Winnipeg to link up with American lines at the U.S.-Canada border, giving transport from Winnipeg to St. Paul and Minneapolis. The major issue of the 1878 campaign, however, was the so-called "National Policy" advocated by the Conservatives. It proposed high tariffs on manufactured imports thereby providing Canadian manufacturers with the protection they had sought, but only received in token, from the Liberals. In this election, the Conservatives won with the largest majority yet.

PROVINCE	CONS.	LIB.	TOTAL
Ontario	59	29	88
Quebec	45	20	65
Nova Scotia	14	7	21
New Brunswick	5	11	16
Prince Edward Island	5	1	6
Manitoba	3	1	4
British Columbia	6	—	6
	137	69	206

It can be seen that 55 seats of the Conservative majority of 68 were won in Ontario and Quebec where the manufacturing interests strongly favored tariff protection.

1880

70. Contract For Railway: Back in office, the Conservatives negotiated terms for the construction of the railway to the Pacific coast. The Canadian Pacific Railway, a newly-formed company sponsored by Montreal industrial interests, was to be provided by the Government, with $25,000,000 in cash, plus a grant of 25 million acres of lands fit for agricultural purposes. The land was to be in a belt 24 miles wide on either side of the railway line, where the CPR was to own every second section while the Government retained the alternate sections. By the agreement, the Government was to sell or dispose of its lands for settlement purposes, first. As this was done, the value of lands held by the CPR increased. A further condition to the agreement was that the CPR would be assured of a railway monopoly for a 20-year term beginning in 1880.

71. Railway To Hudson's Bay: On May 7, the Manitoba Government passed "An Act to Incorporate the Winnipeg and Hudson's Bay Railway and Steamship Company". This company was authorized to build a railway, or combination of railway and steamship links, from Winnipeg to a port on the Hudson's Bay or at Port Nelson, or some other point along the Hudson River. About 40 miles of track were laid out of Winnipeg. The project then came to a halt as the Dominion Government refused to guarantee bonds sold by the Company to finance the project, and the Manitoba Government likewise refused. Evident obstacles were the monopoly granted to the CPR and the fact that Manitoba did not have jurisdiction over the area beyond its borders through which the railway must pass to reach a northern port.

1882

72. Election of 1882: John A. Macdonald's Conservative Government, which had established the National Policy providing tariff protection for manufacturers of Eastern Canada as well as reaching agreement for construction of the railway, was returned to power in the election of 1882, with a majority equal to that attained in 1878:

PROVINCE	CONS.	LIB.	TOTAL
Ontario	54	48	91
Quebec	48	17	65
Nova Scotia	15	6	21
New Brunswick	10	6	16
Prince Edward Island	4	2	6
Manitoba	2	3	5
British Columbia	6	—	6
	139	71	210

73. Farm Organizations Encouraged: Very likely, the earliest farm journal published in the West was **The Nor'-West Farmer,** which began publication at Winnipeg in the summer of 1882. An editorial in an issue of February, 1883, encouraged farmers to join together in organizations.

" The thinking progressive members of nearly every occupation and profession have their groups or associations. The enterprising farmers of every country should sustain one or more. The following are some of the advantages to be derived from them. They bring farmers together and often lead to desirable acquaintance and friendship. They awaken thought on many important subjects and lead to more accurate observations and more accurate conclusions about the results of various methods of cultivating, managing, feeding, etc. They awaken the spirit of enquiry and lead to reading and conversation on subjects connected with farming. They awaken a spirit of healthy emulation, a spirit of enthusiasm, and lead to greater efforts to produce good crops and raise good stock."

74. Crop Failure: In the growing season of 1883, drought and early frost brought ruin to grain crops in many areas of the West. A desperate situation resulted when a large milling company at Montreal refused to handle frost-damaged grain. The grain market was thrown into a state of panic. Wheat prices fell to about 40 cents, oats to 15 cents. The price of farm machinery and other goods, and the cost of transportation, was high. According to the

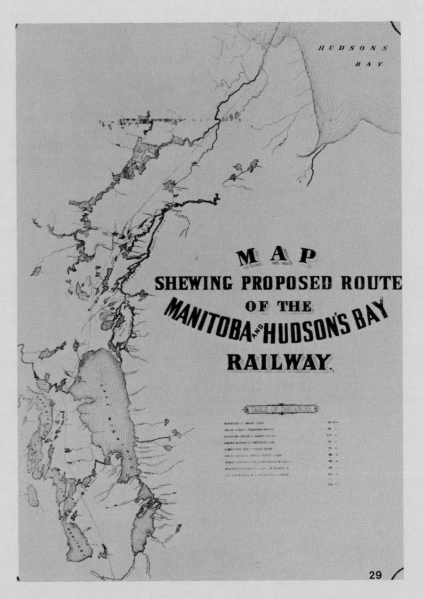

Nor'-West Farmer, "flour is worth $28 a bag at Galgarry (Calgary)." Farmers, ill-prepared with food for the coming winter, were already discontented because of the Government's protective tariff policies, land speculation, and ill-planned immigration.

1882

75. Manitoba Farmers React: As a result of economic and other problems, many frustrated Manitoba farmers began to organize in effort to find solutions.

On November 26, a mass meeting was held at Brandon to discuss grievances. Here, an organization known as The Manitoba and North-West Farmers' Union (and sometimes known as The Farmers' Protective Society) was born. Following the example provided by Louis Riel, the farmers drew up a "Bill of Rights" for submission to Ottawa.

76. North-West Reacts: When the Red River uprising of 1869-70 ended, it was clear that there would be further settlement of the Red River Valley. A number of Metis then left that area for less populated land in the North-West Territories including the Qu'Appelle Valley and the area south of Prince Albert between the North and South Saskatchewan Rivers. At Qu'Appelle, a Settlers' Union was formed to demand land reform and 'adoption of laws for the benefit of the people of the N.W.T. rather than rich politicians.'

On October 16, 1883, a large public meeting of white settlers took place at Prince Albert. The settlers, already concerned because they did not have title to the lands they occupied, were also alarmed over the economic conditions resulting from crop failure. At this meeting, another Settlers' Union was formed "for the protection of the rights and liberties which (we) possess in common with (our) brethren of other more favored parts of the Dominion."

77. Nor'-West Farmer Report: The Nor'-West Farmer, in December, 1883, carried a report on the November 26 meeting at which the Manitoba & North-West Farmers' Union was born. The text is quoted below. It is interesting to note the resolutions which comprised the "bill of rights":

" At Brandon, on the 26th ult. a large gathering of farmers met to discuss their grievances and, if possible, suggest a remedy for the existing state of affairs. The following resolutions were unanimously adopted:

1. That this meeting resolve itself into an Association to be called the Manitoba and North-West Farmers' Union.

2. That the present customs tariff, especially the duties on agricultural implements, is extremely injurious and oppressive to the settlers of the North-West and its imposition has aroused an intense feeling of dissatisfaction with our relation to Confederation. It paralyzes what is to us the most important industry of agriculture while it utterly fails to foster any other. The tariff was adopted entirely in the interests of the manufacturers and producers of the East without any reference to the needs of the country. It discriminates in favor of Dakota and Minnesota and justice to our wants imperatively demand its immediate modification so far as it effects Manitoba and the North-West.

3. That the interests of the settlers of this Province peremptorily demands that the right which under the B.N.A. Act it possesses in common with every other province of the Dominion, of chartering companies to build lines of railway within its bounds should be exercised to its fullest extent. The baneful effects of railway monopoly call loudly for the active and persistent exercise of all the powers of people to maintain their rights and to resist to the utmost every act of arbitrary interference.

4. That the public lands are the sacred heritage of the people to be administered in their interests. We maintain that the possession and management of lands, timber, and mines should be placed in the hands of provincial authorities.

5. That the natural outlet for the products of Manitoba and the North-West is through Hudson's Bay and the great rivers and lakes tributary to it, the feasibility of this route having been proved by 200 years of constant navigation by the ships of the Hudson's Bay Company and by the voyages of the New England Whalers, for the last 30 years. The interest of the North-West demands the construction at an early date of a railway connecting the present railway system with a port in the Hudson Bay. To attempt this is the duty of the Dominion Government to grant the most liberal assistance.

1883

6. We feel that the present arrangements prescribed by the C.P.R. for shipment of grain an exceedingly unsatisfactory one and highly detrimental to farmers and to grain buyers of limited means inasmuch as the C.P.R. prohibits the erection of any

elevators but those of costly description that involves the investment of considerable money thereby placing the shipment of grain in the hands of large capitalists."

1884

78. **Manitoba and N.W. Farmers Union,** formed in 1883, appears to have aroused a bright flame of excitement among farmers, but to have been very short-lived. Locals of the union were quickly formed at Brandon, Pilot Mound, Pomeroy, Ruttanville, and at other Manitoba settlements. However, some extremists of the organization made effort to get the Union involved in politics, a move that was opposed by other members. As a result, the Union came to an end by about 1886. Some of its locals remained active in another form by becoming the nucleus of farmer-owned companies to build local grain elevators.

79. **The Settlers' Union** formed at Prince Albert, 1883, recognized that the Metis of the area had a grievance in common with the white settlers in the matter of wanting title to the lands they occupied. Therefore, the Settlers' Union agreed that an effort should be made to enlist the support of the Metis in making demands. At a meeting at Batoche, March 24, the two groups recognized the need to be assisted by someone able to properly prepare their submission to the Government of Canada. It was suggested, and agreed to, that Louis Riel be asked to come.

Riel, now married and a naturalized citizen of the U.S.A., was then teaching school at St. Peter's Mission, a Metis settlement southwest of Great Falls, Montana.

Riel returned to Canada, to Batoche, where he set up a 'provisional government' as he had done at Red River. At the insistence of the Settlers' Union, he also addressed meetings at Prince Albert, enlisting considerable support and sympathy.

A draft of demands was prepared and submitted to Ottawa. The demands included provision of patents (title) to the lands occupied by settlers and Metis, representation in Parliament, responsible local government with control over natural resources, and the building of a railway to the Hudson's Bay to give the area access to seaports for the export of grain. The demands were similar in several respects to those of the Manitoba and North-West Farmers' Union. They were considered to be both moderate and reasonable, and were given support by members of the clergy, merchants, and other groups. The Government acknowledged receipt of the petition but in answer, strengthened nearby detachments of the Royal North-West Mounted Police.

80. **Grain Flow Begins:** In 1884, the first shipments of Prairie grain were moved to Eastern Canada. The grain was carried by the C.P.R. line to the head of the Great Lakes where it was transferred to boats. Now the Prairies had access to seaports. The farmers of the Prairies could serve the export markets of the world!

81. **Difficult Harvests:** To fully appreciate events that were to follow, one must understand the difficulties under which early grain farmers labored. The implements used to till the land or harvest the crop were crude by today's standards, and drawn by horses or oxen. Among the newcomers there was little knowledge and experience of growing crops amid the extreme climate conditions of the Prairies.

Harvesting was a slow and laborious process. There was danger that an early frost would damage crops before they could be gathered. Further anxiety was caused by the fact that it was necessary to get the grain, by cart, to the railway before the snows came. Each farmer was in a race with his neighbor to get his grain to the railway siding. Those who came too late were apt to discover to their dismay, that the railway had more than it could handle. The railway too, had problems, for it was hard-pressed to move as much grain as possible to the Lakehead before the freeze-up prevented the movement of boats.

At the start of the Prairie grain industry, there was virtually no means of storing grains. The elevator systems had not yet been built, nor were there terminals. Many pioneer farmers lived in sod huts and had no granaries or other facilities for on-farm storage of their surplus.

1885

82. Co-op Store: A co-operative store was in operation at Winnipeg, but little seems to be known of its origin or span of life. Evidence that it did exist is provided by an advertisement appearing in the Winnipeg Daily Sun, May 13th:

> It pays to advertise a good thing! That is why the Winnipeg Co-operative Association has resolved to advertise their tea. 626 Main St.

83. N.W. Rebellion: On the Plains, the buffalo had vanished. Indian and Metis who had depended on the buffalo for food were greatly concerned as settlement caused further inroads upon their way of life. The West was in a state of unrest. At Ottawa the Government placed the blame upon Louis Riel and regarded his petitions to the Government of Canada as evidence that he was an agitator. A strong military force was despatched. At the Battle of Batoche, May 9 to 12, the military was victorious. Riel was captured, tried on a charge of treason, and sentenced to death.

Riel remains as a controversial figure in Canadian history, a hero to some, a rascal to others. It is not easy to deny, however, that the demands he presented to government were reasonable. Indeed, it was only a matter of time before all of the more important requests were fulfilled.

84. North-West Territorial Council: By 1885, the population of the North-West—that area which became Alberta and Saskatchewan—consisted of 48,362 inhabitants, of whom 20,170 were Indians; 4,848 were Metis or half-breeds (577 English half-breeds; 3,387 French Metis; 762 Scotch; 65 Irish, and 57 other); and 23,344 were white settlers.

When Lieutenant Governor Dewdney called the 1885 session of the Territorial Council to order, he found that the members had adopted a firm and determined attitude; they were no longer content to be obedient "aids" to the governor, nor were they willing to accept further slights from the Dominion Government which had ignored the pleas and recommendations of the Council as well as the Governor. In this respect, the Council appears to have had an experience similar to that of Riel and his followers whose demands had been ignored.

In events that followed, a delegation of three was chosen by the Council, to present a Bill of Rights to the federal government. Demands included in the Bill were:

1885

"That the council have power to incorporate companies having purely territorial objects.

Old established trails to be surveyed and vested in the North West Council.

Immediate settlement of old settlers' claims, and the right to transfer.

Freight rates on the C.P.R. being a severe tax on the products of the North West, the government should use its influence to have them reduced, especially on lumber from British Columbia.

No charge to be made to settlers for wood for fuel and that each homesteader be allowed 4,000 lineal feet of building timber on free permit.

Early improvement of the Northern Saskatchewan.

Granting of the right of Habeas Corpus to the North West.

Opening for settlement of cancelled lands.

A Territorial Court of Appeal.

Construction of a trail to Peace River.

Representation in the Senate and Commons, and that for representation purposes, references should be had to territorial area as well as population.

Introduction of the Torrens system.

Right to enter a pre-emption as a second homestead.

Encouragement by the Dominion Government of railways north and south through the territories.

Benefits derived from the National Policy by the older Provinces do not apply here as regards agricultural implements and lumber and that a rebate be given equal to the duty now imposed on agricultural implements and lumber.

Immediate steps to be taken by the Government to acquire the odd-numbered sections and have them opened for settlement.

Monies voted by Parliament for the expenses of Government in the North West, including printing, roads, bridges, ferries, aid to schools, etc., should be vested in the North-West Council, as representing the people.

Early and rapid construction of the Hudson Bay Railway if practicable and liberal encouragement of the scheme by the Government.

1885

Immediate appointment of a commission to settle outstanding half-breed claims.

Early settlement of claims for compensation from rebellion losses and the payment of settlers and merchants who flourished supplies to the troops in good faith.

Stock and tree planting to count as cultivation duties.

Appointments to positions of trust and emolument in the Territories from amongst the residents of the country.

All food supplies for the Mounted Police and Indians to be purchased in the Territories.

We are aware that an issue of beef to the Indian instead of American pork would be satisfactory to all tribes. We would suggest that contracts be called for in smaller quantities, the security deposit not to exceed five per cent, and without the official routine which has attended the letting of contracts before. In this manner we believe settlers will be helped, and the Government will receive a better and cheaper article.

That steps be taken to have the Prince Albert Colonization Co., and the Edmonton and Saskatchewan Land and Colonization Co., inspected, in accordance with the representations of the members from Prince Albert, Saint Albert and Edmonton that the said companies have not complied with agreement. If such representations are correct, that they should insist upon the companies carrying out their agreements.

The recognition of the services of the Mounted Police and the Prince Albert and Battleford special forces in a manner similar to the volunteers."

The delegation from the N.W. Council, it was said, had an extremely favorable visit at Ottawa, perhaps because the N.W. Rebellion earlier in 1885 had jolted legislators out of their apathy toward the Prairies. At any rate, action soon followed.

85. Experimental Farms: In 1885, Parliament took the first steps to establish a system of government-owned experimental farms to help improve agricultural methods and production. A fund of $20,000 was provided for preliminary investigation of the merit of such farms. The decision of the government was influenced in good measure by its disappointment over the failure of agricultural settlement in the West to proceed as rapidly as had been expected.

The fact that many pioneer farmers had not been successful in their efforts to produce crops was discouraging others from attempting to do so. As the Selkirk Settlers had discovered, farming on the Prairies with its severe climate, long and cold winters, danger of early frosts, and often sparse rainfall, was hardly comparable to farming in the Old Countries.

1885

1886

86. Territorial Representation: Following the presentation in 1885, of the Bill of Rights by a delegation from the Territorial Council, Sir John A. Macdonald, prime minister, introduced a Bill to the House of Commons, to provide the Territories with a representation of four seats. At that time, Quebec, by terms of Confederation, held 65 seats in the House, and a comparable number were held by Ontario. Thus, in terms of voting strength in the House of Commons, the Territories hardly held enough power to influence any decisions.

The Bill had originally provided for election of members by a secret ballot, but this provision was deleted by the Senate. This meant that

1886

1887

87. Co-op Legislation: On June 10, "An Act Respecting Co-operative Associations", was passed by the Manitoba Legislature. It provided that 7 or more persons could form a co-operative society, with each of the members having but one vote. It required that all business be done for cash, and provided for two types of shares (transferable shares and withdrawable shares) with a limit on the number of each type which a member could hold.

The Turtle Mountain Creamery Association and the Winnipeg Co-operative Trading Association are both said to have been incorporated in 1886, with the Manitoba Co-operative Society being incorporated in 1887. It is possible that all 3 were, in fact, incorporated under the 1887 legislaiton.

From then on, however, the co-op legislation appears to have been filed away and forgotten. It was not until March 19, 1913, that the Grain Growers' Guide reported: "It will be a surprise to many to know that there is already on the Statute Books of Manitoba a Co-operation Act. ... The Act seems to be fairly satisfactory, though possibly the severe restrictions on credit may be a slight handicap in regard to purchasing supplies wholesale. ... So far as we know the Act has never been used since it was passed many years ago, but since it was unearthed recently one incorporation has already occurred."

voters had to continue to walk up to the returning officer and publicly declare their choice so that it could be recorded. Of this practice John Hawkes wrote in **Saskatchewan and Its People:**

" It might be thought that the ballot was not needed; but it was and badly. Political conditions were not ideal. A settler who had to depend on the favorable report of a government official if he was to get a patent for his homestead, needed a little courage to vote against the government, and so did the man who wanted to tender his hay and oats to the police to go through. The member of those days held absolutely the patronage of his district if his party was in power, and considered himself righteously aggrieved if the smallest government appointment was made, or any favor bestowed, over his head."

The secret ballot was adopted for Dominion Elections in 1874. Why it did not apply to the Territories is difficult to say. A likely reason is that many residents in the Territories were illiterate; they could not read the names printed on the ballot.

88. Territorial Assembly: The North-West Council, begun in 1873, was replaced by a Territorial Assembly of 22 elected members plus three advisors from the legal profession. The Lieutenant Governor appointed by the Federal Government did not preside over the assembly as had been the case under the previous council. The assembly did not, however, achieve the status now recognized of a provincial government, for through the Lieutenant Governor who was responsible to Ottawa, the federal government continued to have final say in financial, legal, and other affairs in which authority was needed by the assembly if it was to provide responsible government to its electorate. Thus, the elected members of the assembly were, in reality, acting only in an advisory capacity while the Governor was still a subordinate of the Minister of the Interior.

89. Co-op Cheese Factories: At a place about 40 miles south of Moosomin, Sask., Captain Edward Michell Pierce erected a stylish home for his family, and called it Cannington Manor. He built the home in 1883. Then, Pierce, who was destitute, set up a form of agricultural college with the idea of teaching young men of wealthy English families how to farm; this despite the fact that he is not known to have had any knowledge of the subject himself. A village soon developed adjacent to the Pierce holdings, with such ventures as a pork packing factory, flour mill, saw mill, wagon shop, stores, and two co-operative cheese factories. This enterprise did,

1887

however have some co-operative features in that Pierce had knowledge of the colonies organized by Robert Owen. The two cheese factories failed for reasons that included an irregular supply of milk, lack of access of markets, and competition from Ontario.

90. Winnipeg Grain Exchange: In 1887, the Winnipeg Grain & Produce Exchange, forerunner of the Winnipeg Grain Exchange which continues to exist, was formed. Its creation appears to have been largely due to efforts of the very aggressive Winnipeg Board of Trade. At the time, the Board was both zealously and jealously exploiting every opportunity to get and retain for Winnipeg all possible forms of commerce. The Board exerted pressures that resulted in preferential freight rates being provided for Winnipeg, making it the major distribution centre for the West. In addition the Board was determined that Winnipeg could be the grain handling capital for the West, the place at which all grading was done. Briefly, the Grain Exchange was established as a facility at which

grain dealers, both buyers and sellers, could meet to conduct their transactions. Only members of the Exchange were allowed to enter the trading arena. Farmers whose grain was being bought and sold for profit were excluded. Traders made their profits from within the margin between cost and selling prices. Their interest was in those margins, not in the price of grain. Thus, the lower the price paid to farmers, the better the margin to dealers was likely to be. At a later date, a system of futures trading was introduced to the Exchange. This gave rise to a method of 'hedging' and speculation which often brought rich reward to the traders. References consulted do not agree as to when the futures trading began; dates of 1892, 1897 and 1903 are given.

91. Election of 1887: As the election of 1887 approached, economic conditions in Canada were not favorable. The Liberals advocated reciprocity with the United States, while the Conservatives held to their policy of high tariffs. In the election, in which the North-West (that part which in 1905 became the Provinces of Alberta and Saskatchewan) participated for the first time, the Conservatives were returned with a reduced majority:

PROVINCE	CONS.	LIB.	TOTAL
Ontario	52	40	92
Quebec	33	32	65
Nova Scotia	14	7	21
New Brunswick	10	6	16
Prince Edward Island		6	6
Manitoba	4	1	5
British Columbia	6		6
North-West Territories	4		4
	123	92	215

1889

92. Immigration Encouraged: The Government of Manitoba sought to expedite the flow of Ontario farmers into Manitoba by opening up an immigration office in Toronto. The Premier of the Province at that time also served as Minister of Agriculture and made immigration his personal responsibility. A few months after opening the Toronto office, Manitoba also set up a similar office in Liverpool, England. Some lecturers were engaged to explain to prospective settlers the advantages of settlement in Manitoba where cheap and fertile land was awaiting.

1889

93. Patrons of Industry: In 1889 another farm organization of U.S. origin entered Canada. This organization first appeared in Michigan, then moved temporarily into Quebec before finding a more permanent niche in Ontario. The Patrons of Industry appear to have been confused at times, with the patrons of Husbandry otherwise termed, 'The Grange'. They were, however, distinctly different organizations although the two had some similarities. The Patrons of Husbandry (the Grange) tended to place first priority on

political effort and the interest of that organization in co-operation emerged at a later stage. The Patrons of Industry took an opposite course. The organization was primarily interested in economic matters including the possibility of forming co-operatives. But, after it had begun to operate, a turn to politics evolved.

94. Patrons of Industry: By 1891, the Patrons of Industry had severed connections with the U.S. organization and had begun to spread across Canada as a Canadian farm organization.

1891

95. Manitoba Patrons: In 1891, a local lodge of the Patrons of Industry was formed at Portage la Prairie, and, soon after, lodges were formed in several other Manitoba communities. These lodges quickly became involved in co-operative procurement of such commodities as twine, coal and kerosene.

96. Co-op Elevators: Some locals of the Grange and the Patrons of Industry became the nucleus of companies formed by farmers to build local grain elevators to be operated on a co-operative basis. In so doing, the co-operating farmers at most points were providing themselves with a service that was not otherwise available.

1891

97. Winnipeg Grain and Produce Exchange: Incorporation of the Winnipeg Grain & Produce Exchange was provided by the Manitoba government. The Exchange had, by now, achieved a strong position in the grain trade.

98. Election of 1891: The Conservatives under Sir John A. Macdonald were again returned to office. In the election campaign, Macdonald defended his party's policies of protective tariffs for Canadian industries. He attacked Liberal proposals for unrestricted reciprocity with the United States, saying it would endanger Canada's freedom and independence." A British subject I was born, a British subject I will die," Macdonald declared. Three months after being returned to office, Sir John A. Macdonald passed away.

PROVINCE	CONS.	LIB.	TOTAL
Ontario	48	44	92
Quebec	30	35	65
Nova Scotia	16	5	21
New Brunswick	13	3	16
Prince Edward Island	2	4	6
Manitoba	4	1	5
British Columbia	6		6
North-West Territories	4		4
	123	92	215

1894

99. Patrons of Industry: In 1894, the Patrons of Industry entered the North-West Territories as a result of a meeting held in the home of a farmer of the Regina area. The movement spread quickly until, in 1895, a Grand Territorial Lodge (compared to a Provincial office) was formed.

The importance of the Patrons of Industry as a catalyst for developing Prairie farm organizations seems to have escaped the attention of many writers on co-operatives and farm organizations. Fortunately, John Hawkes, Provincial Librarian for Saskatchewan, recorded activities of the Patrons of Industry in his extensive work of three volumes, **"Saskatchewan and Its People"**, published about 1925. Hawkes had been commissioned by the Saskatchewan Government to record the early history of the Province. He wrote:

" The main object of the lodges in the first stance was to get their supplies cheaper. A lodge might order sufficient goods from a departmental store so as to get a considerable advantage. The County Association embracing a number of lodges, might go a step further. The practice with the County Association at Lumsden, (Sask.), was, for instance, to buy a carload of something if the circumstances warranted it. The secretary would send out cards to the lodges and request them to send

1894

orders to Mr. Hunter, the Grand Lodge secretary. If sufficient orders came in the secretary would buy a carload at the best price he could get. He would then notify the farmers of the arrival of the car at Regina, and the farmers would drive in from the surrounding country. Mr. Hunter would distribute the goods from the car and take the cash."

According to Hawkes: "The farmers' movements of today are all phoenixes which have arisen from the ashes of the Patrons of Industry." Further, he wrote: "The Grain Growers' Association (formed in 1901) grew (indirectly no doubt, but none the less in reality) out of the roots of the Patron movement; and to the Patrons must be accorded a high meed of praise for the courageous way in which ... they endeavoured to help themselves by making a frontal attack on the established political order."

100. Patrons of Industry: Across Canada, the Patron Movement had grown rapidly. It was now reaching a peak of 50,000 members. It had displaced the Grange (Order of the Patrons of Husbandry) as the most prominent farmers' organization. By 1895, the Patrons of Industry had become very active in politics, seeking to enter

candidates in both federal and provincial elections. To the Patrons, and with good reason, it appeared that election campaigns too often hinged on matters related to industrial trade and commerce without proper consideration of agriculture which concerned the larger number of people.

1895

33

101. Harmona Colony, An Owen Influence: In 1895, near Tantallon, Sask., an association called the Harmona Colony, but also known as the Harmony Industrial Association Limited, formed a 'village of co-operation' along the lines of that attempted by Robert Owen in the U.S.A. in 1828. Homes in the Harmona Colony were grouped together and served by a blacksmith shop, carpenter shop, laundry, a community kitchen, and a co-operative store. The Colony, led by Samuel W. Sanderson, a Quaker of Beulah, Manitoba, was disbanded about 1900 as a result of disappointment and frustration among its members.

1895

102. Hudson's Bay Railway: Sir Charles Tupper, who became leader of the Conservative Party in 1895, tried to gain support in the West in the election of 1896. He promised, that if he returned to office, his party would build a railway line to the Hudson's Bay.

103. Election of 1896: In the election of 1896, the Liberals, led by Sir Wilfred Laurier, replaced the Conservative administration. The Liberals, during the campaign, attacked the Conservative policy of tariff protection for Canadian industry while promoting the idea of a limited reciprocity agreement with both Britain and the United States. In the background of the campaign, and a factor in its outcome, was a religious conflict. The Manitoba legislature had passed, in 1890, a bill withdrawing its financial support of separate schools for French Catholics of that Province. In addition, the legislation made supporters of separate schools pay taxes for public schools, as well. French Catholics across Canada protested against this withdrawal of religious freedom, but other factions, notably Orangemen, partially took an opposite stance. The Conservatives in Ottawa introduced remedial legislation and ran on this platform in the 1896 election. The issue undoubtedly is the reason for strong Liberal support in Quebec in the 1896 election.

PROVINCE	LIB.	CONS.	INDEP.	TOTAL
Ontario	43	44	5	92
Quebec	49	16		65
Nova Scotia	10	10		20
New Brunswick	5	9		14
P.E.I.	2	3		5
Manitoba	2	4	1	7
B.C.	4	2		6
N.W.T.	2	1	1	4
	117	89	7	213

104. Patrons' Candidates: In the North-West, the Patrons of Industry entered candidates in the election of 1896, as did Patrons elsewhere in Canada. In East Assiniboia constituency (S.E. Saskatchewan), a Tantallon farmer, Rev. (Dr.) James M. Douglas, was elected as an independent candidate but with Liberal support. At Ottawa, Douglas soon joined the ranks of the Liberals as did most of the few Patrons who were elected.

CHAPTER VI
CONFLICT FROM 1896 to 1912

1896
to
1912

105. The revolt of 1885 within the Territorial Council coupled no doubt with uneasiness after the execution of Louis Riel, resulted in representation of the North-West in the House of Commons. With 5 seats held by Manitoba and 4 by the North-West, the agricultural Prairies had a total representation of 9, or 4% of the membership of the House of Commons.

At the time, industrially and commercially oriented Provinces of Ontario and Quebec accounted for 73% of the seats in the House, or enough to dominate both the party in office and the opposition party. Both parties appear to have given top priority to commercial interests, that were frequently divided Manufacturers had favored tariff protection, which the Conservatives had provided, while the merchant class engaged in foreign trade, opted for reciprocity. Both, however, were wont to change political direction with a turn of economic conditions.

Engrossed by the affairs of the commercial provinces, the House,

**1896
to
1912**

with only scant representation from the West, found little reason to concern itself with affairs of the West—at least, not until the two rebellions of 1885 and the election of Patrons to the House of Commons. The West, it should be noted, is separated from Eastern Canada by a natural barrier of rock, muskeg, lakes and forests some 700 miles wide. Only on rare occasions did politicians from the East cross that barrier to get a first-hand view of the West.

Around 1854, George Brown had called for 'rep by pop' to replace equal representation in the House of Commons—a means of ensuring that English-speaking Canada West (Ontario) would have supremacy in the House over French-speaking Canada East (Quebec). It is an interesting question as to whether Brown would have taken the same stance if he had been an early settler of the North-West which the Government of Eastern Canada had designated as an agricultural area.

Manufacturing and allied commerce, it should be kept in mind, lead

to a concentration of population. On the other hand, farming results in a low density of population over a wide area of land. As may be seen from election results, the seating in the House of Commons reflects the disparity.

Be that as it may, the representation given to the North-West in the 1887 election was important. The North-West was no longer regarded, politically at least, as a colony of Confederated Canada, although Westerners, at the time, still thought it did. It did not mean, however, that the West was no longer to be an economic colony of Eastern business interests. The latter seems well confirmed by the events of 1896 to 1912—the efforts of the eastern-based business sector, through its Winnipeg outpost, to take full charge of the grain trade, and to stop enactment of legislation that would lead to development of co-operatives through which farmers might gain control over their own affairs.

**1896
to
1897**

34

106. Co-operative Creameries: A further debt is due to John Hawkes for recording the events which led to the formation of co-operative creameries in the North-West. He wrote, circa 1925:

" As far as butter was concerned the local market, under expansion of the country, was sufficient. The demand kept pace fairly with the supply. Barter was the principle means of trading. The settler took butter, eggs, and other produce to the merchant, and received in exchange, clothing, tea and other household necessities, with an exception in the case of flour. The miller demanded cash from the merchant, so the merchant had in this regard to insist on cash from the settler. In a few years the initial rush of settlers flagged, and the local demand (for butter) was outstripped by the supply. The merchant now had to find an outside market for butter he received 'in trade' for the majority of his customers were settlers who made more butter than they could use instead of buying it.

" By this time, Vancouver, after having once been destroyed by fire, was forging ahead and British Columbia was beginning to absorb a good deal of the prairie butter. Winnipeg was growing fast and this was another market. The country merchant would consign butter to commission men in these cities, but necessarily these markets were limited.

" Then the farmers had to turn their attention to making creamery butter, suited for export, so we find creameries established at various points. Most of these were economic failures. Farmers

**1896
to
1897**

and townspeople would meet and decide to establish a creamery. The necessary capital would be subscribed, and a creamery erected and operated only to find out that to run a factory, make saleable butter for a more or less fastidious export trade, and market it to advantage, required expert knowledge and management which in the majority of cases were woefully lacking.

'' For years, the Dairy Commissioner for the Dominion did his best to instruct farmers in the making of both dairy and creamery butter, but failure, or at the best the most modest success, was the result. ... In some seasons seven cents a pound was the top price and the overstocked merchant did not want it at that. Tons of butter went for the making of axle grease. ... One exasperating feature to the merchant was that he practically was compelled to allow the same price for axle grease butter as for the best article, for the woman who made the axle grease would be insulted beyond measure if she found her gilt-edged neighbor got more than she did.

'' A North-West Dairyman's Association was at length formed and duly incorporated at Regina in the hope of coping in some way or another with this desperate state of affairs.

'' In the winter of 1869, the Government made a small grant to the Association and on the strength of this, dairy conventions were held at the principal points in the Territories. At each meeting a plan conceived by William Watson ... was explained. Watson had committed to writing a detailed scheme for the establishment of creameries on the co-operative principle with government assistance and government control. Both merchants and farmers endorsed Mr. Watson's plan.

'' At the conclusion of the series of meetings, the case was presented in a written statement to authorities in Ottawa. The government accepted the plan, advanced money, saw that the equipment was right, appointed a buttermaker and sold the product. So much per pound of butter produced was directed to the government to pay the interest and repay principal on the monies advanced. The farmers received so much per pound as advances, and the balance at stated intervals."

John Hawkes' writing is of value for several reasons. It tells something about economic conditions of the time. It explains how it was that the Dominion Government assisted in the start of co-operative dairies in the North-West even before the Provinces of Alberta and Saskatchewan were formed.

**1896
to
1912**

Another point of interest is the payment of cash advances to farmers as they delivered their butter, followed by additional payments as the produce was sold. This same method, it will be seen later on, was later adopted in the handling of grain by the wheat pools and by the Canadian Wheat Board.

107. Immigration Promoted: In 1897, the Minister of the Interior for the Dominion Government, launched a mammoth campaign to attract immigrants to the Prairies. Through thousands of newspapers and enormous numbers of pamphlets and posters, advertising was carried out in Ontario and Quebec, the United States, Great Britain, and in several European countries where the

offer of a free grant of 160 acres of land had vast appeal to landless peoples. The campaign was given further impetus by the C.P.R., the Hudson's Bay company, and land companies, all of which offered to sell to settlers the land which they held. From now on, the population of the Prairies grew quite rapidly.

1897

108. Crows Nest Pass Agreement: The Dominion Government granted a charter to the C.P.R. for the building of a railway from Lethbridge, Alberta, to Nelson, B.C. A further cash subsidy plus an additional grant of land was provided to the railway. This agreement, known as the "Crows Nest Pass Agreement", required that, in return for government aid, the C.P.R. would reduce, to 14

cents per CWT, the freight charges on grains moving to the East. In addition, the railway was to carry rates established therein to be provided in perpetuity. In the decades that followed the railway was successful in efforts to persuade the Government to eliminate from the agreement the fixed rates on all commodities except grain.

1897

109. Elevator Monopolies: Prairie grain production was rapidly increasing. Production in 1886 was 11 million bushels; by 1890 it had reached 22 million and would reach 45 million bushels by 1899. Farmers rushed most of their grain to the railway siding during a short period in the fall. The result was a congestion which the railway was not equipped to handle. Its funds depleted by the building of the transcontinental line, the railway was not in a position to obtain additional rolling stock, especially since the boxcars would only be needed for a relatively short period in each year.

In an effort to relieve the situation by creating additional storage, the railway offered a monopoly on grain handling to any interests building an elevator at given shipping points. This attractive offer resulted in the building of a large number of elevators. However, to create the promised monopolies, the railway was obliged to issue an order which prevented farmers from loading their own grain into boxcars. The railway argued that the loading by farmers was a slow process that did not permit efficient use of the boxcars.

110. Patrons Of Industry React: Depriving farmers of the right to load their own boxcars and the provision of monopolies for elevators strongly aroused the Patrons of Industry as well as farmers generally. It was charged that the railways and elevator interests had conspired against the farmers by creating a closed, monopolistic channel to the grain markets. As a result, the elevator operators were able to dictate terms to the farmers, and to exploit them by arbitrarily offering low grades, shortweights, unfair prices and excess dockage. The farmers alleged that the elevator companies operated in collusion with one another in opposition to the farmers' interests, and that there was no competition between the companies.

Rev. James M. Douglas, MP, elected with Patron support in 1896, effectively pleaded the farmers' case in the House of Commons. As a result of his efforts, a Royal Commission was formed to study the matter of grain handling.

The Royal Commission held numerous meetings throughout the West between October, 1899, and February, 1900, hearing from both farmers and elevator interests.

Following a meeting of the Commission held at Regina, an independent newspaper, **The Regina Standard**, published its views on the matter:

" The evidence reveals a shameful condition of affairs. It was shown in several instances buyers had admitted theft by restoring the stolen weight. Then again, the most inexplicable instances of dockage were shown. That an elevator monopoly making all this possible should be allowed to exist is nothing short of shameful. The one remedy for it all is the abolition of the monopoly."

1899

111. Co-op Store At Lacombe: In 1899, farmers of the Lacombe (now in Alberta) district formed an organization called the Co-operative Purchasing Association. A branch of that organization also existed at Ponoka. The Association was modeled on the lines of the Rochdale Pioneers. It appears to have been short-lived, existing only until 1902.

1900

112. Manitoba Grain Act: The Report of the Royal Commission formed to study the grain handling industry largely confirmed the charges made by farmers. The Commission reported that 477 grain elevators existed, with 206 owned by three companies, 95 owned by two milling companies, 120 by smaller concerns, and 26 by farmers.

As a result of this Report, the Dominion Government passed the

Manitoba Grain Act. Hugh Boyd, in his book, **New Breaking**, gives the following explanations:

" Briefly, the Act, which in spite of its name applied to the whole Dominion, regulated the railways and elevators in the interests of the grain growers. It called for an official to supervise the grain trade in the West, and to whom farmers might send their future complaints as to weighing and grading. ...

1900

" (The) early statutes had to do chiefly with weights, measures, grades, and so on, and while of advantage to producers were more directly of concern to dealers and indeed were largely suggested by them. The Manitoba Grain Act, on the other hand, was a measure to regulate those middlemen themselves, and resulted from agrarian pressure."

The Manitoba Grain Act of 1900, it should be noted, required the

railway to erect platforms at sidings so that farmers could, if they chose, load their grain onto boxcars.

The Manitoba Grain Act of 1900 was amended in 1903 and again in 1908. In 1912, when still further amended, it became known as the Canada Grain Act. At that time the supervisor was replaced by the Board of Grain Commissioners.

113. Canada's First Credit Union: A veteran newspaperman and Hansard reporter, Alphonse Desjardins, was responsible for founding the credit union movement in Canada. Tired of reporting on leisurely debates about usury and 'loan sharks', he decided to do something about it. During the Commons' Christmas recess, he returned to his home town of Levis, across the St. Lawrence from the City of Quebec. There he gathered about 100 relatives and friends in a church basement, and persuaded them to form a caisse populaire (people's bank). On the fist day of business, deposits totalled only $26.40.

Desjardins borrowed ideas from the pioneer credit union

movements of Germany and Britain, but he also gave the caisse populaire a distinctive French-Canadian character. His efforts were favorably regarded by the Catholic clergy. Desjardins' next step was to endeavour to persuade the Dominion Government to enact legislation for incorporation of caisse populaires or credit unions, but he was not successful (see events of 1908). He then turned to the Quebec Government which soon provided the necessary legislation. Soon afterward, Desjardins was invited to the U.S.A. where he became a leading figure in the start of the credit union movement in that country.

114. Election of 1900: In the 1900 general election, the Liberals were returned with a stronger majority than they had achieved in the 1896 election:

PROVINCE	LIB.	CONS.	TOTAL
Ontario	37	55	92
Quebec	58	7	65
Nova Scotia	15	5	20
New Brunswick	9	5	14
Prince Edward Island	3	2	5
Manitoba	3	4	7
North-West Territories	4		4
British Columbia	4	2	6
	133	80	213

1901

115. Boxcars Refused: The Manitoba Grain Act of 1900 was at first acclaimed as a victory for the farmers. In 1901, however, a bumper crop was harvested and the railway was not prepared to handle such a volume. When farmers sought to do their own

loading of boxcars it was discovered that the railway had given first priority to the elevators, hence almost none were available to the farmers. The latter then raised their voices in angry protest.

116. Territorial Grain Growers' Association: On December 18th, farmers of the district met at Indian Head. It is believed this meeting was called by the president of the Indian Head Agricultural Society. At any rate, in 1896, the town of Indian Head was acclaimed as "the

1901

biggest initial shipping point for wheat in the world." At the December 18 meeting, the prime topic for discussion was the refusal of the railways to honor the clause of the Manitoba Grain Act which required the railway to allocate boxcars to the farmers. The meeting resolved to form an organization known as the Territorial Grain Growers' Association (TGGA) to press the farmers' demand for fair play. Seventy-five farmers immediately joined TGGA. W.R. Motherwell, a Wolseley farmer, was chosen as president, and a drive to sign up members along the CPR line between Moosomin and Regina was begun.

117. Elevator Companies Organize: The elevator companies, closely tied to flour milling interests of Montreal and eager to advance their interests, formed the North-West Elevator Association.

Without doubt, this was done in response to the formation of the Territorial Grain Growers' Association and the determination of farmers to have more control over matters affecting them.

1902

118. Territorial Grain Growers' Boxcar Demands: At its first annual convention, the Territorial Grain Growers' Association soundly backed a strong resolution demanding that the railway allocate boxcars according to the sequence in which orders were received.

119. Lacombe Farmers Association: The Co-operative Purchasing Association at Lacombe had failed. Some of its members, however, continued to act together for group purchasing of necessities. Seeing need for a new organization they formed The Lacombe Farmers' Association which soon after became known as the Farmers' Association of Alberta.

120. Territorial Grain Growers' Interests Manitoba Farmers: At Virden, a Manitoba community near the Saskatchewan border and on the CPR line, members of the local Agricultural Society became keenly interested in affairs of the Territorial Grain Growers' Association. The Society expressed desire that an officer of the TGGA pay a visit to Virden to provide first-hand information.

121. American Society of Equity: In 1902, in the State of Indiana, U.S.A., an organization known as The American Society of Equity was created by a group of farmers. By chance, a farmer of the Edmonton, Alberta, district received some literature giving an explanation of this Society and its aims. He was impressed and undertook to set up a local of the American Society of Equity at Edmonton.

Briefly, the main aim of the Society was to improve the prices received by farmers for produce. A price schedule was established and copies posted in markets as well as published in newspapers. Members of the Society were pledged to refuse to sell at prices below those listed. The Society did not, however, prove to be successful.

1903

122. Manitoba Grain Act Amended: Responding to the resolution of the Territorial Grain Growers' the Dominion Government amended the Manitoba Grain Act. As a result, the railway was compelled, by law, to allocate boxcars to both farmers' platforms and to elevators, in fair rotation and according to the sequence in which orders were received.

123. Railway Disobeys: It became apparent to farmers that the railway was not abiding by the amendments to the Manitoba Grain Act which required that boxcars be made available to farmers in fair rotation. At Sintaluta, farmers carefully noted an incident of violation. The Territorial Grain Growers took the matter to court and won their case against the railway. The railway then complied with the terms of the Manitoba Grain Act respecting boxcar allocation although it did appeal the decision, unsuccessfully, to the Supreme Court of Canada.

The winning of the court case was an important victory for the T.G.G.A. and for farmers who could save themselves as much as 10 cents a bushel by loading their own grain.

124. Manitoba Grain Growers': At Virden, the Agricultural Society invited W.R. Motherwell to address a meeting to discuss the Territorial Grain Growers' Association. The meeting, held January 9, sparked formation of the Manitoba Grain Growers' Association, an organization similar to the T.G.G.A. Enthusiasm was so high that within 6 weeks' time over 15 locals had been formed. On March 3, the Manitoba Grain Growers' Association was born at a convention of 100 delegates from 26 locals.

1904

125. Lacombe Farmers Association, now known as the Farmers Association of Alberta (F.A.A.) became involved in politics when the organization's president ran as a candidate in the federal election. He was soundly defeated. His defeat added fuel to a rift that existed within the organization where some favored while others opposed entry of the F.A.A. into politics. Following this incident, the F.A.A. declined rapidly.

126. Election of 1904: In the general election of 1904, the Liberal Party was returned to office with a majority of 54 seats:

PROVINCE	LIB.	CONS.	TOTAL
Ontario	38	48	86
Quebec	54	11	65
Nova Scotia	18		18
New Brunswick	7	6	13
Prince Edward Island	1	3	4
Manitoba	7	3	10
North-West Territories	7	3	10
British Columbia	7		7
Yukon		1	1
	139	75	214

1905

127. Provinces of Alberta and Saskatchewan: In response to growing agitation, the Dominion Government organized the Provinces of Saskatchewan and Alberta from the North-West Territories. Provision was made for both Provinces to have their own responsible legislatures; they were also extended all rights that Confederation bestowed on other provinces of the Dominion with the exception that, as in the case of Manitoba, the Dominion Government retained control of Crown-owned lands.

1905

128. Co-operative Creameries: The Dominion Government transferred to the Provinces of Alberta and Saskatchewan, its jurisdiction over the co-operative creameries to which assistance had been provided since 1896.

129. Territorial Grain Growers': At meetings held at Edmonton on February 20 and March 2, a local of the Territorial Grain Growers' Association was formed. The meetings were called by a number of farmers of the Strathcona district who felt need for an organization but did not favor the Society of Equity's controlled marketing plan because they did not believe it to be practical. Further, the farmers did not favor an organization of U.S. origin.

131. Grain Exchange: The workings of the Winnipeg Grain & Produce Exchange were viewed suspiciously by many farmers. The Sintaluta local of the Territorial Grain Growers' Association decided to send one of its officers, E.A. Partridge, to Winnipeg for a month-long study of the Exchange so that he might make an assessment of the fairness of its practices.

130. Society of Equity: Formation of the local of the Territorial Grain Growers' Association was opposed by the Society of Equity. The Society had, by now, bought a timber limit and had ambitions of owning lumber mills and flour mills. The plans aroused considerable interest with the result that farmer-shareholders were signed up in nearly all parts of the Province.

132. Co-op Grain Marketing: Among officials and members of the Manitoba Grain Growers' Association there was keen interest in the mission of E.A. Partridge to Winnipeg. An invitation was extended to Partridge to address the annual convention of the M.G.G.A. on his return journey to Sintaluta.

Partridge told the M.G.G.A. convention that control of the grain export business appeared to rest in the hands of five companies which, to a large extent, regulated the profit margins of the farmers. He was convinced that there was a successful and organized effort to exploit farmers and to put farmer-owned elevators out of business. He proposed that farmers form a co-operative through which to market their own grain. The M.G.G.A. responded to the proposal by establishing a committee to investigate the matter.

133. Partridge Returns: Returning to Sintaluta, Partridge provided a report to his T.G.G.A. local on his study of the Grain Exchange. The report was similar to that given to the M.G.G.A. convention. He repeated his proposal that a co-operative organization be formed to conduct grain marketing activity but no action on the proposal was immediately taken.

134. Legislation For Creameries: The Saskatchewan Legislature, in its first session, enacted legislation providing for the organization and operation of co-operative creameries with the assistance

1906

1906

of the government. The effect was to continue, under provincial control, measures and assistance previously provided by the Dominion Government. The new legislation provided that when a group of farmers had raised a certain amount of capital for a creamery, the Province would lend them the balance at a modest rate of interest.

135. Grain Co-op: In January, a large number of farmers who were dissatisfied with the existing grain marketing system, rallied for a meeting at Sintaluta. Here, they discussed Partridge's plan for a grain marketing co-operative and found the idea to be acceptable.

136. Grain Co-op: At a meeting held February 28, the Manitoba Grain Growers' Association gave approval to the Partridge plan for a grain marketing co-operative.

137. Grain Growers' Grain Company: With support from the Manitoba and the Territorial Grain Growers' Associations, a co-operative to market grain was formed in April. It was known as the Grain Growers' Grain Company and was intended to serve farmers in all three Prairie Provinces. Except for the forgotten co-operative legislation in Manitoba there was no legislation to provide for incorporation of a co-operative either federally or provincially. Thus, the GGGC was obliged to seek incorporation under the Dominion Companies Act. The Secretary of State refused to grant incorporation. He pointed out that the Act stipulated that

companies having a share capital in excess of $250,000 were required to issue shares of a par value of not less than $100 each. The GGGC proposed to sell shares at $25 each, aware that many farmers could not afford to invest more.

Frustrated in efforts to obtain a Dominion Charter, the GGGC applied for a charter under the Joint Stock Companies Act of the Province of Manitoba. The Charter was granted, and the organization then obtained licenses to operate in Alberta and Saskatchewan.

138. Grain Growers Grain Company & Grain Exchange: The Grain Growers' Grain Company was successful in obtaining membership in the Winnipeg Grain Exchange. The Company then undertook to sell carlots of grain through the Exchange on behalf of its farmer-members. A circular mailed in October, 1906, by the Company explained its plan to rebate to farmers a portion of the commissions earned through selling their grain. Claiming that such

a practice violated one of its rules, the Exchange expelled GGGC from membership. GGGC was, at the time, holding for sale a large quantity of grain and seemed faced with disaster because the Company had no means of selling. The Scottish Co-operative Wholesale Society, however, came to the rescue by purchasing, outside of the Exchange, most of the grain held by GGGC.

139. Government Intervenes In Grain Exchange Dispute: Responding to numerous complaints by farmers, the Dominion Government formed a second Royal Commission of Inquiry to study practices of the grain trade. The Commissioners arrived at Winnipeg just as the Grain Growers' Grain company was expelled from the Exchange. Investigating affairs, the Commissioners strongly suspected the existence of a secret agreement for wrongful conspiracy among three large elevator companies. The

Commissioners sought to have the GGGC restored to its seat in the Exchange and questioned the rule that had led to the Company's expulsion. The Exchange refused to accept the return of GGGC to membership and argued that the rules of the Exchange were necessary. Without power to establish and enforce its rules, the Exchange claimed, it could not ensure integrity in dealing, equality of treatment, or uniformity of practices, and would be forced out of existence.

1906

In December, 1906, the GGGC's Board of Directors reluctantly decided they must withdraw their plan to pay patronage refunds to farmers on grain sold. This decision should have cancelled out the reason why GGGC was expelled, but the Exchange did not permit the Company to resume its membership. The Manitoba Government then acted on behalf of GGGC, demanding that the Company be readmitted to the Exchange. To back up its demand, the Government threatened to deprive the Exchange of its powers and to impose governmental regulation.

140. Saskatchewan Grain Growers: At the annual convention, it was agreed that the name of the Territorial Grain Growers' Association be changed to Saskatchewan Grain Growers' Association.

142. Farmers' Co-op Store: At Milestone, south of Regina, a co-operative store was operating under the name, Milestone Co-operative Association. It was a farmer-owned joint stock company, and was closed out in 1908.

141. Alberta Farmers' Association: The local of the Territorial Grain Growers' Association formed at Edmonton in early 1905 became known as the Alberta Farmers Association after being reorganized. The AFA was then Alberta's counterpart to the Grain Growers' associations of Manitoba and Saskatchewan.

1907

143. The Winnipeg Grain & Produce Exchange, yielding to pressures from the Manitoba Government, restored membership privileges to the Grain Growers' Grain Company. There was, however, a condition attached. The GGGC was required to give assurance that it would not provide patronage refunds or rebates from the sale of grain to its farmer-members. Thus, the Company was forced to conform to the established order of the grain trade by abandoning a basic principle of co-operative enterprise.

144. Interprovincial Council of Grain Growers': The early Grain Growers' had great faith in their motto, "in unity there is strength". An expression of this faith resulted in the formation of an Interprovincial Council of Grain Growers' and Farmers' Associations.

This provided a basis for co-ordination of efforts by the Manitoba and Saskatchewan Grain Growers' Associations, the Alberta Farmers' Association, and the Grain Growers' Grain Company.

145. Co-operative Legislation: One of the first acts of the Interprovincial Grain Growers' was to send a small delegation to Ottawa to urge the Dominion Government to provide legislation under which co-operative organizations could incorporate.

Simultaneously, Alphonse Desjardins was active in seeking Dominion legislation for the incorporation of caisse populaires or credit unions.

146. Society of Equity: Farmers who had backed the Society of Equity lost their investment when the organization's ventures into lumber and flour milling failed.

147. Co-operative Legislation: In December, Bill No. 5, "An Act Respecting Co-operation", was placed before the House of Commons by F.D. Monk, member for Jacques Cartier. Mr. Monk explained that he was speaking on behalf of a committee set up to study the Bill at the 1906-07 session of Parliament. The committee, Monk said, had met many times, examining employees of the Department of Agriculture and many other witnesses. The committee, he said, has given the Bill 'unanimous' and 'complete' approval, recognizing it as "one calculated to help the development of agriculture and fruit culture, and as (being) a very useful credit and loan measure". The committee recommended that the Bill be passed as quickly as possible.

1908

148. Co-operative Legislation: On March 6, Bill No. 5, "An Act Respecting Co-operation", was still before the House of Commons. Hon. R. Lemieux, chairman of the committee of the House which had studied the Bill, explained that the committee had also studied co-operative legislation existing in other countries. He told the House:

" Co-operation offers very great advantages to the farming classes, particularly in certain branches of agricultural pursuits such as dairying, market gardening, and fruit culture. Co-operation has also been proven of great use in the purchase by farmers of agricultural implements and fertilizers. ... Co-operation offers a means for the laboring classes to purchase under the most favorable terms the necessities of life and the articles required for the exercise of any trade. It also provides a system by which wage earners can either build or acquire their own homes by means of a small loan from credit and savings committees...I may say His Excellency the Governor-General (Earl Grey, original donor of the Grey Cup football trophy) is one of the leading authorities in Europe on the co-operative move-

ment. For many years he was president of the International Co-operative Alliance..."

Mr. Monk, who had introduced the Bill to the House in December, spoke: "Some objections to a measure of this kind have been raised by retail merchants; but it has been abundantly proven in every country where co-operation has been put into practice that far from being a detriment to retail dealers, it has, in the end, been a great help to them by advancing the general welfare of the community, by encouraging thrift, industry, and accumulation of savings."

Mr. Monk pointed out that Manitoba, Quebec and British Columbia had enacted co-operative legislation. "But," he said, "in all these Provinces a very serious obstacle meets those interested in this movement. It is immpossible for a province to enact provisions regarding what I might call the credit-loan feature of this Bill, or what might be termed its banking feature."

On being put to its third vote in the House of Commons, Bill No. 5 received unanimous approval. It now needed only approval by a majority in the Senate to become law.

1908

149. Senate Defeats Co-op Bill: On March 10, Bill No. 5, "An Act Respecting Co-operation," was given first reading in the Senate. On second reading, March 24, the Bill was referred to the Standing Committee of the Senate on Banking and Commerce, for further study.

On July 10, the Standing Committee reported to the Senate that the Provinces of Ontario, Quebec, British Columbia, and Saskatchewan, claimed to have legislative jurisdiction over some matters contained in the Bill, and were, for that reason, opposed to it. The Committee recommended that the Bill be rejected. On July 14, the Senate again discussed the Bill during the afternoon when 56 of the 96 members of the Senate were present. Discussions carried on into an evening session when only 47 members were in attendance. Bill No. 5 was put to a vote. Of the 47 members present,

10 abstained from voting, 19 opposed the Bill, and 18 voted in favor of it. Thus, by a vote in which only 38% of the members of the Senate took part, Bill No. 5 was defeated in the Senate by a majority of one vote after unanimously passing in the House of Commons.

It appears reasonable to assume that Senators were influenced by both banking and mercantile interests. Bankers could hardly be expected to support an intrusion by credit unions or caisse populaires into their domain. And, as Mr. Monk had noted, merchants had expressed opposition to the Bill, a matter that was made more clear in 1913 by a spokesman for the Retail Merchants Association. For more than sixty years to follow the defeat of Bill No. 5 by a majority of but one, the vote was remembered with anger and frustration by Canada's co-operative movement.

150. Manitoba Government Curbs Grain Exchange: On February 19, 1908, the Manitoba Legislature amended the Charter granted in 1891 to the Winnipeg Grain and Produce Exchange. The

amendments curbed the powers of the Exchange. Reacting against what it termed "interference" and "regulation" by the Government, the Exchange closed its doors five days later.

151. Winnipeg Grain Exchange: In November, 1908, members of the erstwhile Winnipeg Grain and Produce Exchange formed a new organization to replace the former Exchange. It was known as the

Winnipeg Grain Exchange and operated as a non-incorporated, self-regulating body that was to play a long and prominent role in the Prairie grain trade.

152. Public Ownership Of Elevators Is Proposed: Farmers continued to hold suspicions that the elevator companies were combined against them. The Manitoba Grain Act had resulted in some improvement from the farmers' point of view, but the fact remained that a very few large milling companies dominated the grain-gathering system. Another "Partridge-plan" was conceived by E.A. Partridge. He proposed that the provincial governments of Manitoba, Saskatchewan and Alberta take over and operate

country elevators and that the Dominion Government do likewise with the terminal elevators. Early in 1908, this "Partridge plan" was firmly adopted by a meeting of the Interprovincial Council of Grain Growers' and Farmers' Associations. In May, Premiers of the three Prairie Provinces met to discuss the plan but came up with a set of alternate proposals that were not acceptable to the Council. A long series of negotiations between the Council and provincial governments then followed.

153. Grain Growers' Guide: Grain Growers Grain Co. began to publish a paper of special interest to farmers. Called **The Grain Growers' Guide,** the paper quickly became an important source of information to farmers, helping to increase their understanding of farm problems and the efforts of farm organizations to cope with

them. **The Guide's** editorials reflected a strong crusading spirit, a firm stand on matters pertinent to the interest and welfare of farmers, and gave much encouragement for development of co-operative trading.

154. Group Purchasing: Although the Patrons of Industry had, by now, almost vanished from the Prairie scene, the practice it had encouraged by which farmers clubbed together to buy in quantity was not forgotten. Indeed, many profit enterprise concerns, particularly those offering bulk goods such as lumber, flour, and

wire were actually encouraging farmers to club together in buying. The encouragement was given in advertisements published in farm papers. One such advertisement appearing in the GRAIN GROWERS' GUIDE, December, 1908, reads:

1908

155. Manitoba Grain Growers': It was reported that the Manitoba Grain Growers' Association now had 133 locals.

156. Saskatchewan Grain Growers': At least 104 locals of the Saskatchewan Grain Growers' Association now existed.

157. Society of Equity: Founders of the local of the American Society of Equity formed in 1902, were concerned that, with formation of the Edmonton local of the Territorial Grain Growers in 1904, there had been evidence of opposition to the Society because of its U.S. origins and ties. Thus, it was decided to reform the Society as a Canadian Society of Equity, free of any U.S. connections. There were plans for the new Society to build co-operative elevators and marketing facilities. However, these plans were not realized because of shortages of capital.

158. Election of 1908: The Liberals were again returned to office:

PROVINCE	LIB.	CONS.	INDEP.	TOTAL
Ontario	36	24	2	86
Quebec	53	11	1	65
Nova Scotia	12	6		18
New Brunswick	11	2		13
Prince Edward Island .	3	1		4
Manitoba	2	8		10
Saskatchewan	9	1		10
Alberta	4	3		7
British Columbia	2	5		7
Yukon	1			1
	133	85	3	221

1909

159. M.G.G.A. Examines Coal, Lumber: At their annual convention held in January, at Brandon, the Manitoba Grain Growers' backed a resolution asking the Grain Growers' Grain Company to get into the business of supplying lumber to farmers. The preamble to the resolution said that "the prices now paid by farmers for different grades of lumber required for building purposes are exhorbitant."

160. S.G.G.A. Examines Coal: At their annual convention held in February at Weyburn, the Saskatchewan Grain Growers' passed a resolution asking the Provincial Government to build coal sheds "at crucial points". The sheds, it was proposed, were to be stocked in the summer months with coal to be sold "at cost in times of emergency."

161. United Farmers Of Alberta: In January, the Canadian Society of Equity met in Housten's Hall, Edmonton, while the Alberta Farmers' Association was meeting in the Mechanics' Hall of the same city.

At both meetings, the matter of amalgamation of the two organizations was considered and agreed upon. The new

1909

The same meeting also resolved to investigate an alleged combine operating in the coal business. A committee of three was appointed to carry out the investigation. In May, the committee discovered that the price at the mine for "mine-run" coal was $1.65 per ton while the price of screened coal was $2.15 per ton. Coal dealers would buy half of each kind, mix them together, and sell for $4.25 per ton. Freight from mine to dealer usually cost about $1.20 per ton. The mines would supply only members of the Coal Dealers' Association.

An amendment added to the resolution called on the Provincial Government to either purchase coal or operate the Estevan mines "in the interests of the people." The resolution further said: "We protest against the mine companies giving one man in town a monopoly on the trade therein as it lowers the amount in store and tends to create a coal famine."

organization then formed was named United Farmers of Alberta (UFA). Its total founding capital was $1.67 inherited from the A.F.A.

The new UFA was involved in the purchasing of farm supplies from its start. This is shown by the fact that in May, the Strathcona UFA local called a special meeting to consider tenders from local and other dealers for the supply of binder twine and formalin.

162. Government-Owned Elevators: In February, a petition bearing 10,000 names was presented to the Manitoba Government. The petition called upon the government to set up a line of elevators to be operated as a public utility under the administration of an independent commission. In December, the Government anounced it would agree to the proposal.

163. Elevator Commission: The Saskatchewan Government could not agree with the plan suggested by Partridge, which called for public ownership of all elevators.

Instead, the Government announced that it would appoint a Royal Commission to investigate the grain handling business within the Province.

164. UFA Studies Elevators: At the convention which gave birth to the United Farmers of Alberta, a resolution expressing favor for the "Partridge Plan" for publicly-owned elevators was given support.

165. Grain Growers' Grain Company: Both growing and expanding, the GGGC opened an office in Calgary to provide more intimate contact with Alberta farmers. In addition, the Company began to supply grain seeds.

166. Winnipeg Grain Exchange: Rules of the Grain Exchange required sellers to charge a commission of one cent per bushel on all grain sold through the Exchange. In addition, sellers were prohibited from rebating commissions to farmers. The Grain Growers' Grain Company had abided by these rules since returning to its seat on the Exchange in 1907. Commissions earned by the Company were used to finance its operations and extension of services.

In a sudden move, the Exchange suspended the ruling on commissions. Immediately, grain elevator companies began to sell through the Exchange for a commission of one-half-a-cent per bushel. Some charged no commission. The effect was to deprive the GGGC of its source of revenue. The Company was convinced that there was a plot to drive the GGGC out of business.

Quickly, the GGGC polled its farmer-shareholders for their view as to what commissions the Company should charge for handling their grain. About 98% of the shareholders agreed to a charge of one cent per bushel on wheat and flax, three-quarters of a cent on barley, and a half-cent on oats. These rates were followed by the GGGC until the Exchange restored the original commission rule. In the end, the incident worked to the advantage of the GGGC for it convinced many more farmers that they ought to patronize the co-operative.

1909

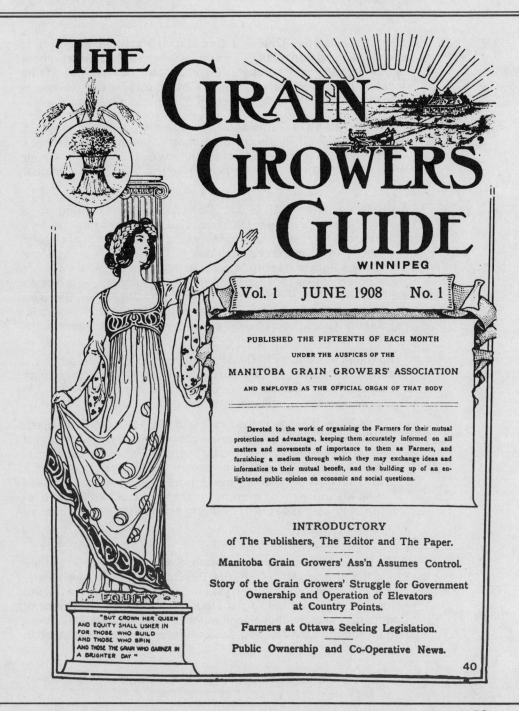

1909

167. Co-operative Union of Canada: At Hamilton, March 6, in premises of the Canadian Co-operative Concern, Limited, a number of representatives of co-operatives in Eastern Canada met. At this meeting the Co-operative Union of Canada was formed. Its objects were to assist in the development of the co-operative movement in Canada, conduct educational work, and to seek the enactment of favorable legislation for co-operatives. The CUC then attempted to obtain legislation for incorporation of co-operatives by the Dominion Government.

1910

168. Co-operative Legislation: In January, a bill that would provide legislation for the incorporation of co-operative societies was introduced to the House of Commons by Lloyd Harris, MP for Brantford, Ontario. This Bill was referred to a Standing Committee on Banking and Commerce for study. It is reported that the committee met on March 9, "and threw out the Bill in half an hour by a vote of 10 to 8."

169. Grain Growers' Guide Comments: Commenting in a January issue, the **Grain Growers' Guide** said: "At the present time there is no machinery available, and no legislation suitable to the needs of co-operative societies in Canada. The Joint Stock Companies Act provides for a division of profits on capital and not for a co-operative organization which provides only interest on capital and division of profits among consumers or between producers and consumers. It is generally agreed that provincial legislation would not be suitable and that Dominion legislation is what is needed. ...

"The Retail Merchants of Canada are opposed to this Bill and have shown their strength through their organization," the **Guide** continued. The **Canadian Grocer,** in dealing with the bill introduced by Mr. Harris, commented:

" ' This Bill will not be in the interest of the retail trade and especially will it be detrimental to the grocers should it go through. If the merchants were united all over the Dominion, such pressure could be brought to bear against the passing of such a Bill that it would scarcely ever be heard of. Nevertheless those who are united can do a great deal and also others who are interested can assist in preventing any legislation detrimental to their interests.

" ' A co-operative society working in every city or town will do much to separate the merchant and his customers even if it does not continue to become a success. Every association and every individual merchant should carefully watch this co-operative Bill and make it a point to interview or write the member representing his constituency in the House of Commons, to oppose it.' "

A further editorial in **The Guide** of February 9, said: "There are a great many interests combined to fight against the Bills now before the Ottawa Parliament providing for machinery for the operation of co-operative societies. The Retail Merchants' Association seems to be the leading spirit in this opposition and many of the statements that are being made are wide of the facts. Co-operation seems to be the best method of the present day by which the producer and consumer can get a fair deal. Co-operation provides no rake-offs for any private individual or corporation. ...The co-operative spirit is strong today in Western Canada and also in Eastern Canada. ...There is no reason why Canadian producers or consumers should not have the opportunity and privilege of conducting their own business if they desire to do so. ..."

170. Retail Merchants Incorporate: Soon after the defeat of the Co-op Bill proposed by Mr. Harris, Bill No. 210 was received in the House of Commons. This Bill had been given approval of the Senate before being presented to the House. 'Debates of the House of Commons' indicates that a good number of Members of Parliament had objection to Bill No. 210. One member, W.H. Sharpe MP, told the House:

" The parties who are asking for this incorporation are a very important class of people. I think they represent the largest amount of capital of any class in Canada. I understand they do not intend to go into business as an association, but if we allow this Bill to go through and give them incorporation, it will combine all the retail merchants throughout this country and they will be able to control prices, the number of stores, and everything of that kind in every town in Canada. They will also be able to control the wholesale people. Suppose there are five or six stores in a town and a man wants to start another store.

UNITED FARMERS & EQUITY ASSOCIATION OF ALBERTA

A. RAFN
DIR. SOC. EQUITY, BON ACCORD

R. C. OWENS
VICE-PRES. SOC. OF EQUITY

HARRY BELL
PRESIDENT SOCIETY OF EQUITY

H. JAMIESON
DIRECTOR FARMERS ASSN.

E. CARSWELL
DIR. FARMERS ASSOC'N.

G. H. THAMER
SEC. SOC. EQUITY

G. MacDONALD
DIR. FAR. ASSN.

W. R. BALL
DIRECTOR SOC. EQUITY

GEORGE LONG
DIRECTOR SOCIETY OF EQUITY

J. FLETCHER
PRES. ALTA. FARMERS ASS'N.

E. J. FREAM
SEC'Y FARMERS ASSN.

RICE SHEPPARD
VICE-PRES. FARMERS ASSN.

The Committee representing the Alberta Farmers Association and The Farmers Society of Equity responsible for the Amalgamation of the two associations now known as The United Farmers of Alberta.

September 1908 — January, 1909.

41

1910

These people will have such power that they will be able to go to the wholesale men and say: 'We do not want you to sell goods to this store; if you do, the retail dealers throughout the country will not buy goods from you. In that way they will be able to

control the retail business from one end of the country to the other. ..."

Despite opposition, Bill No. 210, granting incorporation to the Dominion Retail Merchants Association, was passed.

171. Boycott Co-ops: The remarks by Mr. W.H. Sharpe MP, when speaking in opposition to the Bill providing for incorporation of the Retail Merchants, proved to be remarkably prophetic. It was only a matter of weeks later that the Brockville (Ontario) Co-operative Society reported to the Co-operative Union of Canada that three wholesale houses had refused to supply the Society with goods. One of the wholesalers wrote to the Society as follows:

" Am sorry to say that according to the rule of the Wholesale Grocers' Guild, we are unable to supply you. Am sorry about this, because when speaking to you I was not aware of this fact, but all members of the Guild are unable to sell to any co-operative society."

172. Legislation Promised: During the summer of 1910, the Premier of Canada, Sir Wilfrid Laurier, made a tour of the Western Provinces. He met many delegations. Publications of the time report that the United Farmers of Alberta met Sir Wilfrid at Vegreville. The U.F.A. asked that government-owned terminal elevators be established at Fort William and Port Arthur (Thunder Bay), and at Vancouver. Legislation for co-operative societies was also requested. There was also a request for co-operative

legislation by delegations meeting Sir Wilfrid at Edmonton where, it is said, the retail merchants 'put in a counter petition on the subject of co-operation.'

A day or two later, Sir Wilfrid was at Red Deer where he replied to the farmers' petitions saying: "At the last session, a Bill was passed in favor of the merchants. I see no reason why a Bill should not be passed in favor of any other group which desires co-operation."

173. Co-op Bill Fails: In December, 1910, the House of Commons was again in session. Mr. Smith, MP for Nanaimo, introduced Bill No. 29 respecting co-operation. It was a copy of the Bill that had met its demise in the January session. Bill No. 29 was quickly turned

over to the Standing Committee on Banking and Legislation which immediately rejected it. Thus ended a series of three attempts to obtain Dominion legislation for co-operatives.

174. Manufacturers' Association: The Winnipeg Free Press of February 3, and **The Grain Growers' Guide** of February 9, each carried an account of a "brilliant" banquet held on February 2, at the Royal Alexandra Hotel, Winnipeg. Highlight of the evening was an address by G.M. Murray, the secretary of the Canadian Manufacturers' Association, who was quoted as saying:

" The re-organized Canadian Manufacturers' Association is like a young giant, ignorant of its own powers. By the exercise of these powers it could, if it chose, bring several millions of people to

starvation, or paralyze the industries of the whole Dominion. From the half-hearted 132 who comprised the whole membership of the Association in 1899 (the year of its organization), it has now grown with such strides that now, in 1910, its members number more than 2,500."

These remarks appear to have caused great concern to the **Guide**. It made a good many references to the remarks in the years to follow, including one as late as April 10, 1918.

175. Attacked Through The Press: A series of letters attacking the Grain Growers' Company and organized farmers generally, began appearing in newspapers and periodicals. These were

signed, "Observer", and conveyed numerous misrepresentations and falsehoods. After some sleuthing, the editor of the GRAIN GROWERS' GUIDE identified "Observer" as a newspaperman hired by

1910

the elevator association at $4,000 per year (a good salary at that time) to carry on a campaign of propaganda against the Grain Growers'. "Observer" was said to have had an up-to-date office in the Merchants' Bank Building, Winnipeg. As soon as he was exposed, the campaign came to an end. However, campaigns of a similar kind were waged against co-operatives in the years that followed.

176. The Canadian Council of Agriculture: At a meeting at Prince Albert, Saskatchewan, on February 11, 1970, the Interprovincial Council of Grain Growers' and Farmers' Organizations formed in 1907, was replaced by a new organization, The Canadian Council of Agriculture. The new CCA aimed to unite farm organizations from Alberta to Ontario. Ten months later, the Council called a convention attended by 500 farmers from the West and 300 from Eastern Canada. The convention drew up a set of resolutions for presentation to the Dominion Government. Chief demands included a reduction of tariffs, eventual free trade with Britain, and reciprocal trade with the U.S.A. in farm machinery and agricultural products. The Government gave the demands a sympathetic hearing but not immediate attention.

179. Credit Union: An organization which had characteristics of a credit union was formed in a settlement of Jewish Lithuanians. The settlement, known as the Edenbridge Colony, was in the Carrot River Valley area. The settlers borrowed $1,000 as capital, from the Jewish Colonization Association and used the fund for the making of loans to needy farmers. An interest rate of 8% was charged. The savings feature so essential to credit unions does not appear to have been promoted by the Colony; hence, even though this venture may have been called a credit union, it was, in reality, a loan society.

178. Elevator Study: The United Farmers of Alberta appointed an "Elevator Committee" to undertake a study of the 'Partridge Plan' and other means by which elevators might be provided outside of the control of the 'elevator interests'.

177. Elevator Plan: Early in the year, the Manitoba Government introduced its plan for a publicly-owned elevator system. It put responsibility for the purchase or erection of elevators on the Manitoba Department of Public Works, with administration of the system under a commission appointed by the Government. Terms of the Act required that 60% of the farmers of a given shipping point had to sign a petition of request to the Commission before an elevator was provided.

The Government's plan was different in several important respects, to the scheme proposed by the Manitoba Grain Growers. The MGGA had proposed that control be provided by a 3-man Commission nominated by MGGA and appointed by the Government. There was a condition in the MGGA proposals, that required a two-thirds vote of the Legislature for removal of a member of the Commission. The Government plan provided the cabinet with the power to both appoint and remove Commission members without consultation with the MGGA.

The Committee was appointed at the first annual convention of the UFA, held in January. Premier Rutherford of Alberta, who attended the convention, urged the UFA to work with other farm organizations of the Province to prepare a plan for providing elevators that could be given consideration by the Alberta legislature. He promised to carry out whatever plan was created provided it was practical.

The Convention endorsed 45 resolutions, including a demand for Dominion legislation for co-operatives.

180. Saskatchewan Purchasing Company: An organization that must be regarded as being a type of consumers' co-operative, was formed. It was known as The Saskatchewan Co-operative Purchasing Company, and incorporated under the Joint Stock Companies Act by the Province. There was no legislation at the time for incorporating co-operative societies other than creameries.

The organization's promoters openly declared it to be a co-operative and

There was also a resolution directed to the Alberta government, asking that one-third of the seats in the legislature be for farm representation. Other resolutions called for a system of low-cost farm loans, a consolidated school system, etc.

1910

1911

commonly substituted for its legal title, the name, "Saskatchewan Co-operative Association."

Head Office of the Purchasing Association was established at Broadview. Shares were $100 each, but no person could hold more than 100 shares. At first, each share was entitled to one vote and proxy voting was permitted. The organization's ambitious plans called for the handling of lumber, coal, dry goods and farm implements, and the manufacturing and selling of flour and feed.

183. First Manitoba Credit Union: At the French Catholic village of St. Jean Baptiste, Abbe Clovis St. Amant, Cure for the village, established a Caisse Populaire (credit union) to serve his parishioners. There was no legislation for the incorporation of credit unions or caisse populaires at that time, but, nevertheless, the organization continued to exist until 1918.

184. Consumer Co-op: At Arborg, a co-operative creamery, organized in 1907, began supplying goods on a co-operative basis to its members. This activity was to lead to the founding of the Arborg Farmers Co-operative Association in 1919.

181. Saskatchewan Co-operative Elevator Company: In March, the Provincial Legislature approved a plan by which the Government would assist in setting up a co-operative elevator system throughout the Province. The plan was very similar to the scheme advanced by the Saskatchewan Grain Growers'.

The Saskatchewan Co-operative Elevator Company was granted incorporation with the executive of the SGGA acting as a provisional Board of Directors, and a campaign to sign up farmer-members was begun.

Terms of the legislation provided that when farmers had raised 15% of the capital needed to erect a local elevator, the Government would loan the balance at 5% interest, repayable over a 20-year term.

185. Elevator Company Convention: In July, the Saskatchewan Co-operative Elevator Company held its founding convention.

Delegates were present from 46 locals, and of that number, 40 were already in the process of constructing elevators.

The SCEC's membership was open only to

182. Elevator Study: The Committee of the U.F.A. set up to study the matter of elevators took a keen interest in the plan that was approved by the Saskatchewan Legislature, but decided to await the result of the Saskatchewan venture before devising a plan of their own.

RALPH SMITH, M.P.,
MEMBER FOR VANCOUVER ISLAND.

42

1911

farmers. The organization was incorporated under the Joint Stock Companies Act, but there was provision for certain co-operative features such as one member, one vote.

It was agreed, at this convention, that the Grain Growers' Grain Company would act as selling agent for the elevator co-op in the Winnipeg Grain Exchange, at least for the first year.

1911

186. Saskatchewan Grain Growers': The Saskatchewan Grain Growers' Association had its offices at 34 Russell Block on First Avenue West, between River and High Streets, in Moose Jaw. The city was then a major railway centre.

187. Saskatchewan Purchasing Company: At its first annual convention, the Saskatchewan Purchasing company took steps to amend its bylaws so as to include more co-operative characteristics. Voting was limited to one vote per shareholder regardless of number of shares held; a system of 'purchase dividends' was provided; and a set rate of interest on capital stock was established.

In the spring, the Company opened a branch at Percival. This was the first of a number of other branches that were soon set up.

SASKATCHEWAN CO-OPERATIVE ELEVATOR Cº LIMITED LOCAL Nº 157

44

188. Grain Growers' Grain Company: In 1911, the Grain Growers' Grain Company, which had been incorporated by the Province of Manitoba in 1906, again sought a Dominion Charter. A Special Act of Parliament was required for there was no legislation for incorporation of co-operatives. In the initial draft of the Act, there was a provision empowering the Company's Board of Directors to allocate and distribute patronage refunds when profits exceeded 8% after reserves had been set aside. The proposal respecting patronage refunds was rejected by the Senate and was, therefore, deleted. The Charter was then granted, empowering the Company to undertake a wide range of activities from grain handling to coal mining, etc.

189. Grain Growers' Export Company: Soon after receiving a Dominion Charter, the Grain Growers' Grain Company set up a subsidiary known as Grain Growers' Export Company. The object of the subsidiary was to sell grain direct to millers or to foreign countries rather than through the Grain exchange. The GGGC had determined some time earlier that it could often get better prices for farmers by selling outside the Exchange.

190. Election of 1911: The campaign climaxed by the General Election of September 21, 1911, was a turbulent affair. The Liberals under Sir Wilfrid Laurier had, in 1910, passed a Bill to provide for creation of a Canadian Navy. French Canadians deplored this action on grounds that it could lead to their involvement in British wars. The main issue, however, was reciprocity—free trade with the United States—which the Liberals had long desired, but which initially had been rejected by the U.S. where it was suspected that reciprocity would mainly benefit Canada. President Taft of the U.S., confronted by a slump in trade, reversed the U.S. attitude toward reciprocity, going so far as to put a bill through Congress. The Liberals attempted to do likewise in

1911

Canada, but their bill was held up by opposition in the House of Commons where it remained when the election was called. Farmers of the West favored reciprocity, considering it to be an injustice that they should be required to buy farming needs at tariff-protected prices while forced to sell their produce at whatever price could be had in open competition for world markets. Reciprocity was one of the demands placed before the Laurier administration by the Canadian Council of Agriculture, and in the election campaign, Laurier promised that if returned to office, his government would accede to the Council's demands. However, the Canadian Manufacturers Association, the railways, grain traders of Eastern Canada, and other interests that benefitted from East-West trade within Canada, were opposed to reciprocity. One of their fears was that instead of flowing through Canadian channels grain from the West would be diverted to U.S. railways, terminals and trading concerns. To add to the furor of the campaign, some American politicians made utterances that were anything but discreet. The Speaker of the U.S. House of Representatives, Champ Clark, for example, believing that reciprocity would end Canada's ties with Britain and result in annexation of Canada, declared: "I hope to see the day when the American flag will float over every square foot of the British North American possessions clear to the North Pole...the day is not far distant when Great Britain will joyfully see all her North American possessions become part of this republic." On another occasion Clark predicted, "We are going to annex Canada."

PROVINCE	CONS.	LIB.	INDEP.	TOTAL
Ontario	72	13	1	86
Quebec	27	37	1	65
Nova Scotia	9	9		18
New Brunswick	5	8		13
P.E.I.	2	2		4
Manitoba	8	2		10
Saskatchewan	1	9		10
Alberta	1	6		7
B.C.	7			7
Yukon	1			1
	133	86	2	221

45

1912

191. Elevator Problems: Both farmers and government agreed that the 1910 plan for government-owned elevators was a failure. In all, the government had acquired 174 elevators at 100 shipping points. Some were old or poorly built and bought at inflated prices.

More important, farmers were not patronizing the government elevators, but preferred to load their grain onto boxcars at the loading platforms. There was no advantage to the farmers in using the government's facilities because these elevators did not buy grain from the farmer but provided only an assembly and forwarding service. The net result was an operating loss of $84,145 in the first year.

To get rid of an embarrassing problem, the government offered to lease its elevators to the Grain Growers' Grain Company. The offer was accepted.

195. Bowsman Farmers' Co. Ltd.: In the farming community of Bowsman, an organization called Bowsman Farmers' Co. Ltd. was incorporated under the Joint Stock Companies Act. It operated a co-operative store, open to all, saying: "Its object is the reduction of prices of all kinds of merchandise and the securing of the highest possible price for product. Any farmer can join for $5, and each farmer will have only one vote."

After operating for 12 months during which expenses of incorporation and organization were paid. The Bowsman Farmers' Co. Ltd. realized a surplus of $275. This surplus was divided as follows: 40% as interest on shares; 40% as a rebate on all cash purchases (including those paid for within 30 days); and 20% to a reserve fund. Plans called for branch

192. Saskatchewan Purchasing Company: Membership of the Saskatchewan Purchasing Company had now grown to nearly 500. New branches were set up at Red Jacket, Whitewood, Dubuc, St. Hubert, Qu'Appelle, Moose Jaw, and Kipling.

Assets of the Company at the close of 1912, were stated as being $98,892, with $23,000 paid up in shares. The organization, having operating losses, was not in a sound financial condition.

193. U.F.A. Women: At the 4th annual meeting of United Farmers of Alberta, it was proposed that clubs for women be formed as a means of bringing the women into the U.F.A. organization. This was to be the start of an effort by the organization to obtain for women the right to vote in the election of governments.

194. Eckville & Gilby Co-operative Incorporation was granted to an organization, The Eckville and Gilby Co-operative, which proposed to 'sell general merchandise and give rebates on purchases in proportion to purchases made.' It was also proposed to offer memberships, and to provide patronage rebates to non-members at half the rate provided to members.

It was the aim of the organization to carry on "the business of general merchants, importers and exporters of meats and live stock; dealers in cattle, sheep, pigs and poultry; erect and build stores, freezing houses, warehouses, sheds, and other buildings; carry on manufacturing enterprises and generally do anything which may be of material assistance."

1912

stores to be set up in other towns of the
Swan River Valley.

196. Grain Growers' Grain Company: The Grain Growers' Grain
Company established an elevator department to operate the
elevators the Company had leased from the Manitoba Government.
In this year, the GGGC was also busy with other ventures:

* At Fort William, a terminal elevator owned by the CPR was
leased by GGGC on October 4.

* At Rapid City, Manitoba, the Company obtained a flour mill with
a capacity of 150 barrels per day, to manufacture flour and feed.
The products were sold to locals of the Grain Growers'
Associations, all sales being for cash. As a direct result,
competitive prices for flour dropped by as much as 80 cents per
sack. Some mills cut prices below their cost in an effort to
discourage patronage of the GGGC mill. The Rapid City mill was
a success. But soon it simply could not meet all demands. The
Grain Growers' packed flour under their own brand, the first
private label goods to be sold by Prairie co-ops.

* GGGC acquired a timber berth. It was estimated to hold about
232-million feet of lumber, but the Company did not
immediately obtain a sawmill in order to make use of its timber.

* GGGC was under increasing pressure to enter into wholesaling
of farm supplies and other commodities. One writer in **The
Grain Growers' Guide**, urged the Company to "organize a
Rochdale system of co-operation with a wholesale department

at Winnipeg, and local retail branches." The Rochdale system,
however, required that interest on capital be limited, and that
surpluses remaining after operating costs were paid, be turned
back to members as patronage refunds on their purchases.
These features were in conflict with the Joint Stock Companies
Act under which GGGC had been forced to incorporate due to
lack of legislation providing for incorporation of co-operatives
(Co-operative legislation enacted by Manitoba in 1887 was
inoperative).

By this time, many semi-co-operative organizations had been
organized in communities across the Prairies. Like the GGGC,
those that were incorporated were chartered under the Joint Stock
Companies Act. Many of them did, however, adopt and practise
features of Rochdale-type co-operatives. In addition, a considerable
amount of informal co-operation was prevalent among farmers
who clubbed together to buy commodities in bulk lots. In its first
annual report, published in 1914, the Co-operative Organizations
Branch of the Saskatchewan Department of Agriculture explained:

" There are in the Province a considerable number of so-called co-
operative stores, farmers' elevator companies, and
organizations of a kindred nature, but as these are all registered
under the Companies Act, and in almost every case conduct
their business on capitalistic lines, they cannot be considered as
co-operative institutions."

197. Winnipeg Retail Co-operative: The formation, in 1912, of a
retail co-operative in Winnipeg, aroused interest of **The Grain
Growers' Guide** which reported in its November, 1913, issue:

" In the summer of 1912 a movement was set on foot to organize a
Co-operative Society in Winnipeg, and after a good deal of
spadework by a number of the moving spirits who were
thoroughly imbued with the principles of co-operation, they
succeeded in raising capital sufficient to open their first store, at
350 Cumberland Avenue, for the sale of groceries and
provisions, in June of the present year, with a membership of
over 400 drawn from all parts of the City.

This being the first society that has been formed in the City on a
thoroughly co-operative basis, a keen interest is being taken in

the new venture, and high hopes are held as to its success.
Since the opening in June, sales have continued to increase
month after month, the latest accounts going to show an
increase in trade of forty percent for the month of October over
the previous month, while the share capital paid up has
increased from $2,000 to $5,500, and the shareholders number
540.

" A small pamphlet issued a few weeks ago sets forth the
particulars as to how to become a member of the Society. The
modest sum of $3 constitutes one share, which may be
deposited with an application for membership, or a member may
make a deposit of $1 and pay up the balance at the rate of 50¢
per month. Each shareholder can purchase fifty shares, this
being the maximum holding that any one shareholder may

1912

deposit according to the Co-operative Societies Act of Manitoba under which this society is registered and holds it Charter. (NB—This appears to be the legislation of 1887 which was 'discovered' after being inoperative during the intervening decades.)

" The trading operations are carried on, on a strictly cash basis, absolutely no credit being allowed, according to its bylaws. Supplies are drawn from local wholesale houses and every advantage is taken in procuring the best terms by arranging prompt settlements.

" With the object of following up more closely the true co-operative ideal, the Society is getting in touch with the Co-operative Wholesale Society, Manchester, England, and in the course of a few weeks delivery is expected of the first order of various productions manufactured by that gigantic concern which had a turnover of seventy-five million dollars. By this means the Society will be dealing direct with the producers and thus the middleman's profit will be saved to the Society.

" The system of retailing is similar to that adopted in the Old Country, the merchandise being retailed in any quantity at the lowest market prices and, after meeting operating expenses, including depreciation on equipment, and paying interest at six percent per annum on paid-up capital, the surplus will be divided amongst the shareholders in the form of dividends on their purchases, at the end of each balancing period, in January and July, when an inventory of the stock is taken and the accounts audited by a chartered accountant.

" The management of the society is vested in a board of directors consisting of seven members who are elected by the shareholders at the half-yearly business meeting, all of whom give their services to the Society gratis, and a manager with Old Country co-operative experience is responsible for the general organization and supervises the buying in the Society's interests. The Society is now in a position to undertake a mail order business and in the future will no doubt develop a large business with farmers throughout the West."

(**NB:** Subsequent activities of the Winnipeg Co-operative Society are somewhat vague. It was noted, however, that the Society advertised in the May, 1914 issue of the **Grain Growers' Guide** inviting locals of the Grain Growers' to place orders for "groceries at rock bottom prices!"

1912

CHAPTER VII

CO-OPERATIVES ESTABLISHED 1913 TO 1926

198. By one lone vote, a bill that would have provided for incorporation of co-operative societies was defeated by the Senate in 1908, while two further bills for co-operatives were rejected in 1910, all by legislative bodies mainly composed of members elected in Eastern Canada.

Obviously, commercial interests were not prepared to submit themselves to competition by another type of enterprise, particularly one which could, if permitted to develop, establish standards of ethics and prices that may be so appealing to farm producers and to consumers as to interfere with their assumed role in profits and control of trade.

199. In the United Kingdom, by 1907, the Co-operative Movement begun in 1844 had become an important factor. There were, by 1907, 1,441 co-operative retailing societies serving a total of 2,222,000 members. These societies were, in turn, served by two co-operative wholesales which they owned and controlled—the Co-operative Wholesale Society of Manchester, and the Scottish Wholesale Society. The latter, in 1906, had assisted the Grain Growers' Grain Company to overcome a difficult situation arising from its expulsion from the Winnipeg Grain Exchange.

As well as providing wholesaling service to Britain's co-operative stores, the two wholesales had expanded into the manufacture of many goods, including biscuits and other confections, boots and shoes, textiles and clothing, and furniture. In addition, the co-operative wholesales owned tea plantations abroad, and in 1876 had begun to acquire a fleet of ships. In other directions, the English wholesale had set up a banking department in 1872, and a Co-operative Insurance Company, through which local societies could provide insurance for members and their families, had been established.

Interestingly enough, the most important legislation concerning co-operative societies was provided in 1862 and earlier, a time when Britain's House of Commons was controlled by a small electorate of about 7% of the adult population, and consisting of aristocrats, landed gentry, and the upper business class.

As will be seen, legislation for co-operative societies was enacted by all three Prairie Provinces in 1913, and was undoubtedly done as a result of the report of a Royal Commission which examined agricultural problems in Saskatchewan. The legislation was passed against strong opposition from shopkeeping interests who, in Canada, adopted the more prestigious name of 'retail merchants'. This was not, however, to be the only occasion in which legislatures of the Prairie Provinces served the interests of Prairie people by helping them overcome needs that were ignored at Ottawa.

Excepting co-operative creameries, there was, before 1913, no means of incorporating co-operative societies of the true Rochdale type. Incorporation under the Companies Act was not satisfactory, for the Act was designed for profit business, not for co-operatives. But with legislation provided, a period of co-operative development of local co-operative stores, and in the early 1920's, of the wheat pools, began.

1913

200. Co-operative Buying: The Manitoba Grain Growers' Association, at a conference held at Brandon in January, discussed co-operative buying and selling. The president of the Grain Growers' Grain Company, T.A. Crerar, opened discussion by describing the success of co-operatives in Britain, Denmark, Germany, Ireland, and other countries. He told the meeting that "the need for co-operation in this country is very great," and that members of the Grain Growers' Associations were "making considerable savings" by purchasing goods by the carload through

201. Saskatchewan Purchasing Company was in financial difficulty but proceeded with a plan to set up a wholesale to serve its retail outlets. However, the Company could not overcome its problems which were variously blamed on management, the directors, and on efforts of private business and the banks to discourage co-operative selling. The manager, J.M. Hill, in a letter to an MLA, spoke of "interests" attempting to crush Saskatchewan's first large co-operative. Hill also quoted from a circular of the Co-operative Union of

202. Co-operative Elevators: The Alberta government agreed to assist in financing a co-operative elevator system by lending 85% of the cost of an elevator. The Alberta Farmers Co-operative Elevator Company was then formed, and was assisted by loans from the Grain Growers' Grain Company which also agreed to act as selling agent for the elevator co-op on the Grain Exchange. Alberta's largest lumber company refused to supply the elevator co-op with lumber needed for the building of elevators so supplies had to be obtained from smaller

1913

locals of their organizations."

The conference adopted a resolution calling for the MGGA to form county or district associations "for the purpose of co-operating in the purchasing of large orders to be done preferably through the Grain Growers' Grain Company. A further resolution asked that GGGC negotiate with the dealers of gasoline and coal oil with a view to providing these commodities to members "at a reduced rate on a cash basis."

Canada, dated May 10, 1913, which said:

"At the recent convention of the Retail Merchants' Association it was, I understand, decided to use the united influence of its members to prevent wholesale houses supplying co-operative societies with merchandise..."

companies and from sources in Montana and Idaho.

203. Grain Growers' Grain Company opened an office in Calgary, and from this location it undertook to handle farm supplies.

204. Alberta Farmers' Co-operative Elevator Company set up a farm supplies department. The elevator agents handled the goods locally while orders for supplies were arranged by UFA locals.

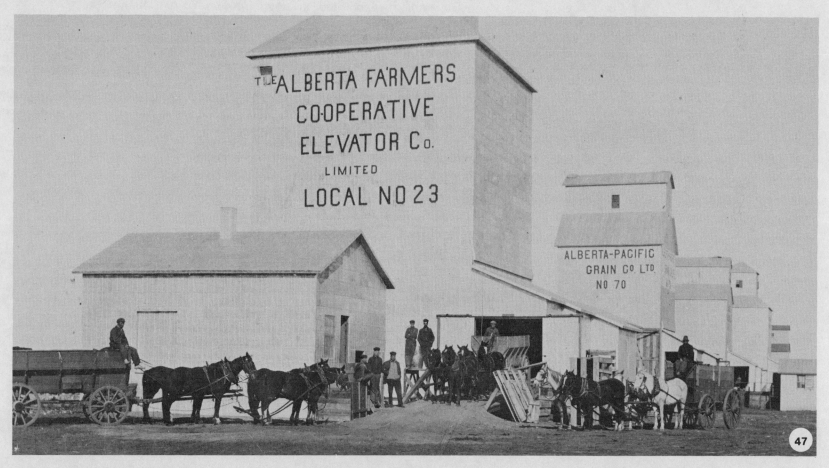

1913

205. The Grain Growers' Grain Company refunded to members, $62,819 of savings arising from 1912 operations. The refunds were paid to members by Dominion Express money orders. A week or two later, the Company received a stern letter from a farmer who objected to the use of the Dominion Express money orders saying that company "is one of the enemies the farmer must fight." The incident, though not of historical importance in itself, illustrates the zeal with which farmers stood by their cause.

Also in 1913, the Grain Growers' Grain Company:

* Purchased a terminal elevator at Fort William (now Thunder Bay), and a small terminal at New Westminster, B.C.

* Formed a Farm Supplies Department to handle apples, coal, lumber, fence posts, barbed wire, binder twine, and a few other commodities. The Department was quickly frustrated in attempts to purchase twine when it was found that not a single supplier in Canada would sell to it. It was then necessary to import twine from Ireland.

207. Co-operative Legislation: The Manitoba Government, responding to demands of the Manitoba Grain Growers, enacted legislation providing for incorporation of co-operative societies. The new legislation was essentially the same as that which had been enacted in 1887, but with some revisions.

J.H. Haslam

206. Royal Commission: In effort to resolve some of the major problems confronting farmers, the Saskatchewan Government appointed an Agricultural Credit Commission. This Royal Commission was to seek ways to improve the position of Saskatchewan grain on European markets and to study ways and means for establishing agricultural credit.

The chairman, J.H. Haslam, Regina, was interviewed by the press on his return from Europe. He was quoted as saying that "the farmer gets a raw deal, and suffers under the greatest handicap in the world in the matter of borrowing money. He is obliged to pay anywhere from 8 to 50 percent on advances...and becomes the victim of a money system which makes a number extremely wealthy while he is restrained in all his farming operations and Canadian agriculture is severely crippled." Haslam said farmers in the West pay $200 for binders costing $54.11 to make, and that most implements were bought on credit.

208. Co-operative Legislation: The Report of the Agricultural Credit Commission was tabled in the legislature. Among its recommendations was one that urged provision of an Act that would enable the formation and incorporation of co-operative enterprises among farmers. This recommendation was acted upon by

209. Co-operative Legislation: The Alberta Legislature, on March 26, 1913, enacted that Province's first Co-operative Associations Act.

The Farmers' Co-operative Association of Huxley, on July 5, 1913, was the first association to incorporate under the new legislation. This organization was short-lived however, because wholesales refused to fill its orders for goods. In 1913, eight other associations were incorporated, but all have since disappeared from the scene.

1913

the passing, in 1913, of the Agricultural Co-operative Associations Act. Terms of the Act enabled co-operatives to incorporate without the restrictions of the Joint Stock Companies Act, for activities such as marketing, production, and purchasing on a co-operative basis. The Act did not provide for incorporation of credit unions. Further, it applied only to farmers who were members of the Saskatchewan Grain Growers' Association.

210. Retail Merchants: There had already been evidence of a boycott against co-operatives. In a number of instances, wholesalers refused to serve co-operative societies. As a result, a number of early associations were either impaired or destroyed. There had also been opposition to the proposed federal legislation for co-operatives. As the following will indicate, a main source of the boycott and opposition to legislation was the Retail Merchants Association. The Dominion secretary of that organization, E.M. Trowern of Toronto, toured the West in 1913 at about the time the legislatures of the Prairie Provinces were considering adoption of legislation for co-operatives. While evidently attempting to form more chapters of the Retail Merchants Association, Trowern was also outspoken in opposition to co-operatives. On the evening of July 13, 1913, he addressed a gathering of retailers at Saskatoon. Two newspaper accounts of his address have been discovered:

Regina Leader of July 14, 1913. The same account also appeared in a Winnipeg daily newspaper of about the same date and was quoted by **The Grain Growers' Guide:**

" Saskatoon, Saskatchewan, July 13-E.M. Trowern, secretary of the Dominion Retail Merchants' A'ssn., at a meeting of the local association held here last night, made a strong attack on co-operative trading societies saying 'they are the greatest frauds that ever struck the community. The Grain Growers' know no more about running a co-operative business than a cat knows about its grandmother. I make this statement publicly and wish the press to make special mention of it.

" We have gone to the government from time to time opposing co-operative societies. I have never seen an honest co-operative store yet, and there has not been one found in Europe. They are a fraud from top to bottom. We have asked every wholesaler by

letter what he thinks of co-operative societies and if he sells to them we will cease doing business with him.

" Mr. Trowern opposed strongly city markets saying that it was an unfair competition to the merchants. He also intimated, during a discussion on the principle of selling for cash only, that the Eaton Company, although it was not generally known, did a certain amount of credit business."

The Saskatoon Daily Star of July 14, 1913, carried a very lengthy report on page 1, from which the following is excerpted:

" He (E.M. Trowern) condemned the trading stamp craze. He hotly denounced co-operative societies. 'The greatest fraud that ever struck a community are co-operative societies. I make this statement publicly and I want the press to make note of it. There is no use in being afraid of these people. If you see a head you don't like, don't be afraid to hit it.

" ' With these co-operative societies we have a great work ahead of us. We have been four times to Ottawa opposing them. In connection with their methods, they have dividends which are nothing but bribes. They are frauds from top to bottom. That's all there is to them. They are either robbers or liars. In Toronto they enlisted the favor of the church and threw the glamour of philanthropy over their operations.

" ' Fear is the mother of all crime. Be right and you'll win,' was the forcible advice thrown out by Mr. Trowern at this point. 'The object of this association is to eliminate fraud from trade...!'"

1913

211. Retail Merchants: As well as Saskatoon, E.M. Trowern, Secretary of the Dominion Retail Merchants' Association, visited a number of other centres in the West. Included were Regina, Moose Jaw, Swift Current, and other points in Alberta and British Columbia. In the wake of his visit, there was retailer-inspired controversy over other matters besides co-operatives:

(a) As Trowern's address indicates, retailers opposed City Markets which were then becoming fairly common. These were establishments providing rows of stalls which farmers could rent as a place to sell eggs, poultry, butter, cream, garden produce, and other commodities direct to the public. In doing so, farmers bypassed both wholesalers and retailers, and the public received the advantage of lower prices. **The Regina Leader,** May 5, 1913, told about a market that had been newly opened at Brandon:

" The Public Market fully justified itself as the best factor against the high cost of living when on Saturday it was the means of transferring many tons of garden and dairy produce from producer to consumer without the costly intervention of the middlemen.

" Dairy butter in stores sold for around forty cents but in the market changed hands at twenty-five cents; eggs sold for nineteen cents a dozen, potatoes for thirty cents a bushel, and other produce at like substantial reductions."

(NB - On that same day, a Regina firm was advertising potatoes at 75 cents a bushel, eggs at 25 cents a dozen or 3 dozen for 70 cents, and butter at 35 cents a pound.)

(b) Retailers were also aroused by the appearance of the mail order houses such as T.Eaton Co. Said an editorial in **The Calgary Herald** of September 9, 1913:

" The retail merchants of this city have thought it necessary to urge upon the public the fairness and even necessity of doing their shopping at home. One chief reason for this campaign is that the Eaton Company, a large Eastern organization, has commenced a raid on Calgary by circular letters, catalogues, and personal canvass.

" There is no profit to a single Calgary citizen in shopping with Eastern houses by mail or otherwise. We are all here together in this fair province and still fairer city. Each one of us is doing his share to build it up. ...It is not square that an outside mail order house should be allowed to come in here and take from our citizens the dollars that should, and otherwise would, go to our own stores ... The newspapers of Calgary have been consistently loyal to the city in refusing to insert in their daily issues the advertisements of these mail order houses."

212. Retail Merchants: Although strongly opposed to co-operation practised by farmers or by consumers, the Retail Merchants saw merit in co-operation to benefit themselves. This is evident from the following excerpt from the **Regina Leader** of May 6, 1913:

" Mr. J. Evans, secretary of the Retail Merchants' Association at Prince Albert, spoke in favor of co-operative buying of staple articles by merchants. This resulted, he said, in greater profits or greater discounts, which are the same thing, and less delay in shipment. In England this system was followed largely. A secretary was appointed, whose duty it was to get the best prices on articles, and the best discounts, as well as the best terms of credit.

" Mr. Paynter, of Tantallon, said that the last speaker had struck the right chord when he advocated co-operative buying. He told of an incident which illustrated this. They had been paying $4.10 per single box to the wholesalers for Sunlight soap. A woman submitted to him a list of goods which she wanted prices on, and as he was buying Sunlight soap by the single box he could not give her as low a price as if he had been buying it in quantities. She protested, saying she could get it from Eaton's for $3.85 a box. He investigated and found that she was right.

" He, therefore, went to a number of neighboring merchants and they clubbed together and got a price from a Sunlight Soap agent of $3.70 a box, by the carload, delivered in any part of Saskatchewan. The wholesalers, hearing of it, raised a kick, and the Sunlight Soap Company tried to cancel the order. The merchants threatened legal action with the result that the carload was delivered.

" The result was that we were able to make a better price to customers and at the same time a better profit. We treated every one of our club members alike, whether he took one box or two, whereas the wholesalers were charging us more on small orders than on large. We started doing this in other things and had a fine organization when the secretary went into the real estate business and the organization broke up. (laughter)"

The meeting on which the above news item reports, was a convention of over 400 retailers held at Regina. At this meeting, the retailers decided to form a provincial organization, the Retail Merchants Association (Saskatchewan Section). Some local chapters of the RMA already existed in the Province.

1913

213. Co-operative Wholesaling: Throughout 1913, **The Grain Growers' Guide** editorials urged that action be taken to form co-operative wholesale societies:

March 19: "In the struggle for economic freedom the prairie farmers can take no better step that to organize into co-operative groups for the purchase of their supplies and the sale of their produce. Such action will not only ease the economic burden but it will bring men into a better understanding with their neighbors and create a bond of mutual sympathy that will develop the very highest type of citizenship. When met together in such a way they are able to work side by side for the general uplift. From the material aspect no other plan will prove so effective in bringing farmers into the organization. We are now half a century behind Europe in co-operation. Let us be up and doing!"

April 16: "The farmers of the West are crowding the Company into co-operative buying and selling. The only impediment is the lack of capital. All are agreed that the saving will be immense. Provide the capital and the question is solved. Buy stock in, and ship your grain to:

THE GRAIN GROWERS' GRAIN CO. LTD.,
Winnipeg, Man. — Calgary, Alberta."

Sept. 10: "The establishment of a co-operative wholesale society for the purpose of supplying the co-operative stores which are springing up in various parts of Western Canada is an enterprise which will undoubtedly be given practical consideration in the near future.

"If E.M. Trowern, secretary of the Dominion Retailers' Association is successful in his attempt to induce the existing wholesale agencies to refuse to supply co-operators, a co-operative wholesale will become an absolute necessity, but in any event the establishment of such a society, as soon as there are sufficient retail stores to warrant it, would be the best kind of business proposition.

"Through the establishment of a wholesale of their own, Western co-operators will be able to retain for themselves the profits now made by the private wholesalers; they will be independent of any organization of private traders which may at any minute refuse to supply them on any terms; they will have a medium through which the country co-operators will be able to dispose of their surplus dairy and farm products in the cities; and they will have an organization of their own which will be able to import and manufacture the necessities of life especially for their own consumption. In addition, they will have an organization which will bind together the co-operators throughout the West, make their system of business uniform, and promote the interests of the co-operative movement generally."

214. Petroleum: A Manitoba farmer wrote to the **Grain Growers' Guide** on prices of petroleum products. He said he recently bought a barrel of coal oil (kerosene) at Hanna, N.D. On this, he paid duty of 2½ cents per gallon which brought his total cost to 16⅞ per imperial gallon. At Pilot Mound, Manitoba, coal oil was selling for 20 cents a gallon. Gasoline, he said, cost 23 cents from the U.S. but sold at home for 30 cents.

216. Women: The SGGA established a women's section within its structure to encourage women to become more active in the organization's programs. In addition, the organization began to campaign for the right of women to vote in the election of governments.

215. Co-operation: Thos. Balaam, secretary of the Vegreville local of the UFA, wrote to the **Grain Growers Guide** on the progress of that local. He said: "By co-operation the farmers feel they have a chance to scuttle the treasure ships of the buccaneers who have waxed fat in times past, off the farmers!"

217. Women: At a January, 1913, meeting at Calgary, the United Farmers of Alberta unanimously approved a resolution providing for women to be granted equal rights to men in U.F.A. membership.

1913

218. Hudson Bay Railway: The Conservative Government headed by Sir Robert Borden began construction of the long-demanded and often-promised railway to Hudson Bay. The project would, however, be halted with the outbreak of World War I.

219. Retail Lumbermen: At Edmonton, July 14, a Retail Lumbermen's Association was formed by lumber dealers to co-ordinate effort in their interests. It was patterned after U.S. organizations and has, on several occasions, expressed opposition to co-operatives.

1914

220. GGGC Begins Co-operative Wholesaling: The refusal of wholesalers to supply co-operative farmers caused mounting pressures on the farm organizations to begin the physical handling of goods. Previous efforts by these organizations were confined, in the main, to receiving orders from locals and pooling them to buy in large quantity. The Grain Growers' Grain Company responded to the farm demands, setting up large supply warehouses at Winnipeg, Regina and Calgary. Flour sheds were built by GGGC at points where flour prices seemed to be unreasonably high. In addition, GGGC elevator agents arranged for carlot shipments of coal, saving members $2 to $3 per ton.

As a further step in the provision of farm supplies, the GGGC decided to handle farm implements. It was hoped that supplies could be obtained from Canadian manufacturers. However, those manufacturers refused to supply GGGC, claiming that they had already set up ample systems for sales and services. The GGGC was then forced to turn to U.S. sources for cultivating implements, seed drills, and other implements. This arrangement was satisfactory but short-lived, for on July 1, 1916, new customs regulations were imposed and severely curtailed the import of farm equipment.

223. Consumer Co-ops: With the enactment of new legislation for co-operatives there was a great deal of activity for organizing co-op stores and other societies.

At Moline, a consumer co-operative was organized at a meeting called by the Moline Branch of MGGA. The Moline Co-operative Limited continued to operate until 1958 when the association amalgamated with the Hamiota Co-operative. After amalgamation, the Hamiota Co-op operated the Moline facilities as a branch.

At Mulvihill events that showed the zeal for consumer co-operatives took place. Local members of the MGGA, determined to build a co-op store, but short of funds, volunteered their labor to cut trees and saw them into lumber. The lumber was hauled to a site where the volunteers erected a two-storey building. The plan was to use the lower storey for a co-op store, and the second as a community hall for meetings, dances and social events. To raise money to finish the building and start their store, members held regular dances in the not-yet-completed premises. The Ladies' Auxiliary of the MGGA local assisted by serving lunch at the dances and by conducting raffles, with all the proceeds going to the building fund.

221. SGGA Farm Supply: The annual convention of Saskatchewan Grain Growers' Association adopted a resolution instructing the organization "to make immediate arrangements to act as purchasing agents for any locals of the Association." SGGA responded by setting a Farm Supplies Department with offices at 502 Walter Scott Building, Moose Jaw, and providing $8,000 as working capital. Goods were not stocked, but as orders were received from SGGA locals they were placed with mines, mills or manufacturers. The department sold to organized SGGA locals only, and in turn, the locals served only their own members. In the first season, the Farm Supply Department handled orders for flour, apples, cordwood, building supplies, groceries, and 25,000 tons of coal.

224. Consumer Co-op: The success of efforts to reduce costs by co-operative action were explained by the secretary of the Lampman Grain Growers', G.E. Niggle, to that organization's annual meeting. He said the auditor's report showed receipts of $677.82 and expenditures of $677.82, and that the handlings of the association had grown yearly from $82 in 1909. He reported:

" No. 1 flour has been reduced by the

222. Alberta Co-op Elevator Farm Supply Department was frustrated in attempts to handle flour. A railway superintendent advised that only elevator companies owned and operated by flour mills were permitted to carry stocks of flour at elevators located on railway property. The obstacle was eventually cleared aside, but illustrates the extent by which efforts to stop co-operative trading were conducted.

225. UFA Supply Services: The UFA was able to report that it had recently received a number of offers from business which were now anxious to supply the organization with such commodities as paints, building materials, etc. Like other organizations handling commodities on a co-operative basis, UFA had been refused supplies by wholesalers. But once supplies were obtained from other sources, wholesalers who had previously refused to provide services reversed their stand.

1914

Unfortunately, it was not possible to locate information as to the eventual success of the Mulvihill project.

merchants from $3.35 to $2.90 a sack, while the Association put out a car at $2.60 per sack. No. 1 apples sold for $4.80 and $5.00 per barrel, but would have cost us $6.50 or $7.00 had we not made arrangements to get a carload in."

226. Grain Growers' Grain Company and Lumber: Although many suppliers refused to sell to co-operating farmers and their organizations, there were others anxious to obtain orders from farmers. In the issue of March 4, the **Grain Growers' Guide** editorials complained about a company which appears to have resorted to deceptive tactics to get farmers' orders. Said the editorial:

" We have noticed in several journals that circulate among

Western farmers, an advertisement signed by the 'Grain Growers' Lumber Company, Vancouver, B.C.' We wish to state that this company has no connection whatever with the Grain Growers' Grain Company. Neither, so far as we are aware, is the company morally entitled to use the term 'Grain Growers' in its name. The term, 'Grain Growers', has become a valuable business asset in Western Canada and entirely because of the great struggle and great success of the Grain Growers' organizations..."

227. Lumber Offered To Farmers: In this era there was a great demand for lumber, for the West was growing. On farms, new homes and barns were being built. In both rural and urban centres, homes, business establishments, and buildings of every kind were being constructed. In the forest areas, many small lumber companies were engaged in a lucrative business. some of them gave special attention to opportunities to serve farmers as the following advertisement appearing in the May 13 issue of the **Grain Growers' Guide** will show:

CHEAP LUMBER FOR FARMERS

The Co-operative Lumber Co.
901 Hornby Street   Vancouver, B.C.

We are now selling carloads of coast lumber to farmers direct from the mill, co-operatively, in mixed cars of dimension, shiplap and boards, finished lumber, doors and windows, shingle, lath, mouldings, etc. We can save you $150 per car and upwards. All lumber guaranteed first quality. Shiplap, all widths $21 per 1000 square feet, delivered to your station. All other lumber equally as cheap. Write for price list. Agents Wanted.

228. Vanguard Co-op: The manager of the Vanguard Co-operative Supply Company, L.J. Walter, in a letter published in the October 21 issue of the **Grain Growers' Guide,** wrote as follows:

" More than one year ago the Vanguard Co-operative Supply Company decided to go into the lumber business, notwithstanding the fact that six old line companies were doing business in our town of perhaps three hundred inhabitants.

" For a number of months these

1914

companies ignored us saying we would soon go out of business. They tried in every possible way to find out where we were getting our lumber, but the jobbing firm with which we did business billed in such a way that no one could tell where it was shipped from. Failing to cut us off from the base of our supply, they decided it would be necessary to freeze us out. The general superintendents of these companies met frequently in Vanguard, in fact far more frequently than our own Board or Directors met. After a while they commenced cutting prices.

"A very clear idea of the way they combined to fix prices may be gained by taking fence posts as an illustration. A year ago the superintendents met to fix prices of fence posts at 18 cents and finally decided upon 17 cents. Now, since they have decided to freeze us out, they are selling at 11 cents. Their cut on lumber prices is, however, still more marked. Their price on dimension stuff, 12, 14, and 16 feet in length, was $32 per M cash, or $34 on time. Now such lumber can be bought from them for $18 per M cash and common lumber for $15 per M, cash.

"As we all know, the methods being used now at Vanguard are exactly the same as the methods used by the Standard Oil Company of the U.S. to freeze out small competitors. They can well afford to sell at Vanguard, Kincaid, Morse, and a few other places where farmers have endeavoured to gain relief from exhorbitant prices by engaging in the lumber business themselves, because, as I understand, they still sell at their old prices in other places.

"If we were in the U.S. we would be protected. These companies would be taken for combining in the restraint of

1914

trade and punishment administered that would put a stop to such practices. I understand that in North Dakota a law has been passed making it unlawful for a line company to charge more at one point than at another, except when warranted by differences in freight rates. If we had such a law in Saskatchewan we would be protected and the farmers of this great province would be assured of being able to purchase lumber at reasonable prices. When will our government furnish us relief?"

229. Legislation: Although the legislatures of Manitoba, Saskatchewan and Alberta had each provided, in 1913, legislation to enable incorporation of co-operatives, **The Grain Growers' Guide** continued to press for federal legislation. Said the **Guide:**

" The government of Canada has provided legislative machinery for organizations of every kind, and it is only reasonable that a good co-operative Bill should be enacted."

230. Co-op Organizations Branch: As provided by the Agricultural Co-operative Association Act of 1913, the Saskatchewan Government formed a 'Co-operative Organizations Branch' within the Department of Agriculture to administer legislation respecting co-operatives. The Branch, in its first annual report published in 1915, said that, by the end of 1914, there had been 113 co-operative societies incorporated under the new Act. The first to be granted incorporation was the Juniata Co-operative Association.

231. World War I: On August 4, 1914, World War I began. The Grain Growers' organizations had feared the coming of war, and had expressed themselves on many occasions as favoring disarmament. With the outbreak of war, the Grain Growers' exhibited strong patriotism, yet continued to uphold the view that

no one should be permitted to profit from war. As a means of ensuring that no one would profit from war and the sufferings it created, the Grain Growers' organizations soon began to advocate a tax on profits.

233. MGGA and Coal: At the annual convention of the Manitoba Grain Growers' Association there were complaints that individuals and

232. World War I: In a practical demonstration of patriotism, the Saskatchewan Grain Growers' Association sponsored a "Patriotic Acre"

1914

associations buying carlots of coal "frequently found they received from a ton to five tons less than they were required to pay for." A committee was formed to study the matter and, if necessary, to take action.

plan by which farmers were asked to donate the grain from one or more acres as a gift to the United Kingdom.

51

1915

234. Women In UFA: Acting upon a resolution from the 1913 UFA annual convention, a group of 58 farm women met at Edmonton to begin organization of a women's auxiliary to the UFA.

1916

235. Canadian Council of Agriculture: At its annual meeting, the Canadian Council of Agriculture extended an invitation to affiliate to four commercial, farmer-owned organizations. They were: The Alberta Farmers' Co-operative Elevator Company; Saskatchewan Co-operative Elevator Company; the United Farmers' Co-operative Company of Ontario; and the Grain Growers' Grain Company. The invitation to these commercial organizations required a change in the constitution of the Canadian Council of Agriculture which, to this time, did not permit commercial organizations to join. Until

1916, members of the Council included United Farmers of Alberta, the Saskatchewan Grain Growers' Association, the Manitoba Grain Growers' Association, and United Farmers of Ontario. At its meeting, held at Winnipeg in December, the Council adopted a national political platform. The platform was aimed to benefit not only farmers, but all Canadians. It was concerned with such matters as tariffs and trade, taxation, proposals for nationalization of Canada's railways, and demands that women be granted the right to vote.

237. Legislation: A revised Co-operatives Act was approved by the Manitoba Legislature. It provided for the Province's first Registrar of Co-operative Associations. Other terms of the Act restrained co-operatives from either buying or selling on credit.

236. Nonpartisan League: An organization known as the Nonpartisan League, which had origins in the Dakota states of the U.S., began to arouse attention in Saskatchewan. A Canadian Nonpartisan League was begun near Swift Current. It rapidly gained support in southern areas of Saskatchewan and in some parts of Alberta, though it went almost unnoticed in Manitoba. The League's philosophy was that farmers could best solve their problems through political action. In the Dakotas, it was said, attention directed to the League caused farmers to neglect their co-operative organizations.

239. Credit Union: In the Roman Catholic parish of Albertville, a predominantly French-speaking community, about 25 miles NE of Prince Albert, a priest, Rev. Fr. Albert Lebel, together with 14 founding members, formed a credit union. It was known as La Caisse Populaire d'Albertville and had its office in the rectory. There was a limit to the sum that members could invest in shares but they were encouraged to put money into deposit accounts. This is regarded as the first attempt to apply orthodox credit union principles and methods in Saskatchewan. Although there was no legislation for incorporation of credit unions during the time, the

238. Women: The women's auxiliary to the UFA which had been formed in 1915, adopted its name, "United Farm Women of of Alberta."

240. "UFA Sunday": At the annual UFA convention a resolution was passed providing "that the Sunday nearest May 24th, Empire Day, be set aside for the discussion of UFA affairs from a religious standpoint."

It appears that among those present at the convention were representatives of the Chamber of Commerce.

Manitoba　　　　Saskatchewan　　　　Alberta

1916

243. Women Enfranchised: Manitoba was the first Canadian province to grant women the right to vote in provincial elections.

organization lived until 1936 when it was dissolved and share capital was repaid in full.

242. Farm Supplies: The SGGA proposed that the operation of its farm supplies department begun in 1914, be transferred to the Saskatchewan Co-operative Elevator Company. The Elevator Company was not anxious to be involved in handling farm supplies. At the same time, some of the officials of SGGA opposed the transfer for they believed that the farm supplies service encouraged SGGA members to be loyal to their locals. No action was taken to press the proposal.

244. Women Enfranchised: The Saskatchewan legislature provided women with the right to vote in provincial elections.

241. Alberta Farmers' Co-operative Elevator Company, at its fourth annual meeting, reported a surplus for the year of $282,426 after providing for depreciation in the years of 1914 and 1916, and setting $175,000 aside in reserves.

At this meeting there was a discussion of a proposed merger between the Alberta Farmers' Co-operative Elevator Company, the Saskatchewan Co-operative Elevator Company, and the Grain Growers' Grain Company. Action on the proposal was taken in 1917.

245. Women Enfranchised: The Alberta legislature passed an Act to give women the right to vote in provincial elections.

1917

246. General Election of 1917: Conscription of manpower for military service was the great issue in the election of 1917. The Conservatives, under Robert Borden, elected in 1911, had held office since that time, there being no elections in the interval because Canada was at war. Canada had made a commitment to supply four divisions to fight the war. By early 1917, enlistment of volunteer recruits for the army fell far behind the number of casualties. Conservative leader Borden, aware that conscription would be vigorously opposed by French Canadians and hence would divide the electorate, proposed that a Union Government be formed. A number of Liberals, including several from the West, joined Borden's government, forming a Union Government. Liberal Leader Sir Wilfrid Laurier did not join the Unionists.

On July 11, 1917, The Compulsory Military Service Act was introduced to the House of Commons where it was passed, after strenuous debate, on August 28, 1917. Laurier had argued that the matter should be placed before the electorate for decision, but Borden would not agree. He did, however, plan to call an election after passage of the conscription bill, but, for the first time, before doing so, the government passed special legislation to apply to the election:

1. Overseas soldiers were enfranchised.

2. Wives, mothers and sisters of men serving overseas were given the opportunity to vote in a federal election.

3. Immigrants who had arrived in Canada after 1902 from countries with which Canada was at war, were deprived of the right to vote.

4. Borden's cabinet allocated the votes of overseas soldiers, placing their votes in ridings most likely to oppose conscription.

PROVINCE	UNIONISTS (Borden)	OPPOSITION (Laurier)	TOTAL
Ontario	74	8	82
Quebec	3	62	65
Nova Scotia	12	4	15
New Brunswick	7	4	11
P.E.I.	2	2	4
Manitoba	14	1	15
Saskatchewan	16		16
Alberta	11	1	12
B.C.	13		13
Yukon	1		1
	153	82	235

The popular vote was much closer than the placement of candidates suggests. The Unionists, with 65% of the seats in the new government, had but 53% of the popular vote (total ballots counted), indicating that allocation of the soldiers' votes determined the outcome at a number of ridings.

1917

247. Nonpartisan League, which had emerged in 1916, entered a slate of 8 candidates in the Provincial election. These candidates received only a small number of votes. Disappointment over the result caused rapid decline of the League in Saskatchewan.

248. Nonpartisan League of Alberta held its first annual convention at Calgary. It had attracted the support of many UFA members thereby causing a strong alliance between the League and UFA to develop. In the Provincial election of 1917, the League endorsed 4 candidates, 2 of whom won seats in the legislature.

249. Legislation: The Saskatchewan Co-operative Creameries Act was enacted by the Saskatchewan legislature. It provided that co-operative creameries scattered throughout the Province become federated as one organization known as the Saskatchewan Co-operative Creameries Association. The legislation also provided for government loans to assist development of branches, warehouses, and required building. A development program followed, most of the development being in the form of butter plants.

250. Income Tax: The Dominion Government enacted legislation providing for a War Income Tax. It provided that personal and corporate incomes be taxed on a graduated scale with high incomes and profits being the more severely taxed. The Grain Growers', opposed to profiteering from war and its consequences, had favored such a tax. Said **The Grain Growers' Guide** editorials of March 27:

" This year farmers and others are to be called upon to pay an income tax. This is the most direct form of federal taxation we have yet had instituted and infinitely more desirable than some of the more indirect means of increasing public revenue. The organized farmers have favored the application of this form of taxation in their endorsement of the Farmers' National Platform."

251. Income Tax—Co-op Union of Canada: The War Income Tax Act was the subject of several letters exchanged between the Co-operative Union of Canada and the Finance Department of the federal government. George Keen, secretary of the C.U.C., was seeking to clarify terms of the Act insofar as it affected co-operatives. The Department informed Mr. Keen that cash savings of co-operatives applied as payment of interest on capital, were regarded as "profit" or "income" and were, therefore, taxable. However, dividends on purchases (partonage refunds), or surpluses applied to any other purpose, were not considered to be

taxable. Mr. Keen, still in doubt as to precisely what was meant by the Department, wrote a further letter of enquiry. To this he received a reply dated November 17, 1917, from R.W. Breadner, Commissioner of Taxation, Ottawa, saying:

" In reply to your letter of the 12th inst., I may state that refunds made to customers which represent savings effected in purchases should not be classed as dividends or income and, therefore, are not liable to taxation under the Income War Tax Act."

1917

252. Orderly Marketing: Abnormal conditions caused by World War I created enormous increases in demand for Canadian wheat, especially in British markets. As a result, there was a great deal of speculation and fluctuation of prices on the Winnipeg Grain Exchange. In the midst of an already troublesome situation, a British Purchasing Commission was successful in cornering the future markets in both the Winnipeg and Chicago grain exchanges, creating a most chaotic condition. There was fear that powerful financial interests, adopting the scheme of the British Purchasing Commission, would acquire a monopoly on the wheat supplies desperately needed by Britain.

Action to correct the dangerous situation was taken by the Canadian Government on June 11 when, by Order-in-Council, a Board of Grain Supervisors was set up "to prevent to the utmost extent possible, any undue inflation or depreciation of values by speculating, the hoarding of grain supplies, or by any other means." The Board assumed control of all wheat supplies in Canada and a monopoly on both domestic and export sales. The Board, in consultation with the Canadian Council of Agriculture, established prices to be paid to farmers. The result was a uniform price system based on grades and types of wheat. For 1917-18 crops, farmers received $2.21 per bushel, basis No. 1 Northern.

This wartime measure marked the first time that farmers had any say in determining the prices they were paid for their grain. It also resulted in the closing of the Winnipeg Grain Exchange for the duration of the period in which these governmental controls remained in effect.

253. Merger—United Grain Growers' Formed: The Grain Growers' Grain Company, serving in all three Prairie Provinces, and the Alberta Farmers' Co-operative Elevator Company, amalgamated under the GGGC Charter, to form United Grain Growers' Limited. Five basic principles were chosen to guide the new organization in its operations:

1. Sell grain at the highest possible price.
2. Pay a part of the profit as a return on shareholders' capital. (Only farmers could hold shares.)
3. Devote a portion of the profits to educational work.
4. Set aside a portion of the profits to reserves.
5. Distribute a part of the profits or earnings as patronage refunds to customers.

With completion of its 1917 construction programs, UGG was operating 332 country elevators, 184 coal sheds, and more than 200 warehouses. Large, central warehouses were operated at Winnipeg, Calgary and Regina to supply farm machinery and other commodities. UGG also operated terminal elevators at the Lakehead and at the West Coast, and a feed business at New Westminister. A timber cutting permit was held at Hatton, B.C., where a sawmill was built and lumber production was begun in 1917.

254. Manitoba Grain Growers' were not affected by the merger by which UGG was formed. MGGA was operating a farm supplies service for its own locals by receiving orders and combining them for placement with various suppliers. MGGA did not stock goods or operate wholesale warehouses.

255. Saskatchewan Grain Growers' resolved to continue operation of its Trading Department independent of any affiliation or reliance upon the newly-formed UGG. A grocery service which the GGGC had operated at Winnipeg was taken over by the SGGA.

In the same year, SGGA began to market a "Rein-drive" tractor, and also introduced, under its own brand name, a gopher poison. The many locals of the SGGA which were by now operating stores were warned time and time again of the dangers of credit.

1917

256. Saskatchewan Co-op Elevator Company declined an invitation to be a party to the merger by which UGG was formed. This organization had not ventured into the handling of farm supplies.

1918

257. Canadian Council of Agriculture—Co-ordination With Business Interests: In an evident attempt to find common ground for co-ordination of the interest of farmers and businessmen, the Canadian Council of Agriculture, about 1916, took steps to organize a body known as "The Joint Committee of Commerce and Agriculture." The two sectors had difficulty in finding common ground, a matter made evident by this report published in **The Grain Growers' Guide** of March 20, 1918:

" Twenty-five leading representatives of commercial, financial and transportation interests met last week in Regina with an equal number of the Canadian Council of Agriculture, to discuss matters vital to the development of the West.

" The Joint Committee of Commerce and Agriculture, as the organization is known, was organized two years ago to discuss every question of mutual interest to farmers and what are called the business interests.

" On the program for discussion at this meeting were two important subjects. The first was co-operative trading as it is now carried on by the farmers' organizations. A number of business organizations are opposed to this method of trading among farmers...A paper was read by C. Rice-Jones, vice-president of United Grain Growers' Ltd., showing reasons why it is necessary for farmers to enter into co-operative trading to keep down the cost of production and ensure fair prices from retailers and wholesalers.

" In reply to this paper was one prepared by H.H. Piggott, Credit Manager of the J.H. Ashdown Hardware Company, which opposed the entry of the farmers' organizations into co-operative trading and maintained that it would drive the retailers out of business, destroy the country town, and would not supply the service now being rendered by the retailers.

" A considerable discussion developed. The farmers made it clear they were in the co-operative trading business to stay because they found it necessary. If, however, they could be shown it was wrong or that the present system could give better service than the farmers were given, then it would not be necessary for the farmers to continue their business.

" It was discovered that neither the wholesalers nor retailers were, represented by men with authority to speak for their organizations. The bankers' representative explained that their opposition to granting credit to farmers' co-operative organizations was due entirely to the nature of the legislation in Saskatchewan. They were quite prepared to loan to these associations but the Act prevented them from taking any security the same as they would do with a retailer. It was agreed that the Bill should be amended and the bankers agreed to extend credit in the usual way.

" One representative of the wholesalers said that they were quite prepared to sell to the co-operative associations providing they were selling goods over the counter, but not to associations conducting their business in any other way..."

258. Credit Union: An unincorporated credit union which had operated at St. Jean since 1911, was dissolved because no trained person was available to carry on its management. No member lost money as a result of the dissolution.

259. Saskatchewan Grain Growers launched a drive to increase its membership by 20,000, to reach 60,000. **The Saskatoon Star,** in an editorial on December 10, displayed support for SGGA and its campaign, saying:

" It should not be difficult to accomplish this task, for farmers have seen the value of co-operation and unity if they

260. United Farmers of Alberta had not been involved in the 1917 merger by which UGG was formed, and in 1918 was granted a Provincial Charter that gave the organization power to do business with members. UFA then considered entry into the trust and insurance businesses as a means of raising funds to finance activities of the organization. These plans were not, however, carried out due to a post-war

Manitoba	Saskatchewan	Alberta

1918

mean to get anywhere, and only the mentally lazy must fail to realize the need for full accession of strength if the greater problems of the future are to be met.

"For a Saskatchewan farmer to stand aloof from this organization...is not justified on any ground whatever. It has deserved well of him in his farming business; it has presented a consolidated front when matters of political and economic influence affecting him were under discussion; it has done more than any other institution to foster the community spirit. ...Membership in such an organization becomes a bounden duty to the farmer."

depression and the entry of UFA into the political arena.

Locals of the UFA were involved in group purchasing of farm supplies and other necessities. This was considered by the UFA central chapters and at this time there was no attempt by the central office to become involved.

261. Uncertainty Over Orderly Marketing As War Ends: With the signing of an Armistice on November 11, 1918, World War I came to an end. Farmers and farm organizations, having experienced the advantages of orderly marketing of grains, were concerned that the end of the War would see the federal government abandon its control of the grain trade adopted in 1917. For the present, however, the government gave no hint as to its intentions. Naturally, the matter was an important item of the agendas of the farm organizations at their conventions held in January of 1919. The Canadian Council of Agriculture, during 1918, demanded that a wheat board be set up by the Government of Canada to market grains under methods similar to those that had been followed during the war years.

1919

262. Manitoba Grain Growers' Becomes U.F.M.: The Manitoba Grain Growers' Association, begun in 1903, was reorganized as United Farmers of Manitoba, a move that reflected an intention to emphasize greater involvement in political affairs.

Meeting in annual convention, the UFM was at first in favor of continuation of government control of grain marketing with a fixed price to farmers for the 1919 crop. However, a controversy arose after UFM adopted a National Platform of measures aimed at assisting farmers. Included in the platform was a demand for lower tariffs on imports. It appeared that if farmers persisted in demands for a fixed

263. SGGA Wants Orderly Marketing: At annual convention, Saskatchewan Grain Growers' Association adopted a resolution demanding that the federal government fix the price paid to farmers for grain at the 1918 level.

265. Legislature Favors Orderly Marketing: The Saskatchewan legislature urged the federal government to fix the price paid to farmers for grain. It proposed that the price be comparable to that in effect in the U.S.A. where a government-sponsored agency, United States Grain Corporation, was controlling the marketing of grain.

264. UFA Favors Lower Tariffs: The annual convention of United Farmers of Alberta debated the subjects of tariffs and government control of grain marketing. The debate followed a course much like that of the UFM convention. The farmers were in favor of government control of grain marketing and a fixed price to farmers, but feared demands for this would impair prospects that the government would respond to their simultaneous demand for lower tariffs on imports.

The convention compromised by adopting a resolution asking that all dealings in grain for future delivery be transacted on a cash basis, a method that was aimed at curbing speculation.

1919

price for their grain they would ruin their chances for getting lower tariffs. So, after much debate, UFM, withdrew its demand for government control of grain marketing.

266. Canadian Council of Agriculture Favors Orderly Marketing: When the Canadian Council of Agriculture met on July 11, delegates from United Farmers' organizations of Manitoba and Alberta acted in accord with resolutions passed at their annual conventions by opposing government control of grain marketing and the fixing of the price paid to farmers. However, Saskatchewan Grain Growers' Association, the Saskatchewan Co-operative Elevator Company, and United Grain Growers', supported demands for government control. The conflict of opinion on this matter was the first incident of major dissention within the C.C. of A. By majority vote, the Council resolved to demand that the Canadian Government set up an organization similar to the United States Grain Corporation, and to declare that the Council was "strongly opposed to the opening of the Canadian markets for unrestricted sale of wheat." The Council argued that it was logical for the Canadian Government to control grain exports because governments of European countries regarded as customers for Canadian grain were controlling imports of this commodity.

267. Grain Exchange Opened But Again Closed: On July 22, the Canadian Government ceased to control grain marketing, and the Winnipeg Grain Exchange opened for business. At the time, inflation was rampant. As the Exchange opened, wheat sold for $2.24 per bushel. There was fear that a continued rise in prices could have serious consequences to the already inflated economy. The Government quickly acted, closing the Grain exchange and setting up a Wheat Board to operate for one year to market the 1919 crop. This Board was a genuine marketing agency that aimed to obtain the best possible price for grain for farmers. An initial payment of $2 per bushel (basis No. 1 Northern at Fort William, now Thunder Bay) was made to farmers on delivery, and the farmers were also provided with 'Participation Certificates' entitling them to further payments if their grain was sold at a higher price. Farmers were inexperienced with this method of selling, and many traded their certificates for paltry amounts while others either lost or destroyed them. However, when the 1919-20 crop year came to an end it was shown that the Board had sold the grain at a good price so that farmers were entitled to additional payments of 40 cents per bushel. Only those able to present participation certificates, however, could claim a share of the additional payments. Several million dollars of final payments were not claimed because farmers had traded, lost or destroyed their certificates. Eventually these unclaimed funds were set up in a trust for agricultural scholarships which are still available to young farm people.

268. UGG Livestock Subsidiary: In Manitoba, United Grain Growers' set up a subsidiary to handle livestock. It operated until 1927 when the Manitoba Livestock Pool was organized.

269. Saskatchewan Grain Growers' annual report told of opposition which confronted the organization in its efforts to carry on co-operative trading. Said the report:

" The central organization has had almost innumerable enemies to contend with and the methods and means resorted to and the weapons employed by them have been too many to fully enumerate.

" Of all the hostile forces which have endeavoured to frustrate your democratic co-operative movement, none is so outstanding as the Retail Merchants' Association. This body has

270. UFA Political Action: At its annual convention of 1919, the United Farmers of Alberta decided to offer facilities of its central office to assist in organizing the membership by electoral constituencies for political action. This was done, and the UFA Political Association was set up as a branch of the UFA. In previous months, there had been a number of discussions between the UFA and the Nonpartisan League but no formal amalgamation of the two organizations had emerged.

1919

consistently endeavoured to defeat every effort to establish co-operative distribution. Their wicked efforts have been successfully frustrated and are proving but a boomerang to themselves.

"At the present time there is being put forth a strenuous effort to create a Coal Dealers' Association, the object of which is, through the organization of all the coal dealers throughout the west, to bring such pressure to bear upon the coal mines that they will not dare to sell to any except those self-styled 'legitimate' coal dealers. It is well that you bear in mind that in no other western province is the farmer able to purchase coal as cheaply as from the Association in Saskatchewan....The fight is, therefore, aimed at us....The imperative need is for the Association to have a controlling interest in a couple of mines..."

271. Co-op Wool Growers: At the urging of the Saskatchewan government, Canadian Co-operative Wool Growers established a Saskatchewan branch to handle the marketing of wool produced in the Province. The Co-operative Activities Branch of the Department of Agriculture then withdrew from a commercial activity which it had been carrying on for a number of years when it prepared an annual program for the assembly and marketing of wool, rented the necessary warehouse space, and made shipments to wool markets. The government had provided this service at no cost to wool producers. It was part of a government program to initiate and test co-operative ventures of benefit to farmers; the government, once the co-operatives were functioning well, would withdraw and let the farmers operate them themselves.

272. Co-operative Union: A group of consumer co-operatives in Alberta established a new organization, Alberta Co-operative Union. It was hoped that through this body the associations might co-ordinate their efforts and establish a co-operative wholesaling service. The organization was, however, but short-lived and its history is obscure.

55

1920

273. Canadian Council of Agriculture Seeks Continued Orderly Marketing: The Wheat Board set up in 1919 was to exist for one year only. As 1920 began, it was clear that the federal government was under pressure from grain interests who desired reopening of the Winnipeg Grain Exchange.

In January and again in June, 1920, the Canadian Council of Agriculture demanded that the Wheat Board be continued, and that the Grain Exchange remain closed. The demands were made at a time when a federal election campaign was in progress, so received little, if any, attention.

274. UFA Seeks Orderly Marketing: In July, the United Farmers of Alberta pressed the federal government to continue control of grain marketing through the Wheat Board, for at least another year.

Suspecting that their demand would be ignored, the UFA passed another

Manitoba	Saskatchewan	Alberta

1920

resolution to urge that the boards of directors of the United Grain Growers' and Saskatchewan Co-operative Elevator Company consider the possibility of organizing a co-operative pool for the purpose of selling wheat direct to European markets. This appears to be the first time that the "wheat pool" idea was proposed on the Prairies.

275. Wheat Board Ends: The federal government, in late August, disbanded the Wheat Board set up in 1919. On August 18, the Winnipeg Grain Exchange resumed operations. Prices moved upward to $2.85 per bushel but began to decline as deliveries of the 1920 crop started arriving at elevators. By December, the price had dropped by $1 per bushel. A post-war depression had now begun, but grain prices were falling faster than prices of any other commodity.

276. Canadian Council of Agriculture Studies UFA Plan: Dismayed by the ending of the Wheat Board, the Canadian Council of Agriculture met in October, repeating its demands of January and June that the Wheat Board be continued and the Grain Exchange remained closed. In addition, the Council took note of the UFA's suggestion for a co-operative pool. A committee was set up to study the idea of a voluntary pooling method by which farmers could market their grain. Members of the committee included the UFA president, who acted as the chairman, J.R. Murray of United Grain Growers', and F.W. Riddell of Saskatchewan Co-operative Elevators Limited.

277. UFM Into Politics: The United Farmers of Manitoba entered into the provincial political arena with plans to contest the forthcoming election.

278. UFA Political Activity: The UFA Political Association set up in 1919, was given further consideration. In order to comply with legal requirements, it was necessary for the central organization to act as a clearing house for political funds, and that full autonomy and authority remain entrusted with constituency associations. In short, it was not practical to divide the UFA central from the political arm. By resolution, UFA delegates reaffirmed their desire for political action by their organization.

279. Co-op Creameries: A new organization, Manitoba Co-operative Dairies, was incorporated. Its formation was the result of dissatisfaction among producers over the wide spread between producer and consumer prices.

280. Canadian Council of Agriculture Into Politics: At a Winnipeg convention called by the Canadian Council of Agriculture, a new political party, The National Progressive Party, was formed. It was the result of discontent, in agricultural circles, over policies of both the Liberals and Conservatives and their alignment to commercial interests. The Progressive Party had, as its object, to promote a "New National Policy". This policy called for public ownership of some utilities; provision of old age pensions, and of allowances to widows; and for removal of high tariffs that added to farmers' cost of machinery and other production needs. The "Farmers' Platform", by which the policy was also known, was enthusiastically accepted by many, and particularly in Ontario, Manitoba and Alberta, led to involvement in Provincial politics by United Farmers organizations.

1921

282. Legislation: The Manitoba Legislature amended the Co-operative Associations Act to relieve its rigid restrictions against credit. The amendment permitted credit to be extended for 90 days.

281. Farmers' Union of Canada: At a meeting of farmers held at Ituna on December 17, there was discussion of a proposed new organization to be known as the Farmers' Union of Canada. It was intended that this organization avoid commercial activity and direct political involvement, and be a big industrial union that would offer a means "for the farmers to assume control of their own affairs."

The Farmers' Union of Canada was formed, and its membership grew at the expense of the Saskatchewan Grain Growers' Association. Affairs of the Union were conducted behind closed doors, and it was said to have had a system of signs and passwords.

283. SGGA Favors Pooling Plan: The pooling plan for the marketing of grain met with the approval of the Saskatchewan Grain Growers' which called for "the fullest measure of interprovincial co-operation among farmers' organizations" to get the plan into operation. In the meantime, however, SGGA, in September, again demanded that the Wheat Board be continued.

285. Co-op Branch: The Co-operative Organizations Branch of the Department of Agriculture, formed in 1914, became known as the Co-operation & Markets Branch. Its responsibilities had increased as a result of further legislation and growth in the number of co-ops.

284. UFA Forms Government: United Farmers of Alberta contested the Provincial election and was swept into power, forming the UFA Government that was returned in 1926 and again in 1930 before being defeated by the Social Credit party in 1935.

286. General Election of 1921: The Union Government elected in 1917 had, to some extent at least, disturbed the traditional two-party concept, encouraging some factions of the electorate to consider political action through other than the Liberal and Conservative parties. Thus, in the election of 1921, the choice of parties and candidates was larger than in the past.

The new Progressive Party, led by T.A. Crerar, contested a good number of ridings. The Liberals were led by W.L. Mackenzie King, who had replaced Sir Wilfrid Laurier. Likewise, the Conservatives had a new leader, Arthur Meighen, who had been a member of Robert Borden's Union Government. In the election, a minority government was placed in office:

1921

PROVINCE	Lib.	Cons.	Prog.	Labor	Indep.	Total
Ontario	21	37	24			82
Quebec	65					65
Nova Scotia	16					16
New Brunswick	5	5	1			11
P.E.I.	4					4
Manitoba	2		12	1		15
Saskatchewan	1		15			16
Alberta			10	2		12
B.C.	3	7	2		1	13
Yukon		1				1
	117	50	64	3	1	235

57

1922

287. UFM Forms Government: The United Farmers of Manitoba entered the Provincial election. Winning power by a strong majority, the UFM took over reins of the Provincial Government.

288. Legislation: The Agricultural Co-operative Associations Act of 1913 provided that farmers who were members of the Saskatchewan Grain Growers' Association, could form or become members of co-operative associations. In 1922, the Act was amended to enable any bona fide farmer to form or to be a member of a co-operative.

289. Demand For Orderly Marketing: In 1921, the Liberal Government, headed by Mackenzie King, was elected to office. Awaiting attention were numerous demands for reinstatement of the Wheat Board. The Government declared that it would not respond to the demands for it could not exercise wartime powers by which the 1917 Board had been set up. The Government's stand was that it could act on the matter only with the consent of the provinces concerned, and that it would consider establishment of a Wheat Board if the legislatures of at least two of the three Prairie Provinces voted in favor of it.

291. Manitoba Defeats Board: The Manitoba legislature considered the proposed federal wheat board. By a vote free of party ties, the proposal was defeated. Demand for a board was not as strong in Manitoba as it was in Saskatchewan and Alberta. As well, grain trade interests in Manitoba who favored operation of the Winnipeg Grain Exchange strongly opposed the proposed wheat board.

290. Saskatchewan and Alberta Legislatures Favor Board: The legislatures of Alberta and Saskatchewan were immediately summoned into session. Both legislatures gave approval to proposals that the Federal Government be requested to establish a Wheat Board.

It was then discovered, however, that the proposed Wheat Board would have no power over the flour trade nor in the movement of wheat. The 1917 Board had power to control these two areas and found such power to be essential to proper control. Consequently, efforts to set up a wheat board under federal jurisdiction came to a standstill.

292. UGG Ends Farm Machinery Service: United Grain Growers' ended the farm machinery supply service begun in 1913. At first, the service had been a financial success but was now operated at a loss as farmers preferred to deal at nearby outlets of other companies rather than order by mail from UGG. Although ending its service, UGG directors were satisfied that it had done a good job of helping keep farm machinery costs down.

1923

293. Canadian Council of Agriculture Proposes Pooling Plan: The special committee of the Canadian Council of Agriculture, set up in 1920 to study the pooling plan, completed its report. The committee recommended a system of pooling provided for:

a) A contract between the farmer and marketing organization. It was proposed that the contract be legally enforceable and require the farmer to market all wheat through the pool for a five-year period. In return, the pool would sell grain on behalf of the farmer, paying each farmer the average price received by the pool for all sales. The farmer would receive an initial payment upon making delivery to the pool, and a final payment would be made after the year's crop had been sold by the pool and the average price was then known.

b) It was the aim to have at least 50% of all wheat acreage under contract. It was considered that the pooling plan could only succeed if accepted by a majority of farmers and included more than half of the total wheat crop.

1923

Farmer Government for Manitoba

U.F.M. Sweeps Rural Manitoba, Winning Decisive Victory Over Both Old Parties.

AS a result of the provincial elections held on July 18, Manitoba becomes the third province of Canada to place a farmer government in power. The Liberal government, headed by Hon. T. C. Norris, which has ruled the province since 1915, was overwhelmingly defeated, only seven of his candidates securing election, while the representation of the Conservative party in the House will be confined to six members. Independents elected eight and Labor six. Twenty-four U.F.M. candidates were elected, and with one Progressive from Winnipeg the dominant party in the legislature will have 25 supporters, with a strong probability of securing the three deferred elections. It is understood that some of the Independent and Labor members have also signified their intention to support the new government, thus assuring a working majority.

Premier Norris retained his seat in Lansdowne by the substantial majority of 461 votes, but only one other member of his cabinet, Hon. Robert Jacob, attorney-general, was elected. Hon. Dr. Thornton, Deloraine; Hon. John Williams, Arthur, and Hon. C. D. McPherson, Portage la Prairie, were all defeated, the two former by U.F.M. candidates and the last named by the Conservative leader, Major F. G. Taylor.

The election in Winnipeg was conducted under the proportional representation system, the city electing ten members in one constituency. The total vote in the city was 44,328, making the quota necessary for election 4,030. Out of 43 candidates nominated, two were elected on first preference votes, F. J. Dixon, the leader of the Independent Labor party, receiving 7,394 votes, and Hon. Robert Jacob, the recently appointed attorney-general, 4,030, the exact number required for election. The counting and transferring of the votes occupied three days, the final result being the election of four Labor

men, two Liberals, two Conservatives, one Independent and one Progressive.

Results by constituencies are given below. The majorities shown are unofficial figures and in a few cases are from incomplete returns. It is unlikely, however, that the result will be changed in any case.

Farmers Elected—24

Arthur—D. L. McLeod, 323 majority.
Beautiful Plains—George Little, 589 majority.
Birtle—W. J. Short, 596 majority.
Carillon—A. Prefontaine, 348 majority.
Deloraine—D. S. McLeod, 207 majority.
Dufferin—W. Brown, 113 majority.
Fisher—M. V. Bachinsky, 177 majority.
Gilbert Plains—A. G. Berry, 568 majority.
Gladstone—A. McGregor, 837 majority.
Hamiota—T. Wolstenholme, 408 majority.
Iberville—A. R. Boivin, 513 majority.
Killarney—A. E. Foster, 214 majority.
Lakeside—D. L. Campbell, 493 majority.
LaVerandrye—P. A. Talbot, 272 majority.
Manitou—G. Compton, 31 majority.
Minnedosa—Neil Cameron, 835 majority.
Morris—W. R. Clubb, 379 majority.
Mountain—Chas. Cannon, 608 majority.
Norfolk—John Muirhead, 147 majority.
Rockwood—W. C. McKinnell, 596 majority.
Russell—I. B. Griffiths, 397 majority.
Springfield—C. Barclay, 180 majority.
Swan River—R. W. Emmond, 789 maj.
Virden—R. H. Mooney, 675 majority.

Progressives Elected 1

Winnipeg—R. W. Craig.

Liberals Elected—7

Dauphin—A. Esplen 84 majority.
Fairford—A. W. Kirvan, 396 majority.
Glenwood—J. W. Breakey, 530 maj.
Lansdowne—Hon. T. C. Norris, 461 maj
St. George—S. Sigfusson, 574 maj.
Winnipeg — Hon Robt. Jacob, Mrs Edith Rogers.

Continued on Page 13

HON. JOHN BRACKEN—MANITOBA'S NEW PREMIER

58

59

1923

294. Saskatchewan Premier Offers Alternate Plans: Premier Charles Dunning of Saskatchewan opposed the Canadian Council of Agriculture's plan because of its compulsory features. He proposed that a voluntary plan be pursued, and urged that United Grain Growers and the Saskatchewan Co-operative Elevator Company combine their marketing services and form a new company called Canadian Farmers' Export Company. The suggested merger would combine about 700 elevators into a marketing system.

The Saskatchewan Co-operative Elevator Company rejected Premier Dunning's proposal, saying it was unlikely to either succeed or curb the influence of the Winnipeg Grain Exchange.

295. United Grain Growers' Propose New Organizations: At a meeting of the Canadian Council of Agriculture held July 4, the president of United Grain Growers advanced a further proposal respecting the pooling plan. He proposed that the pools be organized apart from the existing grain handling co-operatives. However, the existing grain handling co-operatives would, he proposed, provide the necessary elevator services and, if necessary, financial assistance to help the pools get started.

296. Sapiro Speaks For Orderly Marketing: For months there had been efforts to bring to the Prairies an American lawyer, Aaron Sapiro, to tell farmers about the pooling plan. In the U.S.A., Sapiro had assisted raisin growers to form marketing pools. He had also helped the California orange growers who had formed the Sunkist Orange Growers' Co-operative. Accounts of these activities were published in **The Grain Growers' Guide** around 1920.

Many organizations claim credit for inviting Sapiro to the Prairies. The list includes United Grain Growers; United Farmers of Alberta; United Farmers of Canada, and others. In addition, the **Edmonton Journal, Regina Leader, Swift Current Sun,** and other newspapers advocated that Sapiro be invited. The **Calgary Herald,** however, brought Sapiro to the first meeting held at Calgary in August, 1923.

Sapiro spoke at many meetings on the Prairies, particularly in Saskatchewan and Alberta. He told his audiences that he did not favor a voluntary plan, but proposed a united effort. Sapiro's proposals generally supported the idea of firm contracts with farmers.

Speaking at Third Avenue United Church, Saskatoon, Sapiro warned farmers that it was themselves who broke the price for wheat by dumping onto the market more than it could absorb at one time. "Every farmer who sells as an individual is dumping his product and breaking his own price in the process," Sapiro stressed. "If a thousand men are trying to sell to five, the five will name the price. But if the five are trying to buy from one central office, that office will have something to say about the price!"

Sapiro advised farmers to stop dumping their wheat onto markets, and to set up their own merchandising system so as to control the flow of wheat onto world markets. He proposed a co-operative organization to operate the pooling plan—an organization democratically controlled thorugh a system of district representation, and with contracts between the pool and farmers. He warned against involving such an organization in politics, in handling grains for non-members, and against individual selling.

298. Saskatchewan Co-operative Wheat Producers Formed: Steps toward formation of Saskatchewan Co-operative Wheat Producers were almost simultaneous to those taken in Alberta.

On August 9, 1923, Sapiro spoke at Regina. Next day, a select committee representing organized and unorganized farmers, the Provincial government, Line Elevators, Retail Merchants, and others, met in the offices of Saskatchewan Grain Growers' Association, resolving to take definite steps to form a pool.

297. Alberta Co-operative Wheat Producers Formed: Alberta farmers were the first on the Prairies to take definite steps toward forming a wheat pool, to gain incorporation and to begin operations.

A definite decision to form their pool was made at a meeting held on August 7, 1923, when a committee of farmers, UFA officials plus representatives of the grain trade and elevator interests, Board of Trade, banks, and the Alberta government was given the task of initiating organizational work.

1923

299. Initial Steps To Form A Manitoba Pool

By resolution of the Board of Directors, United Farmers of Manitoba, on August 21, 1923, set up a "Wheat Pool Committee" for the purpose of taking the action necessary to establish a pool similar to those being developed in Alberta and Saskatchewan. The initial committee was soon enlarged to include representatives of rural municipalities, agricultural societies, the Government of Manitoba, United Grain Growers', line elevators, and Retail Merchants. It was named "the Manitoba Wheat Pool Committee."

While widespread support for a Manitoba pool was evident among farmers and farm organizations, it seemed evident that the press, Retail Merchants, and Chambers of Commerce were not inclined to offer the support and encouragement that had been provided from those sources in Alberta and Saskatchewan. No doubt the influence of the Winnipeg Grain Exchange and at least some officials of the North-West Line Elevator Association was a countervailing factor. Nevertheless, the Committee set about its tasks with enthusiasm in hope of having the pool in operation in time to handle the 1924 crop.

Saskatchewan Co-operative Wheat Producers Limited was incorporated on August 25, 1923, under the Companies Act. This incorporation was a temporary measure and incorporation under a Special Act followed the next year.

A campaign committee formed a province-wide organization of canvassers who visited farmers to persuade them to sign pool contracts. There was wide support for the campaigning. Boards of Trade, the Retail Merchants' Association, Association of Rural Municipalities, Kiwanis Club, Saskatchewan Government, and other bodies gave strong support. On August 26, pastors of many churches encouragingly brought the matter to the attention of their congregations.

The Campaign resulted in the sign-up of 3,079,560 acres through contracts with 22,328 farmers—only about 25% of the total seeded acreage and about one-half of the objective. Saskatchewan, with 12.8 million acres sown to wheat, presented a much larger sign-up task than did the other two provinces. The combined wheat acreage in Alberta and Manitoba was 8.1 million, or 2/3 of the Saskatchewan total.

When it became clear that the sign-up campaign had not yet reached its objective, it was decided that the Saskatchewan Co-operative Wheat Producers would not attempt to market the 1923 crop, but would continue its organizational work with the aim of marketing the 1924 crop.

On August 17, Alberta Co-operative Wheat Producers was granted incorporation under the Alberta Co-operative Act.

On August 20, a two-week campaign to sign up farmers to pool contracts was begun. It was hoped that by September 5, 50% of the acreage sown to wheat would be under contract. Meetings were held throughout the Province but as it was harvest time and many farmers found it difficult to attend the meetings or else delayed signing the contract. Still, 45% of the wheat acreage was signed, and more contracts were coming in. It was decided to go ahead.

Operations of the Wheat Producers began October 9, 1923, when a delegation went to Winnipeg in an effort to reach agreement with the North-West Line Elevator Association on the matter of handling grain for the pool. This was not a successful meeting. However, in Alberta, United Grain Growers' and the Alberta Pacific Elevator Company did agree to handle pool grain.

On October 29, the Wheat Producers opened its first office, at Calgary, and put the pooling scheme into operation. Farmers were paid 75¢ per bushel (basis No. 1 Northern) on delivery to the elevator—an initial payment—with an interim payment to follow when substantial sales had been made, and a final payment after the year's sales and operations had concluded.

On November 13 and 14, delegates met for the first annual meeting of Alberta Co-operative Wheat Producers. There were 10 elected delegates from each of the 7 districts set up within the Provinces.

Sapiro, speaking to large and enthusiastic

Manitoba	Saskatchewan	Alberta

1923

audiences, had aroused much interest in the pooling plan among people of all walks of life and particularly among farmers. At a meeting of 3,500 people at Calgary, where he was introduced by the mayor of that city, he said:

" Alberta can be organized for a wheat pool in thirty days. ...I never saw a Province so ripe for it. Do this, men, and you are making the greatest contribution toward world freedom and in the right handling of the greatest commodity that has ever been."

It was Sapiro, too, who was responsible for outlining the program by which the pools of the three Provinces were organized.

300. Credit Union Concepts: The federal government appointed the President of the University of Alberta, Dr. Marshall Tory, to investigate the various systems for agricultural credit across Canada. In his report, Dr. Tory advised the government that:

" There can be no doubt that the establishment in Canada of a short term credit system based upon formation of local associations for co-operative purposes would be much more

difficult than for most European countries, or even in the U.S.A. ...Yet, I think...a sound plan along these lines could be worked out under proper supervision and control and, therefore, independence of the farmers themselves. ...I am further of the opinion that organization of this type of credit should be left to the Provinces..."

1924

301. Manitoba Co-operative Wheat Producers Formed: During the fall and winter the organizational committee formed in August 1923, prepared drafts of proposed articles of incorporation and bylaws for a Manitoba pool. The drafts were approved by the United Farmers of Manitoba. Application was then made for incorporation of the Manitoba Co-operative Wheat Producers Limited. Incorporation was granted on January 28, 1924.

Plans to organize the farmers were then launched. Sapiro was enlisted to speak at large gatherings held at Portage la Prairie, Brandon, Morden, Carman and Winnipeg.

302. Saskatchewan Co-operative Wheat Producers; In early 1924, the annual conventions of the Saskatchewan Grain Growers' and the United Farmers of Canada (Saskatchewan Section) were held. Both meetings called for the sign-up of pool members to be expedited. Sapiro was called back to address a further series of meetings and, when he had done so, the sign-up campaign was pursued with renewed vigor. By June 10, the campaign had succeeded with 6,247,086 acres being under contract making the Saskatchewan Co-op Wheat Producers the largest co-operative marketing organization in the world.

303. Alberta Co-operative Wheat Producers, first to market a crop under the pooling plan, had handled 25 million bushels for its members by the end of January, 1924.

By now the Pool had acquired seats on the Winnipeg Grain Exchange, the Clearing House, and Lake Shippers' Associations. Alberta Wheat Pool had also developed its own selling agency. As a result, the organization had quickly accumulated experience and know-how that was of valuable help to pools of the other two provinces.

1924

He was as successful as he had been in the other two provinces.

On March 10, immediately after Sapiro's visit, urgent steps were taken to get a sign-up campaign under way in hope that it would be possible for the Wheat Producers to market the 1924 crop. The goal was to sign up 1,000,000 acres by April 1st. By that deadline, 712,000 acres were signed up. Confident that the objective could be reached, the Wheat Producers launched a further campaign after spring seeding, and set the date for a general meeting at July 2 and 3. It was a successful effort.

Meanwhile, the Wheat Producers had taken steps to set up a democratic control structure. The Province was divided into 16 districts with 10 sub-districts each. One delegate was elected by pool members in each sub-district, with the 10 delegates electing a director for the district.

304. Canadian Co-operative Wheat Producers Formed: Before the Wheat Producers' (pools) of Alberta, Saskatchewan and Manitoba were formed, there was a question as to whether there should be a separate organization for each Province, or a single body serving in all three Provinces. The matter was resolved when it was decided that farmers of each Province should form their own pool and the three pools would co-ordinate and combine efforts for purposes of strategy and selling.

Directors of the three Wheat Producers' Co-operatives met on May 31, 1924, agreeing to form a central marketing association to serve the three pools. The new organization, Canadian Co-operative Wheat Producers was incorporated on August 6, 1924, under the federal Companies Act and held its organizational meeting on August 20, 1924. Each of the pools subscribed for $50,000 in shares of the central selling agency, and each named three members to its Board of Directors.

The Charter of Canadian Co-operative Wheat Producers described

its purposes as follows:

" To be an agricultural organization for the purpose of mutual help; to serve as the central marketing association for the three pools, but for no others; to reduce speculation, manipulation and waste of unnecessary transactions in such marketing; to increase consumption, build up new markets and develop new uses for grain; marketing same directly and with regularity so as to furnish it economically to the users thereof; and preserve to the growers and the public their proper profits and economies."

Their new organization had to act quickly to arrange for bank credits of $25,000,000 and otherwise prepare to handle the 1924 grain crop on behalf of the three pools. Valuable assistance was provided by the Alberta Co-operative Wheat Producers which turned over to CCWP seats held on the Winnipeg Grain Exchange, the Clearing House and Lake Shippers Association, together with its selling agency.

305. Manitoba Co-operative Poultry Marketing Association was formed and granted incorporation during 1924.

1925

306. Legislation: The Saskatchewan Co-operative Marketing Associations Act, passed by the Saskatchewan Legislature, provided for incorporation of co-operatives to market farm produce.

308. Central Alberta Dairy Pool was formed, serving producers of the central region of Alberta.

1925

309. Co-op Wholesale Desired: In December, the Souris local of the United Farmers of Manitoba held its annual meeting. Unanimous support was given to a resolution calling for the formation of a purchasing organization which would act as a central for locals which were involved in co-operative buying.

307. Saskatchewan Egg and Poultry Pool, incorporated under the new Co-operative Marketing Association Act, was formed with assistance by the Saskatchewan government which provided a grant of $10,000. This organization was similar to the Co-op Poultry Marketing Association which was formed in Manitoba during 1924.

310. United Grain Growers: A sawmill, erected by United Grain Growers in 1917, was destroyed by fire. It was decided that the mill should not be rebuilt, and the venture was abandoned.

311. Canadian Co-operative Wheat Producers reported on 1924 operations, indicating that 55 million bushels had been marketed on behalf of the three wheat pools. Farmers had received an initial payment of $1 per bushel (basis No. 1 Northern) from the pools. It was intended that an interim payment of 35 cents per bushel be made to farmers by late March, 1925. Before this interim payment was announced, however, grain prices began to decline from 2.17.87. on January 28 to $1.93 on March 1, and $1.72 by March

17. By April 3 the price had slipped to $1.36. The executive of Canadian Co-operative Wheat Producers then purchased large quantities of grain on the Chicago market for future delivery, causing prices on the Winnipeg Grain Exchange to quickly rise. The Wheat Producers' purchases were then sold at a profit and, more important, the action taken had served to stabilize the Canadian price for the benefit of farmers.

312. Elevator Problems: The Wheat Producers organizations of the three Prairie Provinces were formed for the purpose of marketing wheat in an orderly manner to achieve improved returns to farmer producers. The organizations were not begun primarily to operate country elevators but it was obvious that the two functions were interdependent. Existing at the time were the elevators owned by United Grain Growers', some locally-owned co-operative elevators, and the system of the Saskatchewan Co-operative

Elevator Company. These facilities were outnumbered by those of the line elevator companies. UGG, the Saskatchewan Co-operative Elevator Company, and some others, agreed to handle pool grains. But an obvious demand-supply problem emerged with respect to elevator space since the pools had signed up 50% of the acreage but had less than that proportion of the total elevator space at their disposal. Steps were needed to remedy the situation.

314. Manitoba Pool Elevators Limited was incorporated under Special Act of the Manitoba Legislature, April 9, to provide elevator services needed by the Manitoba Co-operative Wheat Producers.

The new organization, operating with funds provided by the Wheat Producers, was to build or buy elevator facilities. The elevators would be leased to local associations formed at points where farmers signed up to pool contracts representing at

315. Saskatchewan Pool Elevators Limited was incorporated early in 1925, as a subsidiary of the Saskatchewan Co-op Wheat Producers to provide the latter with elevator services and facilities. It was the policy to acquire elevators at points "where there was a minimum of 10,000 acres under contract to the pool, except at such points now served by one or other of the Farmer Elevator Companies." Where farmer-owned elevators already existed, it

313. Alberta Wheat Producers acted to secure elevator space by appointing an Elevator Committee with instructions to select 50 points at which elevators could be either built or purchased to advantage. The organization obtained its first elevator in the fall of 1925, at Leo, soon followed by others at Esther and Sedalia.

There was then a series of extensive discussions between the AWP and UGG, on proposals that the elevator facilities of the

1925

least 10,000 acres. The associations also had the option of purchasing the pool elevators.

was decided, SPE would not build an elevator unless there were 30,000 acres under contract. Construction was financed by a 2¢ deduction for each bushel handled.

two organizations be combined under a joint board. At times near agreement, the discussions failed to result in a mutually acceptable plan; hence, they were ended. At the time there were 979 country elevators at 406 Alberta shipping points, with UGG owning 185 of the elevators.

1925

316. Election of 1925: In the election of 1925, the Liberals, led by Mackenzie King, won fewer seats than did the Conservatives. However, Mackenzie King was able to obtain the support of Progressive Party and Labour Party members, convincing them that his Party was more sympathetic to their aims than was the Conservative Party. Thus, Mackenzie King was able to carry on with a minority government.

PROVINCE	LIB.	CONS.	PROG.	LABOR	INDEP.	TOTAL
Ontario	12	68	2			82
Quebec	60	4			1	65
Nova Scotia	3	11				14
New Brunswick	1	10				11
P.E.I.	2	2				4
Manitoba	1	7	7	2		17
Saskatchewan	15		6			21
Alberta	4	3	9			16
B.C.	3	10	1			14
Yukon		1				1
	101	116	25	2	1	245

317 Progressive Party Declines: As a result of its support of the Liberals in the House of Commons, the Progressive Party soon lost its identity and its initiative as a distinct political party. It was, in essence a repetition of the situation by which the Patrons' candidates were absorbed into the Liberal ranks. To the credit of the Progressives, however, is the fact that, through their actions, they had injected into the House of Commons more respect for the needs of the agricultural West, thereby providing a countervailing opinion against the commercial interests of Eastern Canada. In other words, the Progressives contributed to an improvement of democracy.

1926

319. Co-op Wholesale Desired: The resolution passed in 1925 by the Souris Local reached the annual meeting of United Farmers of Manitoba held January 13 in the city hall, Brandon. The meeting agreed that formation of a wholesale or purchasing agency to serve local associations should be considered and a committee to study that matter was formed.

Subsequently, there was another meeting held in 1926 in the Brandon city hall. The widely scattered "buying clubs" were invited to send representatives to this meeting at which definite steps were taken by appointing a committee which was instructed to obtain a Charter for a co-operative wholesale. This meeting was, it appears, arranged by an organization called The Manitoba Marketing Board of which very little is known.

318. Saskatchewan Co-op Wheat Producers, in annual meeting, heard reports that 50,202,599 bushels representing about 47% of Saskatchewan's 1924-25 crop, were handled by the pool. In some areas wheat had been marketed before the pool was able to accept deliveries. The reports also said that:

* Field men were making a check of growers signed to pool contracts who did not deliver grain to the pool during the past year.

* Arrangements had been made with publishers of **The Western Producer,** a farm journal, to place two pages at the disposal of the pool's publicity department.

* It had been necessary to build 52 new elevators and was found to be difficult to purchase elevators from Line com-

320. Alberta Pool Elevators Organized: Discussions between the Alberta Co-operative Wheat Producers and United Grain Growers on proposed joint ownership of elevators did not lead to agreement between the two organizations.

Alberta Co-op Wheat Producers then took steps to form a subsidiary, Alberta Pool Elevators, which was incorporated February 2, 1926, to provide elevator services for pool grain.

Alberta Pool Elevators took charge of 3 elevators already built by its parent co-operative and began the task of acquiring more. Capital for acquisition of elevators was provided by farmers through a deduction of 2¢ on each bushel handled plus 1% of the final price received on the sale of grain. In 1926-27, the pool elevator

1926

panies at a realistic price.

Efforts had been made to develop a closer relationship with Saskatchewan Co-op Elevator Company and United Grain Growers, both of which were handling grain through their elevators on behalf of the pool. It appears that some differences of opinion stood in the way of the desired close relationship. UGG, for example, considered that the building of elevators by the pool was an unnecessary duplication.

321. Saskatchewan Co-op Wheat Producers and Saskatchewan Co-op Elevator Company: The Saskatchewan Co-op Wheat Producers and its pooling system had diverted much of the interest of farmers away from the Saskatchewan Co-op Elevator Company, and some conflict of interest had developed between the two organizations.

At the Wheat Producers' annual meeting, delegates approved a proposal that their subsidiary, Saskatchewan Pool Elevators Limited, offer to buy out the Elevator Company. The subsequent offer was accepted by the elevator company with the price of $11,059,000 being reached by arbitration. The Pool thus became owner of another 451 elevators, bringing its total to 540 elevators plus four terminals.

company operated 42 elevators handling 5,274,000 bushels for an earning of $327,000.

322. United Grain Growers': While it had given strong financial and moral support to formation of the Wheat Producers' organizations, UGG had misgivings over the entry of the Producers into ownership of elevators. UGG's argument that unnecessary duplication of farmer-owned elevators was being created was interpreted in other circles as indicating opposition to the pools. On November 25, UGG was officially notified that the Co-operative Wheat Producers of Alberta, Saskatchewan and Manitoba were prepared to negotiate for the purchase of UGG's elevator system. At the UGG annual meeting in December, 41 resolutions on the matter were received with 19 in favor of selling the facilities to the pools. When the matter came to a vote, the proposed sale was turned down by a strong majority. However, unanimous approval was given to another resolution providing for UGG to assist the pools through other means including the leasing or sale of UGG elevators where necessary to avoid duplication of services at shipping points.

1926

323. Amalgamation To Form United Farmers of Canada (Saskatchewan Section): The Saskatchewan Grain Growers' Association begun in 1901, and the Farmers' Union of Canada formed in 1921, amalgamated to form a new organization known as United Farmers of Canada (Saskatchewan Section). The choice of a name for the new organization was influenced by a belief that it would soon become a Canada-wide movement with chapters in each of the provinces.

Inherited by the United Farmers of Canada (Saskatchewan Section) was the Trading Department set up by the Grain Growers' in 1914. This Department can be regarded as being a 'misfit' in the new organization which was not designed for commercial activity but as an educational body that would exert political influence on behalf of farmers.

324. Saskatchewan Co-op Livestock Producers Formed: A new organization to consolidate operations of many local co-operative livestock shipping associations existing in the Province, was formed. It was known as Saskatchewan Livestock Producers Limited, and incorporated under the Saskatchewan Co-operative Marketing Associations Act. The Saskatchewan Government assisted in the start of the Livestock Producers (otherwise known as the Saskatchewan Livestock Pool), by making a grant of $25,000.

325. General Election of 1926: Following the election of 1925, a report by a parliamentary committee charged that corruption was rampant within the Canada Customs Department, and that a massive two-way trade of smuggled goods was being carried on between Canada and the U.S. This was the era of prohibition in the United States when the sale of liquor was banned. The committee reported that the illegal trade was operating "not merely (with) the tacit connivance of a multitude of Customs officials but in many cases their active co-operation in making a wholesale mockery of the Customs laws of Canada." Fearing withdrawal of Progressive support, Mackenzie King resigned and Arthur Meighen, Conservative leader, was asked to form a government. Meighen counted on support of the Progressives, but was defeated in the House over a constitutional technicality so that he too, had to resign. An election

1926

was then called, and another majority government placed into office, led by Mackenzie King.

Of special interest in this election was the entry of candidates by the United Farmers of Alberta who won a majority of the seats in that Province.

PROVINCE	LIB.	CONS.	U.F.A.	PROG.	LIB. PROB.	LABOR	INDEP.	TOTAL
Ontario	23	53		4	2			82
Quebec	60	2					1	65
Nova Scotia	2	12						14
New Brunswick	4	7						11
P.E.I.	3	1						4
Manitoba	4			4	7	2		17
Saskatchewan	16			5				21
Alberta	3	1	11			1		16
British Columbia	1	12					1	14
	116	91	11	13	9	3	2	245

61

1926

1927 to 1941

CHAPTER VIII
CO-OPERATION DIVERSIFIES—1927 TO 1941

326. Before moving into the next chapter, let us ponder for a moment, on the formation of the wheat pools in the mid-1920's, and the earlier complaints of farmers which led to the passage of the Manitoba Grain Act in 1900, the formation of the Grain Growers' Grain Company, the Growers' Associations, and Co-operative Elevator systems. Were these complaints and actions on the part of farmers justified, or did they merely reflect non-rational, emotional feelings aroused by difficulties for which the farmers themselves were at least partly to blame?

The answer to the question is yes, the farmers did have just cause for complaint over their subordination by the grain trade. The justification was firmly established by Royal Commissions as well as by the farmers themselves. The farmers expected only fair treatment, but, instead, they were exploited. Their only means of relieving themselves from an unjust predicament was to create organizations owned by themselves to act for them in the assembly and marketing of grain. In other words, the farmers found it necessary to seek independence from an oligarchy.

Fifty years after the wheat pools were formed, evidence of the worth of orderly marketing and co-operative intervention in the grain business was provided by reports from the United States. In that country, in 1975, according to **The Chicago Tribune**, a "scandalous" situation existed in the grain business, involving mixing and blending of grades, 'shaving' of shipments, short weighing of farmers' deliveries, and other practices curbed by farmers of the Canadian Prairies through their co-operatives and their demand for orderly marketing. The story published by **The Chicago Tribune**, June 29, 1975, is reprinted herein as Appendix B.

The wheat pools that had by now been formed, had as their aim an orderly marketing system under the direct control of farmers. The collapse of the economy in 1929, followed by the Great Depression of the 1930's—a depression made worse on the Prairies by prolonged drought and grasshopper plagues—diverted the pools, from their aim of building an orderly marketing system. The pools like the co-operative creameries, were severely injured by the rapid fall of prices in 1929. Provincial governments, aware of the value of these farmer-owned organizations, averted their demise by extending loans and guarantees of loans, all of which were repaid.

The federal government, in 1935, restored orderly marketing by setting up the Canadian Wheat Board, an institution which was given full support by the pools.

Meanwhile, farmers turned to other co-operative ventures. In all three Prairie Provinces, embryo co-operative wholesales were set up by 1929 to serve consumer-owned retail co-operatives which, for the most part, existed in agricultural communities. Of great importance to the co-op wholesales and retail co-ops, was the outstanding success of the farmer-owned Consumers' Co-operative Refineries begun in 1934-35. Its success provided great encouragement for the formation of many more retail co-operatives.

But in the Great Depression era, the start of the Co-op Refinery was not the only major co-operative advance. Of equal importance was the provision of legislation by all three Provinces, for incorporation of credit unions and caisses populaires. In essence, the two serve the same function—that of encouraging thrift among members, and of providing members with loans at reasonable interest.

Caisses Populaires are credit unions designed to serve French-speaking members. In Manitoba, in particular, formation of caisses populaires was fostered in French Catholic villages by the clergy. One purpose was to help the people of the parishes to overcome their social and economic problems. Another was to provide French-speaking institutions that would help French people to retain their cultural and religious heritage.

The credit union movement, on the other hand, developed in answer to the need of farmers for credit. A farmer is never certain what his year's income will be, for it depends upon weather conditions and marketing conditions and prices, matters beyond his control. And, as they say, farmers have but one 'pay day' each year, so that it is often necessary for them to resort to credit in order to buy machinery or plant the next crop. Thus, short-term credit is a great farm need.

And so is long-term credit. When establishing a farm or purchasing more land, farmers must finance the cost of building homes, barns, and other facilities, as well as the cost of their holdings. This involves long-term mortgage loans.

In his book, **Conflict and Co-operation**, Norm Bromberger has noted that, "In 1931, the majority of farm mortgage loans in the Prairies, totalling an estimated 650 million dollars, were held by Canadian life insurance, trust and loan companies, as well as private individuals. Most of the corporate mortgage lenders were

Manitoba	Saskatchewan	Alberta

1927 to 1941

Eastern concerns." The Depression, crop failures, and low prices for agricultural production, made the farmers a poor mortgage risk, hence prudent business practise curtailed this source of credit."

An alternate source of credit was the banks, but as Bromberger points out, "By law, the banks could not make loans on the security of land or buildings in the first instance. Therefore, they were short-term lenders. Consequently they held only about 7.4 per cent, or 48 million dollars, of the total Prairie farm debt in 1931. The experience of all commercial lenders with the cyclic nature of the agricultural economy tended to raise interest rates in the Prairies from 1 to 3 per cent higher than for similar kinds of loans in Ontario. Whether those higher interest rates were legitimate or not, they aroused considerable resentment among Prairie people. By law,

bank loan interest rates were limited to 7 per cent, but in practise, actual rates were 9 per cent to 10 per cent."

In addition to the restriction on bank services to farmers, further problems arose as the banks, faced with need to economize during the Depression years, closed out their branches in many agricultural communities. In Saskatchewan alone, Bromberger says, the number of branches operated by chartered banks was cut by almost 50%—from 447 to 233.

Thus, the need for agricultural credit, coupled with knowledge obtained elsewhere that provided convincing evidence of the value of credit unions as a means by which people could solve their own financial problems, led to the enactment of Credit Union legislation in 1937.

1927

327. Co-op Wholesale Proposed: A proposal that the Trading Department of the United Farmers of Canada (Saskatchewan Section) be linked up with interested bodies of Manitoba and Alberta "in a vast wholesaling scheme", was considered at a conference held at Regina early in 1927. According to the

proposal, Davidson, Saskatchewan, would be chosen as a central distributing point for all locals served, with the cost of freight from Davidson to destination being equalized. Although the proposal was not acted upon at the time it was nevertheless a vision of co-operative wholesaling of the future.

328. Co-op Wholesale: The Manitoba Marketing Board organized a conference held March 1 at Brandon. The committee formed in 1926 to take steps for formation of a co-operative wholesale reported on its work. A report was also given on the proposal that the UFC trading department be expanded to serve Manitoba and Alberta. Attending this conference were representatives of 13 co-operative trading societies of Manitoba. It was decided by the meeting that a co-operative wholesale should be formed within Manitoba.

331. Manitoba Co-operative Wholesale: As a result of the March 1 meeting at Brandon, a new organization, Manitoba Co-operative Wholesale, was incorporated on November 17 under the Manitoba Co-operatives Act. Its initial purpose was to pool the purchasing of retailing co-operatives so as to obtain larger discounts and more favorable prices.

329. SGGS - FUC Merger Officially Approved: By an Act of the provincial legislature on February 7, the merger of Saskatchewan Grain Growers' and Farmers' Union of Canada to form United Farmers of Canada (Saskatchewan Section) became official.

At the time, UFC was said to have a membership of 23,500 farmers organized into 900 lodges throughout the province. More than 1,500 delegates attended the first UFC annual convention held at Moose Jaw in the month of March. Only members were admitted to the convention which was held behind closed doors.

332. Co-op Wholesale: United Farmers of Canada (Saskatchewan Section), **The Grain Growers' Guide** said in an editorial, was seeking to bring together "the co-operative stores, the Trading Department of the UFC, and its own trading units, for the purpose of establishing a co-operative

330. Credit Union Formed: At Killam, the manager of the Killam Co-operative Association, William Halsall, initiated steps to set up a credit union. There was no legislation providing for incorporation of credit unions, hence the new venture was set up as a savings and loan department of the Killam Co-operative's store to serve the members of that association and to reduce need for the co-operative to sell on credit. This pioneer Alberta credit union service, operated according to Desjardins concepts, was continued until 1933.

1927

wholesale. At a meeting of the Canadian Club, the president of the United Farmers of Canada (Saskatchewan Section), spoke on co-operative buying. He said his organization's aim was to develop co-operative retail stores and trading units, and to link them together "to increase their buying power and return to patrons all the surplus over the actual cost of administration."

333. Manitoba Livestock Pool: A new co-operative, Manitoba Livestock Pool, was organized. Its purpose was similar to that of the Saskatchewan Livestock Producers formed in 1926, being that of providing a system for province-wide assembly and shipping of livestock to a producer-owned selling agency.

334. Dairy Co-operative Marketing Association: Within the Saskatoon milk shed, the Dairy Co-operative Marketing Association, otherwise known as the Dairy Pool, was organized. It was in answer to an acute problem resulting from the production of milk in surplus quantities. The Dairy Pool soon expanded its area of activities to include the milk sheds of North Battleford and Prince Albert.

335. Technological Change: In the early pioneering days, teams of oxen were often used to draw implements for tilling the soil. As time went on, oxen gave way to horses and, in many instances, to steam engines. By now, however, tractors and trucks were rapidly increasing in a number of prairie farms. Unlike the horse for which fodder could be grown on the farmstead, the new means of power and transport required fuel that had to be bought. In a good number of communities, farmers began to club together, on an informal basis, to buy petroleum in sizeable quantities at wholesale prices. They were following methods that had previously been used to buy lumber, twine, and other commodities by the carlot. The Board of Transport Commissioners took note of the farmers' petroleum-handling activities, and ruled that the unloading of petroleum into drums on the railway property was a fire hazard. New regulations were introduced, limiting the handling of petroleum on railway property to those who had set up proper storage facilities. Farmers who had been clubbing together were either forced to cease their petroleum operations, or to comply with regulations by establishing acceptable bulk petroleum plants.

336. Petroleum Co-ops: At Oakville, farmers formed a co-operative for the purpose of providing a petroleum service that would comply with regulations. The Oakville Co-operative Oil & Supplies Association was the first of a number of co-ops to be formed for the handling of petroleum. Between 1927 and 1930, 23 such associations were begun by Manitoba farmers.

63

1927

337. Canadian Livestock Co-operatives: At a meeting of the Saskatchewan and Manitoba Livestock Producers' Associations, attended by representatives of Alberta livestock producers, steps were taken to create a central livestock selling agency to serve producers of the three Provinces. This organization was known as Canadian Livestock Co-operative (Western) Limited.

1928

338. Legislation: The Agricultural Co-operative Associations Act of 1913 enabled farmers who were members of Saskatchewan Grain Growers' to form co-operative trading societies. In 1922, the Act was amended to enable all farmers to form such societies. In 1928, it was again amended to permit any group, whether farmers or not, to form co-operatives. The legislation was then named The Co-operative Associations Act.

339. Alberta Pool Elevators, in a vigorous effort, increased the number of its country elevators from 162 to 317 during the 1928-29 crop year.

In addition, construction was begun on a terminal elevator at Vancouver. The Alberta Pool, being closest to the Western seaboard, had focused in that direction while the pools of Manitoba and Saskatchewan exported most of their handling via the Lakehead and Eastern ports.

340. Canadian Pool Agencies Limited: The three provincial wheat pool organizations, formed a jointly-owned organization, Canadian Pool Agencies Limited, to handle and serve their insurance requirements.

341. United Grain Growers, at its annual meeting held on November 14, 1928, reported handlings for 1927-1928 of 41,233,000 bushels. Surpluses earned, which were subject to income tax, amounted to $715,000. A patronage dividend to customers, in the amount of $115,000 was paid, and shareholders received a dividend on shares of 8 per cent. The organization was operating many elevators and other facilities which, broken down by provinces, included the following:

MANITOBA: 122 country elevators, 1 annex, 62 flour sheds, 60 coal sheds.

SASKATCHEWAN: 120 country elevators, 4 annexes, 35 flour sheds, 69 coal sheds.

ALBERTA: 218 country elevators, 35 annexes, 141 flour sheds, 132 coal sheds.

343. Petroleum Co-ops: Across the province, a gasoline price war broke out. In Winnipeg, prices dropped by 3 cents a gallon. In some southern areas of the province, prices were cut by as much as 5 cents.

The press, in feature stories on the price war, said there were two causes: First, it was due to the growth of co-operative buying of petroleum amongst farmers who had formed more than 70 co-ops to supply petroleum products. Secondly, there were rumors that the petroleum market was to be invaded by a number of new companies. The event added to farmers'

342. Saskatchewan Co-operative Council: In 1928, a body known as the Saskatchewan Co-operative Council, was formed to provide a means of liaison, co-ordination, and possibly education, among and between the various co-operative organizations of the Province.

344. United Farmers of Canada: An invitation to become a member of the Canadian Council of Agriculture was declined by the United Farmers of Canada (Saskatchewan Section). The UFC advised that it desired to remain aloof from commercial activity hence could not join the Canadian Council of Agriculture which

1928

suspicions that petroleum prices were higher than necessary.

347. Manitoba Co-op Wholesale: A progress report to the annual convention of United Farmers of Manitoba said that associations at Lauder, Killarney, Elgin, Minto and Hartney had already joined Manitoba Co-operative Wholesale, and others were expected to do so. By the end of 1928, MCW had a membership of 32 associations.

1929

348. Manitoba Co-operative Wholesale, reporting in January, said that 32 associations were now signed up as members. The members had subscribed $2,000 in MCW shares but had only paid up $610.

Eleven new members were oil co-ops. Some locals had coal sheds, and one had a flour shed. An average local had 116 members.

On February 28, MCW opened its first office at 460 Main Street, Winnipeg, with a staff of two—the president and a secretary. Arrangements were made with a Minneapolis firm for the supply of petroleum fuels and oils.

In effort to provide a source of income to defray operating costs, MCW set up a small printing department. It was hoped that the department would serve other central co-ops as well as MCW members. However, other printing plants soon cut prices in order to win back business that had been diverted to MCW.

was comprised largely of members and organizations engaged in that kind of activity.

345. Co-operative Wholesale: At annual convention held in Third Avenue United Church, Saskatoon, February 29, United Farmers of Canada (Saskatchewan Section) considered the matter of forming a co-operative wholesale. It was proposed that the UFC's Trading Department, begun in 1914, be the nucleus of the new organization. Definite action was taken with the appointment of a committee of 9 members—3 of them from co-operative retailing associations—to act as a provisional board that would proceed with organizational plans.

The committee acted quickly with the result that a co-operative wholesale, the Saskatchewan Wholesale Society, was incorporated under the Companies Act of Saskatchewan, July 30, 1928. Further pertinent steps took place early in 1929.

346. Alberta Co-operative Wholesale Association (ACWA): At Killam, representatives of 9 co-operative associations of nearby communities met to discuss a proposal that an organization be set up to pool the purchasing power of their associations for better discounts and lower prices. The proposal was accepted, and the Alberta Co-operative Wholesale Association incorporated on March 10. The Association set up its first office in the premises of the Killam Co-operative.

1929

349. Saskatchewan Co-operative Wholesale Society (SCWS): Saskatchewan Wholesale Society, incorporated under the Companies Act in 1928, was incorporated by a Special Act of Saskatchewan Legislature under the name, Saskatchewan Co-operative Wholesale Society, on February 2,1929.

SCWS assumed the operations and the assets of the Trading Department of the UFC (Saskatchewan Section). SCWS also assumed the liabilities of the Department, imposing upon itself a substantial burden of debt. The accounts receivable included in the assets were of doubtful value for many accounts were old and impossible to collect.

At the start, 29 co-operative associations joined SCWS, each subscribing to a $100 share. Net capital available to begin operations was $4,700.

351. Politics: A small group of trade unionists and teachers, most of them from urban centres, formed the Independent Labor Party of Saskatchewan. The party soon developed connections in many towns and cities of the Province although it did not acquire a large number of members.

350. Alberta Wheat Pool: The Alberta Co-operative Wheat Producers formed in 1923, had always been referred to as "the pool". After Alberta Pool Elevators had been organized in 1926 as a subsidiary to the Wheat Producers, the name of the parent organization became even more obscure. By popular request, the name of the organization was changed by an Act of the Alberta legislature, to Alberta Wheat Pool.

352. Hudson's Bay Railway: After nearly 50 years of agitation, promises and expectations, a railway line at last reached the shores of Hudson's Bay. The erection of a terminal elevator of 2-million bushels capacity then began. Though the movement of grain through the Port of Churchill on the Hudson's Bay did not begin until 1931, promotion of the Port was immediately begun. A ton or more of wheat, in two-pound bags, was carried by the railway to the new port. It was then loaded on a ship of the Hudson's Bay Company, S.S. Nascopie, for delivery as souvenirs to European grain buyers.

353. Canadian Co-operative Wheat Producers, acing as the central selling agency for the three prairie pools, handled 51.55% of the total Prairie wheat crop. The volume was an evidence that farmers had recognized the value of the pooling system for marketing grain. As will be shown, however, serious problems were not far ahead.

354. Great Depression Begins: On Tuesday, October 29, the bottom fell out of the New York stock market, creating financial havoc, and starting the Great Depression that was to last for a decade. The consequences of the Depression were severe and

1929

miserable, affecting not only millions of people in North America, but the people and economies of nations all around the world. Countless numbers became unemployed, making it necessary for governments to undertake massive programs to provide welfare or "relief".

The already difficult conditions on the Prairies were made even more desperate by drought. In the early years of the 1930's, rainfall was sparse if it came at all. Crops could not be grown. As the cultivated land dried out, Prairie winds created blinding dust storms that left "snowdrifts" of topsoil. Then came the grasshopper plague to further darken skies and hopes, and to destroy what grain could be grown. Misery, poverty and despair thrust their savage way into every corner.

During this terrible era, many farmers from the Great Plains were attracted to the Peace River area of Northern Alberta, an area that

had not yet been greatly settled and was not affected by the drought. At this point, the growth of population and number of farms in rural areas of the Prairie Provinces came to a halt, then commenced to decline. As statistics reveal, the decline began between the 1932 and 1936 census years.

The 'Dirty Thirties' as the decade was called, affected farm organizations and co-operatives. Some organizations suffered severe setbacks. Others thrived because desperate farmers made determined efforts to help them succeed. Among the latter were consumer co-operatives. In many rural communities, merchants were encouraged by the declining population and economic difficulty to either sell or abandon their enterprises. The attraction the communities had once held for private capital had vanished. Many co-ops stores were begun to provide local services that were no longer available.

1930

355. Wheat Pools Suffer Setback: In preparation for the 1929 crop, the wheat pools in each of the three provinces borrowed funds from banks to finance an initial payment of $1 per bushel to farmers delivering to pool elevators. The 1929 crop was sparse in many

areas, much of the scarcity being caused by drought. With prospects of a light harvest, wheat prices began to rise, justifying the proposed initial payment of $1 per bushel basis No. 1 Northern. But after the New York stock market crash of October 29, prices for

1930

all commodities tumbled. The price for No. I Northern wheat fell to 85 cents a bushel—15 cents less than the initial payment by the pools. The pools were in a difficult financial position for they owed money to the banks and had overpaid farmers as follows:

Alberta	$ 5,649,000
Saskatchewan	13,300,000
Manitoba	3,375,000
	$ 22,324,000

Fortunately, governments of all three Provinces came to the assistance of the pools, guaranteeing payment of the loans from the banks and providing loans to enable the pools to continue operations. All obligations to the governments were repaid by the pools by the late 1940's.

1930

356. Canadian Council of Agriculture: When the Canadian Council of Agriculture met at Prince Albert, there were serious differences of opinion as to how to cope with the grave situation in agriculture being caused by the Great Depression. On a note of grave disharmony, the organization ceased to function.

357. Canada Grain Act: The Canada Grain Act was completely written. It now provided for a Board of Grain Commissioners to be appointed, each for a 10-year term. The Act also established new grading and sampling standards, inspection and weighing procedures, and rules governing movement of grain by railway and by boat.

358. Income Tax: The War Income Tax Act of 1917 was amended to exempt from the tax, co-operatives which either:

(a) Market products for members on a basis by which members receive full proceeds from the sale less necessary expenses and reserves; or

(b) Purchase supplies and equipment for members and provide them at cost plus necessary expenses and reserves.

The amendments also provided that co-operatives could serve non-members on condition that the services to non-members did not exceed 20% of a given association's total transactions.

The amendments were in response to many resolutions by co-operatives, and to the request of a delegation which had asked that the terms of the Act, insofar as they were intended to apply to co-operatives, be clarified beyond doubt. The matter had seemed to be clarified back in 1917 when the Commissioner of Taxation stated, by letter, that patronage refunds were exempt from tax. However, a number of producer co-operatives had nevertheless received tax assessment notices. The co-operatives drew attention of the Canadian Government to the fact that in Britain patronage refunds, or savings to members, were not taxed. The British government had adopted a ruling of the House of Lords, which defined co-operative savings as different to net income derived from the public by profit-seeking enterprise.

359. Manitoba Co-op Wholesale had already closed down the printing plant begun in 1929. The venture had incurred a deficit of $5,000.

Affected by the Depression, MCW, its retail co-operatives, and farmers generally, had strong need for borrowing capital. The banks, however, declined to extend credit on the modest assets of the wholesale. MCW directors solved the problem and demonstrated their faith in MCW by individually signing guarantees and pledging their homes and personal property as security for a loan of $15,000 to MCW.

MCW sales in 1930 reached $334,000. The organization moved to a larger office at 316 McIntyre Block, Winnipeg.

360. Saskatchewan Co-op Wholesale sales to members reached $586,000.

361. Alberta Co-op Wholesale, like the pools, was placed in a dire predicament by the effects of the Depression. ACWA had contracted to purchase a large quantity of lumber at a fixed price. But when the Depression set in and lumber prices fell, ACWA's contract price was more than the current retail selling price. ACWA's supplies could only be sold at a loss, a situation that put the organization heavily in debt and quickly insolvent.

ACWA, with 1930 sales of $62,000, was not a large organization and could not absorb the deficit resulting from the lumber venture.

362. Co-operation Between Wholesales: Meeting in November, representatives of the Alberta, Saskatchewan and Manitoba co-op wholesales, discussed possibilities for joint purchasing arrangements. A plan for co-ordination in the purchasing of some commodities was adopted.

1930

363. **Politics:** At a February convention, United Farmers of Canada (Saskatchewan Section) voted in favor of political action. As a result, the Farmers Political Association was formed some weeks later, to contest the 1930 federal election. The FAA was supported by the Independent Labor Party formed in 1929, but was not successful in the election.

364. **Legislation**: The government of Alberta established a Co-operative Activities Branch to incorporate, assist and supervise co-operatives operating under provincial legislation.

365. **General Election of 1930:** The disastrous state of the economy caused by the Great Depression was the issue for the election campaign of 1930. Before the election was called, the Conservatives were demanding that the Liberal Government take action to relieve the acute unemployment situation, and to financially assist the provinces, which, particularly in the West, were made financially desperate. In the heat of debate, Prime Minister King implied that he would consider assistance to the Provinces but stated he had not a "five-cent piece" for a province that happened to have a Conservative government. The new leader of the Conservatives, Calgary lawyer and millionaire R.B. Bennett, did not forget King's "five-cent piece" during the election campaign. He led his party through a determined and often boisterous campaign, promising to turn Canada toward prosperity

1930

by raising tariffs to protect Canadian industry, boosting foreign trade, putting men back to work, and giving help to the provinces.

As often happens when the economy slumps, the government changed hands:

PROVINCE	CONS.	LIB.	UNITED FARMERS	PROG.	LIB. PROG.	LABOR	INDEP. LABOR	INDEP.	TOTAL
Ontario	59	22	1						82
Quebec	24	40						1	65
Nova Scotia	10	4							14
New Brunswick	10	1							11
P.E.I.	3	1							4
Manitoba	11	1			3	2			17
Saskatchewan	8	11		2					21
Alberta	4	3	9						16
B.C.	7	5					1	1	14
Yukon	1								1
	137	88	10	2	3	2	1	2	245

1931

366. Canadian Co-operative Wheat Products: The Board of Canadian Co-operative Wheat Producers met at Winnipeg. The main item on the agenda was the future of their organization and of the pooling system. A course of action was difficult to define under the pessimistic conditions of the time. The Great Depression was taking a further toll, causing grain prices to slide downhill. Also affecting prices and future prospects was the fact that wheat was in surplus supply on world markets. A still further concern was the burden of debt incurred by the pools as a result of the 1929 overpayment of cash advances to farmers.

Confronted by uncertainty and by ridiculously low grain prices, the Board decided that the pooling plan should be suspended for the time being, and that each of the three pools should continue to handle grain through its elevators, and market the grain through the Winnipeg Grain Exchange. The farmers were, therefore, released from their pooling contracts. But not all farmers agreed that the pooling operation should be dropped, so a voluntary pool was then established by each of the three provincial organizations for those who desired to use it. The initial price for 1931-32 wheat was set at 35 cents per bushel.

367. Wheat Producers Attacked: A series of unfounded and malicious rumours concerning the Canadian Co-operative Wheat Producers began to circulate. According to the rumours, the organization, the central selling agency of the three provincial

pools, was disbanded. Simultaneously, a publication known as **The Grain Trade News** carried a series of articles attacking the wheat pools. The articles, reprinted in leaflet form, were widely circulated, even being distributed in schools.

368. Manitoba Co-op Wheat Produ-cers: A prominent member of the grain trade publicly denounced the Manitoba Co-operative Wheat Producers, charging the organization with mismanagement, over-expansion of its elevator system, and other faults. In March, the Manitoba government appointed a Royal Commission to enquire into the charges against

1931

the Manitoba pool. The Commission reported agreement with three charges but not with a fourth charge against the pool. Circumstances since proved that the Commission was in error when supporting the charges.

369. Saskatchewan Co-op Wheat Producers' directors were convinced that the voluntary pooling plan proposed by Canadian Co-op Wheat Producers could succeed only if given 100% support by farmers. This view was shared by United Farmers of Canada (Saskatchewan Section), and a campaign for a 100% pool was begun. As a result, a plebiscite was held in which 32,653 farmers voted in favor of the 100% pool and 12,991 against. The Provincial government then passed legislation for a 100% pool but it was challenged and the courts declared it to be ultra vires. In opposition to a 100% pool was an organization known as The Association Opposing Compulsory Pool. It was said that this organization sought to destroy the Saskatchewan Co-op Wheat Producers and reestablish the Saskatchewan Co-op Elevator Company which the Producers had taken over in 1926.

370. Alberta Wheat Pool did not favor the 100% compulsory pool that was sought by the Saskatchewan Co-op Wheat Producers. However, farmers of Alberta were given an opportunity to decide the matter for themselves. By vote, 3,391 farmers expressed favor for the 100% pool plan, while 4,238 rejected it.

371. Manitoba Pool Elevators: In the wake of the enquiry into the operations of Manitoba Co-op Wheat Producers, a major re-organization took place. On August 1, Manitoba Pool Elevators Limited, previously a subsidiary of Manitoba Co-op Wheat Producers, became the dominating company, operating a grain handling service on behalf of the local co-operative elevator associations of the Province.

372. Saskatchewan Co-op Wheat Producers became the owner and publisher of **The Western Producer** by acquiring the organization which had been producing that farm journal, Modern Press Limited, of Saskatoon, as a subsidiary.

373. Hudson's Bay Railway: In August the first commercial cargo of export grain shipped through the Port of Churchill was loaded aboard the S. S. Farnworth. The railway, terminal elevator, and harbor had been completed.

374. Manitoba Co-op Wholesale was actively assisting farmers to organize more petroleum co-ops, and was purchasing fuels and lubricants on behalf of the co-ops while assisting in other ways such as setting up uniform accounting systems. It was noted that 21 local petroleum co-ops had realized, in 1930, savings averaging 5.89%. MCW's sales of all products in

375. Saskatchewan Co-op Wholesale Society with staff consisting of a manager, a bookkeeper, and two stenographers, was purchasing some petroleum fuels for local petroleum co-ops. Many of these associations were not members of the SCWS at the time. The wholesale had an inventory of overalls and shirts, most of doubtful value, inherited from the Trading

376. United Farmers of Alberta noted that a number of its locals were handling farm supplies, and some had provided leadership for the start of local co-operative associations.

Manitoba	Saskatchewan	Alberta

1931

1931, were $274,321, about $60,000 less than in 1930 due to the adverse economic conditions.

Department of the UFC (Saskatchewan Section).

The Wholesale attempted to interest Saskatchewan Co-op Wheat Producers in joint distribution of bulk goods but the offer was declined.

377. Petroleum Co-ops: At farmers' meetings mounting interest in petroleum co-ops was evident. Farmers regarded fuel prices as being too high, and noted that, while prices of nearly all commodities had declined, petroleum prices remained stubbornly firm. A number of new petroleum co-ops were formed. At least one such association was importing fuel from Tulsa, Oklahoma, achieving savings of as much as 13 cents per gallon.

378. Saskatchewan Co-op Creamery, like many other enterprises at the time, was a victim of the Great Depression. The organization was forced into receivership but was rescued by the Provincial Government which then assumed responsibility for financially assisting and managing the organization.

379. Politics: Leaders of the United Farmers of Canada (Saskatchewan Section) and of the Independent Labor Party formed in 1929, agreed to collaborate to form a large farmer-labor party. A number of meetings of farmers and workers were held. Eventually, these events led to the formation of the C.C.F. Party (Co-operative Commonwealth Federation) in Saskatchewan.

1932

380. Wheat Prices Tumble: The Canadian Press, in a report dated December 16, 1932, told a grim story of declining wheat prices:

"Crushed under five days of falling prices, wheat sold on the Winnipeg market today cheaper than any records show it selling since it was first introduced on this continent by the Spaniards 400

1932

years ago. Number 1 Northern, as fine a wheat as is grown in quantity anywhere, dropped to 38 cents a bushel basis Fort William. . ." (Fort William now known as Thunder Bay since amalgamation of the twin cities of Fort William and Port Arthur).

381. Manitoba Wheat Pool Bankrupt: On November 5, Manitoba Wheat Pool was declared to be bankrupt but carried on with the aid of the Manitoba Government.

In the 1931-32 crop year, the first since reorganization, the Manitoba Pool served 151 local Elevator Associations which were operating 154 elevators. The local associations were autonomous units which in turn owned the central organization, Manitoba Pool Elevators Limited. Of the 151 local associations, 30 were able to meet all commitments and achieve a surplus, repayable to farmer members, of $21,936.

382. Co-operative Abbatoir: At Saskatoon, long-standing demands by livestock producers resulted in establishment of a small co-operative abbatoir. Some custom slaughtering was done for private packers, but the co-operative was not able to develop markets for its own supplies mainly because there was not a regular supply of stock delivered to the plant and markets were strongly served by the major meat packing concerns with which the co-operative had to compete.

383. United Farmers of Alberta Central Co-operative: In response to demands of its locals, United Farmers of Alberta set up, as a wholly-owned subsidiary, UFA Central Co-operative, to perform buying on behalf of the members and the local co-operative associations which they had formed. The latter were eventually disbanded as members and UFA locals diverted their purchasing to the UFA Central Co-operative.

Farmers could join the new organization by acquiring one $5 share. Farm supply depots began to appear in a number of communities, offering UFA members a wide range of farm and automotive hardware, lumber, building supplies, coal, etc.

384. Petroleum Co-ops: The Canadian government imposed a gallonage tax on imported petroleum fuels. The Prime Minister of Canada at that time was a former legal counsel for a major oil company. He said the new tax was intended as a means of encouraging development of the Canadian oil industry. Some such development took place about this time, as a number of small, independent petroleum refineries appeared in the three Prairie Provinces. They were encouraged by the prevailing price of petroleum and the protection against imports provided by the new tax. Moreover, price competition was not great since all refineries generally followed price structure of the major companies. The gallonage tax, however, drastically cut the savings which petroleum co-ops had achieved by importing fuel from the U.S.A.

385. Co-ops and Coal: For many years farmers had clubbed together to buy coal by the carlot. When the car arrived at the railway siding, the farmers unloaded it, each taking his share home by wagon. During the Great Depression many farmers—up to 80% at times, it is said—depended upon government relief (welfare) for sustenance, and had to purchase their coal supplies with relief orders (vouchers).

Coal dealers resented efforts of the farmers and enlisted The Retail Merchants' Association to act on their behalf. The

386. Legislation: The Co-operative Associations Act of 1913, was repealed by the Manitoba legislature. In its place, provision was made for the incorporation of co-operative societies under a special section of the Manitoba Companies Act.

1932

Association influenced the Saskatchewan government to adopt a rule that allowed coal to be distributed only by dealers who operated coal sheds. As the co-operating farmers did not operate such sheds, the co-ops were struck off the list of those authorized to accept relief orders for coal.

387. Politics: At a convention held at Calgary in August, leaders of Saskatchewan's UFC-LIP political party formed in 1931, together with representatives of the United Farmers of Alberta and Manitoba, plus delegates from labor and socialist parties, met together. Some members of Parliament also attended the convention which resolved to form a national political party known as the Co-operative Commonwealth Federation (CCF).

1933

388. Politics: The CCF Party, born at Calgary in 1932, held its first national convention in July at Regina. The convention drew up a lengthy list of goals which became known as the "Regina Manifesto."

389 Politics: On November 2 and 3, the United Farmers of Manitoba met in an annual convention at Portage la Prairie. Speaking to the meeting was J.S. Woodsworth who appealed for affiliation of the UFM with the new CCF party. The appeal was not accepted by the majority, but about 30 UFM delegates stayed for the

390. Credit Union Legislation: At the Congress of the Co-operative Union of Canada, held at Regina, the Provincial Government was urged to provide legislation for the incorporation of credit unions. In response, the Co-operation and Markets Branch of the Department of Agriculture began a study of the matter of co-operative

1933

first annual convention of the Manitoba 4. Elected as provincial CCF President was Jock Brown who later was to abandon the political arena to become president of a farmer-owned machinery co-operative, Canadian Co-operative Implements.

credit. The study led to the enactment of credit union legislation in 1937.

391. Co-ops and Coal: The regulations imposed by the Saskatchewan Government in 1932 prevented many local co-ops from handling coal.

The Saskatchewan Co-op Wholesale Society acted by introducing a plan by which local coal sheds could be built at points where 30 or more farmers subscribed to $5 shares. Each farmer was expected to put up at least $1 toward his share, but could build up the balance of his $5 requirement through patronage refunds earned on coal purchases. Thus, terms of the Government regulations were complied with as sheds were erected. Many sheds were built beside Pool elevators where they were operated by the elevator agent who received 25 cents per ton for his efforts. The Retail Merchants then directed their effort to persuading mine owners not to sell to co-ops.

392. Co-ordination: Delegates to the annual meeting of the Saskatchewan Co-op Wheat Producers carried a resolution in favor of close co-operation between their organization and the Saskatchewan Co-op Wholesale.

393. Petroleum Co-ops: With U.S. fuel supplies shut off by the gallonage tax imposed in 1932, local petroleum co-ops turned to domestic sources for their petroleum. Some savings were still realized by the co-ops. However, these savings were practically eliminated when the major oil companies increased wholesale prices but made no change in retail price levels. The petroleum co-ops then turned to small, independent refineries in quest of more favorable deals. This solution was not long-lived, for, over a very short period, the independent refineries were either bought out by the major oil companies or had, for other reasons, ceased to operate. As a result, the petroleum co-ops were all but put out of business.

1934

394. Petroleum Co-ops: Farmers located in the triangle between Regina, Moose Jaw and Weyburn, held meetings to consider the future of their petroleum co-ops. They were convinced no solutions could be found through appeals to major oil companies and that their need was to build a refinery of their own.

In April, the farmers obtained incorporation of a new organization, Consumers Refineries Co-operative Association. A campaign was launched for both funds and members. It was hoped that $200,000 could be raised. Few farmers, however, could afford to invest in the daring plan. Only $32,000 was forthcoming. Undaunted, the farmers decided in November to go ahead with their plan by erecting a small refinery plant within the limits of their means.

396. Co-ordination and Twine: The Saskatchewan Co-op Wheat Producers agreed to a plan for co-operation with the Saskatchewan Co-operative Wholesale Society in distribution of bulk commodities such as twine and coal supplied by the Co-op Wholesale. However, when the Wholesale attempted to purchase stock twine, not a single company in Canada was willing to sell to the co-operative. The Wholesale was thus forced to buy from manufacturers in Ireland and Britain.

397. Politics: The UFC-ILP political group formed in 1931, operating under the name, Farmer-Labour Group, placed itself under the CCF banner to contest the June, 1934, provincial election. Receiving almost 25% of the vote, the candidates entered by the Group became the official opposition party.

395. Petroleum Co-ops: A number of Alberta farmers collaborated to form a new organization, Alberta Oil Consumers Co-operative, in effort to provide themselves with petroleum products at reasonable cost. The organization was later taken over as the basis of a petroleum department of United Farmers of Alberta Central Co-operatives.

1934

398. Co-ordination: The Co-operation and Markets Branch of the Saskatchewan Department of Agriculture organized a Conference of Co-operative Trading Associations of the Province. Such conferences became an annual event with the Branch providing secretarial services and organizational assistance. At this first conference, George Keen of the Co-operative Union of Canada, gave an explanation of the operation of credit unions, stimulating much discussion of the subject.

399. Saskatchewan Co-op Wheat Producers, at annual convention, endorsed a resolution calling for a committee to be set up to explore possibilities of providing life insurance on a co-operative basis.

400. Orderly Marketing: Since their start, and especially after the difficulties of 1929, the three Prairie wheat pools and their central selling agency, Canadian Co-operative Wheat Producers, had repeatedly urged that there be an effective system for orderly marketing of grain. Such a system, it was argued, was the only means for farmers to get a fair and equitable price for grain. It would eliminate the price fluctuation caused by speculation.

In 1935, the Federal government responded at least partially, to the demands. A voluntarily patronized Canadian Wheat Board was established and empowered to buy wheat if and when the price fell below 90 cents. The wheat pools, however, favored a compulsory system in which the Wheat Board was the sole marketing agent; hence, they were not content with the voluntary scheme. In adopting its plan, the government was evidently acknowledging opposition to a compulsory plan by Grain Exchange interests.

As the new plan came into operation, the Winnipeg Grain Exchange continued its activities. Farmers, however, could now choose between selling through the Exchange or by pooling through the Wheat Board.

401. Canadian Federation of Agriculture: At a November meeting in Toronto, a new organization was formed to take the place of the Canadian Council of Agriculture which had disbanded in 1930. At this founding convention, 75 farm leaders from all parts of Canada determined the aims and objects of the new organization to be:

(a) to co-ordinate efforts of agricultural producers' organizations thoughout Canada for the purpose of promoting their common interests through mutual action.

(b) to promote and advance the social and economic conditions of persons engaged in agriculture; and

(c) to assist in formulating and promoting national agricultural policies, and to co-operate with organized producers of other countries for this purpose.

The new organization was first named The Canadian Chamber of Agriculture, but was later renamed the Canadian Federation of Agriculture.

1935

402. Saskatchewan Federation of Agriculture: At the Saskatchewan Co-operative Conference, it was decided to form a Saskatchewan Section of the Canadian Federation of Agriculture, to co-ordinate efforts of farm organizations of the province and to seek social, economic, and legislative improvement.

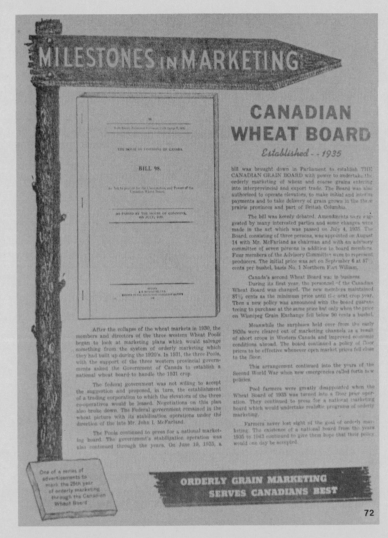

1935

405. Manitoba Co-op Wholesale had 1935 sales of $320,000, but found progress difficult because of the serious economic conditions. Only three new associations were begun between the years of 1932 and 1937.

404. Politics: The UFC-ILP political group, formed in 1929, were known until 1935 as the Farmer-Labor Group. In this year, the name, Co-operative Commonwealth Federation (CCF) was adopted by the Group which then contested the 1935 federal election, electing two of its candidates to Parliament.

United Farmers of Canada (Saskatchewan Section), now withdrew from direct political activity.

403. Politics: The UFA Government, in office since 1921, was defeated at the polls by the Social Credit Party, a newcomer to the political scene. The successful party aspired to pay to all Alberta residents a dividend of $25 per month and to abolish interest on debts.

73

406. Consumers Co-op Refineries: Consumers Refineries Co-operative Association was renamed as Consumers Co-operative Refineries Limited. On May 27, a small farmer-owned refining plant bearing the new name, went "on stream" at Regina, to serve its 10 founding-member petroleum co-ops. The world's first co-operative petroleum, refinery, with a capacity of 500 barrels of crude per day, had 1935 sales of $253,000, and a net savings of $30,000—almost matching the $32,000 farmers had invested to build their plant. The Refinery, in addition to serving its own locals, became the petroleum supplier to locals of the Saskatchewan Co-op Wholesale Society, and supplier of petroleum for Saskatchewan Pool Elevators.

407. General Election of 1935: During the regime of the Conservative Government under R. B. Bennett, elected in 1930 a number of events took place. The first grain shipments via the Port of Churchill, were made in 1931. In 1934, The Bank of Canada was formed as an instrument to regulate currency and credit, to supply financial services to chartered banks, and to advise the Dominion Government on fiscal matters. In 1932, the Canadian Radio Broadcasting Commission (later known as Canadian Broadcasting Corporation or CBC) was formed. The Government also began Crown-owned air transport services which became the basis of Air Canada. Of greater importance to Prairie agriculture, however, was the provision of the Prairie Farm Rehabilitation Act, and the establishment, in 1935, of the Canadian Wheat Board to provide for orderly marketing of grains. Toward the end of their term, the Conservatives enacted a number of measures which, at the time, could be considered as radical. These were part of a "New Deal" program adopted by Bennett who was influenced by the "New Deal" program of U.S. President Roosevelt. The "New Deal"

1935

consisted of measures to alleviate farm debt (Prairie Farm Rehabilitation Act); control of export trade; high tariffs to increase employment by protecting Canadian industry; unemployment insurance; minimum wage scales; and shorter working hours. In the election campaign, Bennett relied on the "New Deal" program to return his Government to office. The Liberals, however, attacked some of the legislation enacted by the Conservatives on grounds that the Dominion Government had exceeded its authority since some measures involved matters for which the provinces had exclusive jurisdiction. In the election, held October 24, the Liberals won a sweeping victory:

PROVINCE	LIB.	CONS.	SOCIAL CREDIT	C.C.F.	INDEP. LIB.	LIB. PROG.	INDEP. CONS.	RECON-STRUC-TION	INDEP.	UFO LABOR	TOTAL
Ontario	56	25								1	82
Quebec	55	5			5						65
Nova Scotia	12										12
New Brunswick	9	1									10
P.E.I.	4										4
Manitoba	12	1		2		2					17
Saskatchewan	16	1	2	2							21
Alberta	1	1	15								17
B.C.	6	5		3				1	1		16
Yukon							1				1
	171	39	17	7	5	2	1	1	1	1	245

As can be seen, the election was contested by candidates of a variety of political faiths, including the Social Credit Party and the Co-operative Commonwealth Federation Party, both contesting federal seats for the first time. The Reconstruction Party, though it did not make an impact, had an interesting background. It was led by H.H. Stevens, Minister of Trade and Commerce in the Bennett Government, who resigned before the election. Stevens had urged Bennett to control big businesses, charging that large retail concerns having huge buying power demanded that manufacturers supply them at prices so low that wages of the factory workers were restricted. Likewise, Stevens charged that prices received by farmers for meat, vegetable and fruit products were unfairly depressed for the same reasons, and that, as a result of being able to purchase at low prices, the large retail interests were able to force small competitors out of the markets.

1936

409. Manitoba Beekeepers Association at the annual convention, formed a committee to explore prospects for establishing a central plant for assembly and processing of honey. No such plant then existed in Western Canada.

408. Petroleum Co-ops: Farmers, in growing numbers, were convinced that they had found an answer to petroleum price problems in the start of their co-operative refinery. Their convictions were caused by the offering of price reductions or discounts, in communities where petroleum co-ops were formed. At other communities, prices remained firm.

410. Alberta Co-operative Council: At a July meeting, a group of co-operative and farm leaders formed an organization similar to a co-operative union. Known as The Alberta Co-operative Council, it operated as an office through which member co-operatives could unite for purposes of co-ordination, education and development. This body was later reorganized as the Alberta Federation of Agriculture.

411. Farm Machinery: A Royal Commission of Enquiry, set up by the federal government, made a study of farm machinery prices. It reported that distribution costs often accounted for as much as 60% of the price of implements of farmers. The Commission recommen-

1936

ded that machinery companies be urged to reduce their distribution costs, and that, in the event the companies did not do so, the government should encourage farmers to set up machinery co-operatives.

1937

412. St. Malo Caisse Populaire: In the French-speaking Catholic village of St. Malo, Rev. Fr. Arthur Benoit, who arrived in 1936 from California guided his parishioners to the start of a caisse populaire (credit union). Fr. Benoit held a number of study sessions where participants discussed their social and financial problems, and the means of solving them. After about a year of such deliberations, the St. Malo Caisse Populaire was formed on March 1, 1937 with 17 founding members—13 farmers, a carpenter, the postmistress, a merchant, and Fr. Benoit. Legislation for incorporation of credit unions had not yet been passed, but, when it was provided later in the year, the St, Malo organization was incorporated.

1937

413. Credit Union Legislation: Fr. A. J. Couture, in charge of the Catholic parish at La Broquerie and an advocate of caisses populaires, was instructed by his superiors to assist in the formation of caisses populaires in French Catholic parishes. There was, however, no legislation for incorporation of such organizations. Fr. Coutoure met with the Manitoba Minister of Agriculture, then responsible for co-operative affairs, with the result that the two visited Quebec and Antigonish to study caisses populaires. The Minister of Agriculture, greatly impressed, prepared legislation for credit unions which was enacted in 1937.

415. Manitoba Co-op Wholesale: At the annual meeting of the Manitoba Co-operative Wholesale there was a feeling of optimism. Delegates believed that the worst of the Great Depression was over, and the economy on the road to at least a slow recovery. In 1937, MCW sales of almost $400,000 established a new record for organization.

414. Credit Union Legislation: An Act providing for incorporation and supervision of credit unions was passed by the Saskatchewan Legislature. The first credit union to incorporate under this was formed in Regina by people of the Jewish faith. Soon after, a credit union was incorporated at Moose Jaw.

416. Co-op Refinery and Wholesale: A close relationship between Consumers' Co-operative Refineries and Saskatchewan Co-operative Wholesale was further strengthened as the two organizations collaborated in a joint venture to market tires. The results were reported as being very satisfactory.

417. Saskatchewan Co-op Wheat Producers had petitioned the Saskatchewan legislature for an amendment to the charter of their organization. The proposed amendments were strongly opposed, and as a result the government called for public hearings on the matter. Retail merchants and other dealers criticized the proposed amendment on grounds that it would enable the Producers to enter the retail field, and that this was evidence that the Producers intended to assume a new role. Officials of the Wheat Producers declared, however, that the amendments were primarily to enable the organization to comply to its members' 1934 request that the organization provide an insurance

75

1937

program, and that the Producers did not intend to offer services already being provided by consumer co-operatives.

418. R.O.P. Breeders' Co-operative: with assistance from the Saskatchewan Department of Agriculture, the R.O.P. Breeders' Co-operative was formed. Devoted to improved breeding of livestock, ROP was the first organization of its kind to be formed in Canada. The government favored the venture because it would contribute to more diversification of the agricultural economy.

419. Co-op School: The first co-operative school for young people was held at the University of Saskatchewan, Saskatoon. It was arranged by the Co-operatives and Markets Branch of the Provincial Department of Agriculture, assisted by Saskatchewan Co-op Wheat Producers, Saskatchewan Co-op Wholesale, and other co-operatives. The co-operative schools became an annual event with attendance growing to the extent that several were held simultaneously in various parts of the Province.

420. Alberta Co-operative Union:The Alberta Section of the Co-operative Union of Canada was in operation at this time, but its history is not clear. In 1937, the organization unanimously adopted a resolution urging that competition between co-operatives in the distribution of goods be eliminated.

421. Rowell-Sirois Commission: Prime Minister Mackenzie King, after assuming office in 1935, had some of the measures enacted by the Bennett administration considered by the Courts. The courts ruled that, as claimed by the Liberals, some measures did encroach upon areas of provincial jurisdiction. In 1937, King appointed a Royal Commission, known as the Rowell-Sirois Commission to study and report on matters relative to Dominion-Provincial jurisdiction and relationships.

1938

422. Credit Union Legislation: Legislation providing for the incorporation of credit unions was adopted by the Alberta legislature. This legislation was given Royal Assent March 31, and administered by the Department of Trade and Industry. The minister of that Department of the Social Credit government was Hon. E. C. Manning who later became the Premier of

1938

Alberta. The Government provided the legislation, which was patterned after credit union legislation existing in the U.S.A., as a part of its program to make credit available to the people of the Province. Ten credit unions were chartered under the new legislation in 1938, and within 5 years, about 50 had been formed in both rural and urban communities.

423. Rural Credit Union: On April 19, Saskatchewan's first rural credit union, the LaFleche Community Savings & Credit Unions, was incorporated.

424. Credit Union Federation: At a meeting attended by 26 delegates of new or forming credit unions, an organization called Saskatchewan Credit Union Federation was formed. There was, at the time, about 16 credit unions formed or in the process of being formed. The Federation was conceived as a means of providing for educational needs, bonding, and other assistance. In 1948, this organization evolved into the Credit Union League of Saskatchewan.

426. Manitoba Beekeepers Association considered the report of the committee formed in 1936 to study need for facilities to process and market honey. No such facilities then existed in Western Canada, and the committee had not been able to interest private enterprise in establishing such facilities. As a result, the Beekeepers' Association decided to form an organization to serve their needs. It became known as Manitoba Co-operative Honey Producers.

425. Co-operative Abbatoir: The co-operative abbatoir operating at Saskatoon since 1932, under the name, Saskatchewan Co-operative Abbatoir, was steadily losing money. With great reluctance, the Board decided to suspend operations. Subsequently, the plant was purchased by F. Mendal who operated it under the name, Intercontinental Packers, with outstanding success.

427. Alberta Wheat Pool rejected a proposal that there be a merger between the Pool and United Grain Growers to form an organization to handle grain across the three Provinces. It was recognized that if such a merger took place there would be direct competition with the Saskatchewan and Manitoba Pools.

428. Co-op Wholesales Form Interprovincial Committee: Since 1930, the co-operative wholesales of the three Provinces had been co-ordinating efforts in purchasing some bulk commodities. In 1938, this co-ordination was placed on a more formal basis. An Interprovincial Committee was appointed, with representation from all three co-operative wholesales. Through efforts of the Committee, purchasing of bulk commodities was increased. Considerable savings were realized, particularly with respect to binder twine.

1938

Manitoba	Saskatchewan	Alberta

1938

429. Alberta Co-op Wholesale Association (ACWA) had a rebirth when it was completely re-organized. Head office was moved from Killam to Edmonton where ACWA received orders from 29 local associations and placed them with suppliers. Any volume discounts earned were held in a fund to be eventually used to finance the start of a wholesaling operation.

430. Co-ops and Coal: The Saskatchewan Co-op Wholesale attempted to purchase coal for its locals, but found it impossible to obtain a single ton from the Lethbridge area. Most mines in that area were owned or controlled by the C.P.R., and output was sold through a Winnipeg-based concern.

A group of unemployed miners, however, located an abandoned mine and began to operate it as best they could. Upon hearing of it, SCWS investigated, and offered financial help to the miners who willingly agreed to provide coal they produced to the Wholesale. When the Wholesale was able to obtain coal by this means, other sources of supply immediately became available.

431. United Farmers of Canada (UFC) entered Alberta on September 4, when a meeting of farmers at Willingdon resolved to form a "non-political" organization, a branch in affiliation with the UFC in Saskatchewan". After a further conference held October 27, the UFC launched a province-wide membership campaign. By January, 1939, 25 locals with a total membership of 506 had been registered.

1939

433. Chamber of Agriculture: At a meeting of representatives from co-operatives and farm organizations, a co-ordinaing body known as the Western Section of the Canadian Chamber of Agriculture was formed. This organization operated under that name until 1945 when it became known as the Manitoba Federation of Agriculture.

432. Co-op Union: The annual Conference of Co-operative Trading Association, initiated in 1934 by efforts of the Saskatchewan Department of Agriculture, Co-operatives and Markets Branch, was held at Regina. It was decided to re-form as the Saskatchewan Section of the Co-operative Union in Canada, with terms of reference and bylaws to be decided in 1940 at a further meeting held in Saskatoon.

434. Credit Unions: An organizer was appointed by the Co-operative and Markets Branch, Saskatchewan Department of Agriculture, to work with the University of Saskatchewan, Wheat Pool, and other co-operatives, to promote and develop credit unions.

1939

1939

435. Saskatchewan Co-op Creameries: The Saskatchewan Government took steps to return to dairy producers the co-operative creameries which the government had controlled since 1931. For this purpose, Saskatchewan Co-operative Creamery Association was then formed, and was able to retire all indebtedness to the government by 1946.

436. Manitoba Co-op Honey Producers brought into existence the first commercial honey processing and packaging plant in Western Canada plus a uniform system for grading honey products. Equipment installed in a rented warehouse processed more than a million pounds of honey which was marketed under the brand name, "Clover Crest".

437. Saskatchewan Honey Producers Co-op: At Tisdale, Saskatchewan Honey Producers' Co-operative was incorporated to receive, process, manufacture, clean, pack, grade, market and sell honey produced by its members. Financial assistance for this venture was provided by the Saskatchewan government.

438. Manitoba Pool Seeds Department: On July 1, Manitoba Pool Elevators established a Forage Crop Seeds Department. Farmers engaged in the production of such seeds were grouped into 10 Co-operative Seed Associations, each of which was incorporated under provincial statute. MPE was responsible for the marketing of seed on behalf of the associations.

439. Saskatchewan Co-op Wheat Producers-Pool Insurance: Saskatchewan Co-op Wheat Producers were successful in their 1937 bid for an increase in the scope of activities permitted by their Charter. As a result, a subsidiary, Pool Insurance Limited was formed to provide insurance coverage for Pool members.

440. Saskatchewan Co-op Wholesale Flour Mill: A small flour mill at Outlook was purchased by the Saskatchewan Co-op Wholesale which operated the plant as a subsidiary under the name, Consumers Co-operative Mills Limited. SCWS invited the Saskatchewan Co-op Wheat Producers to become joint owners of the mill which had a capacity of 250 barrels of flour per day. The offer was declined by the Wheat Producers who held that flour milling was an activity that should be pursued by a producers' rather than consumers' co-operative.

1939

441. Saskatchewan Co-op Wholesale— Farm Tractors: A farm tractor of revolutionary style was imported into Canada by the Saskatchewan Co-op Wholesale. Powered by a Chrysler industrial engine, the tractor was developed through a coordinated effort between U.S. co-operatives and the Ethyl Corporation. One farmer who drove his Co-op tractor on the highway was fined for speeding at an alleged 60 mph. A unit purchased by the Co-op Refinery in 1939 remained in service until 1960.

442. Alberta Co-op Wholesale-Feed Manufacturing: Among the three Prairie co-op wholesales, Alberta Co-operative Wholesale Association pioneered the manufacture of livestock and poultry feed in 1939. Products were distributed under the brand name, Co-op Maid.

443. Manitoba Co-op Wholesale sales for the year were $615,000 on which a net savings of $36,937 was realized. The largest sales were recorded in petroleum.

444. Consumers Co-op Refineries, now serving 146 petroleum co-ops, could not keep pace with growing demands for its products with the original skimming plant which had a capacity of 500 barrels of crude per day. A contract for enlargement of the plant, by addition of thermal cracking processes, to increase capacity to 1,500 barrels per day, was completed.

1939

445. **World War II**: On September 1, Nazi Germany invaded Poland. On September 3, Great Britain and France declared war against Germany, followed on September 10, by a declaration of war by Canada. As the Canadian economy turned to wartime production, opportunities for co-operatives, and for other types of enterprise, were restrained by scarcities of materials and civilian manpower. Gasoline, meat, sugar, butter, and other commodities were rationed, and non-essential commercial construction was at a standstill. Thus, co-operative associations, which had begun to flourish after formation of the wholesales, were restrained in their growth and development, first by the Great Depression of the 1930's, then by World War II.

446. **Grain Trade**: With the outbreak of World War II, the British Government closed the Liverpool Corn Exchange and established a cereal import board. In Canada, the Federal Government announced that the Winnipeg Grain Exchange would be kept open, but a quota system which limited deliveries by any one producer to 5,000 bushels, was established.

1940

447. **Canadian Co-operative Implements Limited (CCIL), Formed**: In 1936, the Federal Government set up a Royal Commission to enquire into costs of farm machinery. In 1939, the matter was further probed by a Committee of the Saskatchewan Legislature. Reports of both bodies revealed concern about the high prices asked of farmers for machinery and implements. It was shown that as much as 60% of the price of some implements was attributed to distribution costs. Both reports recommended that co-operative action be taken in an effort to reduce prices to farmers. On April 23, a group of about 25 co-operative leaders and representatives of the government of the three Prairie Provinces met at Saskatoon. Initiative for this meeting had been assumed by the Saskatchewan Co-operative Wholesale Society. After discussion, this meeting formed an interim body known as The Interprovincial Farm Machinery Committee to consider prospects for co-operative action and to prepare a report and recommendations for a further meeting of the same group.

On July 24, 1940, the representatives met at Regina to consider reports of the Committee. The report proposed that a co-operative be formed to procure and distribute farm machinery. Governments of both Manitoba and Saskatchewan offered financial assistance for such a venture, and it was agreed by the meeting that federal incorporation of the proposed farm machinery co-operative be sought.

As a result, Canadian Co-operative Implements Limited was granted incorporation under the Dominion Companies Act on September 3, 1940. On September 11, the co-operative and government leaders again met to complete organization of the new co-operative. At the time, it was intended that about 35 district co-operative associations—depots to handle farm machinery—would be established throughout the Prairie Provinces. Farmers could become members of the district association serving their area by making an investment based on their acreage, ranging from $10 to $40. The district associations would own and control the central CCIL organization, with farmers exercising control through a delegate system. However, as the manufacture of farm machinery virtually ceased during World War II, Canadian Co-operative Implements Limited did not get into operation until 1946. Soon after, in 1948 the structure of the organization was significantly revised.

448. **Interprovincial Co-operatives Limited**: As early as 1930, and possibly sooner, the three co-operative wholesales serving Manitoba, Saskatchewan and Alberta, were collaborating in an informal manner in the joint purchase of some commodities. After the start of its operations in 1935, Consumers' Co-operative Refineries Limited also took part in these joint puchasing efforts. The bargaining strength thus derived caused increased importance to be placed on joint purchasing, and focused on the need of a formal body to be formed to unite the purchasing power of the wholesales and to manufacture commodities on their behalf. With the three Prairie wholesales as Charter members, a new organization, Interprovincial Co-operatives Limited, was organized and granted federal incorporation on September 17, 1940. British Columbia Co-operative Wholesale Society soon became a fourth member-owner of IPCO. The B.C. Wholesale was formed in 1939. As in the case of CCIL, IPCO was prevented by wartime restraints, from immediately developing as an organization in its own right. It was not until 1947 that IPCO began operating as a separate entity or office. In the meantime, its activities were carried on by representatives of the member wholesales working in collaboration with one another.

1940

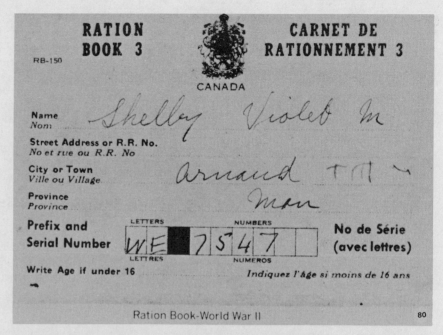

Manitoba	Saskatchewan	Alberta

1940

449. Co-op Refinery Rejects War Profit: Under the British Commonwealth Air Training plan, a large number of air force training stations were quickly constructed across Canada. A good number of them were established within the Prairie Provinces. Consumers Co-operative Refineries was called upon by the government to supply crude oil residues for use in construction of airport runways. The Refinery's Board of Directors recognized that, at the price awarded by the government, the crude residues would return a profit to the Refinery. The Board could not, for reasons of conscience, accept profit from the provision of military needs. The Board adopted a policy by which all profits from sales of military requirements were donated by the Refinery to the Red Cross to help that organization in its effort to reduce the suffering caused by World War II.

450. Manitoba Co-op Wholesale had a growing membership roster, as about 32 new members joined between 1938 and 1942.

451. Saskatchewan Co-op Wholesale— Coal: Confronted on one hand by a growth in demand for coal from the retail co-operatives, and on the other hand by efforts of private interests to keep co-operatives out of the coal business, the Saskatchewan Co-operative Wholesale Society was forced to take action to improve its supply position. A substantial interest was obtained in the Hy-Grade Coal Mine at Drumheller, Alberta.

452. Manitoba Pool Elevators was granted a change to its Act of Incorporation on December 17. As a result of the change, all capital stock was cancelled, and, since that time, federation with the Pool has been through a membership fee assessed each local Pool Elevator Association. In turn, farmers pay a membership fee to join the local Association.

455. Alberta Federation of Agriculture: The Alberta Co-operative Council, formed in 1936, changed its name to Alberta Federation of Agriculture.

454. Co-op Union: The decision of the Annual Conference of Co-operative Trading Associations to form a Saskatchewan Section of the Co-op Union of Canada was carried out, with the adoption, in 1940, of a set of rules and bylaws at a Saskatoon meeting. Soon after, these rules and bylaws were approved by the annual congress of the Co-op Union of Canada held at Winnipeg in July.

453. MPE Buys Elevators: All Manitoba elevators of Western Canada Flour Mills were purchased by Manitoba Pool Elevators.

456. United Farmers of Canada: Following defeat of the UFA government in 1935, some division of the UFA ranks occurred with the result that some members left the UFA to form a new Alberta farm organization—United Farmers of Canada, Alberta Section.

1940

1940

457. Retail Merchants' Association: At the annual conference of Co-operative Trading Associations held June 25 and 26 at the Bessborough Hotel, Saskatoon, Mr. George Houghman of Toronto, who was then Secretary of the Dominion Retail Merchants' Association, was a guest speaker. **The Co-operative Consumer**, July 2, 1940, describes the appearance of Mr. Houghman of Toronto before a co-operative audience as "unprecedented in the history of the co-operative movement in Canada."

"Mr. Houghman told the delegates that he regarded the co-operative movement as one of the most hopeful signs of the times. 'Within your movement lies all hope for the survival of our democratic institutions, he stated. Congratulating the delegates on the reality of their discussions and their acute sense of the value of problems, Mr. Houghman told them that he represented a dying species—the independent retailer. 'There is no room any more for anyone whose sole claim to existence is their independence,' he said. Pointing out that both the independent retail merchant and the co-operatives face a common 'economic autocracy, he foresaw the day when retailers would see the co-operatives in their proper light and work with them instead of in opposition," the **Consumer** reported.

The attitude toward co-operatives displayed by Mr. Houghman was in contrast to that shown by E. N. Trowern, circa 1913, and also in contrast to the nature of events soon to follow as RMA joined in attacks against the income tax position of co-operatives.

460. Study of Co-operative Associations Shows High Failure Rate: The Co-operatives and Markets Branch of Saskatchewan Department of Agriculture, with

458. Alberta Livestock Co-op: A number of local livestock shipping associations created a central marketing agency by forming Alberta Livestock Co-operative. This new organization was provided with financial assistance by the Alberta Wheat Pool, United Grain Growers, UFA Co-operative, the shipping associations, and established sales agencies at Edmonton and Calgary.

459. Alberta Honey Producers' Co-operative, an organization similar to the Saskatchewan Honey Producers formed in 1939 and the Manitoba organization of 1938, was incorporated but did not begin business operations until 1945.

1940

the Economics Branch, Canada Department of Agriculture, reported on a study of co-operatives incorporated in Saskatchewan during the 25-year period, 1913 to 1938. The study showed that 1,091 associations were incorporated during the 25-year period, but by 1939, 531 or about 50% had been either stillborn or had failed and disappeared. Most common reasons for failure included mismanagement and lack of business and co-operative experience on the part of boards of directors, members and managers; inadequate financing; and improper use of credit in both buying and selling. The report stressed "the need for careful control of merchandise credit; the need for more inspection and advisory services insofar as these could be provided by the Branch." As one step toward overcoming the problems, a small economics research division was then set up within the branch. The report was widely publicized within co-operative circles and was undoubtedly an influence upon the central co-operatives in all three Prairie Provinces, encouraging them to put more emphasis on advisory, supervisory and training programs for their members.

461. Producers Fieldstaff Assist Other Co-operatives: When the need to sign up farmers to pool contracts came to an end, fieldmen of Saskatchewan Co-op Wheat Producers were able to devote much of their time to assisting in the formation of new consumer co-operatives, and later, new credit unions. These efforts are credited with having expedited the development of co-operation in rural Saskatchewan.

462. Credit Union National Association (CUNA): In British Columbia, the B.C. Credit Union League joined a U.S.A.-based credit union service organization, Credit Union National Association, formed in 1934. The B.C. credit unions were the first in Canada to affiliate with CUNA which had, prior to this time, operated only in the U.S.A. However other central credit union organizations were soon to follow the B.C. example.

1940

463. General Election of 1940: The outbreak of World War II again raised the issue of conscription. Prime Minister King declared that his Government intended to rely on volunteer recruitment only. While acceptable to those opposing conscription of man-power, King's stance drew criticism from other quarters where all -out aid to Britain was demanded. By, the election, held March 26, 1940, before the fall of France revealed the extent of the war crisis, the Liberals were returned to office.

PROVINCE	LIB.	CONS.	SOCIAL CREDIT	C.C.F.	LIB. PROG.	INDEP. LIB.	INDEP. CONS.	INDEP.	UNITY	UNITY REFORM	TOTAL
Ontario	55	25			2						82
Quebec	61					3	1				65
Nova Scotia	10	1		1							12
New Brunswick	5	5									10
P.E.I.	4										4
Manitoba	14	1		1	1						17
Saskatchewan	12	2		5					1	1	21
Alberta	7		10								17
B.C.	10	4		1				1			16
Yukon		1									1
	178	39	10	8	3	3	1	1	1	1	245

1941

464. Saskatchewan Co-op Credit Society: With the growth in the number of credit unions, it was proposed that a central organization be created to co-ordinate their financial resources. A central organization would accept surplus funds of credit unions, and make loans to others in temporary need of additional funds. As a further benefit, a central organization could provide loans of larger size to organizations such as the Saskatchewan Co-op Wholesale which had been required to borrow from non-co-operative sources because individual CUs could not meet the need. The central organization, with membership open to all credit unions incorporated under the Saskatchewan Credit Union Act, was incorporated under

1941

a Special Act of the Saskatchewan Co-operative Credit Society Limited. Until 1952, the Society shared office premises with Sherwood Co-operative Credit Union, Regina.

465. Manitoba Co-op Wholesale, in need of larger premises, moved on August 1 to the Aldous Building on Donald Street, Winnipeg. Here, MCW set up its first inventory of goods in a small warehouse which was stocked with tire, paint and harness, all worth about $1,000. Staff now consisted of 8 persons, one of whom provided an audit service to retail co-ops on a part-time basis.

466. Saskatchewan Co-op Wholesale, like its Manitoba counterpart, was in need of larger premises. A vacant four-storey office building was purchased in Saskatoon while additional warehouse and office space was rented at Regina.

467. Number of Co-op Associations Peaks: In 1941, the number of consumer co-operative associations in Saskatchewan reached an all-time high at 483. Thereafter, the number began to slowly decline for various reasons including:

*Lack of adequate manpower and opportunity to maintain viable operations under wartime conditions.

*Amalgamation of some local oil co-ops with co-op stores after merger between the Co-op Refinery and Co-op Wholesale in 1944.

*Wartime restraints on farming affected volume handled by retail co-ops.

*Depopulation of some smaller rural communities.

468. Alberta Poultry Producers: A new organization, to provide the marketing services required by producers of poultry and eggs, was incorporated as Alberta Poultry Producers Limited.

469. Grain Markets: The Federal Government restricted deliveries from the 1941 crop to 230,000,000 bushels of wheat, and also introduced a plan to encourage a reduction in the number of acres sown to wheat. The plan provided for cash payments on land that had been sown to crops in 1940 but summerfallowed in 1941.

470. Rowell-Sirois Commission: The report of the Rowell-Sirois Commission was completed in 1940, and a conference of Dominion and Provincial leaders was called to discuss its recommendations. The report pointed out that there was disparity of income between the Provinces. Adversely affected were the Maritime Provinces, Manitoba and Saskatchewan. In the case of Alberta, revenues from crude natural gas helped keep revenues above those of the other Prairie Provinces. The report proposed a

1941

major reform of the allocation of tax revenues by the Federal Government which would have a monopoly on income tax, corporation tax, and succession duties. The Federal Government would then allocate, from its revenues, grants to the provinces as necessary to provide reasonable uniformity and quality of services such as education, social services, and highways. The industrially-rich provinces of Ontario and Quebec, which would be deprived by the proposals, refused to consider them. Alberta's Social Credit administration, which aspired to introduce new economic ideas to that Province, was disinterested. British Columbia, too, did not accept the proposals in belief that it had nothing to gain. Thus, the Report and efforts to implement its recommendations were rejected.

83

1941

1942 to 1961

CHAPTER IX

WAR AND POST—WAR YEARS—1942 TO 1961

471. In the years of World War II, 1939 to 1945, co-operatives, like most other business concerns not involved in producing war material, had almost no opportunity to expand facilities or to begin new ventures. Many co-op annual meetings or conventions opened with a prayer directed towards plans for new progress after the war came to an end. In this time, Co-op Refinery, called upon to deliver material, for military use, declined to profit from the sale of that material, donating all returns over and above cost to the Red Cross.

But, on the home front, hostility of a new kind, directed against co-operatives, came to the fore, mustered by private elevator companies and organized retailers.

The elevator companies had organized themselves in 1901 (see 116) after farmers had been successful in causing passage of the Manitoba Grain Act, and after the Territorial Grain Growers' Association was formed. The organized farmers had scored a victory over grain interests in the boxcar dispute of 1903 (see 122), and another when the Manitoba Government intervened after the Grain Growers' Grain Company was expelled from the Grain Exchange. There had also been attacks on the farm organizations in 1910, and in 1931.

The organized retailers too, had tried to thwart co-operative activities through opposing legislation for co-operatives, organizing boycotts and other means. Now, in 1942 those opponents of co-operation adopted a new tactic, charging that co-operatives were not paying a fair share of income tax.

Co-operatives were, however, complying with the requirements of the Income Tax Act as set forth by the Federal Government. Furthermore, the income tax liability of co-operatives was considered by Britain's Parliament in 1853, and following merchants' protests, the matter was examined in 1879 with the result that principles were established by legislation in 1880. The principles held that (1) Co-operative surpluses belong to the members hence are not taxable income, and (2) business done with non-members does produce a profit which is subject to tax.

The Federal Government established a Royal Commission on Co-operatives in response to the demands of the grain trade and retailers with the result that the terms similar to those of the British legislation of 1880, but also including one or two discriminatory clauses, were applied to Canadian co-operatives.

After the income tax issue subsided, the co-operatives began unfolding plans for development. A new phase also began—that of amalgamation of co-operatives. It was a logical step because of changes taking place in the business arena. One-establishment single-owner stores were being out-paced by the growth of merchandising chains, some integrated with their own wholesaling and manufacturing enterprises. Thus, if co-operatives were to be competitive and fulfill their purposes, amalgamation, to unite purchasing power and to increase strength, became increasingly necessary.

472. Income Tax: In 1917, the Commissioner of Taxation had ruled that "savings effected in purchases should not be classed as dividends or income" by co-operatives for income tax purposes. This ruling recognized that savings returned by a co-operative to members using the services provided were, in reality, a reduction of the price paid by members and not comparable to profit which other forms of business derive from serving customers and retain as income to reward invested capital.

United Grain Growers, as formed in 1917, was essentially a continuation of the organization and structure of the Grain Growers' Grain Company formed in 1906. GGGC was formed before legislation had been provided to permit incorporation as a co-operative, being incorporated under the Manitoba Joint Stock Companies Act. Terms of the Act required that the Company allocate earnings to its shareholders. Only farmers could hold shares. The Company also observed co-operative principles and practices including the offering of patronage refunds to its patrons. The patronage refunds could be deducted by the Company for income tax purposes, but the dividends paid on shares held by farmer-shareholders were not exempt. On this basis, the Company paid, without question, its income tax assessment since the tax was levied in 1917.

In the early 1940's, income tax assessments were substantially increased to reduce the purchasing power of Canadians and thereby help control price inflation, and help finance the war effort. As a result, the earnings UGG was able to allocate to shareholders and patrons were reduced. On the other hand, the three Prairie wheat pools, incorporated as co-operatives, were able to allocate all earnings as patronage refunds to members and were not required to allocate earnings on the basis of share capital as UGG was obliged to do.

1942

Noting the disparity between its own income tax assessment and that of the Pools, and arguing that UGG and the Pools were pursuing similar purposes and activities, UGG made a submission to the federal government requesting a tax status similar to that of the Pools.

The Government provided no satisfactory reply to UGG's request. However, the **North-West Line Elevator Association** was quick to take note of the disparity pointed out by UGG. The Association immediately launched a campaign, not for the purpose of adjusting UGG's tax status to a basis similar to that of the Pools, but to cause the tax status of the Pools to be altered to that of the private elevator companies. Support of other groups, such as retail merchants, was enlisted by the Association. This alliance led to the creation of a

Winnipeg-based organization known as **The Income Tax Payers' Association.** This body launched an intense and well-organized campaign in an effort to arouse public opinion against the tax position of co-operatives. This campaign, in various forms, was continued for many years. Superficially at least, it was conducted as a fight for "fair" taxation. However, to put matters into perspective, one should review events of 1908, 1910, 1913, 1937, and 1938, when private interests demonstrated their strong opposition to co-ops. Many important events of that nature took place before Canada's first Income Tax Act was passed in 1917. Thus, there is doubt as to whether taxation was the issue or merely a tactic.

473. Saskatchewan Co-op Wholesale Begins Feed Production: Wartime restraints on the marketing of grain encouraged many farmers to increase production of livestock and poultry. This created a demand for feeds and for the Saskatchewan Co-op Wholesale to get into the feed manufacturing business. The Wholesale's start in feed production was in an old tin shed with a second-hand bread dough mixer and a shovel as the key production 'machinery'.

475. Saskatchewan Co-op Wholesale Begins Grocery Service: With the opening of a grocery department at Regina, Saskatchewan Co-op Wholesale began a new service as a wholesaler of groceries to co-operative stores.

477. Co-op Refinery Exploration For Crude Oil: Responding to demands of delegates, Co-op Refinery was involved in a search for crude oil. In 1942, wells were drilled at Alameda, Stoughton, Radville and Kamsack. Others were to be drilled in 1943 at Ogema and Simpson. None was successful.

474. UGG Feed Manufacturing: At Edmonton, United Grain Growers built a plant to manufacture livestock and poultry feeds.

476. Alberta Farmers Union: The United Farmers of Canada (Alberta Section) formed in 1938, was reorganized as The Alberta Farmers' Union.

478. Credit Union League of Alberta: October 25, 85 representatives from 30 Alberta credit unions met in the town hall at Red Deer to organize The Credit Union League of Alberta. This body, formed primarily to provide and co-ordinate credit union educational programs, was patterned after similar organizations in the U.S.A., and affiliated with the Credit Union National Association of Madison, Wisconsin.

1943

479. Manitoba Co-op Wholesale Begins Feed Production: In a plant purchased from the Manitoba Poultry & Marketing Association, the Manitoba Co-operative

480. Saskatchewan Co-op Wholesale Has Second Feed Plant: At Regina, the Saskatchewan Co-op Wholesale opened a second plant for the manufacture of

1943

Wholesale undertook the manufacture of livestock and poultry feeds. It was decided to adopt the same feed formulae and brand names as used by the Saskatchewan Co-op Wholesale.

482. Credit Union Federation: At a meeting of a number of representatives of Manitoba credit unions, it was decided to form a co-ordinating body known as the Credit Union Federation of Manitoba.

484. Vegetable Oils: At Altona, a group of farmers responded to recommendations of the federal government that oil-bearing seed be produced in greater quantity, by sowing 5,000 acres to sunflowers. It was a new farm crop in every sense, for no other farming area of North America had ever grown sunflowers as an oilseed crop. The farmers pooled such knowledge and experience as they had, and, as a result, were able to produce an encouraging sunflower crop.

487. Manitoba Pool Elevators purchased 14 country elevators from a line elevator company, Federal Grain Co. Ltd.

488. MPE Publishes "The Manitoba Co-operator": On July 31, Manitoba Pool Elevators began publication of a tabloid, **The Manitoba Co-operator**. An earlier publication of that name had been sponsored by the Manitoba Co-operative Conference from 1931 to 1936.

livestock and poultry feeds. For some years hence, the Wholesale manufactured feeds at both Regina and Saskatoon.

481. Saskatchewan Co-op Wholesale Buys Office and Warehouse Building: An office and warehouse building of good size, was purchased by the Wholesale at Regina, and was officially opened by a ceremony held on November 19.

483. Saskatchewan Co-op Superannuation Society: By Special Act, of the Saskatchewan Legislature, the Saskatchewan Co-operative Superannuation Society was incorporated as an organization through which co-operatives of the Province could provide a superannuation scheme for their employees.

485. Co-operative Fidelity & Guarantee Company, incorporated May 3, under the Saskatchewan Insurance Act, was organized to provide such services as bonding of employees and fidelity guarantees to co-operatives.

486. Saskatchewan Livestock Pool, at its 16th annual meeting, approved a resolution favoring amalgamation with the Saskatchewan Co-op Wheat Producers. The handlings by the Livestock Pool in the previous year were in excess of $12 million.

1943

85

489.   Grain Trade: In 1943, the Prairie acreage sown to wheat was reduced to 16,729,000 acres from the 1942 level of 20,653,000, but the amount of wheat produced was still in excess of demand. Export markets were, of course, severely restrained by World War II. In the U.S.A., however, a large quantity of grain was being consumed for livestock feed and for the manufacture of alcohol. This encouraged U.S. speculators to buy Canadian grain and led to a boom in wheat futures.

On September 28, however, the Canadian government closed the futures market operated by the Winnipeg Grain Exchange. Simultaneously, the Government vested the Canadian Wheat Board with the exclusive right to market Canadian wheat grown west of the Great Lakes. The Wheat Board's program provided that farmers would deliver grain under a quota system. Upon delivery, farmers received an initial payment of $1.25 a bushel, basis No. 1 Northern at Vancouver or Fort William (Thunder Bay). Oats and barley were not included in the Wheat Board program and were still traded on the Exchange.

490.   Income Tax: The federal government levied an income tax assessment against the three Wheat Pools. On the one hand, the government was under pressure of the Income Tax Payers' Association, formed in 1942 and supported by the line elevator interest. On the other hand, it appeared that the government was uncertain as to what decision should be made with respect to taxing co-operatives, and was hoping that the levy against the Pools would result in an appeal to the Courts. A decision by the Courts would then be used as a basis for drafting legislation respecting tax liabilities of co-operatives. The Wheat Pools, however, did not resort to the Courts. The organizations decided that savings created for members were to be taxed, the handling charges which were the source of the savings, should be reduced so as to eliminate the surpluses subject to tax. The Pools, which had been making a handling charge at the same scale as line elevators, reduced their charge by 2 cents per bushel for the 1934-44 season. This resulted in a saving to farmers of about $11-million. The turn of events most certainly did not please the private elevator companies.

The Manitoba

CO-OPERATOR

SERVICE AT COST

Official organ of the co-operative movement in the province of Manitoba, Canada.

Vol. I, No. 1   50 cents a year
Winnipeg, July 1, 1943

CREAM ZONING NOW IN FORCE

Transportation of cream by trucks in Manitoba is now restricted to zoned areas. The new regulation went into force on July 1, and was announced by M. W. McCutcheon, Toronto, Administrator of Services, Wartime Prices and Trade Board.

The regulations apply for a 30-day trial period, but a large number of Manitoba creameries have objected to the zoning on the grounds that the allocation of the zones was unfair and that the map outlining the areas had been rejected more than a year ago.

NO MEETING

A committee of creamery operators was set up to deal with the matter over a year ago, but no meeting of the operators was called by the committee and the plan which was to go into effect a year ago was assailed to have been discarded until pressure developed in the East during the past month.

At the start of the season independent private service vehicle operators were granted their usual permits to operate over their established routes, and trucks owned in the creameries were limited to the localities adjacent to their plants. As a result of the new regulations the situation is now disorganized and the producers, truck operators and creameries are compelled to alter their transportation arrangements.

PRODUCTION PEAK

The purpose of the regulation is to conserve trucks, gasoline, tires and labor. However, many producers and creamery operators fail to see how the order will accomplish this.

It is pointed out that it will be particularly difficult at this season of the year and most disturbing to producers to make the necessary arrangements with cream producers at so late. It is also emphasized that transfer of rates are so disturbed that the creamery must now be sure one of three miles from one end of its territory and anywhere from 20 to 30 miles from the other boundary.

COLLECTION SERVICE

The following is an excerpt from the administrator's order:

have been accustomed to send their cream will continue to collect from them, but certain producers will find themselves in the zone of another creamery and truck collection service will only be available to that creamery."

GARDINER SEES LARGE HOLDINGS CANADIAN WHEAT

The 1943 crop is likely to increase Canadian holdings in wheat available for international distribution up to 900,000,000 bushels, Hon. J. G. Gardiner, Federal Minister of Agriculture, told delegates to the Midwest Farm Bureau conference and training school. The meeting was held at Chicago, June 27.

Mr. Gardiner said Canada's carryover of wheat into the new crop year on Aug. 1 would total almost 650,000,000 bushels, and about 220,000,000 bushels of this would still be on farms.

COST OF LIVING

"We are confident that these vast stocks of wheat produced from reduced acreage will be required at a return which will tend to remove the greatest agricultural problem we have in Canada, namely that of providing a cost of living return to our wheat growers," Mr. Gardiner stated.

Commenting on the problem of explaining why Canadian farmers should take certain prices for their commodities, such as 42 cents for oats, 65 cents for barley, $2.45 for flax and 12 cents for their cattle, Mr. Gardiner said, "we have only one answer. We are fighting a war shoulder to shoulder with our Allies, and our sacrifices must be equal to theirs."

ELECTRIC FENCE WIRE AVAILABLE

The Steel Controller states that, subject to the ability of manufacturers to supply, 13 gauge and smaller wire is now being released for use as electric fence only. Farmers requiring wire for electric fences should place their order with their normal suppliers who may make application to the Steel Controller for release of wire for this purpose.

Born and raised in Manitoba, W. J. Parker, president of Manitoba Pool Elevators Limited, has had his feet firmly planted in Manitoba's acres since boyhood and continues to operate his farms at Union Point and Sanford.

Blackleg Outbreak Reported At Carman

An outbreak of blackleg disease among cattle is reported from the Carman area in Manitoba and eight animals have died as a result. The infection has been confined to one farm and municipal authorities have taken strict measures to check it.

Manitoba Pool Buys Elevators

Manitoba Pool Elevators Limited have announced the purchase of 11 country elevators and 12 temporary grain annexes from the Federal Grain Limited. These elevators are all located in the western and northern districts of the province and boost the total number of country elevators owned and operated by Manitoba Pool Elevators Limited to 212, and the number of annexes to 133. The capacity of country elevators and annexes combined is approximately 9,15,000,000 bushels.

The elevators purchased are located at Alonesdoa, Larga Siding, Silverton, Decker, McConnell, Cardale, Sandy Lake, Sevick, Roblin, Foxwarren and Basswood. Two elevators were purchased at each of the two last named stations.

A Message to Our Readers

A multitude of questions await your consideration and it is our hope and belief that this publication may assist us to achieve the goals we may set as our objectives.

An intelligent, tolerant approach to the solution of any problem must be paved with knowledge and understanding.

Through the medium of these pages during the months and years to come we hope to encourage and to create a wider and better understanding of those factors of a political, social or economic character which affect the lives of the people.

W. J. PARKER, President,
Manitoba Pool Elevators Limited.

Pool Officials Hold Meeting

The two-day inter-provincial meeting of directors and officials of the Western Wheat Pool organizations was held in the Marlborough Hotel, Winnipeg, June 29 and 30. Thirty-five delegates attended with J. H. Wesson, Regina, chairman.

Discussing a coarse grain policy for 1943-44, a motion was unanimously adopted that the Canadian Wheat Board take over full control of the marketing of coarse grains. Another supported the resolution approved at the Canadian Federation of Agriculture convention in Calgary last spring urging a higher price for wheat.

DOLLAR WHEAT

While the price asked for in the C.F.A. resolution was $1 per bushel, basis No. 1 Northern in store Fort William, some delegates expressed the belief that conditions and factors have altered considerably since then and that the price should be increased.

The allocation of cars was discussed fully the the delegates conferred with George McIvor, chief commissioner; D. Kane, commissioner, and W. McNamara, supervisor of car supply, Canadian Wheat Board, on the latter.

Also discussed was the desirability of urging the Dominion Government to make an advance payment on the deliveries portion of grain stored on farms in the 1943-44 crop year. This was prompted by the fact that elevator space will be limited this fall and only small amounts of grain will be delivered thus creating financial burdens for the producers.

PRIORITY ASKED

The interim report of the reconstruction committee dealt at length with the problem of social security for agriculture. A resolution endorsed by all delegates urged that farmers be given priority in securing lumber and nails for the construction of elevators.

Other subjects dealt with included the different phases of international co-operation, a national health insurance plan and a report on industrial alcohol.

The Manitoba Pool Elevators Limited entertained the delegates at a banquet on the evening of June 28.

Members of Manitoba Co-operatives!

We want your authorization for the co-operative of which you are a member to pay for you the subscription for The Manitoba Co-operator in the manner described in the order given below. Please fill in the name of your co-operative and hand the order to your local or mail to be forwarded to the central office at your co-op, or mail to the office. This is where you co-operate and help to give strength to the co-operative movement in Manitoba.

86

1944

491. Income Tax: The federal government, by Order-in-Council on November 16, formed a Royal Commission on Co-operatives with Hon. Errol M. McDougall, Montreal, as chairman. The Commission was directed to enquire into the present position of co-operatives in the matter of the application of the Income War Tax Act, the Excess Tax Act, the organization and business methods employed, and other matters. The Commission began a series of hearings across Canada, beginning at Vancouver on December 15.

87

492. Politics: The CCF Party contested the Provincial election and was swept into office with a strong majority.

493. Department of Co-operation: Soon after the CCF government assumed office, a Department of Co-operation and Co-operative Development was established. The administration of legislation for co-operatives and credit unions was transferred to the new department which was the first of its kind to be created by any government in Canada. With evident heed of the report of 1940 which indicated a high rate of failure among new associations, the Department undertook to provide for inspections and supervision of co-operatives plus research and other allied services. The Deputy Minister, B. N. Arnason, regarded the services as a means to making co-operatives self-sufficient, saying: "Department employees, if they do their job properly, should gradually work themselves out of a job so far as ordinary inspections of any co-operative are concerned."

494. Saskatchewan Federation of Agriculture: The Saskatchewan Section of the Federation of Agriculture, operating since 1935, was re-organized as the Saskatchewan Federation of Agriculture. This event took place at a meeting of the Saskatchewan Co-operative Conference held in April at Saskatoon.

495. Interprovincial Farm Union Council: Provincial chapters of the United Farmers of Canada formed an Interprovincial Farm Union Council for inter-provincial co-ordination. The Council held its first meeting at Macklin, Saskatchewan, October 26 and 27.

1944

496. Canadian Co-operative Implements Limited: As World War II appeared to be on its way to an end, CCIL was making plans for an aggressive operation in the future. A membership campaign was successful in increasing the number of farmer-owner- members to about 50,000. The Manitoba, Saskatchewan and Alberta Governments provided loans totalling $250,000 to assist CCIL to purchase, on October 1, 1944, factory facilities at Winnipeg.

497. Manitoba Central Credit Union, with objectives similar to those of the Credit Society formed in Saskatchewan during 1941, was formed and began to operate in an office provided rent-free by the Manitoba Co-op Wholesale.

498. Credit Union Checking Services became a reality when the Saskatchewan Co-op Credit Society became a member of the Clearing House and undertook to handle negotiable instruments of its member credit unions.

500. Co-operative Union of Saskatchewan: The Saskatchewan Section of the Co-operative Union of Canada was re-organized and granted incorporation under the Sasktachewan Co-operative Associations Act, as the Co-operative Union of Saskatchewan.

501. Saskatchewan Women's Co-op Guild: A provincial organization set up by local women's Co-op Guilds was incorporated by Special Act of the Saskatchewan Legislature.

502. Saskatchewan Federated Co-operatives Limited: There had always been a close working relationship between the Saskatchewan Co-operative Wholesale Society and Consumers Co-operative Refineries. To a great degree, the two organizations were serving a common membership. It was, therefore, logical for the two organizations to amalgamate . The matter was considered and unanimously agreed to, with amalgamation effective on October 31, 1944. The new organizatin operated under the name Saskatchewan Federated Co-operative Limited.

503. Wholesale Expands: In 1944, Saskatchewan Federated Co-operatives greatly expanded its services:

499. Credit Union League of Alberta, in second Annual Meeting at Edmonton, April 22, was presented with its Certificate of Incorporation by an official of the Alberta Government, A. J. Hooke Provincial Secretary. At this meeting, a Constitution and Bylaws dated March 21, 1944, were adopted.

A short time before, on January 1, 1944, a Deposit and Loan Department began operation. Its purpose was to serve credit unions by receiving their surplus funds and providing loans to other credit unions in need of funds. Interest was 4% per annum on loans to credit unions which made application approved by the Supervisor of Credit Unions of the Alberta Government.

Manitoba	Saskatchewan	Alberta

1944

504. Manitoba Pool Elevators built a Seed Plant at St. Boniface to process and sell forage crop and cereal seeds produced by members of the 10 Co-operative Seed Associations served since 1939.

505. Manitoba Co-op Wholesale, now serving 92 local associations, had outgrown the Aldous Building premises acquired in 1941, and acquired larger premises at 230 Princess Street, Winnipeg. The cost was $37,000 plus $11,000 for renovations.

In the same year, MCW purchased the Winnipeg assets of the Penn Oil Co., for $30,000. Facilities included an oil blending plant and a building at 1335 Whyte Ave., where MCW erected a feed plant.

506. Co-op Vegetable Oils Limited: Farmers at Altona, who had produced a successful sunflower crop for oil in 1943, had to ship the seed to Ontario for processing. High costs of freight led to a conclusion that processing should be done close to the area in which the seed was produced. It was decided by the seed producers that a co-operative crushing and processing plant should be built, and a Charter was then obtained for a new organization, Co-op Vegetable Oils Limited. Erection of a crushing plant was begun.

*The annual meeting instructed the Board of Directors to enter into the lumber business.

*A new department to wholesale dry goods was begun.

*Complete ownership of the Hy-Grade Coal Mine at Drumheller was acquired. It had been partially owned since 1940.

*At Saskatoon, a building was purchased for use as a feed plant and lumber storage.

*At Regina, a second building was purchased and put into operation to provide additional warehouse space.

507. Amalgamation-Livestock Producers and Wheat Producers: In 1939 the Saskatchewan Co-operative Livestock Producers approved a proposed amalgamation with the Saskatchewan Co-op Wheat Producers. This amalgamation was consummated in 1944, and the Wheat Producers continued to serve the former members of the Livestock co-op through its Livestock Division.

508. Saskatchewan Co-op Wheat Producers' Oil Plant: At Saskatoon, the construction of an oilseed crushing plant to produce vegetable oils from Saskatchewan-owned crops, was begun with completion scheduled for early 1945.

At the same time, the Wheat Producers' organization gave serious consideration to the erection of a major flour mill.

509. Saskatchewan Co-op Honey Producers, formed in 1939 and now serving 300 beekeepers, reported handlings in the past year had reached 435,450 pounds of honey, with net returns to members being 16 cents per pound. The Honey Co-op was

1944

marketing products under the brand name, SASCO. Honey supplies to consumers were subject to rationing during the war years.

510. Legislation-Co-op Farms: The Saskatchewan Legislature approved amendments to the Co-operative Associations Act. The amendments made it clear that co-operative farming operations could be undertaken through duly organized co-operative associations. This meant that a group of farmers could form an association to jointly operate a farm enterprise.

511. Legislation-Pharmacy Act: Co-operative associations were prohibited from operating drug departments and from handling certain chemical products such as gopher poisons. Existing legislation provided that these services could only be provided by a licensed pharmacist who owned the majority of stock of the retail outlet. An attempt was made to remove these restraints which prevented co-operatives from entering the drug field. However, when a Bill designed for that purpose was finally approved by the Legislature, the only concession it provided was to enable co-ops to handle certain insecticides and gopher poison.

512. Horse Marketing Co-operative: In March, 1944, initial steps were taken at a meeting of farmers held at Val Marie, Saskatchewan, to dispose of a large number of horses owned by farmers but no longer needed since tractors now provided farm power. Events took place quickly, and with a loan by the Government of Saskatchewan, The Horse Marketing Co-operative Association was formed and built abbatoirs at both Swift Current and Edmonton. Horse meat was processed for export for human consumption in Europe, and by-products and some meat was sold for animal feed and other purposes in Canada.

513. Income Tax: The Royal Commission on Co-operatives, formed in 1944, proceeded to conduct hearings across Canada. In total, the Commission was presented with 175 briefs. Many of them were from sectors opposed to co-operatives, including feed manufacturers, flour millers, independent fruit and vegetable producers, some boards of trade and chambers of commerce, the North-West Line Elevator Association, Retail Merchants Association, Western Lumbermen's Association, and the Canadian Automotive Wholesale Association. Many of the same organizations were also represented through the Income Tax Payers' Association which submitted briefs opposing co-operatives.

1945

There were also many briefs submitted by co-operative organizations across Canada. These briefs were given very close scrutiny by the Royal Commission which carefully probed co-operative activities, philosophies, and methods.

On November 26, the Report of the Royal Commission on Co-operatives was tabled in the House of Commons. The Report recommended that co-operative associations be permitted to deduct, for income tax purposes, "such amounts as patronage bonuses, patronage dividends, refunds of excess handling charges, discounts, rebates, and other similar amounts paid or credited to their customers in proportion to quantity, quality, or value, of the goods acquired, marketed or sold, or services rendered."

514. **Canadian Co-operative Implements Limited** entered into a contract, in December, with a major manufacturer of farm machinery, Cockshutt Plow Company. By contract, CCIL was supplied by Cockshutt with such farm implements as tractors, combines, and other machines to be distributed under the CO-OP brand name.

1945

515. Interprovincial Co-operatives Limited: In October, representatives from co-operative wholesales of both Eastern and Western Canada, met at Winnipeg to discuss plans and prospects for greater co-ordination through Interprovincial Co-operatives. Enthusiasm was evident, and it was agreed that IPCO should move into full-scale operations as soon as practical.

516. Manitoba Co-op Wholesale Moves Into Grocery Wholesaling: In response to about 50 associations that were handling groceries, MCW set up a wholesale grocery department.

A hardware department was also established with a buyer in charge.

517. Saskatchewan Federated Co-op Expands Grocery Services: Having had a satisfactory experience with the grocery department operated at Regina since 1942, SFCL set up at Saskatoon, its second grocery department to supply member co-ops.

518. Alberta Co-op Wholesale Begins Wholesaling: Up to this time ACWA was not stocking goods, but was receiving orders from member associations and placing them with suppliers. In 1945, warehouses were established at both Calgary and Edmonton and the physical handling of goods was begun.

Manitoba	Saskatchewan	Alberta

1945

521. Manitoba Federation of Agriculture: The Canadian Chamber of Agriculture (Western Section), formed in 1939, was joined by a number of Manitoba's major co-operatives. As a result, the Chamber was re-organized as the Manitoba Federation of Agriculture and Co-operatives.

519. SFCL Acquires Lumber Mill: In response to a resolution from its 1944 annual meeting, Saskatchewan Federated Co-operatives began production of lumber by purchasing a sawmill and planer at Canoe, B.C.

522. Co-operative Life Insurance Company: After more than 10 years of consideration and planning, Co-operative Life Insurance Company was organized and incorporated on May 15, under Saskatchewan legislation, "to undertake and carry on the business of life insurance..." for the benefit of its members and not for profit." Saskatchewan Wheat Pool contributed $25,000 to enable the Company to be incorporated, and the Pool's 16 fieldmen became the first salesmen for Co-op Life. By the end of May, 1945, 159 policies were sold, and $350,000 worth of life insurance was in effect. Interest in Co-op Life was soon shown by co-operators of other provinces, encouraging a belief that the Company should consider federal incorporation.

523. Co-op Union of Saskatchewan, which had been operating from an office at Saskatoon, was relocated at Regina for more convenient contact with government officials.

524. Legislation—Pharmacy Act: The Pharmacy Act was amended as necessary to permit co-operatives to own and operate drug departments provided that such departments were under the direct supervision of a qualified pharmacist. Sherwood Co-operative, Regina, then proceeded with plans to provide drug store and prescription services to its members.

520. Honey Producers Co-op: The Alberta Honey Producers Co-operative, incorporated in 1940, began active operations by importing packaged bees and dealing in beekeepers' supplies for its members.

1945

525. General Election of 1945: During the war years, the Government had, with approval of the provinces, established the Unemployment Insurance Commission. In 1944, the Family Allowance program, another piece of social legislation, was provided. The Government, which had pledged to avoid conscription, conducted a national plebiscite in April, 1942, asking voters for release from the pledge. Among English-speaking Canadians, the vote was 85% affirmative, but in Quebec, 72% of the voters rejected the proposal which might lead to conscription of manpower for overseas duty. The Government was, therefore, obliged to handle matters very astutely but did make eligible for overseas service, some 16,000 men who had been called up for home duty. In the election of 1945, the Liberals were returned with a slim majority in the House of Commons.

PROVINCE	LIB.	PROG. CONS.	C.C.F.	SOCIAL CREDIT	INDEP. LIB.	INDEP. C.C.F.	INDEP.	BLOC. POP. CAN.	LAB. PROG.	INDEP. PROG. CONS.	TOTAL
Ontario	34	48									82
Quebec	54	1			2		4	1	1	65	
Nova Scotia	8	3	1								12
New Brunswick	7	3									10
Prince Ed. Is.	3	1									4
Manitoba	10	2	5								17
Saskatchewan	2	1	18								21
Alberta	2	2		13							17
British Columbia	5	5	4			1	1				16
Yukon		1									1
	125	67	28	13	2	1	5	2	1	1	245

91

1946

526. Income Tax: After the Report of the Royal Commission on Co-operatives was tabled in the House of Commons in late 1945, the Government of Canada prepared, for the consideration of Parliament, a set of amendments to **The Income War Tax Act.** In summary, the amendments which were adopted, contained these provisions of particular interest to co-operatives:

1. Co-operatives were to calculate liability for income tax by three different methods, and pay income tax on whichever of the three methods resulted in the greatest amount. The three methods, or basis of taxation, were:
   i. Surpluses arising from sales to non-members.
   ii. Monies set aside as reserves and not allocated to members as patronage refunds.
   iii. Three percent of the capital employed by the association.
2. Co-operatives and also profit enterprises, were permitted to deduct from income, before computing income tax liability, volume or patronage rebates to customers.

3. Members of co-operatives who received patronage refunds on purchases of goods or services used in farming, fishing, or otherwise earning an income, were required to include such refunds as income when computing their personal income tax returns. This regulation applied whether refunds were returned by the co-operative to the member in cash, or in the form of additional shares or equity in the association.
4. New co-operatives were exempted from income tax liability for three years.

Generally, the amendments pertaining to co-operatives were similar to recommendations of the Royal Commision. However, the assessment of co-operative income tax on the basis of 3% of employed capital was not recommended by the Commission. For many years hence, the Co-operative Union of Canada sought removal of this provision, arguing that it was a 'punitive' measure against co-ops since it did not apply to any other form of enterprise.

527. Canadian Co-operative Implements Limited began active operations in the distribution of new farm machinery obtained from Cockshutt Plow Company, and also purchased a factory at Winnipeg to begin manufacturing some farm implements.

Operations for 1946 were confined to Manitoba and Saskatchewan. Savings of $220,000 after income tax were realized on sales of $1,486,000.

528. Co-operative Life Insurance Company was granted federal incorporation on July 26, 1946, and as a result was able to

extend operations beyond Saskatchewan to other Provinces of Canada.

529. Wheat Pool Building: The wheat pools of Alberta, Saskatchewan and Manitoba together purchased the Lombard Building at Winnipeg, providing themselves with offices to the key

centres of the grain trade. This building was owned by the three pools until 1956 when it was sold and the pools moved their Winnipeg offices to the Royal Bank Building.

531. Manitoba Co-op Wholesale had a record year with sales increasing by 31% over 1945, to reach $2,952,000. Savings, after income tax, were $193,000. It was estimated that retail co-ops served by MCW had a membership of 32,000.

During 1946, MCW erected a modern new feed plant at Winnipeg.

530. Horse Co-op Marketing Association Limited, which was initiated in 1944, now had a membership of 14,700, and provided employment for 400 persons through its operations at Swift Curent and Edmonton. At Swift Current, 200 horses per day were processed, and another 150 were handled each day at the Edmonton plant. Large quantities of pickled and canned horse meat were exported to Belguim where it was an acceptable food for human consumption. It was estimated that by the end of 1945, the Horse Marketing Co-op had processed 60,000 horses and that the by-products from the plant had provided feed for some 75,000 head of cattle.

534. Co-op Vegetable Oils Limited: The oil crushing plant of Co-op Vegetable Oils was completed and in to operation on March 7. Its cost, $160,000, had been

532. Saskatchewan Federated Co-ops also had a record year. Sales reached $9,500,000, with after-tax savings of $559,000.

533. Alberta Co-op Wholesale took steps to provide petroleum services to the retail associations it was serving, by negotiating a contract with the United

Manitoba	Saskatchewan	Alberta

1946

raised locally through the sales of debentures and by loans. The Manitoba Government provided guarantees to back $25,000 worth of debentures sold, and an additional $40,000 worth of debentures that were not secured were subscribed to locally. Manitoba Pool Elevators assisted by providing guarantees of loans. Thus, North America's first plant for crushing sunflower seeds came into existence.

A building on Avenue D at Saskatoon, originally built by T. Eaton Co., but used for military purposes during World War II, was purchased by SCWS. This building was occupied until 1970.

Farmers of Alberta which provided that the UFA would supply petroleum products to ACWA locals.

535. Saskatchewan Co-operative Superannuation Society: The Charter of Saskatchewan Co-operative Superannuation Society was amended to enable co-operative organizations outside of the Province of Saskatchewan to participate in the Society's pension plans and programs.

1947

536. Co-operative Life Insurance Company, now operating under its federal Charter, was extending operations to other Provinces from its Saskatchewan Home Office. Loans to assist the Company, amounting to $53,560, were provided by co-operatives across Canada, and by May 31, 2,836 policies had been issued. Co-operative Life Insurance undertook to set up, in each province, an advisory committee to guide the organization in the expansion of its services.

537. Federated Agencies Limited, a new co-operative, was incorporated under Saskatchewan legislation to provide insurance brokerage service to co-operatives in Saskatchewan. Creation of this organization had been approved by the annual meeting of Co-op Fidelity and Guarantee Company formed in 1943. The latter did not have enough volume of business to warrant a full-time staff, but it was predicted that, by acting as an agency for other types of insurance required by co-operatives, a full-time office could be maintained. Federated Agencies was, therefore, created to handle fire and other types of insurance.

538. Co-operative Hail Insurance Company, a new and separate organiza-

1947

1947

tion, was organized with support by a group of farmers of the Edenwold district.

539. Legislation—Co-operative Guarantee Act, providing for the guarantee by the Saskatchewan Government of loans made by co-operatives for development purposes, was enacted by the Saskatchewan Legislature.

540. Saskatchewan Co-op Credit Society, now serving 152 credit unions and 131 other associations in Saskatchewan from Regina, opened a branch office at Saskatoon, and also negotiated a Clearing House arrangement for instruments drawn on the Society and its member credit unions.

The Department of Co-operation and Co-operative Development, in its 1947 annual report, explained some of the activities of the Credit Society:

"Apart from its functions as a central credit union for local credit unions and co-operative organizations which are its members, the possibilities of collaboration by the Society with other organizations in other provinces, rendering similar services, is receiving attention and study. This is a further indication of attempts being made to co-ordinate co-operative credit service on a Dominion-wide basis as supplementary to those provided by other lending institutions."

541. The Alberta Central Credit Union Formed: On April 22, 1947, Alberta Central Credit Union was incorporated. Similar in many respects to the Saskatchewan Co-operative Credit Society, ACCU was to serve some 92 credit unions and co-operatives of Alberta and replace the Deposit and Loan Department of the Credit Union League of Alberta which had begun operating in January, 1944. Assets and liabilities of the Department were assumed by the new ACCU on September 30, 1947, and close co-ordination between the two organizations was achieved.

542. Co-op Union of Alberta: At a meeting held in Edmonton in June, delegates representing about 300 Alberta co-operatives voted in favor of forming the Co-operative Union of Alberta.

543. Proposed AFA, AFU and UFA Merger: The Alberta Farmers Union rejected a proposal that that organization together with United Farmers of Alberta and the Alberta Federation of Agriculture unite into a single body. The proposed merger, accepted by both AFA and UFA, had been under consideration for at least a year.

544. Alberta Honey Producers Co-operative began to process and package honey, marketing 300,000 pounds during 1947.

545. Manitoba Pool Elevators made a cash refund to members in the amount of $1,880,000. The return covered rebates on handling charges for the 1943-44 and 1944-45 crop years. Repayments had been held up pending amendments to the Income Tax Act.

546. Saskatchewan Co-op Wheat Producers returned $6,265,000 to members in cash as rebates on 1943-44 and 1944-45 handling charges. The distribution of earnings had been deferred until the effect of pending new Income Tax legislation was known.

Manitoba   Saskatchewan   Alberta

1947

547. Manitoba Pool Elevators purchased from Reliance Grain Company in December, 20 country elevators in Manitoba plus a large terminal at Port Arthur (Thunder Bay). At 17 points not previously served by MPE, new pool Elevator Associations were formed.

548. The Pool Co-operative Seed Association was formed by the amalgamation of 10 Co-operative Seed Associations formed in 1939. The new Association entered into an agreement by which MPE would act as its agent and trustee, and provide facilities for cleaning, handling and selling of the production of the Association.

550. Amalgamation Creates Manitoba Dairy & Poultry Co-operatives: The Manitoba Co-operative Dairies, begun in 1920, and the Manitoba Co-operative Poultry Association, formed in 1924, amalgamated as one organization under the name, The Manitoba Dairy & Poultry Co-operative Limited.

551. Amalgamation Between MPE and Livestock Pool Proposed: At Annual meeting of the Manitoba Livestock Pool formed in 1927, it was proposed that the organization amalgamate with Manitoba Pool Elevators. The proposal was accepted, and the amalgamation consummated in the following year.

553. Manitoba Co-op Wholesale, now serving 121 retail co-operatives, had total 1947 sales of $3,700,000.

549. Saskatchewan Co-op Wheat Producers' Vegetable Oils Division, opened a $300,000 plant at Saskatoon to crush flax. This plant, which first began operating January 17, 1947, was later replaced by more elaborate facilities.

552. Co-operative Farms: After legislation for co-operative farms was provided in 1944, some organizations of this type were formed. By 1947, 8 co-op farms were operating and had assets of $286,000.

554. Saskatchewan Federated Co-operatives established a lumber department to distribute products of the lumber mill purchased at Canoe, B. C., in 1945, and to assist retail co-ops in the development of lumber yard services.

555. Rural Electrification Co-ops: In April, 1947, the first of many co-operatives formed in Alberta to provide electrical services to rural areas was incorporated under the Co-operative Associations Act by the Province of Alberta. Through such co-ops, farmers in areas near power lines were able to contract with the power company, on a 10-year basis, for electrical service to their individual farms. This enabled farmers organized into electrification co-ops, to obtain power under arrangements similar to those by which the power companies supplied electrical service to various incorporated communities.

1948

556.   Credit Unions' 100th Anniversary: In 1948, credit unions around the world celebrated the 100th anniversary of the start of the credit union movement. In 1848, a Belgian by the name of Haeck formed the first successful credit union. There has been a number of earlier attempts to form societies to provide personal credit or banking, but the society formed by Haeck is recognized as being the first to succeed. This society, however, was useful only to well-to-do persons and for that reason it did not attract widespread interest. Haeck's concepts, however, were reflected in subsequent developments in Germany, led by Raiffeisen and Schulze-Delitzsch. From these developments came many of the operating principles and methods that were adopted by credit unions in North America.

In Canada, Alphonse Desjardins formed the Dominion's first credit union in 1900, and soon after he assisted in the formation of the first credit unions in the U.S.A. From the credit union formed by Desjardins at Levis, Quebec, in 1900, the number of credit unions in Canada has grown to 2,500 by 1947. On the Prairies, credit union development began in 1947 when the necessary legislation was provided, although there had been some earlier attempts.

The 100th anniversary of the credit union movement was noted by the Acting Prime Minister of Canada, Right Hon. Louis St. Laurent, in a message of congratulation to Canada's credit unions. He wrote:

"On the one hundredth anniversary of the organization of the first credit union, I am happy to extend congratulations to the members of the Credit Union Movement. Credit Unions represent a successful application of the co-operative principles to the improvement of the material welfare of large numbers of our people."

94

Manitoba   Saskatchewan   Alberta

1948

557. Credit Union League of Saskatchewan: The Credit Union Federation formed in 1938, at its 10th annual meeting, approved a change of name to The Credit Union League of Saskatchewan. The League's operations were complementary to those of the Saskatchewan Co-op Credit Society. While the Society was concerned with financial affairs on behalf of member credit unions, the League provided the credit unions with educational, publicity, and training services.

558. Interprovincial Co-operatives Limited made it first venture into manufacturing by establishing a jute bag factory at Montreal. Production of this plant was mainly required by central co-operatives in Eastern Canada.

559. Manitoba Co-op Wholesale began a new wholesaling service to retail co-operatives by setting up a small inventory of dry goods.

In 1948, MCW also acquired a 30% interest in a coal mine operating as Maple Leaf Coal Company Limited at East Coulee, Alberta. Balance of the mine ownership was then held by United Farmers of Alberta. The Maple Leaf mine was in close proximity to the Empire Coal Mine owned by Saskatchewan. Federated Co-operatives.

561. Dairy Co-op and Egg & Poultry Pool Amalgamate: Saskatchewan Egg and Poultry Pool, formed in 1925, amalgamated with the Dairy Co-operative Marketing Association which was formed in 1927 and commonly known as the 'Dairy Pool'. The amalgamated organization then operated under the name of the Dairy Co-operative Marketing Association.

560. Alberta Co-op Wholesale took steps to expand after the annual meeting approved a proposal that ACWA establish warehouses at both Calgary and Grande Prairie. An issue of bonds was sold to raise the necessary capital, and the two warehouses were put into operation.

562. Livestock Producers Amalgamate With MPE: The amalgamation of Manitoba Co-operative Livestock Producers with Manitoba Pool Elevators, proposed in 1947, took place on November 16. MPE assumed assets of the Livestock Producers, and established a Livestock Department to provide the necessary services.

563. Livestock Producers Amalgamate With Wheat Producers: The Saskatchewan Livestock Producers Limited co-operative amalgamated with Saskatchewan Co-operative Wheat Producers which established a Livestock Division to serve the Livestock producers.

564. Farmers Union of Alberta: By an amalgamation of the Alberta Farmers Union, formed in 1942, and the Educational Section of United Farmers of Alberta, a new organization, Farmers Union of Alberta, was formed.

565. Co-ordination: A Co-operative Services Branch was established in the Manitoba Department of Agriculture, to co-ordinate various government services

566. United Farmers of Alberta Amend Charter: The Charter of United Farmers of Alberta was amended, providing for a change of name to United Farmers of

1948

and legislation respecting co-operatives.

Alberta Co-operative Limited. The organization then assumed direct operation of the trading in farm supplies which had been carried on by its subsidiary, U.F.A. Central Co-operative Ltd.

567. Canadian Co-operative Implements Limited Reorganized: At its seventh Annual Meeting held March 22 and 23, attended by 200 Delegates and visitors, initial steps were taken to reorganize Canadian Co-operative Implements Limited. The reorganization was undertaken to develop both methods of distributing farm machinery, and a more effective means for farmer-members to exercise democratic control of the organization.

Subsequent to this meeting, the original CCIL, which had been incorporated under the Dominion Companies Act in 1940, was incorporated November 1, 1948, under Special Act of the Saskatchewan Legislature and became registered in the other Provinces in which it was to operate. The new CCIL organization

assumed the assets and liabilities of its predecessor.

Structure of the new CCIL differed from that of the old. The 1940 structure provided for the formation of local District Co-operative Associations to handle machinery and implements provided by CCIL. Under this structure, farmers became members of the local associations which owned CCIL and exercised democratic control through a delegate system. The structure of CCIL of 1948, however, provided that the CCIL organization itself would own local depots through which it served farmers. Farmers became members, not of the local depot, but as direct members of CCIL. The members, served by each of the depots from local committees from which representation is provided to CCIL annual meetings.

1949

568. Canadian Co-operative Implements Limited ended its fiscal year at October 31 with a new surplus of $713,093. As well as handling farm machinery procured from Cockshutt Plow, CCIL was both designing and building some machinery and equipment at its Winnipeg plant. CCIL's "Disker" and harrowers were particu-

larly well accepted, being designed to incorporate many suggestions and ideas obtained from Prairie farmers. The "Disker", a new innovation, was not patented by CCIL but its name was registered. It proved so popular that other companies soon introduced similar machines.

95

1949

569. Income Tax: The Report of the Royal Commission on Co-operatives and subsequent amendments to the Income Tax Act provided in 1946, did not altogether end the opposition of private business interests to co-operatives. Perhaps inspired by the success of CCIL, the semi-annual meeting of the board of the Alberta Retail Implement Dealers Association endorsed the following resolution:

"WHEREAS The Canadian Co-operative Farm Implements (sic) are now in the farm implement retail business,

"AND WHEREAS they enjoy special concessions in respect to trade practices that are not available to regular implement dealers,

"AND WHEREAS this practise could very well lead to the disruption and destruction of our Canadian way of living and that if such practises were to grow to engulf all other business it is the opinion of this Association that there would be nothing left but state ownership,

"BE IT THEREFORE RESOLVED that we, of the Alberta Retail Implement Dealers Association, bring to the attention of farm implement manufacturers, the Provincial Government, the Federal Government, and Retail Implement Dealers of Canada, the fact that something should be done as soon as possible to curb the spread of this menace and that we believe that the manufacturers should clamp down on this type of business by refusing to deal with any other than a regular established dealer who sells in the regular way with no special tax or other concession."

570. Canadian Wheat Board, in addition to being the sole marketing agency for wheat, was given extended powers to become the sole marketing agent for Western Canadian oats and barley.

571. Saskatchewan Co-op Wheat Producers Flour Mill: At Saskatoon, Saskatchewan Co-operative Wheat Producers opened a major flour milling facility with a capacity of 2,000 cwt. of flour per day. Erection of such a mill had been under discussion since at least 1944.

572. SFCL Closes Outlook Flour Mill: Upon the opening of the Saskatchewan Co-op Wheat Producers new flour mill, the mill which Saskatchewan Federated Co-operatives had operated at Outlook was closed. This mill, purchased in 1939, had operated under the name, Consumers Co-operative Mills Limited.

573. Interprovincial Co-operatives Handles Flour: Saskatchewan Co-op Wheat Producers' Saskatoon mill packaged flour under both POOL and CO-OP brand names. Interprovincial Co-operatives Limited undertook, on behalf of the Producers, to distribute CO-OP flour to co-operatives across Canada including SFCL.

574. MCW Grocery Services: Manitoba Co-operative Wholesale began to stock and wholesale groceries to retail co-ops. Initially, this service was limited to CO-OP

575. Saskatchewan Farmers Union: United Farmers of Canada (Saskatchewan Section), formed in 1926, desired to rid itself of the image of being a political body.

576. ACWA Feed Plant: Alberta Co-operative Wholesale Association, which had manufactured feeds since 1939, purchased a feed plant at Edmonton from

1949

labelled products which, in the main, were supplied by Interprovincial Co-operatives.

577. MCW Bulk Petroleum Plant: On property at which its feed and lube oil blending plant was located, the Manitoba Co-op Wholesale set up facilities for bulk petroleum distribution. These facilities were to serve those retail co-ops near Winnipeg which did not have their own bulk petroleum plants.

579. MCW Sets Records: With sales of $4,872,000, and net savings of $186,000, Manitoba Co-op Wholesale set new records for itself during 1949.

The image had been acquired as a result of the UFC's involvement in events that led to creation of the CCF Party. In effort to bring about a change of image, UFC Saskatchewan Section) was re-organized under a new name, Saskatchewan Farmers Union. The UFC had held membership in the Saskatchewan Federation of Agriculture (formed in 1944), and this membership was continued until 1951, by the SFU.

581. Saskatchewan Co-op Credit Society, with a membership consisting of 180 credit unions plus 187 co-operative organizations, ended its fiscal year on November 30 with assets of $4,965,000. and a net savings of $102,000.

Commercial Feeders Co-operative. Though small, this plant was more efficient than the existing ACWA feed production facilities, and, with some alterations from time to time, it remained in operation to near the mid-1970's.

578. UFA Co-operative was expanding its farm supplies services through centrally-owned depots. Membership, available only to farmers, was on a direct basis rather than through local associations as in the case of retail co-ops served by ACWA. By now, UFA was a major distributor of petroleum products which it procured from oil companies and sold under the brand name, "Maple Leaf".

582. Alberta Credit Unions, by arrangements provided though the Alberta Central Credit Union, were able to provide chequing services for the first time. Provision of such services was made possible as the Treasury Branches of the Alberta Government (a type of bank) offered to provide clearing arrangements though its offices at Calgary and Edmonton.

1949

580. Credit Unions: There were now 236 credit unions in Manitoba, including 35 French caisses populaires. Administrative services provided to both were amalgamated under the Co-operative Services Branch, Manitoba Department of Agriculture.

583. Co-op Vegetable Oils Ltd.: From 5,000 acres sown to sunflowers in 1943, the number had grown to 30,000 acres in 1948, then doubled to reach 60,000 acres in 1949. The crushing plant which Co-op Vegetable Oils had completed in 1946 now required expansion to cope with the rising volume of sunflower seed being produced. In 1949, a major expansion program was begun; it included erection of an elevator for storage of seed.

CVO also solved a waste disposal problem in a unique and profitable manner by compressing the hulls of sunflower seeds into logs. The logs, sold as "Pres-to-Logs" became popular as a fuel for heating, and for use in open fireplaces, and the sale of these logs also helped to increase returns to the sunflower producers.

97

PROVINCE	LIB.	PROG. CONS.	C.C.F.	SOCIAL CREDIT	INDEP. LIB.	INDEP.	TOTAL
Ontario	56	25	1		1		83
Quebec	66	2			1	4	73
Nova Scotia	10	2	1				13
New Brunswick	7	2			1		10
Newfoundland	5	2					7
P.E.I.	3	1					4
Manitoba	12	1	3				16
Saskatchewan	14	1	5				20
Alberta	5	2		10			17
B.C.	11	3	3			1	18
Yukon & N.W.T.	1						1
	190	41	13	10	3	5	262

1949

584. Federal Election of 1949: Since the election of 1945, World War II had come to an end. In 1947, oil fields were discovered at Leduc, Alberta. In 1948, Prime Minister Mackenzie King retired from political life, and a French Canadian lawyer, Louis St. Laurent, was chosen as Liberal leader. On April 1, 1949, Newfoundland joined Confederation and became involved, for the first time, in a Federal election. The Liberals were again returned.

1950

585. Co-operative Credit Society of Manitoba: The Credit Union Federation of Manitoba, formed in 1943, and the Manitoba Central Credit Union, begun in 1944, amalgamated to form **The Co-operative Credit Society of Manitoba**. The new organization was incorporated April 22 by Special Act of the Manitoba Legislature, and began its active operations on August I, 1950, with assets of $378,504 and a membership consisting of 139 Manitoba credit unions (including about 33 caisses populaires), and 10 co-operative organizations.

586. Credit Union League Adopts Budget Plan: At the annual meeting of the Credit Union League of Saskatchewan, delegates approved a proposal that credit unions undertake to provide a budget plan or time payment plan that could be used by co-op members when purchasing from retail co-operatives. Details of the plan were subsequently worked out at a meeting between League and SFCL officials.

At the time, there was considerable concern among retail co-ops that too much co-op capital was being diverted to the extension of credit. An effort to encourage co-operatives to sell for cash only did not meet with any appreciable success for selling 'on time' had become widespread throughout the retail trade. The proposal of the League, however, offered a means by which credit needs could be served by the credit unions rather than by the retail co-ops:

587. UFA-ACWA Merger Discussed: It was obvious that the UFA Co-operative and Alberta Co-operative Wholesale were, in the end, attempting to develop services in competition with one another. At a series of meetings, officials of ACWA and UFA considered the possiblities of an amalgamation between the two organizations, or, alternately, a means of achieving co-ordination. UFA, at the time, owned and operated 21 retail stores and had given some thought to starting a wholesaling service of its own.

It was agreed that ACWA would purchase from UFA, the stores which the latter owned and operated, and which were valued at about $800,000. ACWA would then concentrate on the development of co-operative wholesaling services while the UFA pursued its petroleum and farm supply activities.

588. MCW Growth Continued: Manitoba Co-operative Wholesale sales for 1950, exceeded $5,000,000. The volume handled by the grocery department begun in 1949, was said to have shown "phenomenal growth", reaching $159,000 in groceries and CO-OP flour.

589. SFCL Shows Growth: Saskatchewan Federated Co-operatives 1950 sales reached $17,047,000, on which net savings, after taxes, of $882,000 were realized.

590. Rural Electrification Co-ops: A number of Rural Electrification Co-ops were incorporated in Alberta following formation of the first such organization in 1947. In 1950 the **Alberta Union of Rural Electrification Associations** became the central body for co-ordination and united strength for negotiation with governments and power companies.

591. Canadian Co-operative Implements Limited achieved sales of $4,919,000 with net savings of $710,000.

1951

592. Interprovincial Co-operatives Limited opened a small plant to process foods at Burnaby, B.C. Teas and coffees were blended and packaged under the CO-OP label for distribution through retail co-operatives. Later, peanut butter manufacturing was begun. Some spices were also packaged.

1951

593.   **Manitoba Co-op Wholesale Dry Goods Services**, begun in 1948, but not greatly successful, were suspended. Saskatchewan Federated Co-ops then undertook to serve Manitoba associations from its Dry Goods Department at Saskatoon.

594.   **SFCL Swift Current Warehouse:** At Swift Current, Saskatchewan Federated Co-operatives opened a small warehouse to serve retail co-ops of SW Saskatchewan with a number of bulk commodities including twine, sugar and flour.

596.   **ACWA Extends Operations:** New warehouse facilities were erected by the Alberta Co-op Wholesale at both Edmonton and Calgary. This enabled ACWA to increase its stock of grocery lines which heretofore had consisted mainly of CO-OP products.

1951

595. SFCL Begins Training Program: To provide training for retail co-op personnel in the merchandising of various commodities, accounting, administration, and co-operative philosophy. SFCL undertook to conduct a number of courses, the first of which was held at Saskatoon in November.

597. SFCL & Dairy Pool-Margarine: Saskatchewan Federated Co-operatives, and the Dairy Co-operative Marketing Association (the Dairy Pool) agreed to a plan by which the Dairy Pool would manufacture margarine for distribution through co-ops stores. The program was soon put into effect but was short-lived.

598. Consumers Co-op Refineries, operating as a subsidiary of SFCL, completed a major expansion project, increasing capacity of the plant to 6,500 barrels of crude per day. At a ceremony held August 24th, to mark the completion, it was announced that a further expansion would begin almost immediately.

599. Saskatchewan Farmers Union Withdraws From Federation of Agriculture: The Saskatchewan Farmers Union, formed in 1949, withdrew its membership and support from the Saskatchewan Federation of Agriculture. SFU contended that some organizations in SFA membership, such as the Saskatchewan Co-op Wheat Producers, Co-op Hail Insurance Company, and others, were exerting undue influence in the making of farm policies. SFU held that such policies should not be created by commerical organizations but should be the responsibility of the direct-membership SFU body.

1951

600 Co-op Trust Company Proposed: At the annual meeting of the Co-operative Union in Saskatchewan, it was proposed that a co-operative trust company be formed to provide long-term credit, administer estates and trusts, and to prepare wills for as many co-operative people as possible. By resolution, the Board of CUS was asked to take steps to form such an organization.

601. Co-operative Hail Insurance Company, formed and incorporated in Saskatchewan during 1947, was granted a license permitting its operations to be extended to the Province of Manitoba.

602. Saskatchewan Co-op Wheat Producers paid the final installment on the loan provided by the Saskatchewan Government. The loan had been provided to sustain the Wheat Producers following the overpayment made on the 1929-30 crop.

603. Saskatchewan Co-op Wheat Producers purchased from Western Grain Co., a terminal at Fort William (Thunder Bay). It became know to the Pool as "Terminal No. 5", and had a capacity of 3,000,000 bushels.

604. Canadian Wheat Board: The Coarse Grain Marketing Referendum Act was enacted, confirming the Canadian Wheat Board as having control of the marketing of oats and barley.

605. Co-op Vegetable Oils Ltd. had won wide recognition as being "an outstanding example of rural industrialization and self-help". It was calculated that the farmer-owned plant at Altona had relieved Canada of the need to import about 28-million pounds of oil plus 22,800 tons of meal since beginning production in 1946. By July 31, 1951, CVO could report that:

* Assets had reached $1,021,000.

1951

* The investment by farmers who had subscribed to $10 shares to join, was $23,290.

* Over $170,000 in patronage dividends had been provided to the farmer-members.

* The CVO plant, which had at first produced only crude vegetable oils, was now equipped with its own refining facilities, producing salad and cooking oils marketed under SAFFLO and CO-OP brand names.

* An agronomy department within the organization was performing breeding and experimental work to produce improved varieties of sunflowers, and was also providing advisory services to the farmer-members.

1952

606. The Winds of Change: The environment of Prairie co-operatives and farm organizations was in the process of change. Some significant trends had begun during the 1930's when it became evident from the 1931 and 1936 census reports, that the number of farms and number of people living in rural areas had generally reached a peak and had begun to decline. In many communities, businesses that had begun in times when rural population was growing, felt the change. As the population declined, so did the attraction of the community for risk and investment capital.

Change was more evident in small communities. Automobiles were both plentiful and efficient, and new highways were being built. In the past, highways were often blocked by snow for weeks on end, but now, Prairie governments were obtaining machinery with which to keep roads open all year long. Thus, rural people were no longer confined to home communities, but could journey with ease to larger centres for their shopping. Many smaller communities were by-passed in favor of larger centres. The pattern by which townsites had been established at intervals of 7 or 8 miles when the railways were built was becoming outmoded.

Co-operative associations were, of course, affected by the changes. In some communities the decline of population and business activity brought about the demise of the local co-op store. But in other communities, those people who remained supported co-operatives as a means by which they could provide themselves with local services no longer available from other sources. In more than one Prairie community, the local businessmen, through their Chamber of Commerce or other organizations, assisted in the formation of consumer co-ops. They were convinced that a local co-op would attract people to the community for shopping and thereby benefit other places of business.

607. La Caisse Centrale De. St. Boniface: In 1952, Manitoba's French Catholic caisses populaires withdrew from the Co-operative Credit Society of Manitoba to establish their own central organization, La Caisse Centrale De. St. Boniface. The purpose was to form an organization to provide services in the French language

608. Co-operative Trust Company: Following direction from the annual meeting of the Co-op Union of Saskatchewan held in 1951, a new organization, The Co-operative Trust Company, was formed and incorporated March 24 by Special Act of the Saskatchewan Legislature. Membership in the Company was restricted to

1952

and which would otherwise be more intimately concerned with the particular cultural aims and needs of the caisses populaires.

consumer, producer, marketing and other co-operatives. The terms of reference of the Trust Company included the following:

1. Accept appointments as executors and trustees in Wills.
2. Administer estates and trusts.
3. Provide long-term loans to members of credit unions and co-operatives.
4. Provide an investment medium for individuals, co-operatives and credit unions.
5. Act as trustee for debenture and bond issues.
6. Receive and administer sinking funds.
7. Manage and administer business enterprises.

609. Co-operative Life Insurance Company expanded its services by providing credit unions with policies to protect them against loss in the event of the death of a borrower, and to insure the savings of members of credit unions. These policies were similar to those being provided at the time by the U.S.-based CUNA Mutual Insurance Society. Thus, Co-operative Life was providing an opportunity for credit unions to obtain protection for themselves and their members through Canadian sources.

610. Co-operative Fire & Casualty Company was formed as a national company following a series of conferences with leadership by the Co-operative Union of Canada. Success of Co-operative Life had encouraged entry into other fields of insurance. Co-operatives and credit unions across Canada provided $325,000 to launch the new company, with $200,000 of that sum being required as a deposit with the Federal Department of Insurance as a provision for incorporation. The new company issued its first policy in June, and quickly began to set up operations in 8 provinces. As a result of its rapid expansion across Canada, Co-operative Fire & Casualty Company incurred operating deficits during the first two years. The deficits were offset by additional infusion of capital from co-operatives and credit unions, and thereafter the company was on the road to success.

611. Co-ordination of Insurance Companies: Co-ordination between Co-operative Life and the Co-operative Fire & Casualty Company was assured by placing the two companies under a common board of directors and management. The two companies retained their separate identities.

612. Interprovincial Co-operatives Limited leased a small cannery at Beamsville, Ontario, and undertook to pack fruits and vegetables under the CO-OP label for distribution through co-op outlets.

613. SFCL Opens Warehouse At Yorkton, Closes Regina Feed Plant: At Yorkton, SFCL opened a warehouse to handle bulk commodities. Its purpose and operation was like that of the warehouse opened in 1951 at Swift Current.

614. ACWA Financial Problems: By the 1950 purchase of 21 retail outlets from UFA, and acquisition of warehouses at both Calgary and Edmonton in 1951, Alberta Co-operative Wholesale Association had made heavy commitment of its

1952

In the same year, SFCL closed down the feed plant it had operated at Regina since 1943, consolidating the production of feeds at the Saskatoon plant.

financial resources. The stores were not being well patronized, and the volume of goods required by Alberta retail co-ops was not enough to economically support three warehouses. The warehouse operated at Grande Prairie since 1948, was closed and other steps were taken to improve ACWA's financial condition. Though able to remain solvent, ACWA could not provide patronage refunds to members.

615. UFA Co-operative, now serving 20,000 farmer-members, reported to its annual meeting that savings for the year were $198,000.

616. Canadian Co-operative Implements Limited: A special committee of the Saskatchewan Legislature reported extensively on Canadian Co-operative Implements Limited. The report credited CCIL with saving farmers large sums of money, and with designing and manufacturing implements that were particularly well suited to Prairie needs. The Committee urged CCIL to establish more local depots and to expand its activities, and also urged farmers to make greater use of the organization.

CCIL sales for the year were $7,500,000, and net savings, after income tax, of $926,000 were realized. Membership stood at 55,929.

617. Saskatchewan Co-op Producers Becomes Saskatchewan Wheat Pool: The Saskatchewan Co-operative Wheat Producers was given a major re-organization and a change of name to Saskatchewan Wheat Pool.

By this re-organization, charters of Saskatchewan Pool Elevators Limited, Saskatchewan Pool Terminals Limited, Saskatchewan Co-op Livestock Producers Limited, and Modern Press Limited were retained with the business of all those subsidiaries to be conducted through the parent organization.

While the re-organization was effective on August 1, 1952, the change of name was not official until the same date of the following year since Legislative approval was required.

618. Alberta Wheat Pool earnings for the year were $2,413,000.

1952

1953

619. Canadian Co-operative Credit Society Limited. A significant event in the financial affairs of Canada's co-operatives occurred when Parliament approved Bill 338, Co-operative Credit Associations Act. The Bill provided for the organization, the powers, and the supervision of central co-operative credit associations that may be incorporated by Parliament. The passing of Bill 338 was the climax of years of efforts by the Co-operative Union of Canada, credit union organizations and co-operatives. It provided a means by which co-operatives and credit unions across Canada could form organizations through which financial resources could be employed both interprovincially and nationally.

Following passage of Bill 338, incorporation was granted to a new organization, The Canadian Co-operative Credit Society Limited. The petition for incorporation was supported by credit union organizations of Nova Scotia, Ontario, Saskatchewan, and B.C., and by Saskatchewan Federated Co-operatives, Canadian Co-operative Implements, and Interprovincial Co-operatives.

Founding members of the Canadian Co-op Credit Society were the Alberta Central Credit Union, Saskatchewan Co-operative Credit Society, and the Co-operative Credit Society of Manitoba. The Act of Incorporation provided that up to 10 co-operative or credit union organizations could participate in the Canadian Co-op Credit Society and not more than 15 natural persons.

A key function of the Canadian Co-operative Credit Society was that of receiving funds from the provincial credit societies or central credit unions, and in turn, providing loans to organizations requiring them. The new Credit Society had an authorized capital stock of $1,000,000 divided into 10,000 shares of $100 each.

620. Interprovincial Co-operatives Limited acquired a small chemical formulating plant at St. Boniface, Manitoba, by purchasing assets of Hastings & Sons Chemical Plant for $80,500. IPCO obtained the plant in order to formulate 2,4-D, Amines and other weed control chemicals, insecticides and rodenticides, seed dressings, glycol antifreeze and similar products.

621. Manitoba Co-op Wholesale Opens Lumber Department: An expansion of MCW's services took place with the opening of a department to provide lumber and building supplies. MCW began to purchase supplies from the SFCL mill at Canoe, B.C.

622. Saskatchewan Federated Co-op celebrated its 25th anniversary with a record year of sales of $29,000,000 and net savings of $1,806,000. In its 25 years of operations, the organization's sales totalled up to $168,000,000, and aggregate net savings were $9,756,000.

623. Saskatchewan Farmers Union announced plans for a strong membership drive that would require the help of some 6,000 canvassers. SFU's aim was to sign up at least 51% of Saskatchewan's farmers as members, and to then bring about an application of the Rand formula by which all farmers in the Province could be compelled to contribute to the SFU. Contributions would be collected by the municipalities on behalf of SFU, and the latter would then become the bargaining agent for all farmers in farm policy matters. The campaign resulted in an increase to SFU's membership, but did not reach its target.

101

1953

624. General Election of 1953: Louis St. Laurent and his Liberal administration were returned to office by the general election of 1953, with a substantial majority.

PROVINCE	LIB.	PROG. CONS.	C.C.F.	SOCIAL CREDIT	INDEP. LIB.	INDEP.	LIB. LAB.	TOTAL
Ontario	50	33	1				1	85
Quebec	66	4			2	3		75
Nova Scotia	10	1	1					12
New Brunswick	7	3						10
Newfoundland	7							7
P.E.I.	3	1						4
Manitoba	8	3	3					14
Saskatchewan	5	1	11					17
Alberta	4	2		11				17
British Columbia	8	3	7	4				22
Yukon	1							1
North-West Terr	1							1
	170	51	23	15	2	3	1	265

1954

625. National Farmers Union Proposed: The Interprovincial Farm Union Council, meeting at Saskatoon on April 13, approved a recommendation "that the various provinces which are members of the Council discuss the feasibility and practicality of establishing a nation farmers union."

626. Consolidation of Co-op Wholesale Proposed: Addressing the annual meeting of Saskatchewan Federated Co-operatives, the President of Alberta Co-operative Wholesale Association proposed that there be a consolidation of the production, consumer goods and farm supplies services being provided by his own organization, Saskatchewan Federated Co-operatives, Manitoba Co-operative Wholesale, and UFA Co-operative. He envisioned a single, large co-operative wholesale providing service "from the Lakehead to the Rockies." At the same SFCL annual meeting, delegates unanimously approved a resolution asking the SFCL Board to explore possibilities of effecting a consolidation such as proposed by the ACWA president.

627. SFCL-MCW Merger Explored: A merger between the Manitoba Co-operative Wholesale and Saskatchewan Federated Co-operatives was seen by the boards of directors of the two organizations as being advantageous. It would enable more effective use of SFCL-owned manufacturing facilities including the Co-op Refinery and the Lumber Mill at Canoe, and assemble a larger volume of purchasing power for procurement purposes. Boards of the two organizations carefully studied the idea throughout 1954.

628. ACWA Desires Consolidation: At the annual meeting of Alberta Co-operative Wholesale Association, the organization's president outlined his proposals for consolidation of co-operative wholesales. The delegates then passed a resolution instructing the ACWA Board to consider possibilities of a merger with SFCL.

629. Co-op Refinery Expansion: On August 18, a large gathering took place at Consumers' Co-op Refineries to mark the completion of a major expansion project. The project costing $7,500,000 involved

1954

the installation of catalytic cracking processes, and enlarged capacity of the plant to 12,500 barrels of crude per day.

630. Oil Drilling Rights Provided by Saskatchewan Government: In the first such agreement of its kind, the Saskatchewan Government (CCF) provided Consumers Co-op Refineries with drilling rights on 2 sections of land in a new field at Smiley. The agreement enabled the drilling of up to 32 wells. The Refinery was to bear all drilling and other costs, and recover its costs from crude production. Until costs were recovered, the Saskatchewan Government was to receive 15% of the value of the crude production, and thereafter, 60%. Oil interests soundly criticized the agreement, charging that the Government was depriving its Treasury of income that would have been received if oil rights had been sold by bids. On the basis of prices then being received by the Government for the sale of oil drilling rights, it was caluulated that the final return to the Crown from the agreement with CCRL would bring more money to the Treasury than would sale of the rights. By July, the 6th co-op well had been drilled at Smiley. CCRL also had 7 at Leduc and 2 in the Princess field, both in Alberta.

631. SFCL Leases Planer Mill: To augment lumber production, SFCL leased a small planer mill at Chase, only a few miles distance from the Canoe lumber mill. The Chase mill, then producing about 16,000,000 lb. feed per year, was later purchased.

632. SFCL-Swift Current Warehouse: At Swift Current, where Saskatchewan Federated Co-operatives had operated a bulk commodities warehouse since 1951, a new warehouse building was completed.

1954

102

1954

633. Interprovincial Co-operatives Limited achieved sales of $9,000,000. At this time, its membership consisted of eight Co-operative organizations:

B.C. Co-operative Wholesale Society
Saskatchewan Federated Co-operatives
United Co-operatives of Ontario
Co-operative Alliance of Quebec

Alberta Co-operative Wholesale Association
Manitoba Co-operative Wholesale Association
Co-operative Federee of Quebec
Maritime Co-operative Services Limited

1955

634. MCW-SCFL Amalgamation Creates Federated Co-operatives Limited: Manitoba Co-operative Wholesale and Saskatchewan Federated Co-operatives held annual meetings simultaneously, at Winnipeg and Saskatoon, respectively. The major topic before the meetings was a proposed merger of the two organizations. On January 4, the proposal was given unanimous approval by Delegates of the SFCL meeting, and on the following day, unanimous approval was also given by the MCW meeting.

The organization created by the amalgamation adopted the Charter of the Sasakatchewan Wholesale. By a Special Act of the Saskatchewan Legislature, the Charter was amended to provide for a change of name, to Federated Co-operatives Limited, and an

increase in FCL's authorized share capital from $10,000,000 to $15,000,000. In June, a Special General Meeting of Shareholders of FCL was held at Regina to consider Bylaws for the organization. Representation on FCL's Board was provided to Manitoba members by increasing the number of Directors from 12 to 19.

In 1954 sales by MCW were $7,635,000. SFCL sales were $31,643,000. FCL sales in 1955 reached $40,694,000. The 1955 sales volume was, however, adversely affected by a lack of grain sales to export markets. The Prairies produced a bumper crop in 1955, but because of low sales to foreign markets, large quantities of grain were piled up in storage in elevators and on farms.

635. Alberta Co-op Wholesale was anxious for a merger with FCL. The FCL Board, however, not anxious to be forced into competition with another co-operative, held that there should be a merger between UFA Co-op and ACWA before amalgamation with FCL was considered. UFA Co-operative, achieving greater success that ACWA, did not favor an amalgamation. There was also an important difference between UFA and ACWA structures—UFA being a direct-membership and farmer-owned organization, while ACWA's members consisted in the main of local retail co-ops with membership open to all. Some co-ordination between UFA and ACWA was agreed to, however, as plans for a joint effort to expand co-op distribution of petroleum and to eventually build a co-op refinery in Alberta, were agreed upon.

1955

636. Co-operative Institute: Among consumer co-ops in Manitoba, the idea of setting up a co-operative institute to provide for the training and education of elected officials and employees had been considered for some time. The proposal was explained to Delegates to the June meeting of FCL.

Soon after, on August 9, the Co-operative Union of Saskatchewan convened a meeting to discuss the same topic. Officials of FCL, and Saskatchewan Wheat Pool, Manitoba Federation of Agriculture and Co-operatives, Saskatchewan Farmers Union, together with representatives of the University of Saskatchewan, and Departments of Co-operation and Education, were present. It was decided to form a Co-operative Institute to be responsible for training programs which SFCL had begun in 1951, as well as to serve other co-operatives.

On November 28, 1955 the Co-operative Institute began instructing its first class which consisted of retail co-op managers.

637. Interprovincial Co-operatives Limited—Fertilizer: Interprovincial Co-operatives, uniting the volume of its members, completed arrangements for the supply of fertilizers. In Western Canada, a contract with Consolidated Mining and Smelting Company, a CPR subsidiary, was agreed to, while supplies for co-ops in Eastern Canada were arranged under contract with Canadian Industries Limited and other manufacturers. Fertilizers for distribution through co-operatives were packaged under the name, "Indian Brand".

638. Legislation: Amendments to the Co-operative Associations Act provided that co-operatives may,in order to raise capital, issue securities such as mortgage debentures and savings certificates. Before making such issues, however, prior approval of a Securities Board was required.

639. Legislation: Several Acts respecting co-operatives were consolidated into a new Co-operative Associations Act by the Province of Alberta.

640. Horse Co-op Marketing Association, begun in 1944, accomplished its mission of utilizing surplus Prairie horses. The plant operated at Swift Current was sold to Quaker Oats Company.

641. Public Relations Federations: A plan to stimulate member involvement and participation was launched by FCL. Under the plan, retail associations and other co-operatives of the various FCL electoral districts, were encouraged to form a Public Relations Federation. The Federations, which were financed by participating co-ops of the districts, would engage full-time Public Relations Officers (PROs) to organize and promote various activities among members and elected officials. First to be formed was District 9 Co-operative Education Federation serving an area in and around Assiniboia.

1956

642. Interprovincial Co-operatives Limited, responsible for control of the use of the CO-OP brand label across Canada, added CO-OP tires to the list of private brands available to member organizations. Tires bearing the name of well-known manufacturers had been handled by IPCO since 1951, and IPCO's sales of such tires had increased each year by about 15%. When CO-OP tires were introduced in April, 1956, acceptance was so great that IPCO's volume increased by about 130% over the previous year. IPCO sales of all commodities in 1956 reached $19,000,000.

643. FCL Lumber Mills Hit By Fires: The planer section of FCL's Canoe lumber mill was destroyed by fire. By improvising and using portable equipment, production was continued. But, only a few weeks later, the FCL-owned mill at Chase, B.C. was put out of commission by fire. Steps to rebuild the damaged facilities were immediately begun.

644. Co-op Refinery Capacity Increased: With a modification of facilities performed by its own staff, the capacity of Consumers' Co-op Refineries, Regina, was increased from 12,500 barrels of crude per day to 15,000. Annual production of the plant, operating as a subsidiary of FCL, was then about 145,000,000 gallons of fuels.

645. FCL Sales Increase in Difficult Times: The sales by FCL in 1956, reached $46,051,000. Net savings, after income tax, were $2,058,000. The annual report of the Board of Directors noted that since 1946, costs of farm operation had increased by 52% while farm prices were up by only 9%.

104

648. MFAC-MFU Merger Proposed: The Manitoba Federation of Agriculture & Co-operatives considered and favored the idea of a merger with Manitoba Farmers Union as a means of achieving farm unity. It was agreed that in the event of such a merger, MFAC's co-operative section should be set apart as the Co-operative Union of Manitoba.

646. Alberta Co-op Wholesale was striving valiantly for progress. The emphasis on increasing petroleum volume was continued in hope that it would lead to the building of a co-op refinery in Alberta. In addition a strong effort was being made to encourage retail co-ops to establish new lumber yards. ACWA set up a lumber department which placed orders with FCL's Canoe mill.

ACWA, now serving 104 locals, had 1956 sales of $4,000,000. At annual meeting, delegates reiterated their proposal that there be an amalgamation with FCL.

647. Saskatchewan Wheat Pool leased from the National Harbours Board, Terminal No. 2 at Vancouver. It has a capacity of 1,650,000 bushels.

1956

649. Credit Union League of Manitoba: The Co-operative Credit Society of Manitoba had applied to the Manitoba Government in 1955 for a change of name to The Credit Union League of Manitoba. The application was denied by the amendments committee of the Legislature which considered that since financial activities comprised the main functions of the organization, these should be reflected in its name.

In 1956, The Credit Union League of Manitoba was set up as a separate organization. The Co-operative Credit Society of Manitoba was then operated under a management contract with the League. Membership in the Society at the time consisted of 153 credit unions plus 10 co-operatives.

651. Caisses Populaires: Membership of La Caisse Centrale de St. Boniface now included 33 caisses populaires which together served 8,231 members and had assets totalling $2,432,000.

650. Calgary Co-operative Association Formed: In 1956, the Calgary Co-operative Association was formed and incorporated. In little more than a decade to follow, this new retailing co-operative became the largest of its kind in Canada.

Behind the new Calgary Co-operative was a story dating back to 1940 when UFA Co-operative opened a retail outlet in Calgary. This store was among the 21 acquired from UFA co-operative in 1950 by Alberta Co-op Wholesale Association, and had continued to be owned and operated by ACWA since that time. ACWA had, however encouraged those served by the Calgary store to communicate through a local advisory board.

At a meeting held in 1953, it was argued that in order to develop and be an effective competitor of the many large retail outlets in the City, the Calgary store needed to be an entity in itself with its own membership that would patronize it and control it. The members being served instructed the Advisory Board to pursue the matter, and with ACWA approval a campaign to sell shares and to raise funds among local people was begun. Sale of ACWA's Calgary store to the newly-formed Calgary Co-operative Association was completed October 31, 1956, and the new association began operation of the store at 11th Ave. & 1st. St. NE with about 1,000 members.

652. Interprovincial Honey Sales Co-operative Limited: In 1956, the honey producers' co-operatives of Manitoba, Saskatchewan and Alberta, collaborated to form a new organization, Interprovincial Honey Sales Co-operative Limited, to assist in marketing their products. The new organization was soon incorporated but remained almost inactive until 1959.

653. Interprovincial Co-operatives Limited leased for one year, a canning factory at Niagara Falls, Ont.

1957

654. FCL Lumber Mill At Canoe Rebuilt: The planer section of the FCL Lumber Mill at Canoe, B.C., destroyed by fire in 1956, was replaced by a new facility. Other sections of the Canoe plant were upgraded. Also, the Chase Lumber Mill which had suffered fire damage in 1957, was restored to operation. At the official opening of the revamped Canoe Mill held in August, the B.C. Minister of Lands and Forests described the FCL plant as being the most modern in the interior of B.C.

1957

OFFICIAL OPENING JULY 3RD. 1957 CO-OP LUMBER MILL

655. FCL Volume Grows: Reporting on 1957 sales to the annual meeting held early in 1958, the Board of Directors said that growth since the 1955 SFCL-MCW amalgamation had been "dramatic".

656. Co-op Refinery Coke Plant: At Consumers' Co-op Refineries, Regina, a contract was awarded for erection of a $1,300,000 plant to manufacture petroleum coke from crude oil residue.

657. Public Relations Federations: It was reported to the annual meeting held in 1958, that Public Relations Federations had been formed in 2 Manitoba districts, and in 4 Saskatchewan districts. In other districts, Federations were in the process of being formed. FCL undertook to assist Federations by providing annual grants of

Sales for the year ended October 31, 1957, were $50,231,000, with net savings after taxes and dividends to preferred shareholders being $2,077,000.

Arrangements were made to sell coke to an aluminum plant at Kitimat, B.C. Erection of the plant solved a problem of disposal of crude oil residues.

up to $15,000 for the first years on the understanding that the Federations would eventually be financially sustained by the co-operatives of their respective districuts, with co-ordination of programs provided by FCL.

1957

658. MFAC Rejects Merger With MFU: The Manitoba Federation of Agriculture and Co-operation, at annual meeting, considered detailed proposals for an amalgamation with the Manitoba Farmers Union. Delegates rejected the proposal, arguing that it had not been well planned.

659. MFAC Changes Name: To clear the way for formation of a Co-operative Union of Manitoba, MFAC approved a change of name to Manitoba Federation of Agriculture.

660. Co-operative Union of Manitoba: At the annual meeting of the Manitoba Federation of Agriculture, a resolution calling for creation of a Co-operative Union of Manitoba was given unanimous approval.

661. Merger-Co-op Fire & Casualty and Co-op Fidelity & Guarantee: At annual meeting, the Co-operative Fire and Casualty Company reported that annual premium income now exceeded $1,000,000. It was noted that some of the Company's reinsurance was being handled by the Co-operative Insurance Society of Manchester, England. Delegates unanimously approved a proposed merger with the Co-operative Fidelity & Guarantee Company. The merger was soon consummated.

Co-operative Fire & Casualty Company showed a substantial increase in 1957 in automobile and fire insurance volume. In Alberta, the Farmers Union of Alberta set up an automobile insurance pool, completing arrangements with the Co-op Fire & Casualty Company for coverage.

662. Co-op Hail and Co-op Fidelity & Guarantee Merger Proposed: The annual meeting of Co-op Fidelity and Guarantee gave encouragement to an amalgamation with Co-operative Hail Insurance Company. The Hail Insurance Company, formed in 1951, was operating in Saskatchewan and Manitoba only, and was to consider the proposed merger at its annual meeting to be held in 1958.

663. UFA Acquires Petroleum Company: The UFA Co-operative purchased the assets of Maple Leaf Petroleum to become a full-scale marketer of petroleum products. The UFA had been served by the Maple Leaf company for some time.

666. Manitoba Pool Elevators, responding to long-standing requests from members, inaugurated an Accident Insurance Plan on May 1. Generally, the plan covered expenses incurred through accidents to members, their dependents and employees.

665. Saskatchewan Farmers Union was experiencing financial difficulties due to a loss of membership. FCL representatives to Saskatchewan Federation of Agriculture proposed that the structure of SFA be altered in a manner that would encourage SFU to return to membership in SFA. As a

664. ACWA Opens Direct — Member Section: Alberta Co-op Wholesale, which had been serving co-operators through local retail associations, set up a new department to specialize in farm supplies. Farmers were able to become direct members of this department. ACWA thereby

1957

result, SFU did return to SFA membership in the following year.

attempted to introduce a membership structure along the lines of that of the UFA Co-operative.

667. Saskatchewan Wheat Pool purchased from the C.N.R., Terminal No. 6 located at the Lakehead, with a capacity of 7,400,000 bushels.

668. Alberta Wheat Pool took over the operations of the Alberta Seed Growers Co-operative, entering the seed grain business to help stabilize the seed grain market and ensure reasonable prices to farmers.

669. Saskatchewan Co-operative Superannuation Society, by amendment to its Act of Incorporation, became known as the Co-operative Superannuation Society.

670. Canadian Co-operative Credit Society finalized its organizational activities and began active operations, ending the year with a surplus of $3,188. Eight organizations held membership in the Society at this time:

    B.C. Central Credit Union
    Saskatchewan Co-operative Credit Society

    Manitoba Co-operative Credit Society
    Ontario Co-operative Credit Society
    Saskatchewan Wheat Pool
    Federated Co-operatives Limited
    Interprovincial Co-operatives Limited
    Canadian Co-operative Implements Limited

671. Manitoba Co-op Credit Society, serving 173 credit unions and 10 commercial co-operatives, achieved a year-end surplus of $2,632 and had total assets of $1,289,000. It was noted that the demand for loans at times exceeded the funds available.

672. Saskatchewan Co-op Credit Society, serving a total of 618 credit unions and co-operatives, returned $305,000 to members as dividends and interest, bringing the total sum returned since formation in 1941 to $1,500,000. Substantial grants in aid of co-op education were provided to the Credit Union League of Saskatchewan, Co-op Union of Saskatchewan, and Co-operative Institute.

673. Canadian Co-operative Implements Limited achieved 1957 sales of $2,848,000, and net savings, after a substantial write-down of trade-in inventories and repair parts, of $68,000. The organization continued to develop machines and implements for Prairie farm needs. The Model D disker was further improved, a 6-gang, 42 blade disker was designed; a new style harrow drawbar was designed; and a new method of tempering cultivator shovels was developed. It was calculated that CCIL could have saved farmers as much as $4,000,000 on Diskers alone if all farmers who had bought this type of equipment during the year had purchased from the organization.

1957

674. General Election of 1957: In the election of 1957, the Liberals were defeated by the Progressive Conservatives under the leadership of John Diefenbaker. In Western Canada, from 1952 to 1957, grain sales to export markets had fallen, partly because European countries had re-established agricultural production after the war, and partly because the U.S. was selling off surplus grain at bargain prices. Unsold wheat was piling up on the Prairies, quite naturally causing farmer discontent. There was, however, another factor: there was, in some quarters at least, concern at the extent to which foreign investors were gaining control of Canada's industries and resources. It was said that in 1956, non-residents, most of them Americans, controlled 66% of Canada's mining, smelting and oil industries, and 57% of the manufacturing industry investment. In the same year, the House of Commons had a stormy debate on a bill respecting a proposed trans-Canada pipeline to carry petroleum from Alberta to Eastern Canada. In part, the debate was on the question of whether an all-Canadian route should be followed, or a route which would, at one stage, dip into the United States. Of more concern, however, was the fact of American ownership of the company which was to build the pipeline. The Bill was not put before the House of Commons until near the time the session was to end, and debate on it was further curtailed when the Government resorted to 'closure', meaning that debate was to be cut off at a precise time. In protest against the closure, most opposition members left the House just before the final vote was taken on the pipeline bill.

PROVINCE	PROG. CONS.	LIB.	C.C.F.	SOCIAL CREDIT	INDEP.	INDEP. LIB.	LIB. LABOR	TOTAL
Ontario	61	20	3				1	85
Quebec	9	63			2	1		75
Nova Scotia	10	2						12
New Brunswick	5	5						10
Newfoundland	2	5						7
P.E.I.	4							4
Manitoba	8	1	5					14
Saskatchewan	3	4	10					17
Alberta	3	1		13				17
British Columbia	7	2	7	6				22
Yukon		1						1
North-West Terr.		1						1
	112	105	25	19	2	1	1	265

1958

675. Manitoba Pool Elevators reported an operating surplus for the 1957-58 crop year, of $1,932,000.

676. Saskatchewan Wheat Pool declared patronage refunds to its members, totalling $5,190,000.

677. Alberta Wheat Pool earnings for the 1957-58 crop year totalled $2,365,604.

678. AWP Accident Insurance: On August 1, Alberta Wheat Pool inaugurated an accident insurance program for members and dependents. The plan was developed and administered by Co-op Fire & Casualty Company, and provided coverage on condition that the member had delivered a specified quantity of grain or forage to AWP during the previous year.

1958

679. Hudson's Bay Route: Through an organization created for the purpose—the Hudson Bay Route Association—Prairie farmers and farm organizations endeavoured to promote use of the Hudson Bay Railway and Port of Churchill which had been completed in 1929. The secretary of the Association, speaking to the annual meeting of Saskatchewan Wheat Pool, asserted that the interests of farmers in Western Canada, and of foreign importers of Cana-dian grain, would be served by greater use of the Port of Churchill. He declared that farmers of Western Canada could save 12¼ cents per bushel of which 11 cents would be due to higher prices obtained by the Wheat Board on Churchill shipments, and 1¼ cents due to savings on freight to seaports. In addition, he said, overseas wheat buyers could get wheat laid down in Britain at a saving of 6¼ cents below the cost of shipping from Thunder Bay.

680. Interprovincial Co-operatives Limited Bag Factory, operated at Montreal since 1948, was moved to a new plant at Dorion, Quebec.

681. FCL Assists Retail Co-ops To Expand: Among the retail co-operatives served by FCL, a great many new stores and other facilities were being built and older premises were being remodel-led and enlarged. FCL assisted by providing services for design and construction, and in some instances, by providing financial help. The retail co-operatives also issued savings bonds to members, and obtained loans through credit unions, credit societies, Co-operative Trust, Co-operative Life, and other financial co-operatives.

The retail expansion programs were to continue for many years hence. It should be recognized that this was, in reality, the first opportunity that the consumer co-operative system had had for expansion of its facilities since the co-operative wholesales were begun in the late 1920's. During the Great Depression of the 1930's, funds for expansion were not available. During the years of World War II, and the recovery period which followed, building programs were restricted by a scarcity of both labor and materials, and by high costs of construction during the early 1950's. Thus, the extensive building programs that began in the latter part of the 1950's were, in reality, a release of a quarter-century of pent-up demand.

683. Co-op Refinery Coke Plant: The coke manufacturing plant, begun at Consumers Co-op Refineries in 1957, was completed. The first shipment of petroleum coke was made in October.

685. Co-operative Union of Manitoba was officially formed and opened an office with a full-time secretary, at Winnipeg. By the end of the following year, 180 organiz-ations had joined.

682. Co-operative Union of Alberta Ends: Meeting on May 5, the Board of the Co-operative Union of Alberta reluctantly decided to suspend operations. Member organizations of the Co-op Union were advised of the fact by letter. The letter suggested that the Co-op Union of Alberta "may have been formed prematurely, and in too great haste. It might have evolved more naturally and been more generally acceptable if it had not been created so soon....Perhaps the difference among Alberta co-ops are too great to be properly served by an overall organization..."

684. Farmers Union & Co-operative Development Association (FU & CDA) Formed: After the Co-operative Union of Alberta suspended operations in 1958, steps were taken by the Farmers Union of Alberta and a number of larger co-opera-tives to form a new educational organiza-tion. This organization was known as the Farmers Union and Co-operative Develop-ment Association. Its objectives included developing rural leaders, promoting un-derstanding of and support for co-ops, encouraging understanding and co-opera-tion between farm organizations, assisting rural people to meet local needs and prob-lems.

1958

1958

686. Manitoba Federation of Agriculture: The change of name from Manitoba Federation of Agriculture and Co-operation, to Manitoba Federation of Agriculture, became official. At this time, a number of agricultural co-operatives withdrew from MFA membership but continued to provide financial support.

687. SFU Rejoins SFA: The Saskatchewan Farmers Union rejoined the Saskatchewan Federation of Agriculture after the latter had effected a change of its membership structure by removing from membership some organizations such as Co-op Implements, Co-op Hail, Co-op Life and Co-op Womens' Guild.

688. Farmers Union of Alberta set up a camp at Gold Eye Lake to provide a facility where leadership training and educational programs could be carried on.

689. The Co-operative Institute, operating at 402 Grain Building, Saskatoon, was conducting many courses for co-op employees. The 1958 program included 24 5-day courses for co-operative and credit union employees, and 7 3-day courses for elected officials. A committee was set up to negotiate for a permanent building site for the Institute, preferably on or adjacent to the campus of the University of Saskatchewan.

1958

690. Royal Commission on Price Spreads of Foods Products In Canada: In response to widespread concern over rising food prices, the Government of Canada formed a Royal commission of Enquiry to study food prices and the spread between prices received by producers and prices paid by consumers. The Commission conducted hearings all across Canada, receiving numerous briefs from individuals and organizations.

691. FCL Brief To Royal Commission On Food Price Spreads: A brief by Federated Co-operatives to the Royal Commission on Price Spreads of Food Products suggested that a number of factors were contributing to higher food prices to consumers. The list of factors included excessive profits of corporate food chains, a multiplicity of brands and sizes, trading stamps, premiums in packages, selling gimmicks, and excessive advertising and promotion.

692. Co-op Union of Canada Brief to Royal Commission proposed that legislation be provided to enable co-operatives to incorporate on a national basis. This was probably the strongest plea put forth for federal legislation for co-operatives, since the efforts of 1907 and 1910, although the subject had been raised by the CUC from time to time.

693. Federated Co-operatives' Cash Returns: During 1958, FCL returned a record sum of $1,920,000 to members in cash. This brought to $7,500,000, the cash returned by FCL and its predecessor organizations since inception.

1958

694. Manitoba Co-op Honey Producers moved in to a newly-erected building providing offices, processing facilities and packaging, at 625 Roseberry St., Winnipeg. The new plant enabled the organization to produce liquid honey for the first time, and to improve production of granulated honey.

695. Co-operative Fisheries Limited and Northern Co-operative Trading Services Limited: The Saskatchewan Government took unique action to assist development of co-operatives among native Indians and Metis of the northern regions. It adopted a plan providing for the operation of Saskatchewan Fish Marketing Services and a group of Co-operative trading stores as Crown corporations until such time as the operations were successful and the native peoples had become able to carry on by themselves. A provisional board of experienced white leaders was appointed to act as a co-op board in an advisory capacity for the transitional period. The organizations then became known as Co-operative Fisheries Limited, and Northern Co-operative Trading Services Limited.

696. Credit Unions Disturbed by Increase in Clearing Charges: In June, the chartered banks took steps to increase substantially the charges made for clearing cheques drawn on credit unions. One credit union source calculated that the increase would be as high as 900%. In credit union circles it was believed that the banks were attempting to restrict the growth of credit unions which had become popular institutions for personal savings and loans.

697. Co-operative Bank Proposed: Meeting in Yorkton on September 26, delegates of 16 credit unions of the district, all members of the Credit Union League of Saskatchewan, unanimously endorsed a resolution asking the League and Saskatchewan Co-op Credit Society to investigate prospects of forming a co-operative bank under a federal charter. The proposal was seen as a means of relieving credit unions from the influence of banking interests.

698. National Association of Canadian Credit Unions (NAACU): In 1958, credit union leagues and provincial credit societies and/or central credit unions across Canada, formed a new organization, National Association of Canadian Credit Unions. NAACU's basic purpose was to serve as a national federation of credit union leagues. Its functions were to co-ordinate educational and legislative activities of credit unions on a national basis, and to procure and supply to credit unions such materials as stationery, literature and educational aids.

NACCU's activities and purposes were designed to be complementary to, rather than in conflict with, functions of the Canadian Co-operative Credit Society which was basically concerned with financial affairs.

1958

699. General Election of 1958: The general election of 1957 had not resulted in a working majority for the Conservatives. Thus, John Diefenbaker called for another election in 1958, and won by a vast majority:

PROVINCE	PROG. CONS.	LIB.	C.C.F.	LIB. LABOR	TOTAL
Ontario	67	14	3	1	85
Quebec	50	25			75
Nova Scotia	12				12
New Brunswick	7	3			10
Newfoundland	2	5			7
P.E.I.	4				4
Manitoba	14				14
Saskatchewan	16		1		17
Alberta	17				17
British Columbia	18		4		22
Yukon	1				1
N.W.T.		1			1
	208	48	8	1	265

1959

700. FCL-ACWA Merger Proposal Reached: The Boards of Directors of both Alberta Co-operative Wholesale Association and Federated Co-operatives Limited, each agreed that an amalgamation of the two organizations should be considered at annual meetings to be held in early 1960. ACWA's financial condition, though improved, was not strong enough to spur development of the consumer co-operative system in Alberta. It was also believed that there was little hope that there would be a merger between UFA Co-operative and ACWA.

701. FCL Shows Growth: Sales by Federaded Co-operatives in 1959, were $61,558,000, on which a net savings, after taxes and other contingencies, of $4,200,000 were realized. Both sales and savings were new records. The co-operative wholesale, hard-pressed to meet increasing demands of the expanding retail associations became much involved in expanding its own facilities:

702. ACWA Sales for 1959 reached a record $6,950,000. Net savings of $152,707 were achieved.

*At Winnipeg, a new warehouse and office building with more that 4 acres under roof, was under construction.

*FCL's feed plant at Winnipeg, was modernized and enlarged.

*Construction was begun on a new feed plant at Saskatoon.

*Consumers Co-op Refineries was involved in a $3,000,000 program to expand refining facilities.

*The Dry Goods Department, which had operated at Saskatoon, was moved to Winnipeg where it had more convenient contact with the needle trade and suppliers.

703. Royal Commission Recommends Federal Legislation for Co-ops: The Royal Commission on Food Price Spreads in Canada, formed in 1958, released a report which recommended provision of "a Federal Statute providing for the incorporation of co- op eratives." Explained the Commissioners:

"The interest of the Commission in the role of co-operatives stems from the particular significance that the co-operative form of organization may have in performing alongside of other forms of business enterprise and operating as a check against excessive price spreads. One of the factors in the participation of co-operatives is that the patronage dividends which are paid either to producers of food commodities or to consumers of food products alter the effective prices and thereby result in reduced price spreads."

704. Wheat Board Amends Allocation of Boxcars: On August 1, the Canadian Wheat Board issued instructions concerning the allotment of boxcars to elevators. The new regulations enabled an elevator agent to order two cars at once to relieve congestion at his elevator. Previously, the elevator that was congested was given the same allotment of boxcars as any other elevator with the result that farmers could not always deliver to the elevator of their choice for if that elevator was filled, the farmer was forced to deliver to whatever elevator had space available. The old system was especially detrimental to the Wheat Pools which were generally first to be filled.

705. MPE Assists Cattle Feeders: Manitoba Pool Elevators established a program for Feeder Cattle Associations within the

1959

Province, providing financial and technical assistance to members forming voluntary associations for the purpose of finishing cattle on their own farms.

706. MPE Purchases Facilities: On November 16, Manitoba Pool Elevators agreed to purchase the Manitoba facilities of Ogilvie Flour Mills Company and the Lake of the Woods Milling Company. The facilities thus obtained included 86 country elevators and resulted in the formation of 15 new Manitoba Pool Elevator Associations during the 1959-60 crop year.

707. SWP Purchase Facilities: In 1959, Saskatchewan Wheat Pool purchased 103 country elevators plus a terminal at Thunder Bay from Ogilvie Flour Mills and the Lake of the Woods Elevator Company. At about the same time, 17 other country elevators were purchased from United Grain Growers and the Federal Grain Company.

708. AWP Adds Fertilizer Service: Alberta Wheat Pool began to serve its members with fertilizers. The Pool, noting that other elevator companies were already providing this service, believed it must do likewise to be competitive. Keen price competition soon developed with the result that prices to all users of fertilizer were generally reduced. AWP had previously made an effort to distribute Elephant Brand fertilizer, but this was refused by the manufacturer, Consolidated Mining & Smelting Co.

1959

709. Co-operative Fire & Casualty Company was provided with the nucleus of a commercial division when a Management Agreement was arranged, August 1, making the Company responsible for the operation of Federated Agencies Limited, then a subsidiary of Federated Co-operatives Limited. Activities of the Agency, when combined with those of the Fire & Casualty Company, comprised a substantial commercial program. Some time later, in 1969, FCL relinquished its interests in Federated Agencies to Co-operative Insurance Services.

710. Interprovincial Honey Sales Co-operative Limited, formed in 1956, began active operation. The Honey Producers' co-operatives of both Manitoba and Saskatchewan agreed to market their total production through the Interprovincial organization.

711. Northern Co-operative Trading Services Limited, with head offices at Prince Albert was formed to take over operation of the Crown-owned Saskatchewan Government Trading stores, as proposed in 1958.

712. Co-operative Fisheries Limited, was incorporated as proposed in 1958, to assume operation of Saskatchewan Fish Marketing Services and to develop the enterprise as a fisherman-owned venture.

713. Western Co-operative College was incorporated in the Province of Saskatchewan, and registration applied for in the Provinces of Manitoba, Alberta, and B.C. The College evolved from the Co-operative Institute which had operated under the sponsorship of the Co-op Union of Saskatchewan since 1955. Plans were laid for erection of a facility for Western Co-op College on a 3-acre site in NE Saskatoon. It was announced, that in 1960, the College expected a number of students from Pakistan and India to be sponsored under the Colombo plan.

714. Co-operative Trust Company: The Saskatchewan Government enacted the Family Farm Credit Act which provided for loans to assist in the establishment and development of family farms. The Co-operative Trust Company was designated as the agency empowered to make the loans to farmers. The program was in operation for 5 years. In that time, Co-op Trust made 575 loans with a total value of $7,139,181.

1959

715. ACWA-FCL Amalgamation Approved: Proposals for an amalgamation of Alberta Co-operative Wholesale Association with Federated Co-operatives were unanimously approved by delegates to the FCL annual meeting on January 20. A week later, on January 27, unanimous approval was given by delegates to the ACWA annual meeting. Terms of the proposal called for a working relationship between the two organizations to be established immediately, with the amalgamation to become effective October 31, 1962.

716. FCL Growth Continues: Federated Co-operatives sales to members in NW Ontario, Manitoba and Saskatchewan, reached $67,310,000 in 1960. The year was highlighted by erection of new facilities:

  *A new $1,500,000 warehouse and office building with more than 4 acres under roof, was completed at the corner of King Edward St. & Notre Dame Ave., Winnipeg.

  *A contract was awarded for a new warehouse building at

717. ACWA Closes Out Direct-Member Department: With merger with FCL definitely set for 1962, Alberta Co-operative Wholesale took steps to adjust its structure and operations to those of FCL. First, attempts were made to turn over to a local membership, stores purchased in 1950 from UFA. Secondly, the wholesale closed

1960

Saskatoon. The building, slightly larger than the new Winnipeg facility, was to be erected on a 17-acre site.

*A new, modern feed plant was completed at Saskatoon and officially opened October 19.

out the direct-membership farm supplies department begun in 1957. ACWA sales in 1960 were $9,146,000.

718. Consumers Co-op Refinery Anniversary: On June 18, a monster rally was held at Consumers' Co-operative Refineries to mark the 25th anniversary of the start of production in 1935. A crowd calculated to number 43,032 persons came from all parts of the Prairie Provinces. By count, 10,758 vehicles entered the parking lot. Displays, rides, tours of the Refinery, and a ceremonial unveiling of a cairn in honor of the pioneers responsible for start of the Refinery, provided an exciting program for the day. By official count, the crowd consumed 38,000 hot dogs; 33,000 chocolate bars and other confections; 25,000 soft drinks, and 10,000 Dixie cups. Surviving members of the Refinery's first Board of Directors were guests of honor.

719. SFU Opposes Bill To Grant FCL Credit Powers: A private Bill put before the Saskatchewan Legislature to exempt FCL from provisions of the Companies Act which prohibited public companies from making loans to shareholders or directors, was opposed by Saskatchewan Farmers Union. Purpose of the Bill was to enable FCL to make loans to member associations desiring to expand services to members.

SFU opposed the Bill, arguing that it would enable FCL to lend money or provide credit to selected members, and work to the disadvantage of small farmers. SFU's concern was evidently caused by a new program by which FCL had provided a type of deferred payment plan for feeds sold to livestock and poultry producers who met required conditions. The Bill was, however given Legislative approval.

720. National Farmers Union: The Interprovincial Farm Union Council formed in 1944, was reorganized at a meeting held in December at Edmonton, and became known as the National Farmers Union.

721. Co-operative Union Manitoba was granted a Provincial Charter on January 12, 1960.

722. Canadian Livestock Co-operative (Western) Limited: By agreement with Saskatchewan Wheat Pool and Alberta Livestock Producers Co-operative, Manitoba Pool Elevators became responsible for the management of Canadian Livestock Co-operatives (Western) Limited.

1960

723. MPE Provides Life Insurance: Effective January 1, Manitoba Pool Elevators provided a Group Life Insurance Plan for its members.

724. Credit Union Federation of Manitoba: A new organization with purposes similar to that of the Credit Union League of Manitoba was formed by a group of credit unions that did not approve of the services and membership structure of the League. The new organization, The Credit Union Federation of Manitoba, duplicated efforts of the League until the two were merged in 1967.

726. Co-operative Housing: With the leadership by the Co-operative Union of Manitoba, steps were taken to promote co-operative housing in that Province.

The Co-operative Housing Association of Manitoba was formed and granted a Charter as a body to assist groups to form housing co-operatives and to act as an agent for development of co-operative housing projects.

The Association assisted in the formation of The Willow Park Housing Co-operative (1961) Ltd., which then began development of a major townhouse project at Winnipeg.

725. Credit Union League of Alberta, following the lead of the Credit Union League of Saskatchewan, established a stabilization fund designed to assist credit unions encountering financial difficulty. All credit unions that held membership in the League were required to contribute annually, 5% of the net earnings to the fund.

727. Interprovincial Co-operatives Limited, which had sales of $24,000,000 in 1960, announced plans to build "Western Canada's first basic pesticide plant." Details of the plans were not disclosed at the time, but it was such as to encourage co-operatives to enter into the manufacturing of such products.

728. Federal Co-op Act: Encouraged by the 1959 Report of the Royal Commission on Food Price Spreads in Canada, a delegation of the Co-operative Union of Canada and its French-speaking counterpart, Le Conseil Canadien de la Co-operation, met the Prime Minister to ask for federal legislation for co-operatives. Resolutions urging the Government of Canada to provide a federal Co-op Act were unanimously passed by FCL's annual meeting in January, and by the Interprovincial Farm Union Council and the Canadian Federation of Agriculture.

1961

729. FCL-ACWA Merger Ahead of Schedule: Amalgamation between Alberta Co-operative Wholesale Association and Federated Co-operatives was completed ahead of schedule, at midnight, Ocotber 31,1961. When approved in 1960, it was agreed that the amalgamation become effective at October 31, 1962. However, by a strong effort on the part of both ACWA and FCL, the necessary co-ordination of activities and programs was achieved earlier than had been anticipated. Combined FCL-ACWA sales for 1961 were $81,757,000. Savings by FCL were $3,208,000, and by ACWA, $102,000. In many districts drought conditions were experienced in 1961, causing failure or near failure of crops.

730. UFA Co-op Declines Merger: UFA Co-operative, after reviewing the matter, declined to consider an amalgamation with FCL, but expressed good wishes for success of the ACWA-FCL amalgamation, and expressed hope for a favorable relationship with FCL. UFA Co-operative considered that important differences existed between the structure of FCL and UFA. UFA owned and centrally directed activities of its retail outlets, while the outlets served by FCL were locally-owned and controlled autonomous retail co-ops. In addition, UFA membership was open only to bona fide farmers while FCL was serving both rural and urban members with consumer goods as well as farm supplies.

731. FCL Defers Amalgamation With B.C. Co-op Wholesale: The FCL Board considered a proposal for amalgamation with the B.C. Co-operative Wholesale Society (formed in 1939). It was recognized that the growth of volume handled would require major investments in new warehouse and other facilities in the near future, and that an effort must be made to consolidate activities and assist retail co-ops in Manitoba and Alberta before further commitments were undertaken. It was decided, therefore that a merger with B.C. Co-op Wholesale should be deferred until it could be undertaken in an orderly manner at some future time.

732. FCL Warehouse Facilities: At Saskatoon, FCL officially opened a new warehouse, slightly larger than the warehouse opened at Winnipeg in 1960. The FCL warehouse at Regina was also substantially enlarged.

733. FCL Begins Meat Procurement Program: Steps were taken by FCL to assist retail co-ops which were handling fresh meats. A meat procurement service was begun. Orders received from the retails were consolidated. Purchases were made by FCL meat buyers from packaging plants. As the program developed, area by area, assistance was also given to retail co-ops in the operation of their meat departments.

734. Consumers' Co-op Refineries undertook a long-term phase-by-phase program, which was to eventually raise the capacity of the refinery to 22,500 barrels of crude per day. Whereas expansion projects of 1952 and 1954 had been performed by contractors, most of the new program was carried out by Refinery personnel.

1961

112

735. Interprovincial Co-operatives' Chemicals Complex: On January 19, Interprovincial Co-operatives Limited announced plans to build a multi-million-dollar chemicals complex at Saskatoon, to produce 2,4-D and other agricultural chemicals. The plant was to be built in stages, with the erection of the first stage costing $1,750,000 to be started in 1962.

IPCO sales for the year ended October 31, 1961, reached $26,500,000. More than one-half of the total volume was purchased by FCL.

736. Canadian Co-operative Implements Limited sales reached $7,717,000, estimated to be about 8% of the total Canadian farm machinery sales. Savings, after taxes, were $583,000. During 1961, ways and means of purchasing the Cockshutt Plow Company which had been supplying machines to CCIL, were considered. CCIL, unable to carry such a venture by itself, sought financial backing from other sources, but was not successful. The Cockshutt Company was purchased by a manufacturer of heavy duty automotive equipment, and its service as a supplier to CCIL, came to an end.

1961

737. Northern Co-op Trading Service, serving members through six locations in remote areas of northern Saskatchewan, distributed $20,596 to members as patronage refunds on goods supplied and furs handled. Also, $42,000 was paid on the long-term debt to Saskatchewan Government by the co-operative which was purchasing assets of the former Crown-owned corporation.

738. Co-operative Hail Insurance Company reported assets of more than $1,000,000, and cash returned to farmers in excess of $550,000. The Company paid a dividend to farmers in the amount of 20% of 1961 premiums, and noted that, "Hail insurance is one of the costs that have been reduced rather than increased." Members having $50 in paid-up shares were paid their dividend in cash. Share capital was also returned to members who had retired from farming and to the estates of deceased farmers.

739. Co-operative Hail Insurance Company, which had been serving in Saskatchewan and Manitoba since 1947 and 1951 respectively, sought a license to permit operation in the Province of Alberta. The application was denied by the Alberta government.

740. Co-op Fire & Casualty and Co-op Life Insurance companies were in search of a practical means by which policyholders could exert influence in their affairs. It was obvious that it was not feasible to depend on a system by which individual policyholders from all across Canada, could be brought together for Annual or Special Meetings of the Companies.

741. Saskatchewan Farmers Union-SGGA: The Saskatchewan Farmers Union held a celebration at Indian Head, marking the 60th Anniversary of the founding of the Territorial Grain Growers Association (after 1905, it was known as Saskatchewan Grain Growers Association). A cairn was unveiled.

742. Politics—CCF Becomes NDP: At a national convention, the CCF party adopted a new name, New Democratic Party, and simultaneously undertook to make an increased effort to enlist the support of organized labor. The Saskatchewan CCF Party did not immediately adopt the new name but compromised by using the name CCF-NDP.

1961

743. Income Tax: It was now evident that a renewed campaign against co-operatives had begun. Letters to the editors of newspapers, and some editorials, charged that co-ops had special tax 'privileges'. FCL's Board of directors urged Delegates and other co-op leaders to counter these attacks by providing factual information to clarify matters for the public.

744. Interprovincial Honey Sales Co-operative Limited, seeking new markets for its production, explored prospects for sales to the United Kindom. As a result, an excellent new market was developed for honey packaged under registered brand names.

New Democratic Party
Manitoba Founding Convention
Fort Garry Hotel, Winnipeg, November 1961.

113

1962 to 1972

CHAPTER X

CANADIAN OWNERSHIP—1962 TO 1972

745. In the 1960's, Canada witnessed what is termed a "consumers' revolt"—mass protest by consumer organizations, homemakers, and co-operatives against misleading selling practices, excessive packaging, deceptive advertising, and high prices. After Royal Commissions had gathered convincing evidence that the complaints were justified, a Department of Consumer & Corporate Affairs was established by the Federal Government. Soon after, almost all provinces of Canada set up similar departments.

During this time, the membership of both retail co-operatives and credit unions grew. New growth was especially evident in urban centres. The growth was a positive sign that the value of co-operatives, long recognized by the Prairies' rural population, was fast becoming known to people of the larger urban centres, especially Calgary, Edmonton, and Winnipeg.

Another highlight of the 1960's, so far as co-operatives were concerned, was their expansion into new ventures such as fertilizer manufacturing undertaken as a joint project by Federated Co-operatives Limited, Alberta Wheat Pool, Saskatchewan Wheat Pool, and later, the Manitoba Pool Elevators. Federated Co-operatives expanded its manufacturing activities by building a plywood plant and developing another lumber mill, while enlarging livestock and poultry feed production capacity.

In 1962, co-operators found new reason for pride in Consumers Co-operative Refineries, for it was then the largest petroleum refinery in Canada which would claim to be totally Canadian-owned. In a few years' time, it would be the only Canadian-owned refinery in the country.

Harry L. Fowler, President of Federated Co-operatives,. took note of the unique position of the Co-op Refinery, and the extent to which Canada's industries and resources were coming under foreign control. Fowler, who had been first general manager of the Co-op Refinery at its start in 1934-35, commented on the matter, saying in effect, that in the past people were conquered by swords and guns, but now it was being done with dollars.

In April, 1961, **The Moose Jaw Times Herald** carried an article revealing that in 1958 foreign investors controlled 51% of Canada's key industries—rubber 98%, autos and parts 97%, electrical apparatus 79%, chemicals 74%, transport equipment 70%, pulp and paper 55%, farm machinery 45%, primary iron and steel 25%, textiles 20% and beverages 14%.

On December 21, 1971., **The Toronto Star** carried an article based on a report tabled in the House of Commons...

"Ownership of Canada's manufacturing industry is becoming concentrated in fewer hands and is much more highly concentrated than in the United States, according to a special government study tabled in the House of Commons. . .

"Using 1965 figures (the report) found that '50 corporations each with assets of $100 million and over, accounted for 40 per cent of the total assets in manufacturing.' In 1965, there were 20,000 manufacturing corporations in Canada with sales mounting to $34 billion. But about half the output of these corporations came from only 453 of them.

"The detailed study of 154 different manufacturing industry groups found there were many oligopolies in Canada. An oligopoly is an industrial situation in which a very small number of companies control most of the production and determine prices for a commodity, as well as the general pace of product improvement, especially environmental and safety features.

"Industrial oligopolies have become the target of many economists in North America who worry about their growing power and ability to by-pass normal competitive forces and even some kinds of government policies."

In another article on foreign investment, **The Toronto Star**, January 21, 1971, said:

"A United States government economist who took a survey of U.S. subsidiary companies' operations in Canada, yesterday said New Democratic Party Leader, T. C. Douglas was probably right when he said that 94 per cent of U.S. subsidiaries' investment in Canada is effected with Canadian funds.

* * * *

". . .Belli's (the U.S. economist) figures showed that U.S. companies operating in Canada in 1968 actually received more Canadian funds than they invested (in Canada)."

On June 14, 1967, **The Toronto Star**, in an editorial declared:

"As long as the bulk of Canada's mines, forests and factories are owned by foreigners, Canadians will never share in the corporate wealth we create."

But foreign investment was not the only matter to come to the fore.

1962 to 1972

The Co-operative Consumer, December 21, 1962, carried an article on the concentration of control within the Canadian economy:

> "One hundred and seventy corporations dominate the Canadian economy. These corporations are controlled and directed by 922 Canadians. These and other conclusions were drawn by John Porter of Carleton University regarding concentration of economic power in Canada.

> "The one hundred and seventy corporations have 1613 directorships—1317 of them held by Canadians, the rest by persons living in the U.S.A.

> "922 individuals held the 1317 directorships.

> "203 of the individuals held approximately half of the directorships." . . .

In this context, it may be well to again recall the comment by Pierre Elliot Trudeau: "Democracy cannot be made to work in a country where a large part of the citizens are by status condemned to a perpetual state of domination, economic or otherwise."

And let us be reminded that:

1. Co-operatives, being owned by the members they serve, are Canadian-owned.

2. Co-operatives, being controlled by the members they serve, are Canadian-controlled.

3. Co-operatives being patronized by the members who own them, help to keep Canadian wealth in Canada by returning surplus earnings to the members.

1962

746. Income Tax—Equitable Income Tax Foundation (EITF): In 1962, an organization called The Equitable Income Tax Foundation was incorporated under Federal legislation "to conduct study, research and investigation into the fields of taxation and its effect on the economy of Canada; to propogate the principles of equitable taxation and to make representation to Government authorities at all levels regarding Tax Legislation."

While objects of the EITF, as described above, appeared to cover the broad area of taxation, it is difficult to find any evidence that the organization concerned itself with the taxation of any but co-operatives. The president of EITF at the start was also general manager of the Retail Merchants of Canada. Of the 9-man EITF board of directors, 4 others were past presidents of RMA (Canada) and 2 others were either past or present RMA officers. Another board member was an officer of the Canadian Manufacturers' Association, and another was associated with the Western Retail Lumbermen's Association. Serving on the management committee were two grain elevator company executives. In general, the EITF appeared to be very similar to the Income Tax Payers Association formed at Winnipeg, in 1942. EITF, however, began operations at a Toronto office where headquarters of the RMA were located.

The EITF president spearheaded a strong anti-co-op campaign, addressing many businessmens groups across Canada. His addresses were given substantial coverage in the daily press.

747. Income Tax—Financial Post: As the anti-co-op campaign mounted, **The Financial Post** carried a story assailing the tax position of co-operatives. Headlines on the story read: "Go Get Tax Cheaters." With initiative from Federated Co-operatives, which viewed aspects of the story as being libelous, the Co-operative Union of Canada, together with FCL, demanded a retraction by **The Financial Post.**

Subsequently, **The Financial Post** advised its readers : "FP desires to make it clear that nothing in the headline nor in the article was intended to imply that co-operatives in general, or any particular co-operative or officer thereof, was not fully complying with our tax laws. FP apologizes for any embarrassment that may have been caused."

748. Royal Commission On Taxation: The renewed attack on co-operatives coincided with an announcement by the Government of Canada, that a Royal Commission was to be formed to study taxation. The Commission, headed by Kenneth Carter, a chartered accountant and tax expert, was directed to enquire into all aspects of taxation generally; it was not created for the purpose of studying the taxation of co-operatives only. However, as the Commission held hearings across Canada, EITF and its affiliated organizations made use of each opportunity to assail co-operatives and the so-called 'tax advantages' which they claimed co-operatives enjoyed.

749. Co-op Union of Saskatchewan Explains Income Tax: In a brief to the Saskatchewan Government, the Co-op Union of Saskatchewan said that the income tax legislation in effect at the time, discriminated against co-ops since the taxation of co-ops on the basis of 3% of capital employed had no counterpart in Canada or any other country. The Government had recently had submissions from business interests on its recently-passed Provincial Income Tax Act, and these submissions not infrequently assailed the tax position of co-ops. CUS noted that there was only one Income Tax in Canada, at the federal level, and with exception of a 3-year exemption for new co-ops, its terms

1962

applied to all business. It recognized that any corporation, whether a co-operative or not, has the right to deduct patronage refunds to customers when determining taxable income. Co-ops thus had no special privileges "and as said by Prof. R. C. McIvor of McMaster University, 'such a provision represents no form of discrimination as between joint stock enterprise and co-operatives'."

750. Royal Commission On Banking & Finance: A Royal Commission, formed by the Federal Government to study Banking and Finance in Canada, displayed interest in the development of credit unions. It was estimated that about 15% of Canadian families were members of credit unions. One question was whether CUs should be regulated under federal or provincial legislation.

751. Saskatchewan Co-op Credit Society, in a brief to the Royal Commission on banking and finance, said that credit unions differ from banks because the credit unions do not, under any circumstances, create credit (i.e. "print money"). The extent by which credit unions make loans is related to the sum of the members deposits.

752. Credit Union League of Saskatchewan, urged before the Royal Commission on Banking & Finance that credit unions remain under provincial legislation rather than be shifted to federal control.

753. Credit Union League of Alberta told the Royal Commission on Banking and Finance that Alberta had 403 active credit unions with a membership of 85,388; share capital of $29 million, and deposits of $1,322,000. The League urged that credit unions continue to be governed by provincial legislation.

754. Federated Co-operatives Limited Closes Coal Mine: The Hy-Grade Coal Mine at Drumheller, which had served FCL and its members with hard coal since 1940, was closed down for lack of orders. Oil and natural gas had by now absorbed almost all the needs once served by coal. In 1955-56, the mine had produced 76,500 tons. In 1960-61, demand was down to 42,000 tons and still declining. With costs of mine operation rising, and need to invest in a program to reach new seams of coal, it was not practical to continue operations. Arrangements were made to obtain coal supplies from other mines that remained in operation. FCL's total sales for the year were $94,826,000, and after-tax savings, $2,896,000. Being served were 504 retail co-ops and 177 other organizations.

755. Consumers Co-op Refineries is Canadian-Owned: As a result of a series of take-overs and mergers in the petroleum industry, only 3.8% of the Canadian petroleum refining capacity now remained under Canadian ownership. The bulk of that 3.83%

1962

represented the capacity of Consumers' Co-op Refineries, Regina, which then accounted for about 2.21% of Canada's total petroleum refining capacity. It was also noted that the nine petroleum co-ops which in 1934-35 had invested $32,000 to start the Co-op Refinery, had returned nearly $6,000,000 to members in cash as savings on petroleum fuels, by the end of 1961.

756. Interprovinvcial Co-operatives Chemicals Plant: In early summer, IPCO announced plans to proceed immediately with erection of a chemicals complex at Saskatoon. The announcement followed a release in 1960, after which a well had been successfully drilled on the proposed building site, for salt required for the manufacture of herbicides. An official sod turning was held on September 10, with the plant expected to be operating by late 1963.

115

757. FCL Takes Initial Steps For Manufacture Of Fertilizer: The volume of fertilizer handled by Federated Co-operatives Limited and its member retail co-operatives had been increasing, rising from 16,000 tons in 1956 to 39,070 tons in 1961, and showing signs of further growth. Delegates to FCL annual meetings asked that consideration be given to erection of a plant for the production of fertilizer. In response, FCL examined the feasibility of such a project. A group of FCL executives studied operations of a number of fertilizer plants in the U.S.A., and a team of skilled outside consultants was engaged to study the market trends and potential fertilizer use in Western Canada and prepare recommendations as to the type of plant needed to serve the area.

The evidence compiled through the studies pointed toward substantial growth in demand for fertilizers. The reduction of soil fertility caused by annual cropping and the need for increased food production to serve an expanding world population were taken into consideration. Encouraged by the information and prospects, FCL then directed attention to the matter of preparing preliminary design, engineering and cost studies in preparation for construction of a fertilizer complex.

1962

758. Manitoba Pool Elevators Considers Farm Supply Service: At the annual meeting held in 1962, Manitoba Pool Elevators was asked, by resolution passed, to consider the matter of entering into the handling of farm supplies.

759. SWP Elevator System: At Leask, SWP built a new style country elevator with a capacity of 140,000 bushels, the largest in its system. At some other centres, however, the abandonment of railway lines and altered patterns of grain movement confronted the Pool with the need to cease operations at some shipping points and to increase its handlings at others. SWP's engineering department developed a means of moving country elevators from one point to another, making the first such move at Fairlight.

760. Alberta Wheat Pool now had a membership of more than 50,000 farmers. Since its start, AWP had returned to its members in patronage dividends, more than $31 million.

761. MPE Expands Terminals: At the Lakehead, Manitoba Pool expanded its terminal facilities to a capacity of 15,100,000 bushels by a project costing about $10,000,000 in which a workhouse and three series of concrete annexes were added to the Pool's No. 1 terminal.

762. Manitoba Pool Obtains Packing Plant: In May, 1962, Manitoba Pool Elevators purchased the facilities of Brandon Packers Limited, for $180,000. On August 7, at a special meeting of MPE delegates, construction of a new packing plant facility at Brandon was authorized. It would replace the inadequate facility acquired from Brandon Packers. It was anticipated that the new plant would be open by January 2, 1964, enabling the Pool to provide its members with a livestock slaughtering, packing, and meat marketing operation.

763. Interprovincial Honey Sales Co-operative Limited, already serving honey producers' co-ops of Manitoba and Saskatchewan, extended its operations to include Alberta by accepting into membership the Alberta Honey Producers Co-operative formed in 1940.

764. Co-operative Superannuation Society, formed in 1943 as Saskatchewan Co-operative Superannuation Society to provide retirement pension plans for co-op employees, had extended its area of operations to cover the area being served by Federated Co-operatives. Membership in the society now included 236 co-operatives and 54 credit unions in Saskatchewan; 72 co-operatives in Manitoba and two in N. W. Ontario; and 50 co-operatives in Alberta. Assets of the Society were $8,843,000.

1962

MANITOBA POOL 1

117

1962

765. Co-operative Insurance Building: Co-operative Life Insurance Company together with the Co-operative Fire & Casualty Company, began construction of a building in Regina that would serve as home office for both companies.

766. Co-op Credit Society of Mantioba assumed responsibility for the management of its own affairs and operations by ending the contract by which management had been under direction of the Credit Union League of Manitoba since 1956.

Also in 1962, CCSM began to provide central clearing services for cheques drawn on Manitoba credit unions.

767. Western Co-operative College, on October 3, held an official opening of its new classroom and dormitory facilities. Since incorporation in 1959, the College had received voluntary donations from more than 30,000 individuals and co-operative organizations to finance the cost of construction of the facilities.

1962

119

1962

768. Co-operative Fisheries Limited, serving 18 local fish production co-operatives in northern Saskatchewan, handled 7,200,000 pounds of fish for its members. On sales of $1,534,000, net savings of $44,900 were achieved.

769. Eskimo Co-operatives: In Canada's far north, Eskimos were forming a number of co-operatives to market fish and handicrafts and to provide themselves with supply services. It was proposed that some of these associations become members of Federated Co-operatives. The FCL Board, however, noted that it would not be possible for FCL to provide these organizations with services supplied to other retail co-operatives, nor did it seem likely that the Eskimo co-ops could, without much difficulty and high cost, take part in the democratic control of FCL. Therefore, it was decided that FCL should not accept the Eskimo co-ops into membership at this time, but would undertake to act as a supplier of goods. Large orders were then received from Eskimo co-ops and shipment was made from FCL's Winnipeg warehouse.

770. Politics—Medicare: Plans for a compulsory medicare scheme were announced by the Saskatchewan Government. By this scheme, the first of its kind in North America, Saskatchewan residents were to pay an annual premium for insurance to cover costs of services by doctors. A compulsory insurance program to cover costs of hospital services was already in effect. The proposed new plan was strongly opposed by the medical profession who sought public support for their stand. A number of co-operative organizations—but not all—endorsed the plan publicly and declared their support. Among co-operative and farm organizations expressing support were the Co-operative Union of Saskatchewan, Federated Co-operatives Limited, and Saskatchewan Farmers Union.

771. Community Health Services (Saskatchewan) Limited: Some co-operative health clinics had been established in Saskatchewan prior to the introduction of compulsory medical care. To provide these clinics with a central body, Community Health Services (Saskatchewan) Limited was organized under the Mutual Medical & Hospital Benefits Act of Saskatchewan,

1962

and registered under the Co-operative Associations Act.

772. General election of 1962: When the election campaign of 1962 began, economic conditions were not favorable and in May, the Canadian dollar was devalued. Before the campaign, the Social Credit Party had become active in Quebec, while the Canadian Labour Congress had joined with the C.C.F. to form the New Democratic Party. The Progressive Conservatives won more seats than any other party, but not enough for a majority in the House of Commons.

PROVINCE	PROG. CONS.	LIB.	SOCIAL CREDIT	N.D.P.	LIB. LABOR	TOTAL
Ontario	35	43		6	1	85
Quebec	14	35	26			75
Nova Scotia	9	2		1		12
New Brunswick	4	6				10
Newfoundland	1	6				7
Prince Edward Is.	4					4
Manitoba	11	1		2		14
Saskatchewan	16	1				17
Alberta	15		2			17
British Columbia	6	4	2	10		22
Yukon	1					1
North-West Terri		1				1
	116	99	30	19	1	265

773. Saskatchewan Wheat Pool—Terminals: By the purchase of three Lakehead terminals from K.A. Powell (Canada) Ltd., Saskatchewan Wheat Pool increased its terminal capacity by 5,250,000 bushels, bringing total capacity at the Lakehead and Vancouver to nearly 38,000,000 bushels.

774. Saskatchewan Wheat Pool—Seed: The assets of the dissolving Saskatchewan Seed Grain Co-op Limited were taken over by Saskatchewan Wheat Pool which then set up a department to handle cereal and forage crop seed.

775. Manitoba Pool Farm Supplies: On February 1, Manitoba Pool Elevators opened a new department to handle agricultural chemicals, fertilizers, and

776. Saskatchewan Pool Farm Supplies: On August 1, Saskatchewan Wheat Pool began to serve fertilizers, agricultural chemicals, twine and other farm supplies

777. Alberta Pool Farm Supplies: The Alberta Wheat Pool began to supply fertilizer through its elevator system, but announced that it did not intend to diversi-

1963 other farm supplies through Pool elevators. | through more than 1,000 of its country elevators. | fy its farm supplies services at that time.

778. Interprovincial Co-operatives Chemicals Complex: Late in 1963, the erection of the first units of the chemical complex was completed, and the first production of the organic and caustic chlorine units was achieved. The new IPCO plant was then producing from salt, basic ingredients required to manufacture 2,4-D and other herbicides which were formulated and packaged at IPCO's St. Boniface plant.

1963

779. Interprovincial Co-operatives Accept Pools Into Membership: It is fair to say that many of the retail co-operatives served by Federated Co-operatives did not favor the entry of the wheat pools into the handling of farm supplies. Delegates to FCL annual meetings expressed dismay at the prospect of competition between co-operatives in the farm supply business, and the duplication of facilities that resulted. A number of resolutions addressed to the FCL Board of Directors called for co-ordination between FCL and the Pools, and urged that the pools be asked to refrain from handling farm supplies at locations where retail co-ops were already providing such services.

The pools, however, indicated that they had entered the farm supply business in response to demands of their members, and that not all pool members were also members of consumer co-ops. It was also argued that since other elevator companies were

780. Fertilizer Plant: the studies of the feasibility of erecting a fertilizer plant were carried on by Federated Co-operatives in considerable detail. It was predicted that a plant of economic size would cost about $21,000,000, and questionable whether the consumer co-ops and FCL could undertake such a venture on their

781. Co-operative Insurance Services: After long and careful study, a plan was devised to ensure that Co-operative Life Insurance Company and Co-operative Fire & Casualty Company would remain in the hands of the Canadian co-operatives and credit unions. The co-ops and credit unions had provided the capital to start the companies, and their members comprised the majority of the shareholders. It was, however, an impossible task to bring the shareholders or policyholders together for annual meetings where they could exercise democratic control of the companies.

The plan devised to overcome these difficulties provided for creation of a new organization known as Co-operative Insurance Services (CIS), a holding company to control both Co-operative Life and Co-operative Fire & Casualty Co., through a common board of directors. CIS was incorporated in September as a joint stock company to own Co-operative Fire & Casualty, and to control Co-

782. Income Tax: Hearings by the Royal Commission on Taxation continued. The Commission was established to study all aspects of taxation; its terms of reference did not apply to co-operatives alone. However, interests opposed to co-operatives seized ever opportunity to state and repeat their views before the Commission. The North-West Line Elevator Association, in a brief to the Royal Commission, took a strong stand on the matter of taxation of co-

operating farm supply services, the pools must do likewise in order to be competitive in terms of services provided. It was also reasoned that if the pools handled CO-OP brand products, such as chemicals, the result would be a substantial increase in volume that would benefit co-operative manufacturing plants.

There was no doubt that the pools had seriously entered into the farm supply business, and that it would be desirable that the pools handle products from co-operative sources rather than a competing brand. On such reasoning, Interprovincial Co-operatives accepted as members, the wheat pools of Manitoba, Saskatchewan and Manitoba. Other members at the time included the B.C. Co-op Wholesale; Federated Co-operatives; United Co-operatives of Ontario; Co-operative Federee de Quebec; Federation des Magasins Co-op de Quebec; and Maritime Co-operative Services. Total sales by IPCO in 1963 were $34,400,000.

own. As the three wheat pools were now in the business of handling fertilizer and in need of an assured source of supply, FCL invited them to consider erection of a fertilizer plant in a joint venture.

operative Life. The shares of CIS were allotted to the major co-operative, credit union, farm and labor organizations of the six Regions in which CIS operated across Canada. In each Region, the CIS shareholders operated a Regional Committee which nominates two members to the CIS Board. This structure, which still exists, provides an avenue by which individual policyholders may, through their local co-ops, credit unions, farm or labor organizations, exercise their control and ownership of CIS and the two insurance companies.

The plan, approved in 1963, became effective on January 1, 1964. To accommodate the plan, Co-operative Fire & Casualty Company successfully petitioned Parliament for a change of status from a mutual to a joint stock company, the shares of the new Company to be owned by CIS.

operatives. The Association argued that co-operatives should be forced to include patronage refunds allocated to members as a part of their taxable income. Alberta Wheat Pool's brief advanced the principle that co-operative revenue should be taxed in the hands of the members who received it in the form of patronage refund allocations, and that only that part of the income of the co-operative which was retained by the organization should be taxed.

1963

783. Caisse Centrale Des Caisses Populaires Au Manitoba: The name of the organization serving French caisses populaires, La Caisse Centrale de St. Boniface, formed in 1952, was changed to Caisse Centrale des Caisses Populaires au Manitoba. The organization, now serving 43 caisses populaires with a membership totalling 15,180, was closely associated with other institutions serving French-speaking people, including the Manitoba Section of Le Conseil Canadien de la Cooperation (French counterpart of the Co-operative Union of Canada), Societe Franco-Manitobaine, the French CBC station at Winnipeg, and La Liberte, a French-language newspaper published at St. Boniface.

784. Chamber of Commerce Helps Form Co-op: While many Chambers of Commerce, merchants' and dealers' associations, elevator companies and the like were advocating to the Royal Commission on Taxation, measures that would be detrimental to co-ops, a unique turn of events took place at Irricana, Alberta. The local Chamber of Commerce, concerned that the community, about 35 miles from Calgary, faced the future with no store, enquired as to procedures to follow in forming a co-operative. The Chamber called a public meeting to form a co-op, and paid the fee for its incorporation.

785. Canadian Co-operative Implements, no longer being supplied with tractors, combines and other equipment by the Cockshutt Plow Company, turned to European sources of supply. Arrangements were made to import tractors from West Germany and combines from Belgium. With the development of regular air services between Canada and Europe, it was seen that repair parts could be received at many centres in less time than was needed for shipment within Canada.

786. Election of 1963: Early in 1963, the Conservatives were defeated by a non-confidence motion in the House of Commons. In the election, held April 18, the Liberals won the highest number of seats, but not enough to form a majority.

PROVINCE	LIB.	PROG. CONS.	N.D.P.	SOCIAL CREDIT	TOTAL
Ontario	52	27	6		85
Quebec	47	8		20	75
Nova Scotia	5	7			12
New Brunswick	6	4			10
Newfoundland	7				7
Prince Edward Is.	2	2			4
Manitoba	2	10	2		14
Saskatchewan		17			17
Alberta	1	14		2	17
British Columbia	7	4	9	2	22
Yukon		1			1
N.W.T.		1			1
	129	95	17	24	265

It will be noted that the Prairie Provinces supported the Progressive Conservatives. Much of that support can be attributed to the fact that the export sales of Prairie grain had greatly improved during the time the Conservatives held office.

1964

121

1964

787. Prairie Wheat—World Food Needs: In 1964, Prairie farmers seeded a record 29,080,000 acres to wheat, surpassing the previous record of 27,750,000 acres set in 1940. The farmers were encouraged to boost wheat production when a report by United Nations, which indicated that world population had reached 3,135,000,000 and was growing at the rate of 63 million per year, led to the conclusion that world food production would soon fall short of need.

788. Western Co-operative Fertilizers Limited: In early 1964, officials of Federated Co-operatives, Alberta Wheat Pool, and Saskatchewan Wheat Pool, announced plans to erect a fertilizer manufacturing plant at Calgary. For this purpose, a new organization, Western Co-operative Fertilizers Limited was incorporated on May 9 under the Dominion Companies Act. The organization was jointly and equally owned by FCL and the two Pools, and its board of directors comprised of an equal number from each. In October, WCFL announced that construction work on the plant was to begin.

789. Manitoba Pool-Fertilizer: Although invited to so do, Manitoba Pool Elevators declined participation in Western Co-operative Fertilizers. At the time, APE had entered into partnership with private interests for erection of a fertilizer plant located in Manitoba, to be known as Border Chemicals Limited. This plant had a capacity of about 50,000 tons of fertilizer per year.

790. Interprovincial Co-operatives-Fertilizer: The supply contract by which IPCO had produced fertilizers from Consolidated Mining & Smelting Co., Trail, B.C., since 1955, expired at the time that plans for erection of the Western Co-operative Fertilizers Limited plant were announced. An effort was made by IPCO to renew the contract for a 1-year term as had been done in each year since 1955. CM&S, however, refused to enter into such a contract, but insisted upon a 10-year agreement with a slight reduction of prices. A 10-year contract could not be considered by IPCO because the major distributors being served would soon be handling production of the WCFL and Border Chemicals plants. With no source of supplies for 1964-65, the co-operatives were obliged to temporarily withdraw from the fertilizer field.

IPCO sales for 1964, reached $38,000,000. It was calculated that about 17% of the goods supplied were obtained from IPCO's own production plants, and that another 25% were obtained from other co-operative sources.

791. Federated Co-operatives Limited—Plans For Future: During 1964, FCL repaid to its members in cash, $2,550,000, and laid plans for the future, including:

* In preparation for the distribution of fertilizers from the WCFL plan, FCL undertook the erection of a number of fertilizer distribution depots. The depots were placed at strategic locations where they could serve a number of retail co-ops with both bulk and bagged products. The retail co-ops were able to lease the FCL-owned facilities and were given the option of purchasing.

* Plans to build a plywood manufacturing plant at Canoe B.C., were announced. The plant to cost about $1,500,000, was to be erected during the summer of 1965.

* At the FCL annual meeting it was stressed that changes were affecting retail co-operatives in smaller communities. Farm and rural population was declining as farm units increased in size; people of small communities were showing a preference for shopping at larger centres; and in some areas retail co-operatives, with modern delivery equipment, were unnecessarily duplicating delivery and other services. In addition, it was evident that centralized chains were replacing independent merchants as the main competitors of co-operatives. It was

1964

agreed that retail associations should adapt to changing conditions by amalgamating with one another on a trading area basis, to form larger associations and reduce costs of operation.

It was considered possible to reduce the number of retail associations served by FCL to about 100 or even less, within five years' time, through orderly and well-planned amalgamations.

792. Saskatchewan Wheat Pool Expands: In 1964, delegates to SWP's annual meeting approved plans to erect a terminal elevator at Vancouver. Plans called for an elevator of 5-million bushels capacity to bolster facilities for handling increasing shipments from Vancouver.

SWP also purchased from the Saskatchewan Government, a seed cleaning plant at Moose Jaw.

In 1964, SWP handled about 55% of the grain marketed in Saskatchewan.

793. Alberta Wheat Pool: About 44% of the grain marketed in Alberta was handled by Alberta Wheat Pool.

794. Calgary Co-operative Association: With 1964 sales of $8,200,000, the Calgary Co-operative Association emerged as the largest retail co-operative in Western Canada to be served by Federated Co-operatives. Calgary Co-operative also had the highest rate of sales per member, averaging $439 in 1964.

1964

795. Northern Co-operative Trading Services Limited, still operating under a provisional Board appointed by the Saskatchewan Government, handled a volume of $682,000 through six northern locations, achieving a savings for members of $43,000. The education of members was given much attention with the aim of developing among the members, the knowledge and skills that would enable them to assume full control of their organization.

796. Co-operative Fisheries Limited, with 1,350 members in northern Saskatchewan served by 18 locals, handled 6,800,000 lbs. of fish. The co-op obtained a contract to supply several carloads of fish to continental Europe. This was the first time that commercial fishermen of Saskatchewan served a European market.

797. Canadian Co-operative Implements Limited - In 1964, 4,662 new members joined CCIL - the largest number to join in a single year since the membership campaigns of 1944-45. CCIL's sales for the year reached a new record of $19,191,220 on which savings of $2,059,743 were realized. Savings were distributed by an allocation of more than 10% on the purchase of new machines and repair parts.

During 1964, CCIL made the final payments to clear off loans which had been provided 20 years earlier by the governments of Manitoba, Saskatchewan, and Alberta to help the organization become established.

798. Politics—NDP-CCF Defeated: The NDP-CCF administration, first elected in 1944, was replaced by a Liberal administration. The new Government placed under one cabinet minister, the previously separate departments of Labor and of Co-operation & Co-operative Development.

799. Co-op Housing Association: In September, a plan of The Co-operative Housing Association of Manitoba Ltd., began moving toward reality as construction of a major co-operative housing complex was begun. The Association, with the aid of the Co-operative Union of Manitoba, had negotiated for the lease of land from the City of Winnipeg; for mortg-

1964

age financing from the Central Housing & Mortgage Corporation; for interim financing by the Co-operative Credit Society of Manitoba; and for a guarantee of its loans by Federated Co-operatives Limited.

The housing project, which became known as The Willow Park Housing Co-operative, comprised 200 housing units of town-house style, designed to provide a high standard of accommodation at costs less than those then asked for comparable facilities. The tenants, as members of the Willow Park Housing Co-op, were owners of the facilities which they occupied.

800. Co-op Credit Society of Manitoba announced plans to set up a subsidiary, Credit Union Financial Services Ltd., to provide mortgage services to credit union members who desired to purchase used homes. At this time, CCSM's membership included 220 credit unions plus 50 co-operatives.

801. Co-operative Trust Company: Assets of Co-op Trust reached $21 million and the organization now had 4,500 wills in which it was appointed executor and trustee. With its business expanding, Co-op Trust announced plans to erect a home office building in Saskatoon.

802. Co-operative Insurance Services, formed in 1963, reported that the two companies for which it was responsible had a most successful year. Co-operative Life Insurance Company now had $567,000,000 of life insurance in effect as compared to $150,000,000 five years earlier. Premiums collected in 1964 totalled $5,933,000. Co-operative Fire & Casualty Company premiums reached $10,662,000, including $6,550,000 worth of automobile insurance premiums. A refund of 21% was declared on Loan and Savings Insurance premiums paid a credit unions.

At Regina, CIS opened a new home office building costing $1 million, providing accommodation for both Co-op Life and Co-op Fire & Casualty companies.

803. Co-operative Hail Insurance Company increased its service to members by adding to its hail coverage, at no extra cost to farmers, a "fire endorsement" clause to protect crops against fire damage including damage caused by lightning. In the three years ended in 1964, Co-op Hail paid out $4,500,000 in settlement of claims from Manitoba and Saskatchewan farmers. In 1964, a record year for business done by Co-op Hail in Manitoba, a refund of 10% of premiums paid was declared.

804. Co-operative Union of Manitoba was reorganized, its amended Bylaws

1964

restricting membership to central co-operatives only.

805. Manitoba Farm Bureau: At a meeting of leaders of various farm organizations held on November 16, the Manitoba Farm Bureau was organized. It was the result of four years of effort to provide a means for greater unity within the total farm movement. It was agreed that any organization having a national affiliation should continue such ties, but the Manitoba Farmers Union was urged to transfer its affiliation from the National Farmers' Union to the Canadian Federation of Agriculture, a proposal that did not receive MFU approval. With the formation of the Manitoba Farm Bureau, the Manitoba Federation of Agriculture, begun in 1939 as the Western Section of the Canadian Chamber of Agriculture, ceased to operate.

806. Wasagaming Foundation: To provide facilities at which a high calibre of educational and recreational programs could be provided for rural people of Manitoba, the Manitoba Farm Bureau, Manitoba Pool Elevators, Federated Co-operatives, and United Grain Growers', agreed to organize the Wasagaming Foundation which was incorporated by the Manitoba Government on April 16. Operating under a Board of Trustees consisting of representatives from the sponsoring organizations, the Foundation assumed responsibility for ownership, further development, and operation, of a camp site at Clear Lake which had been owned by the Manitoba Federation of Agriculture.

123

807. Western Co-operative College, Saskatoon, completed erection of additional residences and could now accomodate up to 84 students. Kitchen facilities were also added. In 1964, 1,550 students attended short courses at the College, and many others were enrolled in correspondence courses offered by the College.

1965

124

808.　World Food Crisis Predicted: The World Food Congress, and the Food & Agriculture Organization of the United Nations warned of an impending world food crisis. It was reported that, around the world, people died of starvation each minute; 4,200 per hour; or 100,000 per day. Yet, world populations increases by 190 births per minute; 11,400 an hour, or 270,000 per day. At the present rates, it was said, world population, now 3 billion, will reach 6 billion in less than 40 years.

Canada's trade minister called upon farmers to increase their production.

1965

809. Income Tax and Federal Co-op Act: The President of Federated Co-operatives, in an address to that organization's annual meeting held in early February, made a strong plea for a Federal Co-operatives Act. He charged that the same interests that were now claiming that co-operatives enjoy an 'unfair tax advantage' had blocked earlier efforts to obtain the desired legislation for co-operatives. He outlined events of 1907, 1908, and 1910 when attempts to provide legislation had been defeated, and described activities of the Retail Merchants Association in 1913. The FCL president also revealed some steps taken by the Retail Merchants in support of the anti-co-op activities of the Equitable Income Tax Foundation. The FCL President's address was given wide circulation among co-operatives, and, as a result, many resolutions were passed to request federal legislation.

In March, the Co-operative Union of Canada, together with its French-speaking counterpart, Le Conseil Canadien de la Co-operation, presented a brief to the Federal Government. The brief asked for a Federal Co-op Act. At the time, the Secretary of State promised that such a Bill would be drafted. On April 6, while the Co-operative Union of Canada was meeting in congress, the Secretary of State sent a telegram to advise the CUC Congress that: "The Government is taking steps to prepare co-operative legislation through the establishment of a special committee. We would intend to proceed with the legislation during this session if the report of the Committee is available."

The Equitable Income Tax Foundation, meanwhile, was circulating a flow of literature to mayors and councillors. One such item charged that co-operatives had been causing rural towns and villages to shrink in size.

During this period, the Royal Commission on Taxation was completing its task. In response to rumours that the Federal Government would be urged by the Commission to alter the tax status of co-operatives, a member of the Legislature asked the Government of Saskatchewan to comment. In reply, a Government spokesman declared: "We would oppose the extension of income tax regulations to have them apply to co-operatives as they apply to other corporations. The (Income Tax) Act is very clear as it stands. We would oppose any change."

810. Consolidation of Major Co-ops is Proposed: The President of Saskatchewan Wheat Pool, in a major address, proposed a program for consolidation of the major co-operatives of the three Prairie Provinces. He proposed that the program begin with an amalgamation of the Alberta, Saskatchewan and Manitoba Wheat Pools, with that step to be followed by amalgamation with United Grain Growers. Subsequently, he proposed, Federated Co-operatives Limited would merge with the consolidating body to create a mammoth central co-operative to serve the three Prairie Provinces.

The proposal aroused considerable interest but no firm commitments at the time. Structural differences obviously stood in the way. For example, Manitoba Pool Elevators was owned by its local elevator associations while the Pools of Alberta and Saskatchewan had centralized structures. The share capital structure of UGG was different to that of the Pools. Also, Federated Co-operatives was serving autonomous retail co-operatives; hence a consolidation of the retailing and wholesaling organizations was needed to conform to the structure of the Saskatchewan and Alberta Pools.

811. Western Co-operative Fertilizers Limited: The manufacturing complex of Western Co-operative Fertilizers Limited, Calgary, was completed on schedule. Some operations were begun in July, and, in October, the plant was officially opened. Production of fertilizers for the 1965-66 season was begun, enabling the Saskatchewan and Alberta Wheat Pools to begin distribution of fertilizers, and enabling Federated Co-operatives and its retail co-op members to return to the business of serving fertilizers. WCFL plant was built at a cost of $24,000,000 shared equally by the Alberta and Saskatchewan wheat pools and FCL. Rated capacity of the plant was 225,000 tons per year. It was predicted at the official opening that an early expansion of the plant to increase capacity would be needed.

812. Interprovincial Co-operatives Limited—Bag Factory: Since 1948, IPCO had been manufacturing jute bags for co-operatives in Eastern Canada. In 1965, IPCO disposed of its bag factory because demand had fallen off as much of the livestock and poultry feed was now being delivered by co-operatives in bulk rather than in bagged form.

1965

125

1965

813. Federated Co-operatives Expands Lumber Operations: The plywood manufacturing plant built by FCL at Canoe, B.C., was completed and officially opened in October. The plant, built at a cost of $1,500,000, was designed to produce 40 million board feet of ⅜ths-inch-thick plywood per year.

814. FCL Launches Wholesale Drug Department: Early in 1965, FCL opened a Drug Department. It was managed by a qualified pharmacist and set up to serve the 21 retail co-operatives which were then operating drug departments offering prescription services. During May, meetings of the retail drug managers were

Also in 1965, FCL purchased for $500,000, a small lumber mill together with timber cutting permits at Smith, Alberta, about 130 miles north of Edmonton. This plant was obtained with an eye to future needs when volume from the FCL mill at Canoe, B.C., might be insufficient to meet requirements of the retail co-operatives.

held. It was generally agreed that much could be done to help lower costs to consumers through pooling of purchasing power, selective purchasing of drugs, and achieving an economic operation of drug outlets.

815. Legislation—Pharmacy Act: In Alberta, a Bill that would limit the operation of pharmacies to those owned by a pharmacist was drafted according to proposals of the Alberta Pharmacists Association. If the Bill had become law, it would have made it impossible for consumer owned retail co-ops to operate drug stores or departments. After protests by the Edmonton Co-operative and FCL were heard, the Government amended the proposed Bill so as to enable co-operatives to operate drug outlets.

816. FCL Defers Merger With B.C. Co-op Wholesale: A possible merger with the B.C. Co-op Wholesale, considered in 1961, was again deferred by the FCL Board of Directors. In the midst of an

internal re-organization, and involved in several expansion projects, FCL was not able at this time to devote the necessary resources for an expansion of its geographic area.

817. FCL Asked To Study Consolidation: The number of retail co-ops served by FCL stood at 50 or 53 less than in 1961, indicating that consolidation of the retails into fewer but larger units as proposed in 1964, would be a slow process. The FCL annual

meeting, after review of the matter, endorsed a resolution calling upon FCL to institute a study of the feasibility of incorporating all segments (local co-ops and FCL) of the consumer movement into one consumer co-operative.

818. Co-operative Fisheries Limited paid off in full its indebtedness to the Saskatchewan Government; it was now sole owner of the filleting plants and other facilities being operated.

819. Credit Unions—Peak Number: In 1965, the number of credit unions in Saskatchewan reached a peak of 296.

1965

Since then the number has tended to decline, being reduced by amalgamations and dissolutions to 264 in 1970.

820. National Association of Canadian Credit Unions (NACCU)—Membership: In 1965, NACCU, which was formed in 1958, opened its membership to all central co-operatives, credit societies, and the Co-operative Trust Company. By so doing, NACCU adopted a membership structure comparable to that of the Canadian Co-operative Credit Society.

821. Manitoba Pool—Pool Packers: After some delay during which the Brandon Packers plant purchased in 1963 was equipped with modern new machinery, Pool Packers Limited began operations in September, 1965. The plant, a subsidiary of Manitoba Pool Elevators, represented an investment of $3,000,000, and began with a staff of 75, marketing products under such brand names as Peter Piper, Pantry Pride, Platter Pride, Crest, and Cameo.

As a further step, MPE made available to selected producers in Manitoba, a meat-type hybrid hog developed by Connaught Medical Research Laboratories, Toronto.

822. Rural Electrification Co-ops: Seventeen years after Alberta's first rural electrification co-op was formed in 1947, it was calculated that 63,000 farms, or about 95% of the number in the Province, were provided with electrical services.

823. National Farmers Union: At a meeting of directors of provincial farm unions, held at Winnipeg, July 19 to 21, a resolution was passed calling upon the National Farmers Union, formed in 1954 but inactive, to assume a more aggressive role in agricultural affairs. Shortly after, the NFU launched a campaign to raise funds to assist drought-stricken farmers of Eastern Canada.

824. Manitoba Farmers Union endorsed the adoption of a more aggressive role in agricultural affairs by the National Farmers Union. By an almost unanimous resolution, MFU undertook to solicit voluntary contributions to help NFU build up its funds for education and research.

825. Saskatchewan Farmers Union gave strong support to the National Farmers Union. The president of SFU was elected as NFU president.

826. Farmers Union of Alberta, in a bid for farm unity, proposed an amalgamation with the Alberta Federation of Agriculture. The proposal was rejected.

On December 8, the Farmers Union of Alberta, in annual meeting, voted in favor of unification of all farm groups to provide "one voice" for agriculture.

827. Hudson's Bay Route: The Premiers of the Provinces of Alberta, Saskatchewan and Manitoba, at a conference, "agreed to consider greater use and expansion of the Port of Churchill."

1965

1965

828. Canadian Co-operative Implements Limited, in addition to manufacturing a number of farm machinery items, had always relied on other manufacturers for supply of tractors, combines, and some other major implements. In earlier years of CCIL, Cockshutt Plow Company had served many needs of CCIL, but after that Company had been purchased by another corporation, CCIL found it necessary to turn elsewhere. Thus, CCIL began to import "Claas" harvesting combines from Belgium. In 1965, the "Claas" manufacturer was bought out by a multinational corporation, Sperry Rand, and CCIL again found it necessary to locate a new source of supply. This time, arrangements were made for the import of combines from West Germany.

829. General Election of 1965: In 1965, the Liberal Government under Lester B. Pearson, faced the electorate, but again failed to win a majority. In 1964, the Government had introduced the Canada Pension Plan, and in 1965, the Canadian flag was adopted.

PROVINCE	LIB.	PROG. CONS.	N.D.P.	CREDITISTE	SOCIAL CREDIT	INDEP.	TOTAL
Ontario	51	25	9				85
Quebec	56	8		9		2	75
Nova Scotia	2	10					10
New Brunswick	6	4					10
Newfoundland	7						7
P.E.I.		4					4
Manitoba	1	10	3				14
Saskatchewan		17					17
Alberta		15			2		17
British Columbia	7	3	9		3		22
Yukon		1					1
N.W.T.	1						1
	131	97	21	9	5	2	265

127

1966

830. The Essential Principles of Co-operatives: In 1966, the International Co-operative Alliance, a world-wide fraternal organization of co-operatives, completed an important work by adopting a statement of "The Essential Principles of Co-operative organizations. "The list of principles was devised by a select committee which had carefully studied records of the Rochdale Pioneers of 1844, and the practices and needs of co-operatives of the 1960's.

By defining "The Essential Principles of Co-operative Organizations." The list of principles was devised by a select committee applicable in general terms to all types of co-operative organizations of all countries.

Equally important, the ICA clarified a confusing situation that had arisen years ago, which had resulted in a popular belief that the Rochdale Pioneers had left for posterity, a terse and precise set of co-operative principles and methods.

The fact is the Rochdale Pioneers did not carve out such a set of principles or methods as is so often believed. An almanac published by the Rochdale Society in the mid-1860's, about 20 years after the Rochdale store was opened, described in general terms, the philosophies and practices adopted by the Pioneers. Writers seeking an abbreviated way of describing these, listed them as 'principles' or 'methods'. Other writers perpetuated the practice but were not always consistent in their choice of either 'principles' or 'methods'. As a result, authors of books on co-operation have listed many so-called 'principles' or 'methods', and often contradict one another in the process.

The ICA has, therefore, done an important work by providing an 'official' list of co-operative principles that are, without question, in harmony with the concepts of the Rochdale Pioneers of 1844.

THE ESSENTIAL PRINCIPLES OF CO-OPERATIVE ORGANIZATIONS

as approved by the
International Co-operative Alliance
September 1966

I. OPEN AND VOLUNTARY MEMBERSHIP

Membership of a co-operative society should be voluntary and available without artifical restriction or any social, political or religious descrimination, to all persons who make use of its services and are willing to accept the responsibilities of membership.

2. DEMOCRATIC CONTROL

Co-operative societies are democratic organizations. Their affairs should be administered by persons elected or appointed in a manner agreed by the members and accountable to them. Members of primary societies should enjoy equal rights of voting (one member, one vote) and participation in decisions affecting their societies. In other than primary societies the administration should be conducted on a democratic basis in a suitable form.

3. LIMITED INTEREST ON SHARES

Share capital should only receive a strictly limited rate of interest, if any.

4. RETURN OF SURPLUS TO MEMBERS

Surplus or savings, if any, arising out of the operations of a society belong to the members of that society and should be distributed in such manner as would avoid one member gaining at the expense of others. This may be done by decision of the members as follows:

(a) by provision for development of the business of the co-operative.
(b) by provision of common services; or
(c) by distribution among the members in proportion to their transactions with the society.

5. CO—OPERATIVE EDUCATION

All co-operative societies should make provision for the education of their members, officers and employees, and of the general public, in the principles and techniques of co-operation, both economic and democratic.

1966

831. Federated Co-operatives—Cash Refunds: In 1966. FCL repaid to its retail co-operative and other members $2,318,000 in cash. It was calculated that, since being formed in 1928, FCL and its predecessors (co-op wholesales of Alberta, Saskatchewan and Manitoba, and Co-op Refinery) had returned at least $26,547,000 to members in cash, with $20,250,000 of that sum being returned in the years 1958 to 1966 inclusive.

Other co-operative organizations had also returned substantial sums to members over the years. The value of such cash returns by co-operatives to the Prairie economy was described by a former U.S. Congressman, Gerry Voorhis, a co-operative leader in the U.S.A. Said Voorhis: "economists tell us that each additional dollar that can be returned to a community to become part of its stream of purchasing power will generate about $5 of additional income in that community....The main purpose of the co-operative patronage refund is to keep purchasing power flowing through the economy. The co-operative accomplishes this by returning to the people or institutions which possessed the purchasing power in the first place, the margins of earnings which, in other kinds of business, are permanently siphoned away into the hands of sellers."

832. Federated Co-operatives—Smith Lumber Mill: A plan for long-term, step-by-step development of the lumber mill at Smith, Alberta; obtained by FCL in 1965, was developed. As a first step, negotiations for additional timber cutting quotas were held with the Alberta Government. The Government provided further quotas on condition that FCL give Indians and Metis of the area first opportunity to harvest timber for the mill. FCL agreed to the condition and also took steps to train a number of Indians and Metis for employment within the mill.

833. FCL Warehouse & Feed Plant At Calgary: In March, FCL officially opened a new warehouse and office building, and a new feed manufacturing plant, at Calgary.

834. Interprovincial Honey Sales Co-operative had record sales in excess of 18-million pounds of honey. More than one-half of the volume was processed and packed by Manitoba Co-operative Honey Producers Limited.

835. Willow Park Co-op Housing Project, Winnipeg, begun in 1964, was completed, quickly occupied, and given an official opening.

836. Co-op Insurance Services— Rochdale Mortgage & Realty: To provide mortgage funds for individual home building, and to assist in the development of co-operative business properties, a new organization, Rochdale Mortgage & Realty Limited, was incorporated. The organization was created as a wholly-owned subsidiary of Co-operative Insurance Services, with capital of $500,000. Initial operations were to be in Alberta.

1966

838. Manitoba Pool—Livestock: On August 1, Manitoba Pool Elevators leased the Brandon Co-operative Livestock Market to Canadian Livestock Co-operative (Western) Limited.

837. Co-operative Development Association: The Co-operative Union of Saskatchewan, formed in 1944, was replaced by a new organization known as the Co-operative Development Association (CDA), with membership open to all co-operatives registered in Saskatchewan. Many functions and features of the CUS were continued by CDA.

839. Co-operative Trust Company, In June, occupied its new Home Office building at Saskatoon. This building, constructed at a cost of $454,000, also provided accommodation for the Company's Saskatoon Area Offices. At the close of the year, assets of Co-operative Trust amonted to $28,660,000.

128

1967

840. Task Force On Agriculture: The Federal Government established a Task Force to study the trends and future development of agriculture in Canada. In co-op circles there was some concern expressed because those appointed to the Task Force did not include representatives of any major co-operatives or farm organizations. At the time there was considerable concern that world food production was not keeping pace with the population increase. Yet, in Canada, sales of wheat did not appear to reflect a rising world demand. Some traditional markets for Canadian grains were purchasing in decreasing amounts as some countries increased their own production while others imported supplies from other major producing countries.

841. Interprovincial Co-operatives—Chemical Plants: On September 20, a sod-turning ceremony was held to mark the start of an expansion program for IPCO's chemicals complex which had begun production in 1963. The new project involved expenditures of more than $5,000,000, and was encouraged by the Saskatchewan Government which was assisting a U.S.-based concern to establish a pulp mill at Prince Albert. The mill, costing $65,000,000, required chemicals of the type produced by the IPCO plant for its operation. To finance expansion of the IPCO plant, the Saskatchewan Government provided a substantial loan through its Saskatchewan Economic Development Corporation (SEDCO).

At Toronto, IPCO opened a $250,000 chemical plant to formulate agricultural chemicals for distribution in Eastern Canada.

Also in 1967, IPCO expanded the chemical plant it had acquired in 1953 at St. Boniface, Manitoba, increasing capacity by five times the original volume.

IPCO sales for the year were $43,000,000, and net savings, $363,000.

842. Western Co-operative Fertilizers Limited realized a savings of $1,512,000 on fertilizer sales of $19,714,000. The Calgary plant, which was completed in 1965 with a rated capacity of 225,000 tons per year, was hard-pressed to meet demands and actually produced about 248,000 tons.

843. Saskatchewan Wheat Pool Farm Supply: Saskatchewan Wheat Pool, now serving farm supplies through its country elevators, announced plans to erect 21 farm service centres by the end of 1968 under a program to cost about $1,121,000.

844. Saskatchewan Wheat Pool Livestock: A stockyard in Ontario was purchased by Saskatchewan Wheat Pool as a facility for marketing Saskatchewan cattle.

845. Grain Markets: For lack of foreign markets, grain was piling up on Prairie farms and in commercial storage. Further problems were caused by poor harvest conditions. With elevators and granaries filled, many farmers had to improvise temporary storage facilities from plywood and tarpaulins.

846. United Grain Growers Limited purchased 86 country elevators and a terminal at Thunder Bay from McCabe Grain Company, for $4,100,000. With this purchase, UGG's facilities included 344 country elevators in Saskatchewan, 143 in Manitoba, and 353 in Alberta, plus three terminals at the Lakehead.

1967

847. Manitoba Pool Elevators Plans Change of Structure: The 43rd Annual Meeting of Manitoba Pool Elevators consented to give the board of directors authorization to ask the Manitoba Legislature to amend MPE's Act of Incorporation to provide for a direct membership. At the time, 213 local elevator associations and 1 seed association had membership in MPE with farmers being members of the associations. The proposed change would create a structure similar to that of the Alberta and Saskatchewan Pools of which the farmers served are direct members.

848. Alberta Wheat Pool Farm Supply AWP's farm supply services, which had been limited to fertilizer only when begun in 1963, were extended to include the distribution of agricultural chemicals through its elevator system.

1967

849. Western Co-operative Fertilizers had sales for the year ended June 30 of $22,574,000. The organization had allocated savings totalling $4,885,000 to its owners–Alberta and Saskatchewan Wheat pools and FCL–since operations begun in 1965. Although the Calgary plant had been taxed to capacity to meet fertilizer demands, plans to undertake a major expansion were deferred because the lack of markets for Prairie grains and poor 1968 harvest conditions warned that a continuation of high demands for fertilizer could not be assured for the immediate future.

850. Co-op Vegetable Oils reported 1968 sales of $5,500,000, and noted that, since its formation in 1944, it had paid out $1,030,000 to its members.

130

1967

851. Federated Co-operatives–Brandon Feed Mill: FCL agreed to collaborate with Manitoba Pool Elevators in development of a farm service complex at Brandon. The complex was being developed on property adjacent to the Pool Packers Plant which MPE had opened in 1965. As its contribution, FCL announced an immediate start of construction of a $450,000 feed mill.

852. Federated Co-operatives–Edmonton Warehouse: At Edmonton, FCL completed construction of a new warehouse and office building. It was recognized at the time that replacement of the FCL-owned feed plant, first acquired in 1949 by Alberta Co-operative Wholesale, could not be long delayed.

854. Co-op Vegetable Oils Limited purchased facilities of Co-op Prairie Canners at Winkler, Manitoba. CVO planned to expand facilities for canning of vegetables and juices to be marketed under the name of Gardenland Canners, and to enter into the packaging of frozen foods.

855. Northern Co-operative Trading Services sales for 1967 were $1,091,000, and savings were $68,000. During the year cash payments totalling $49,000 were made to members most of whom were Indians and Metis. NCTSL had also reduced to $61,000, its indebtedness of $275,000 to the Provincial Government. The debt was incurred in 1959 when NCTSL was created from the previously Crown-owned Saskatchewan Government Trading Stores.

853. United Feeds Limited, a new organization, was incorporated as a joint venture of United Grain Growers' Limited and the United Farmers of Alberta Co-operative. Purpose of the new organization was to manufacture livestock and poultry feed products for distribution through UGG and UFA facilities.

857. Credit Union League of Manitoba 1967 Limited: The Credit Union Federation of Manitoba, formed in 1960, and the Credit Union League of Manitoba, formed in 1956, amalgamated as The Credit Union League of Manitoba 1967 Limited.

856. Calgary Co-operative Association, now with a membership of 33,000, opened a farm service centre and began construction of its fifth major shopping centre in Calgary. When this centre was opened, the event was attended by an estimated 16,500 persons.

858. Credit Union Federation Of Alberta: A firm of management consultants, after study of the credit union movement in Alberta, recommended a merger of the Credit Union League and the Central Credit Union. Unanimous approval was given by the annual meetings of both organizations which then merged as a new entity, Credit Union Federation of Alberta Limited, which was granted incorporation April 7, 1967. The new organization assumed assets and liabilities of both predecessors, and continued their services to Alberta Credit Unions.

1967

859. Co-operative Trust Company of Canada: The Co-operative Trust Company Limited, incorporated in 1952 by the Saskatchewan Legislature, received a Federal Charter in December, and became known as Co-operative Trust Company of Canada. Under the new Charter, the Company became able to extend its services and activities to other provinces of Canada. The Company's policy was to extend services to other provinces when invited to do so by the central co-operative organizations concerned. The Company adopted a control structure providing for seven regions–one embracing the Maritime Provinces, and one for each of the other Provinces. Each of the regions became entitled to nominate directors to the Board of Directors when 30 organizations within the region were accepted as members of the Company.

860. Canadian Co-operative Implements Limited, in 1967, completed arrangements for the importation of Volvo tractors and combines from Sweden.

Manitoba	Saskatchewan	Alberta

1967

861. Co-operative Union of Manitoba, formed in 1958, ceased to function and closed its offices when Manitoba Pool Elevators withdrew its financial support. However, the Charter of CUM was retained and its Board of Directors carried on as a Board of Trustees responsible for custody of the Charter and the funds of CUM.

862. Saskatchewan Farmers Union Withdraws From Saskatchewan Federation of Agriculture: In 1958, Saskatchewan Farmers Union had rejoined the Saskatchewan Federation of Agriculture, but in 1967, SFU again withdrew from SFA which it charged with violation of terms by which SFU had agreed to rejoin SFA. There were also basic differences in policies and views of the two organizations.

863. Goldeye Lake Camp: The Junior Farmers Union of Alberta Goldeye Lake Camp was officially dedicated on June 30. Representing an investment of $175,000, the camp was to serve as a training centre for rural people, operating with an emphasis on youth groups and concerned with such topics as citizenship, community leadership, co-operation, etc.

864. Food Prices Again Studied: In early 1967, consumers' complaints concerning high food prices and industry practices provoked the formation of two major enquiries. A federal enquiry was undertaken by The Special Joint Committee of the Senate and House of Commons on Consumer Credit (Prices). Simultaneously governments of the three Prairie Provinces launched an enquiry through an appointed body, The Prairie Provinces Cost Study Commission. Briefs were presented to both bodies by Federated Co-operatives Limited and by other co-operatives, consumers' organizations,etc.

Both of the enquiring bodies made favorable mention of co-operatives in their reports. In its report, the Senate-Commons Committee put forth a recommendation that the Government of Canada provide federal legislation under which co-operatives could incorporate. In its report, the Prairie Provinces Cost Study Commission expressed the view that co-operative food stores offered lower prices than did chain supermarkets.

1968

865. Federated Co-operatives–Consolidation: Delegates to the annual meeting of FCL called for a study to be made of changes required to FCL Bylaws to permit retail co-operatives to merge with the organization in order to operate on a centralized basis. FCL's membership included 440 retail co-operatives plus 156 other co-ops and non-profit organizations. It was now evident that the plan to reduce the number of retail co-ops through amalgamations on a

trading area basis, was not likely to be successful. At best, it would be very slow. In the period, 1965 to 1968, 49 retails had amalgamated with others.

FCL sales in 1968, were $176,387,000, and savings, after taxes, $4,262,000. During the year $2,568,000 was returned to retail co-ops and other members in cash.

868. Manitoba Farmers Union, in 18th annual convention, gave support to a proposal that there be a single National Farm Union organization on a district rather than provincial basis. The B.C. Farmers Union had already expressed its support of the plan, and support of the Saskatchewan Farmers Union and the Farmers Union of Alberta was anticipated.

866. Saskatchewan Co-op Credit Society and Credit Union League Amalgamation is Proposed: At annual meetings of the two organizations, amalgamation of the Credit Union League of Saskatchewan, formed in 1948, and Saskatchewan Co-operative Credit Society, formed in 1941, was given approval in principle. The two organizations then began to co-ordinate activities in preparation for the eventual amalgamation.

867. Alberta Pool Rejects Idea of Amalgamation: In 1965, the President of Saskatchewan Wheat Pool proposed an eventual amalgamation of the three Prairie wheat pools, UGG, and FCL. The proposal was discussed by the annual meeting of Alberta Wheat Pool and was rejected. It was felt by Delegates that it would be difficult for members to control such a large organization.

1968

1968

869. Farmers Union of Alberta Delays Decision On National Union: A few days after the Manitoba Farmers Union expressed support for the proposed National Farmers Union, The Farmers Union of Alberta voted in favor of delaying for one year,decision as to whether to support the proposed new NFU body.

870. Co-operative Trust Company of Canada, now operating under the federal Charter granted in 1967, established its first office outside of Saskatchewan with the opening of an office at Vancouver. Total assets of the Company rose to $45.7 million, and a 6% dividend was returned to shareholders.

871. General Election of 1968: Before the general election of 1968, both Conservatives and Liberals had chosen new leaders. Robert Stanfield of Halifax, Premier of Nova Scotia, replaced John Diefenbaker as Conservative leader, while Lester B. Pearson was replaced as Liberal leader by Pierre Elliott Trudeau. In the election of 1968, Trudeau led the Liberals to the first majority government since 1962:

PROVINCE	LIB.	PROG. CONS.	N.D.P.	CREDITISTE	INDEP.	TOTAL
Ontario	64	17	6		1	88
Quebec	56	4		14		74
Nova Scotia	1	10				11
New Brunswick	5	5				10
Newfoundland	1	6				7
Prince Edward Is.		4				4
Manitoba	5	5	3			13
Saskatchewan	2	5	6			13
Alberta	4	15				19
British Columbia	16		7			23
Yukon		1				1
N.W.T.	1					1
	155	72	22	14	1	264

1969

872. Grain Markets: The Task Force Set up by the federal government in 1967 to study agriculture issued its first reports. It was noted that an estimated 850 million bushels of grain were in storage on farms and in commercial elevators at July 31, and when the 1969-70 crop year ended it was predicted that more than 1,000,000,000 bushels would be in storage. The Task Force asserted that Canada had not been adequately aggressive in its quest for grain markets. The report said the U.S.A.'s competition for world markets was increasing, and that Australia was becoming a strong competitor. The Soviet Union, the report said, could produce as much grain as Canada, U.S.A., Australia and Argentina combined.

The Task Force recommended that the acreage sown to wheat in Canada be reduced to 20 million by 1980, from the current 29-to-30 million acres, and that land retired from wheat production be used to increase production of feed grain.

1969

875. MPE Sells Pool Packers Plant: Pool Packers Limited at Brandon, owned by Manitoba Pool Elevators and in operation since 1965, was sold to Burns Foods Limited for $3,500,000. Problems encountered in getting products of the plant established in markets had resulted in operating losses. Effective date of the sale to Burns was April I.

873. FCL-SWP Plan Livestock Study: A major study of the potential for an increased livestock industry in Saskatchewan was jointly undertaken by Saskatchewan Wheat Pool and Federated Co-operatives. The study was to examine the long-term potential for livestock production and to determine means by which the co-operatives could assist producers in such a development.

874. Credit Union Federation of Alberta: It was found that the Charter granted in 1967 in accordance with The Credit Union Act did not permit sufficient latitude for operations of the Credit Union Federation of Alberta. Thus, in 1969, the organization petitioned for incorporation under a Special Act of the Alberta Legislature, and this was granted on May 7, 1969. CUFA was also appointed to administer the Stabilization Fund which was made compulsory on all credit unions in 1966. Credit Unions contributed to the fund on the basis of ¼ of I% of the total shares and deposits held.

1969

876. MPE Reforms Structure: As proposed in 1968, Manitoba Pool Elevators adopted a new structure to enable the previously autonomous local elevator associations to merge with MPE so that their members would become direct members of MPE. Provision was made for local associations not merging with MPE to participate in election of directors. The offer to merge was accepted by 173 associations but declined by 37.

877. Manitoba Pool Joins Western Co-operative Fertilizers: In 1964, when Federated Co-operatives and the wheat pools of Alberta and Saskatchewan took steps to establish Western Co-operative Fertilizers Limited and its Calgary plant, Manitoba Pool Elevators declined an invitation to join in the venture. MPE had, instead, acquired an interest in Border Chemicals Ltd., a Manitoba-based fertilizer plant which was to supply its requirements. In 1969, however, Manitoba Pool Elevators disposed of its interest in Border Chemicals and was accepted as a shareholder of Western Co-operative Fertilizers Limited.

878. Federated Co-operatives Sales in 1969 were $174,000,000, a decline of $2,000,000 from 1968. The lower sales were a result of grain marketing problems experienced by farmers. Their cash income reduced, farmers were forced to curtail spending and production costs, and the effect was felt in almost every quarter. Savings for 1969, however, reached $5,015,000, and during the year the sum of $2,482,000 was paid to retail co-operatives and other members in cash.

879. Federated Co-operatives—Consolidation Plan: In response to a resolution from the 1968 annual meeting, FCL proposed a plan for consolidation of retail co-operatives. The plan called for a new retailing co-operative to be established as a body with which existing retail associations could amalgamate and eventually consolidate as a single retailing co-operative serving in communities across Western Canada. At the annual meeting held in 1969, delegates gave approval in principle to the plan and asked that details as to structure, bylaws, and other respects of the proposed new organization be provided for consideration during 1970.

880. Canadian Co-operative Implements Limited Proposes Consolidation Plan: At annual meeting held February 12 and 13, delegates to Canadian Co-operative Implements supported by resolution, a proposal that the three Prairie wheat pools and United Grain Growers merge as a single organization, with CCIL then joining the new organization to help round out a diversified service to farmers. It was also suggested that Federated Co-operatives should not be a party to the proposed merger because retail co-operatives "are rapidly becoming more urban in membership."

881. Canadian Co-operative Implements—Combines: CCIL ceased to import combines from West Germany which had been handled since 1965, when Ford Motor Company was awarded exclusive distribution rights for North America by the manufacturer. The import of Volvo combines and tractors from Sweden was continued by CCIL. It was CCIL's practice to channel all procured machinery through its Winnipeg plant for inspectioon before making delivery to its depots.

882. Income Tax—White Paper On Taxation: After study of the Report on the Royal Commission on Taxation formed in 1962, the Government of Canada prepared a White Paper outlining a number of proposed tax reforms. This document included proposals respecting the taxation of co-operatives. Under these proposals, the three-year exemption from income tax for new co-operatives would be eliminated, and a new method introduced for calculation of taxable income based on the amount of capital employed. The

1969

Co-operative Union of Canada together with Le Conseil Canadien de la Cooperation, formed a committee to give the tax proposals careful study.

883. Canadian Federation of Agriculture Seeks National Farm Organization: At annual meeting held January 28 to 30, the Canadian Federation of Agriculture adopted a resolution favoring a change of the CFA constitution to provide for increased representation by individual farmers. The proposed change was suggested in the hope that individual farmers would become members of CFA and thereby bring about a strong, national farm organization.

135

884. National Farmers Union: At a convention held at Winnipeg, July 30 and 31, a proposed new structure by which the National Farmers Union would replace the existing provincial farm unions was overwhelmingly accepted. Farm unions of British Columbia, Saskatchewan, Manitoba, Ontario and the Maritimes participated in this convention, but those of Alberta and Quebec did not send representatives.

1969

885. Politics-NDP Elected: In a Provincial election held July 15, the New Democratic Party defeated the incumbent Conservative Party to provide Manitoba with its first NDP administration.

886. Unifarm: In January, the Farmers Union of Alberta (FUA), and the Alberta Federation of Agriculture (AFA), formed a joint committee to examine prospects for unifying the Canadian Federation of Agriculture and National Farmers Union. Reports of the Committee were considered by a meeting of the FUA held December 9 and after debate it was resolved that FUA and AFA amalgamate to form a new organization known as Unifarm. By this move, FUA expressed rejection of the National Farmers Union.

1970

887. Grain Markets: For the agricultural sector, the winter of 1969-70 was a time of despair as the lack of grain sales to export market, and reports of the Task Force on Agriculture, were studied and debated. At July 31, 1,008,000,000 bushels of wheat were in storage on farms and in elevators and terminals. It was the highest wheat inventory in Canada's history, a result of four consecutive years in which production far exceeded sales.

In effort to reduce inventories, the Federal Government introduced what was called the LIFT program (Lower Inventories For Tomorrow). By this program, Prairie farmers were induced to cut back on the acreage sown to wheat in the spring of 1970. A subsidy of $10 per acre was offered to farmers who used land that had grown wheat, for perennial forage crops. Farmers responded by cutting the acreage sown to wheat from 24.4 million in 1969, to 12.0 million in 1970.

The Prairie economy, urban as well as rural, was affected by the depressed grain markets and the LIFT program. Farm demands for such commodities as petroleum, fertilizers, agricultural chemicals, lumber, and machinery, and for consumer goods, was curtailed.

During the early months of 1970, many comments causing further dismay were voiced. It was suggested in some quarters that Canada could no longer expect to make large sales of grain to foreign markets as in the past. It was also suggested that by 1980, about one-half of the farmers would be forced to abandon their occupation. Absent during the furor, was mention of the rise in world population and earlier predictions that world food demands would outstrip the supply. According to demographic reports, world population stood at 1.5 billion at the start of the 20th Century. By 1969, it had reached 3.6 billion. It was predicted that world population would reach 3.7 billion by 1971; 4.9 billion by 1985; and 7 billion by the year 2004.

By late 1970, after vigorous efforts by the Canadian Wheat Board, governments, the wheat pools and other farm organizations, and the grain trade in general, markets were found for some Canadian wheat and grains. As the calender year drew to a close, the outlook was considerably improved.

888. XCAN Grain Ltd., an organization to vigorously promote sales to export markets, was formed in a joint venture of the three Prairie wheat pools and United Grain Growers. XCAN quickly established contacts in England, and through Eurograin—an agency operation of European co-operatives—made other useful contacts in Holland and Germany through which to promote sales to European markets.

889. Palliser Wheat Growers Association, a new organization, was formed in April at a meeting of farmers held at Pense. It was described as "...a producer organization—a commodity group...to

890. Unifarm: The merger of the Farmers Union of Alberta and Alberta Federation of Agriculture, as proposed in 1969, quickly moved forward to a successful founding convention of Unifarm held in

1970

promote and safeguard their interest in the production, handling, and marketing of wheat. Palliser is non-commercial and non-political." The new organization was given much attention by the press as it expressed views to the Wheat Board, governments, and other bodies, and made efforts to stimulate sales of grain. Activities of the organization were carried on among Saskatchewan farmers.

March, 1970.

Following the official birth of the new Unifarm organization, the National Farmers Union made efforts to solicit members from among Alberta farmers.

1970

891. Income Tax: Proposals affecting co-operatives, contained in the White Paper on tax reform released in 1969, were studied by the committee set up by the Co-operative Union of Canada. The committee's findings caused alarm in co-operative circles. the most important objections were:

1. Co-operatives would be required to compute taxable income before, rather than after, the allocation of patronage refunds to members.

2. It would be possible for co-ops to reduce taxable income by paying interest to members on the share capital or equities they had in their organizations. However, this would:

   (a) Discourage co-ops from following their basic purpose of reducing costs of goods or services to members as the payment of interest on capital would mean reduction of sums available for patronage refunds.

   (b) Require co-operatives to ignore a basic co-operative principle which stipulates that interest paid on share capital, if any, shall be strictly limited.

   (c) The Co-operatives would be required to pay out interest on share capital in cash. Thus it would be deprived of the use of capital provided when members agree to the retention of patronage refunds by the co-operative. As co-operatives do not have other means of accumulating capital, the result would have been to reduce the working capital with each payment of interest.

3. Also included in the proposals was a new and complex formula for taxing co-operatives on the basis of capital employed. It would ensure that tax liability was not reduced by the lowering of prices of goods or services to members in order to eliminate an operating surplus. The "capital employed" technique, first introduced in 1946, was regarded by co-operators as being both punitive and discriminatory, since it did not apply to any other form of business.

Through the Co-operative Union of Canada, strong presentations were made to the Senate Committee on Banking, Trade & Commerce, in May, and to the Parliamentary Committee on Trade & Commerce & Economic Affairs, in June. It was evident that many members of both the Senate and House of Commons were not familiar enough with the purpose and operation of co-operatives so as to be able to understand, without explanation, the dire consequences of the tax proposals.

During the latter part of 1970, co-operators were united all across Canada in opposition to the proposed tax changes, and in urging the Government to adopt instead, a practical system for taxing co-operatives which had been devised by the CUC.

892. Federal Co-op Act Passed: Bill C. 177, An Act respecting Co-operative Associations, was given unanimous approval by members of all parties in the House of Commons when given third reading on December 1. On December 17, similar approval was given by the Senate. Thus, the federal legislation for co-operatives, sought as early as 1907, was finally a reality. In debates on Bill C. 177, members of all parties in the House of Commons expressed praise and support for co-operative enterprise.

893. Federated Co-operatives—B.C. Co-op Wholesale—Amalgamation: On May 1, the B.C. Co-operative Wholesale Society, formed in 1939, was offcially merged with Federated Co-operatives. The amalgamation was a necessity for the B.C. wholesale had incurred a substantial operating deficit as a result of efforts to sustain diversified services with a relatively small sales volume. The 1969 sales by BCCWS were $14,000,000. Soon after amalgamation, FCL created two new electoral districts in B.C., to provide for representation by its new members. This brought to 18 the number of members serving on the FCL Board of Directors, there being 4 from Manitoba, 8 from Saskatchewan, 4 from Alberta, and 2 from B.C.

894. Interprovincial Co-operatives Limited—Managed By FCL: In the fall of 1970, it was evident that financial affairs of IPCO required urgent attention. The main cause of the problem was the chemicals complex at Saskatoon where an expansion program begun in 1967 had been completed in 1968. The project was undertaken to enable the IPCO plant to produce increased quantities of caustic soda and chlorine for sale under contract to Prince Albert Pulp Mill. The expansion program had cost $7,500,000, but had been estimated at $5,400,000, hence financing costs were greater than had been anticipated. Furthermore the price at which the IPCO plant contracted to supply the pulp mill proved to be too low, especially since inflation, which was rampant at the time, caused costs of plant operations and production to rise. Still further problems were caused by the drastic

1970

cutback in farm use of agricultural chemicals during the LIFT program of 1970.

Representatives of the organizations having membership in IPCO met in December to ponder the situation. It was evident that quick decisions as to what should be done could not be reached, and it was agreed, therefore, that pending further action, the affairs

of Interprovincial Co-operatives should come under the management of Federated Co-operatives Limited. FCL then took steps to examine in detail all aspects of IPCO operations, and made efforts to negotiate a more favorable contract with the pulp mill as well as more favorable terms with the Saskatchewan Economic Development Corporation which had financed expansion of the chemcials complex.

895. Federated Co-operatives—Consolidation: During 1970, detailed plans for consolidation of retail co-operatives into a single organization were the object of a great deal of study. It had been proposed in 1969, that consolidation be provided through creation of a new retail co-operative with which existing associations could

amalgamate. The studies were not completed in time for consideration at the annual meeting held in early 1970, but detailed reports were provided at meetings held in the fall. The matter was then placed on the agenda for the annual meeting to be held in early 1971.

896. Federated Co-operatives—Lumber, Oil And Home Office: FCL's sales for 1970 reached a new record of $183,388,000, but savings were reduced to about one-half of the 1969 sum, to $2,628,000. The higher sales were, in good measure, the result of serving B.C. members for the first time. Also in 1970, FCL:

* Suspended the crude oil exploration program carried on since the early 1940's.

* Moved into a new Home Office building at Saskatoon.
* Undertook a major expansion of lumber mill facilities. At Canoe, $1,656,000 was spent to install equipment for handling cedar logs, provide further drying kilns, and to increase the mill capacity from 73 million board feet per year to 100 million. At the Smith lumber mill, expenditures of $1,165,000 were involved in a general improvement and expansion project.

897. FCL-SWP Livestock Study: The study, undertaken in 1969 by a joint effort of Federated Co-operatives and Saskatchewan Wheat Pool, indicated that a potential for increased livestock production existed on the Prairies. As a next step, it was proposed by FCL that the two organizations examine possibilities of creating a new organization that would take over the pertinent programs

and facilities of FCL and SWP and provide a complete service to the livestock industry including such activities as research, breeding, veterinary services and supplies, feeds, and marketing. The proposal was declined by SWP which suggested that FCL proceed and keep SWP informed with a view to possible joint action in the future.

898. Federated Distributing Company: As a wholly-owned subsidiary of Federated Co-operatives, Federated Distributing Company was incorporated to distribute CO-OP feeds and allied services on a direct basis to large feeders. Until now, FCL had distributed feeds through member retail co-operatives. However, it was recognized that large-scale producers of livestock and poultry could not be effectively served in the traditional manner, since

those producers purchased feeds in large quantity and were able to deal directly with various feed mills. Federated Distributing Company, set up to provide direct mill-to-farm service to large producers, did not intend to compete with retail co-operatives in the sale of feeds. Its policy was to serve only those farmers who could not be served through retail co-operatives, and to do so with the consent of the retailing association serving the customer's area.

899. Canadian Co-operative Implements Limited: Depressed economic conditions in the agricultural sector were reflected in sales of CCIL. The organization's 1970 sales of $9,438,603 were 33% lower than in 1969. Already handling Volvo tractors and combines which it had been importing from Sweden since 1967,

CCIL expanded activities by becoming distributor for Volvo's line of industrial equipment. In doing so, CCIL anticipated that through sales of a more diversified nature the organization would be less vulnerable to the effects of the uncertainties of the agricultural economy.

1970

900. Legislation: Credit Union Act: On September 30, the Manitoba Legislature enacted a new Credit Union Act, removing credit unions from jurisdiction of the Companies Act. The new Act also broadened the scope for credit union activities by enabling them to work with other agencies in the financing of homes and to do business with municipal, provincial and federal government agencies. Under terms of the new Act, the work "society" was dropped from credit union names.

901 Saskatchewan Co-op Credit Society and Credit Union League Amalgamate: An amalgamation of the Credit Union League of Saskatchewan, formed in 1948, and the Saskatchewan Co-operative Credit Society, formed in 1941, became effective in 1970. The amalgamation had been given long and careful consideration after being given approval-in-principle in 1968. The organization resulting from the amalgamation then operated under the name and amended Charter of the Saskatchewan Co-operative Credit Society.

902. National Association of Canadian Credit Unions (NACCU): At a meeting held at Vancouver, December 4 and 5, the National Association of Canadian Credit Unions was re-organized and revitalized. Originally formed in 1958, NACCU had assumed a more active role in 1965. As a result of its re-organization, NACCU was to become, on January 1, 1971, the nucleus of a federation of the central credit societies and credit unions of all ten Canadian Provinces, as well as the Co-operative Trust Company of Canada.

The organization, supported by a dues structure, is similar to credit union federations of the U.S.A. and Australia which, together with NACCU, became, in 1971, first members of the World Federation of Credit Unions.

As an additional step in its revitalized role, NACCU became responsible for providing management services to the Canadian Co-operative Credit Society, and possibilities of an eventual NACCU—CCCS merger began to receive consideration.

903. Co-operative Trust Company of Canada announced plans to open an office at Winnipeg.

904. Co-operative Insurance Services declared a dividend of 25% on premiums paid by credit unions for loan and savings protection. It was reported that CIS was serving 393 credit unions across Canada.

CIS also adopted a Bylaw amendment providing for election to its

Board of Directors of two additional members who would represent the newly-formed Quebec region. CIS had extended its service to Quebec when Co-operative Fire & Casualty Company began writing automobile and fire insurance through a Quebec co-operative, "Assurance U.C.C." With its entry into Quebec, CIS was now writing insurance in all ten Provinces of Canada.

906. Co-op Housing Association of Manitoba announced plans for further development of the Willow Park Co-op Housing complex at Winnipeg, to provide for additional housing units and for accommodation for 52 senior citizens. Other facilities planned included a child day-care centre, recreation hall, and a wholly-owned convenience store to serve residents.

905. Manitoba & Saskatchewan Honey Producers Amalgamate: In 1970, the Saskatchewan Co-operative Honey Producers formed in 1939, amalgamated with the Manitoba Co-operative Honey Producers, begun in 1938. The resulting new organization continued operations under the name and Charter of the Manitoba Co-operative Honey Producers. The plant at Tisdale, through which Saskatchewan Co-op Honey Producers had been serving 250 members, also continued to operate.

1970

907. Keenozae Co-operative Limited, a fishermen's co-operative with a membership including a number of Indians and Metis in Northern Manitoba, acquired a fish processing plant with the aid of the Manitoba Government, co-operatives, and credit unions.

908. Northern Co-op Fisheries Limited, aided by loans from the Saskatchewan Economic Development Corporation, undertook expansion of a number of its fish filleting plants and to erect a new plant at LaRonge. NCFL was serving 1,500 fishermen through 17 fishing co-ops, its members including many Indians and Metis.

909. Saskatchewan Federation of Agriculture: To this time, the membership of Saskatchewan Federation of Agriculture consisted of farm organizations, including commodity groups, and co-operatives. In 1970, SFA set up a committee to devise a new type of structure which would provide for direct membersip by individual farmers as well as for representation of various farm organizations.

1971

910. Income Tax: In early December, amendments to the Income Tax reform bill before the House of Commons were adopted. Members of all parties had vociferously denounced the measures for taxing co-operatives as proposed by the White Paper. It appeared that these measures had been drafted by persons unfamiliar with the nature, purpose, principles and capital structure of co-operative organizations. At any rate, the final result was that the tax reform measures were considered by co-operatives to be both reasonable and practical. Briefly, the revised Act provided:

1. The taxation of co-operatives on the basis of capital employed was abolished.

2. Co-operatives were to be taxed at regular corporate rates on earnings retained or on earnings derived from business done with non-members if patronage refunds were not allocated to both members and non-members.

3. The co-operatives were to deduct and remit to the government, a withholding tax of 15% of any patronage refunds in excess of $100 allocated to individual members. Members could deduct the withheld tax when computing their own income tax, and any overpayment would be returned by the Government to the taxpayer.

4. Patronage refunds earned on the purchase of consumer goods were not taxable in the hands of recipients. Refunds earned on goods used in farming or other operations were to be included as income when recipients calculated their own income tax. This applies whether or not the patronage refunds are immediately returned to members in cash.

The new measures became effective on January 1, 1972. Co-operative organizations across Canada lauded the Co-operative Union of Canada and Le Conseil Canadien de la Co-operation for their successful efforts in averting a disastrous situation.

911. Interprovincial Co-operatives Limited: Early in 1971, representatives of the organizations having membership in IPCO met to decide on the future of the organization. At the time, FCL was responsible for managing IPCO affairs and had compiled reports which were studied by the meeting. It was agreed that each of the present members would relinquish its membership and equities in IPCO thereby making FCL the sole owner of the organization. Thus, IPCO became an FCL subsidiary. After assuming responsibility for

1971

ownership as well as management, FCL, after further studies, took the following steps:

1. It was agreed that so far as practical, commodities and services provided to the former members would be continued. Some administrative changes were introduced to reduce costs of these services.

2. IPCO's home office at Winnipeg was closed. Staff necessary to continue IPCO operations were provided with accommodation in the FCL Winnipeg Regional office, Winnipeg.

3. The IPCO food processing plant at Burnaby, acquired in 1951, and the chemical plant at Toronto, obtained in 1967, were sold. Other arrangements were made for the supply of CO-OP brand products previously served by these plants.

912. Federated Co-operatives Limited achieved sales of $232,345,000 with savings of $2,880,000. During 1971, it was noted that:

* **FCL's New Home Office Building**, erected at Saskatoon at a cost of $4,200,000 and occupied in late 1970, was officially dedicated ". . .to co-operative people of the past, present and future. It reflects their desire for a social and economic order built on the ideals of freedom, democracy, and justice."

* **Chargex,** a bank sponsored credit card program was adopted by by FCL for introduction to retail co-operatives desiring such

913. Economic Benefits to Prairie Economy: During 1971, a survey of major co-operatives of the three Prairie Provinces, showed that in the 10-year period, 1961 to 1971–a period that included difficult times for agriculture–the co-operatives concerned had returned to their members in cash, an aggregate sum of more than $143,100,000.

Included in the sum was $60,764,000 returned in cash by Canadian Co-operative Implements Limited, UFA Co-operative, and the retail co-ops served by Federated Co-operatives.

The three Prairie Wheat Pools and United Grain Growers returned cash totalling $72,595,000, and the credit unions of the three Provinces effected cash returns amounting to $9,773,000.

4. **Northern Industrial Chemicals Ltd.** (NICL) was incorporated as an FCL subsidiary to be responsible for operations of the chemicals complex at Saskatoon. Thus, the plant was divorced from IPCO and operated as a separate entity. On September 1, arrangements were made for the operation of the NICL plant under management of Canadian Industries Limited.

5. FCL's Board of Directors agreed, and accordingly advised the former IPCO members, that when the operations of IPCO had been restored to a viable state and FCL losses had been recovered, it was the intent of FCL to invite the former members to return to their former status as member-owners of Interprovincial Co-operatives.

services. This was done with prior consultation and approval of central credit union organizations. It was considered that the program would benefit retail co-operatives by reducing the amount of capital necessary to carry accounts receivable.

* **Retail Co-ops** served by FCL achieved 1971 sales of $349,000,000, and net savings of $8,605,000. The sales were almost double the 1970 total of $4,546,000, indicating that as a result of improved grain markets the Prairie economy was quickly improving. It was also calculated that the retail co-operatives returned $4,750,000 to members in cash, during 1971.

When calculating the cash returned to members, care was taken to avoid including sums which the members might have been paid if they had dealt elsewhere. For example, the cash returned by the credit unions did not include interest paid on members' deposits since the deposits would also earn interest if placed in a bank.

The benefit of the $143,100,000 returned in cash by the co-operatives was pointed out in 1966 by Gerry Voorhis who quoted economists as saying that each dollar a co-op returns to a community will generate $5 worth of business activity in that community.

914. Calgary Co-operative Association, now Canada's largest consumer owned retail association, opened its 6th shopping centre in Calgary, December 9 to 11. It was estimated that 24,000 persons attended the opening, and that 3,000 were on hand for the ribbon cutting ceremony.

1971

138

1971

915. Co-op Housing Association of Calgary, formed about 1967, made an auspicious start of its activities by opening Scarcee Meadows, a 380-unit co-operative housing development on a 35 acre site.

916. Co-op Vegetable Oils Limited began a $500,000 project to double the capacity of its oilseed refining plant, from 50,000 to 100,000 pounds per day. A new administration building and other facilities were included in the project.

CVO also closed its Gardenland canning plant at Winkler, acquired in 1967, when the Manitoba government announced plans to open another such plant. CVO believed that there was only sufficient produce available to support one plant.

917. SWP—Vegetable Oil Plant: Saskatchewan Wheat Pool began a major expansion of its vegetable oil plant at Saskatoon with the aim of increasing capacity from 100 to 300 tons daily. The expanded plant, it was estimated, would utilize about 3,600,000 bushels of rapeseed annually.

918. UGG-United Feeds: An offer by United Grain Growers to buy out the interest of UFA Co-operative in United Feeds limited, begun in 1967 as a joint UGG-UFA venture, was accepted. UGG, then operating 16 feed plants in Alberta, planned to extend feed service to Manitoba and Saskatchewan.

919. XCAN Grain Ltd., formed in 1970 by the three Prairie wheat pools and United Grain Growers, was successful "beyond expectations" in efforts to sell Prairie wheat to foreign markets. The organization completed its first year of operation with a small earnings.

920. Northern Co-op Trading Services Limited achieved record sales of $1,517,000 a savings to members of $132,179, or 8.7% of sales. The home office of NCTSL was moved from Prince Alberta to La Ronge to be closer to the 8 northern co-ops being served.

921. Co-op Fisheries Limited completed repayment of its debt to the Saskatchewan Government and became a bona fide co-operative owned and controlled by its members who were mainly Indians and Metis. The debt was assumed in 1959 when steps were first taken to convert a Crown-owned company into a co-op. From 1959 to 1971, CFL had operated under an appointed Board of Directors, but at an annual meeting held February 10 to 12, the members elected a Board from their

1971

own ranks. CFL's net surplus in 1970 was $94,535. On May 1, 1971, $34,000 was repaid to members in cash,

922. Canadian Co-operative Implements Limited, importing Volvo combines from Sweden, announced that plans had been made with the manufacturer for the manufacture of these machines in Canada by CCIL. Both self-propelled and pull-type models were to be built and would ensure continuity of supply to CCIL's 80,000 farmer members in Western Canada.

923. Credit Unions Reject Higher Bank Charges: On April 1, chartered banks increased their charges to customers for the receiving of deposits and handling of cheques. For entering of both deposits and withdrawals to current accounts, the charges were increased from 15¢ to 20¢ per entry. Charges for entries to checking accounts were raised from 11¢ to 14¢. While co-operatives generally tend to follow competitive prices, the credit unions did not comply with the higher charges. Most credit unions in the Prairie region had, in fact, been following a rate that was lower than the banks had charged before the April 1 increase. A good many credit unions made no charge whatever for entering deposits or withdrawals to members' accounts.

139

1971

924. Co-operative Bank Proposed: Officials of the Co-operative Credit Society of Manitoba, and of the Credit Union League of Manitoba, expressed interest in a proposal by a member of the Manitoba Government who advocated that a bank be established in Manitoba to be responsive to Western needs. CCSM and CULM officials agreed that a logical place in which to form such a bank would be among the co-operative and credit unions. A committee was set up to study the matter with the resulting reports to be circulated for consideration by the major financial co-operatives of Western Canada, the National Association of Canadian Credit Unions, and the Canadian Co-operative Credit Society.

925. Co-op Credit Society of Manitoba and Credit Union League Merge: On April 16, The Co-operative Credit Society of Manitoba, formed in 1950, and the Credit Union League of Manitoba 1967, Limited, amalgamated to create a single central body to serve English-speaking credit unions of the Province. The organization thus created continued operations under the Charter and name of the Co-operative Credit Society of Manitoba, serving 180 credit unions.

926. Co-operative Superannuation Society entered into an agreement with Co-operative Insurance Services by which CIS became responsible for managing the investment portfolio of the Society.

927. Co-operative Trust Company of Canada—New Offices: A new office providing full services was opened by Co-operative Trust Company of Canada at Winnipeg. The Company also announced plans to establish a Branch Office at Calgary. With an increase of approximately 40% over 1970, total assets of Co-operative Trust at the close of 1971 had reached $84,600,000.

928. Co-operative Hail Insurance Company returned to its farmer-policyholders, a dividend of 25% of the premiums paid for crop coverage in 1970. The Hail Insurance co-operative also announced that it would reduce rates in some of the areas it served, but do so with no reduction of the protection being provided.

929. Rural Education and Development Association: The Farmers Union and Co-operative Development Association, formed in 1959, was replaced by a new organization known as Rural Education and Development Association (REDA). The new organization was to be an educational association serving rural people. REDA also assumed responsibility for administration and development of the Goldeye Lake Camp begun in 1958 by the Farmers Union of Alberta and now owned by Unifarm. Sponsoring organizations of REDA included Unifarm and its member organizations plus Co-operative Insurance Services and Federated Co-operatives Limited.

1971

930. Department of Co-operative Development: Manitoba's NDP Government established as a new department of government, a Department of Co-operative Development. This new department became responsible for incorporation and registration of co-operatives, and for administration of pertinent legislation. It replaced the Co-operatives, and Credit Union Services branch of the Department of Agriculture and assumed responsibility for administration of that part of the Manitoba Companies Act which pertained to co-operative organizations.

The new department also aimed to encourage more co-operative development among native Indian and Metis people of Northern Manitoba, and to assess the need for legislation specific to the needs of co-ops.

931. NDP Party Returned to Office: The New Democratic Party which had been replaced by a Liberal administration in 1964, was again returned to office.

932. Saskatchewan Federation of Agriculture: Studies by a committee that was formed in 1970 to devise a new structure for Saskatchewan Federation of Agriculture resulted in a plan by which farmers could be provided with direct membership in SFA, with representation being based on rural municipalities. In addition to the direct members, SFA's membership would continue to include farm organizations, co-operatives, and commodity groups. The plan was explained to the annual convention of the Saskatchewan Association of Rural Municipalities where it received support.

933. National Farmers Union: The revitalized NFU was active on several fronts in efforts to increase it membership and influence. In Alberta, NFU was competing with Unifarm in efforts to gain the support of farmers. In Saskatchewan, NFU opposed efforts of the Saskatchewan Federation of Agriculture to enlist farmers as direct members of SFA. In Ontario, NFU launched a Canada-wide campaign by which consumers were urged to boycott Kraft Foods Limited. This campaign was begun as a means of pressing NFU's demands that Ontario farmers be accorded higher returns for milk.

1972

934. Grain Markets—Grain Handling System: As part of its effort to relieve the acute grain marketing problems of the late 1960's, the federal government established a "Grain Council" in 1969. In a report, July 20, 1972, the Council urged that steps be taken to improve the systems for assembly and transportation of grain between farms and seaports. The Council offered two proposals: one providing for a system of 80 inland terminals to which farmers would deliver their grain; the other called for reduction of country elevators from the existing 4,849 to 2,300 by 1980.

There had been mounting interest in grain assembly and movement since 1969. Some reports suggested that Canada was losing sales to foreign markets due to inability to meet shipping commitments or to provide a specified grade at the right time.

Transportation delays were incurred for a number of reasons, including strikes in the shipping industries, winter snowslides that halted trains enroute to the West Coast, and the slow process of assembling trains from boxcars picked up from the large number of country elevators. Other problems were caused by the abandonment of many branch lines. It was also claimed that the railways were not allocating enough boxcars to the movement of grain. The Government of Canada, in an effort to improve the situation, made government-owned inland elevators available to augment the country elevator system. The Government also directed the railways to experiment with "unit trains" during the winter of 1970-72, and undertook to purchase a large number of special 'hopper cars' for grain movement by the railways.

1972

1972

935. Western Grain Elevator Association, a new organization to be concerned only with the matter of grain handling and movement, was formed at a meeting of representatives from the three Prairie wheat pools, United Grain Growers, and five private elevator companies. The organization's area of concern was to be matters affecting country elevators and terminals; it was not to be involved with such matters as grain marketing or sales promotion.

936. Palliser Wheat Growers Association, meeting July 15 at Regina, advocated closer co-ordination between plant scientists, producers, marketers, and consumers, to enable Canada to produce those grains that best meet requirements of the world markets. The PWGA president called for the erection of more government-owned inland terminal elevators to help expedite grain movement.

937. XCAN Grain Limited, with the support of the Federal Government, invested in a new flour mill in Venezuela under an agreement by which more than one-half of the wheat milled was to be of Canadian origin. The mill's capacity is in excess of 1,000,000 bushels per year.

938. Wheat Pools Purchase Assets of Federal Grain Company: The Directors of Federal Grain Company accepted an offer by the three Prairie wheat pools, for the purchase of the Company's country elevator system and related facilities. The price, $90,000,000, included the inventories of grain on hand plus the physical facilities which were: 1,100 country elevators; 2 terminals at the Lakehead; 1 terminal at Vancouver; 3 seed plants and several farm supply warehouses.

939. Western Co-operative Livestock Markets, a new organization to "modernize nationwide movement of livestock, was formed by joint action of the Alberta Livestock Co-operative, B.C. Livestock Co-operative, Manitoba Pool Elevators, and Saskatchewan Pool. The organization was to seek ways to improve the transportation of livestock from Western Canada to the markets in Eastern Canada and to export markets. In addition, it was to set up an efficient system for the communication of price information.

941. Co-op Vegetable Oils achieved record sales of $15,893,000 and net earnings of $957,000 for the year ended July 31. Crop purchases from Manitoba farmers were $8,500,000. An allocation of $775,000 was made, bolstering returns to farmers by 60¢ CWT for sunflower seed and 12¢ per bushel for rapeseed. On seed purchases by farmers from CVO, a 10% patronage refund was allocated. CVO's oil refining plant was to be doubled in capacity by 1973, and farmers were encouraged to increase their oilseed acreage.

940. Saskatchewan Wheat Pool Livestock: On August 9, a 70,000-lb shipment of cattle from SWP's stockyard at North Battleford was shipped by air from Saskatoon to Toronto. It was an experimental project to determine whether the higher cost of air transport would be offset by a reduction in weight loss that occurred when cattle were shipped by surface means.

1972

942. Saskatchewan Wheat Pool Oil Plant: Expansion of SWP's oilseed crushing plant begun in 1971, was completed and the enlarged plant was officially opened.

943. Dairy Producers Co-operative Association Formed By Amalgamation: On June 14, Saskatchewan Co-operative Creamery Association, formed in 1917, and the Dairy Co-operative Marketing Association (also known as the 'Dairy Pool') formed in 1927, amalgamated as the Dairy Producers Co-operative Association. At the time the Co-op Creamery operated 22 manufacturing plants plus 3 others used as distribution depots in Saskatchewan. The Dairy Pool operated 7 manufacturing and 8 distribution plants.

944. UFA Co-operative reported that record sales of $28,200,000 were achieved in the year, and that the organization now had a membership of more than 45,000 Alberta farmers.

945. Calgary Co-operative Association reported sales for the year ended October 31, of $37,500,000 and savings of $1,491,000 which enabled a patronage refund of 4% to be allocated to members on their purchases. In 1972, 12,000 new members joined the association, bringing its total membership to 67,000. A staff of 940 was employed. The association's president reported that ". . .in 16 years of operation as a co-operative we have never failed to pay a patronage refund."

946. Canadian Co-operative Implements Limited announced plans to erect on a 40-acre Winnipeg site, a $7,200,000 manufacturing plant to permit the manufacture of Volvo combines then being imported from Sweden, and to increase production of the implement co-operative's own line of swathers, diskers, cultivators, harrows and other machines. The plant, with 7.5 acres under roof, would be among the largest in the Winnipeg area and include facilities for research and development, raw material storage, machinery fabrication, painting, assembly, etc.

In 1972, the organization discontinued use of its full legal name for public identification and advertising purposes, using instead the name, Co-op Implements and the abbreviation, CI. Sales for the year were $22,091,472 on which a savings of $319,614 was achieved.

1972

947. Federated Co-operatives Limited set new records in 1972 with sales of $285,600,000 and net savings, after income tax, of $9,103,000. After applying about $1,000,000 against the deficits of Interprovincial Co-operatives, and setting aside reserves, FCL allocated patronage refunds of $7,734,000 to its members. During 1972, about $4,500,000 was returned to retail co-operatives in cash.

The FCL records were reflected in activities of the retail co-operatives served. The retails recorded sales of $401,507,000 in 1972, with total savings, including refunds from FCL, of almost $17,000,000. Savings were nearly double the 1971 figure of $8,605,000.

948. Consumers' Co-operative Refineries, Regina, a wholly owned FCL subsidiary, began erection of a new administration building that would enable the present building to be used as a laboratory. Additional storage tanks were erected to bring storage capacity of the plant up to 70,000,000 gallons. The Refinery now

949. Westland Co-operatives: At the FCL annual meeting held in early February, delegates gave approval to plans for creation of a new retailing co-operative which autonomous associations could join to achieve an eventual consolidation of retail associations into a single organization. Plans had been developed through extensive studies of such aspects as democratic control, capital structure, repayment of savings and equities to members, and methods of operation. Following the annual meeting, a new organization was

950. Co-operative Trust Company of Canada: As announced in 1971, Co-operative Trust Company of Canada opened a Branch Office at Calgary. The organization also made application for registration and a license to operate in Ontario. Other offices then

Other FCL activities of 1972 included:

* **Feed Plants:** A feed plant at Melfort, Saskatchewan, which had been operated by the Melfort Co-operative Association, was purchased by FCL. Two other feed plants, one at Weyburn and the other at Moosomin, were purchased from Inter-Ocean Grain Co. Ltd. The two plants each had a capacity of 20,000 tons of feed per year. FCL was operating other feed plants at Winnipeg, Brandon, Saskatoon, Calgary Edmonton and Prince George.

* **Plywood Plant**: A project costing $600,000 to increase the capacity of the plywood plant at Canoe, from 40-million square feet per year to 56-million, was begun with completion expected in May, 1973.

occupied a site of 400 acres and was capable of producing 230,000,000 gallons of light refined products per year. Steps to increase the present productive capacity of 22,500 barrels of crude oil per day, were being planned.

incorporated under the name, Westland Co-operatives. Incorporation was under the Canada Co-operative Associations Act passed in 1970. It was stressed that the amalgamation of retail co-ops with Westland Co-operatives was to be done in an orderly manner. The pace of amalgamations was to be regulated, particularly until experience in the operation of the centralized organization had been acquired. By the end of 1972, four retail co-operatives had made application for amalgamation into Westland.

being operated outside Saskatchewan were at Winnipeg and Vancouver. Assets of Co-op Trust now exceeded $100,000,000, while membership consisted of 425 credit unions and other co-operatives located as follows:

Saskatchewan	296
Manitoba	69
Alberta	44
British Columbia	14
Ontario	2
Yukon Territory	1

1972

951. Co-operative Superannuation Society: Over the year, Co-operative Superannuation Society had grown. Co-operative organizations and credit unions joined as 'employer members' of the Society in order to provide their employees with a retirement pension program. Employees of an 'employer member' were then eligible, after one year of service, to become 'employee members' of the Society. At January 1, 1972, the Society was serving 5,470 employees of 467 employer members. The employee members, by Provinces, were as follows:

British Columbia	229
Alberta	704
Saskatchewan	3506
Manitoba	1017
Ontario	14
	5470

Employee members contributed to the Society, 5% of their monthly wage, and, on behalf of its employees, each employer member matched these contributions with a like amount. The

952. Proposed Merger of Canadian Co-op Credit Society and National Association of Canadian Credit Unions: At a March meeting held in Halifax, terms and conditions of a proposed merger involving the Canadian Co-operative Credit Society, formed in

953. Co-op Housing Association of Manitoba announced plans to establish a co-operative resort costing about $590,000 at Child's Lake in Duck Mountain Provincial Park. It was hoped that the first phase of the project, which when completed would provide accommodation and commercial services in a natural setting, could be completed by June, 1974.

954. Nor'-West Co-op Health and Social Services Centre: Meeting on October 24, representatives of a number of co-operatives, labour groups, and interested Winnipeg citizens, formed and elected a provisional board of directors for a new organization, Nor'-West Co-operative Health & Social Services Centre Inc. This organization was granted incorporation November 27 by the Department of Co-

funds thus accumulated by the Society were then invested in bonds, securities, shares, and as loans to co-operative organizations. From the investment income derived, the Society paid its operating costs, then allocated the balance to employees in the form of interest on their accumulated funds. Interest paid to employees in 1972, and added to their accumulated funds, was 7.1% of the amount accumulated by each.

Until 1972, it was the practice of the Society to use the accumulated fund of an employee member to purchase an annuity providing a monthly income on retirement. Annuities were purchased from government sources or from financial houses, whichever produced the greatest benefit to the retiring employee. In May of 1972, however, the Society ceased the purchase of annuities from outside sources and assumed responsibility for issue of pension cheques to retiring employees. The change was adopted when it was determined that the strength of the Society was adequate, and that it could administer its own pensions at lower cost and thereby increase benefits to retiring employees.

1953, and the National Association of Canadian Credit Unions, begun in 1959, were developed. It was agreed that the proposals be given careful study by the two organizations before a final decision was reached.

1972

operative Development. The object of the organization was to render "comprehensive programs of integrated health, social and related services" as well as programs of preventative health and social care. Effort was then directed to a campaign to solicit both members and funds with the aim of establishing a co-operative medical and health clinic in Winnipeg as soon as possible.

955. Department of Co-operative Development, in response to many requests made over past years and in co-operation with the Department of Education, took steps toward providing students of Manitoba schools with more information on co-operative enterprise and methods. It was noted that an 'imbalance' existed as students received a considerable amount of information on the profit form of enterprise but very little explanation of the co-operative form.

In the fall, credit courses on co-operation were offered by the University of Manitoba and the University of Winnipeg.

956. Co-operative Development Association Ceased: Offices of the Co-operative Development Association, which was formed in 1966 as successor to the Co-operative Union of Saskatchewan were closed. It had proven to be increasingly difficult to define a useful and effective role for CDA. The central co-operative organizations which has sustained CDA and its predecessor by financial grants, had long reached the stage at which they were able to conduct their own liaison educational, and development activities. it was agreed by representatives of the central organizations, however, that the Charter of CDA should be retained, and that some of CDA's activities would be continued as necessary through ad hoc committees financed by the centrals.

957. Rural Education and Development Association, formed in 1971, was given additional support as Canadian Co-operative Implements Limited joined Unifarm, Co-operative Insurance Services, and Federated Co-operatives Limited as an active member.

958. Western Co-operative College—Change Of Name: At annual meeting attended by delegates from five provinces, approval was given to a change of name from Western Co-operative College to The Co-operative College of Canada. It was expected that the change of name could be effected during 1973. The change of name reflected the fact that the College was extending its services to all Provinces. It was, in fact, providing services to many countries, particularly to developing nations which either requested instructors from the College to journey to them or sent students to attend special courses at the College.

959. National Farmers Unions: In a brief presented to the Saskatchewan Government, NFU requested that legislation be provided to certify that NFU as the sole bargaining agent for Saskatchewan farmers when it was shown that 5% of the farmers of the Provinces had become NFU members. The Minister of Agriculture did not, at the time, give encouragement for the proposal. NFU, however, proceeded to place similar proposals before governments of other provinces.

1972

960. General Election of 1972: In the general election of 1972, the Liberals, led by Pierre Elliot Trudeau, won only two seats more than did their major opponent, the Conservatives led by Robert Stanfield. The NDP, with 31 seats, then held the balance of power.

PROVINCE	LIB.	PROG. CONS.	N.D.P.	SOCIAL CREDIT	INDEP.	UNAFFIL— IATED	TOTAL
Ontario	36	40	11			1	88
Quebec	56	2		15	1		74
Nova Scotia	1	10					11
New Brunswick	5	5					10
Newfoundland	3	4					7
Prince Edward Is.	1	3					4
Manitoba	2	8	3				13
Saskatchewan	1	7	5				13
Alberta		19					19
British Columbia	4	8	11				23
Yukon		1					1
North-West Terri.			1				1
	109	107	31	15	1	1	264

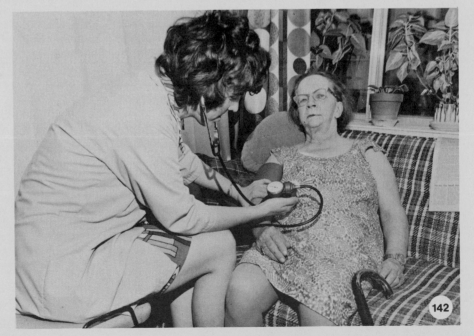

1972

1972

CHAPTER XI

THE FUTURE HAS BEGUN 1972 TO ?

961. This Diary has been constructed in such a manner as to enable it to be extended to cover the years that follow. At this stage, it is too early to comment on events of the 1970's, but as will be seen, there are trends and signs of an eventful future.

I AM A CONSUMER

I am a consumer. I must have goods and services in order to live. I pay for these with my dollars. I alone decide where and how I shall do my spending.

To myself I owe the duty of spending my dollars wisely, for I can spend away my freedom. I can be a servant or a master of my own destiny, according to my acts.

I live in a world where most men are divided against one another in a struggle for profits. If I spend my money in a business place operated for profit, I am but a part of a system for building profits for others—a mere servant of the business.

And it is the spending of servants that builds giants and leads to monopoly—concentrations of wealth, power and control in the hands of a few to be used to draw greater yields from the servants.

When a man is a servant of business, he has no dignity except that granted by his master, for no servant is really free.

My other choice is to clasp hands with my neighbors so that we, together, might own and control our own business which shall be our servant, and we, its masters.

This could make us men who are truly free and who are not divided against one another, but share a more abundant life in harmony.

These are my two choices. I can be a master, or I can be a servant. I am a consumer and help to build all business, but only through co-operation am I a master of what I help to build.

1973

962. A Troubled Year: Inflation, a world-wide problem that had been worsening for many years, had become a topic of major concern by 1973. In response to angry demands by consumers, the Federal Government launched yet another enquiry into the high cost of foods. Prices for meats and other farm produce had risen, but not as fast as farm production costs. In other lines of industry, acute shortages of materials and finished products developed. Conditions were further aggravated when, in the latter months of 1973, shipment of crude oil from the Middle East to the Western World were curtailed and prices of available crude sharply advanced. The result was an 'energy crisis' that affected the quantity and price of petroleum and of products derived from petro-

1973

chemicals or otherwise requiring petroleum in their manufacture.

Grain prices reached levels never before achieved in the history of Western Canada. Said the president of Saskatchewan Wheat Pool to that organization's annual meeting held in November, 1973:

> "Who among us would have predicted even a year ago now that Wheat Board selling prices for top grade bread wheat at Thunder Bay would have reached $5.75 per bushel, or that durum wheat would be sold for $9.00 per bushel? Who would have predicted fed steer prices of $56.40 per hundred pounds at Saskatoon? On the other hand who among us would have predicted that the index of farm costs would increase by some 13 percent from mid-1972 to the same time this year?"

Amid the already difficult situation, still other causes for concern and debate emerged:

1. The Government of Canada proposed a new marketing policy for feed grains. Whereas the Canadian Wheat Board previously had full jurisdiction of feed grains moving beyond provincial boundaries, the new policy would limit the Board's authority to the export market for feed grain. Further, the Board would be required to give priority to domestic buyers of feed grain, while domestic buyers were free to purchase their requirements on a direct basis from Western sources.

2. Exports of Canadian grains were at a high level, but shipments lagged. The railways were accused of complacency in their effort to move the grain to seaports, and there were also claims that the existing grain collection and handling system was outmoded and inefficient. Reports indicated that the number of boxcars suitable for grain, owned by Canada's two railways, had dropped from about 88,000 in 1963 to around 48,000 in 1973. Said the **Wheat Pool Budget,** a publication of Alberta Wheat Pool, in November, 1973:

> "The truth is that Canadian railways have not built rolling stock for moving grain for about twenty-five years. The replacement cars they have and are building, are specialized for hauling products other than grain, and are not suitable for grain. In addition the revenue for handling lumber, newsprint and a variety of other clean cargo is better than for grain, and cars tend to be assigned to the higher revenue commodity."

3. There was controversy as to whether rapeseed should be placed under the Canadian Wheat Board for marketing purposes. The Rapeseed Association of Canada opposed the proposal which was supported by the wheat pools and by National Farmers Union.

---

963. Manitoba Pool Elevators had record handlings during the 1972-73 crop year, its volume reaching 91.6 million bushels, or 10.3 million more than in 1971-72. The organization's total earnings for the year were $5,670,157.

In February, it was reported that MPE had purchased a small number of country elevators that had been owned by the Scottish Co-operative Wholesale Society Limited, in Manitoba.

In August, MPE announced purchase of a livestock marketing facility at Virden, from Virden Auction Mart Co. Ltd. The purchase was to be effective September 1 when the facility would be operated by the MPE livestock division to complement the Pool's Brandon stockyard operations.

964. Saskatchewan Wheat Pool had a net operating surplus after taxes, of $21,255,000 on 1972-73 operations. The sum was allocated as a patronage dividend to members. Delegates to the Pool's 49th annual meeting held at Regina in November, devoted much time to discussion of grain handling and transportation, and by resolutions asked that:

* SWP support development of a rationalization program for the railway network in Western Canada, with consideration given to needs on a regional basis rather than line by line as railways sought to abandon individual branch lines.

* Governments develop a Canadian

965. Alberta Wheat Pool met at Calgary in November, for the organization's 51st annual meeting. It was reported to the meeting that members doing business with the Pool during the 1972-73 crop year would share savings of $5,714,000. In that crop year, the Pool handled a record 164,362,529 bushels or 68.7% of all grains delivered in Alberta and British Columbia.

Additionally, AWP:

1. Supported proposals that the marketing of rapeseed be placed under jurisdiction of the Wheat Board.

2. Called for urgent action to end grain transportation problems.

1973

144

1973

transportation policy that would serve needs of Western Canada, encourage industrial development in the region, and make it economically possible to move products of all kinds from the Prairies to other Canadian and overseas markets.

* Steps be taken to improve and ensure continuous movement of grain and other commodities, particularly to West Coast seaports.

* That the Government of Canada provide more hopper cars, and the railways upgrade tracks so that full use of the cars may be had on branch lines.

966. XCAN Grain Limited, the organization formed in 1970 by the three Prairie Pools in an effort to stimulate export sales of grain, achieved an operating surplus of $286,329 during the 1972-73 crop year. Reports emphasized that marketing conditions were "entirely different" from those existing in 1970 when there was a surplus of grain and markets were lacking. The report noted that the Canadian Wheat Board had assumed an increased role in the marketing of those grains for which it was responsible, and this resulted in correspondingly less opportunity for export firms to participate in the sale of wheat or course grains. "Under these circumstances, it has been difficult for XCAN to increase its volume of handling," the report said. "In addition, violent price fluctuations of recent months have made trading extremely hazardous. However, the serious losses which are always possible under these circumstances have been avoided by XCAN."

967. Palliser Wheat Growers' Association: As the Palliser Wheat Growers met at Regina, December 11 and 12, in annual convention, the organization's president charged that Canada was losing ground to the U.S.A. in exporting wheat to Russia and China. He attacked the Canadian Wheat Board and its sales policies and also the existing grain handling system. He suggested that "relaxation of the Crow's Nest rates might be the beginning to a turnaround", and proposed more use of the 5 existing inland terminals, an increase in freight rates, and a more flexible elevator tariff plan. Another speaker to the meeting was the president of Cargill Grain, a U.S.-based concern, who asserted that "the Pools in

1973

particular are hell bent to ensure that no changes are made in the system that they have perpetuated since the 1930's." Still another speaker was the president of United Grain Growers who favored higher tariffs for country elevators to allow "proper rebuilding" of the system.

968. The Farm Commodity Group Alliance, a new body formed earlier in 1973, announced plans to hold its first annual meeting in late November, with only six voting delegates—two from each of the Palliser Wheat Growers Association, Saskatchewan Stockgrowers Association, and the Rapeseed Growers Association. A spokesman for the Palliser Wheat Growers explained that one goal of the Alliance was to reduce the influence of the Saskatchewan Wheat Pool within the Saskatchewan Federation of Argriculture.

969. Hudson Bay Route: The Minister for Industry and Commerce, Province of Manitoba, speaking at Lloydminster to the annual meeting of the Hudson Bay Route Association, declared that more grain should be shipped via the Port of Churchill to alleviate the current critical grain transportation problem. He described the Churchill port as 'under-used' and expressed concern over the lack of response by the federal government to suggestions for changes to the Churchill port which had been offered by the Manitoba government. He expressed the opionion that "there is the potential in Western Canada of shipping at least 1,000,000 tons of bulk commodities a year through Churchill."

970. Western Co-operative Fertilizers Limited, on July 20, announced its purchase of a fertilizer production plant at Medicine Hat, Alberta, which had operated under the name, Northwest Nitro-Chemicals Ltd. The Medicine Hat plant, with annual capacity of 220,000 to 240,000 tons would augment production of WCFL's Calgary plant which was being expanded, providing WCFL with about one-fifth of the total fertilizer production capacity in Western Canada. An increased capacity was needed by WCFL to meet demands of its owners, Federated Co-operatives Limited, Alberta Wheat Pool, Saskatchewan Wheat Pool, and Manitoba Pool Elevators. Amid distressed grain markets of the latter 1960's, total fertilizer sales by all companies in Western Canada had dropped from 1,008,265 tons in 1968 to 521,502 tons in 1970, then began to recover, reaching about 1,055,000 tons in 1972. Even higher demands appeared in 1973 and it was then evident that in the spring of 1974 available supplies would fall short of requirements. Particularly short in supply were ammonia and urea-based fertilizers. The latter were not produced by WCFL, but procured when available from other sources.

971. Western Co-operative Fertilizers—Consortium For New Plant: In late 1973, it was announced that three major co-operatives had agreed to form a new organization to establish at Medicine Hat, a new plant costing in excess of $80,000,000, for production of anhydrous ammonia and urea fertilizers. The three co-operatives were Western Co-operative Fertilizers Limited, United Co-operatives of Ontario, and CF Industries Inc., of Chicago. CF Industries was formed by a federation of 18 regional co-operatives in the U.S.A. where it served about 1,500,000 member-owners. Announcement of the new venture stressed that a majority of its ownership would be held by Canadians, and that it was hoped the plant would be producing in time to serve 1976 needs.

1973

972. Canadian Co-operative Implements Limited completed construction of its new factory at Winnipeg and marked the occasion by an official opening held July 7 with over 20,000 members and other visitors present. The plant was built at a cost of $7,200,000 about one-half the sum being provided by CI's own members through thier purchase of bonds. The balance was borrowed from other co-operative organizations. It was estimated that Co-operative Implements was now supplying about 8% of the farm machinery market in Western Canada, and employing 1,104 persons at its Winnipeg plant and country depots.

CI sales for the 1973 year reached $37,000,000—an increase of 67.8% over 1972 sales. In anticipation of the high expenses incurred in starting its new factory, a substantial loss on 1973 operations was predicted. The year-end net loss was, however, only $36,454. During 1973, CI added nine new products to its lines, ranging from large tractors to manure spreaders, augers and garden equipment. Steps were under way to upgrade CI's country depots, with 5 new depots being completed in 1973 and 4 more under construction.

973. Federated Co-operatives Limited completed a record year at October 31, 1973, with sales of $358,218,000 and an allocation of $14,582,000 to retail co-operatives and other members, as patronage refunds on 1973 purchases. During 1973, FCL returned $8,235,000 to its members in cash. The annual report noted that

FCL earnings for the year had been reduced by as much as $1,750,000 by deliberate steps taken to help retail co-operatives hold down the effect of price increases to members, and to hold prices, so far as possible, at fair and reasonable levels.

974. Westland Co-operatives, formed and incorporated in 1972, officially began operations on January 1, 1973. On that date, amalgamation with Westland, of retail co-operatives at Carrot River, Hudson Bay, Kelvington and Kindersley, all in Saskatchewan, was effective. A fifth unit of Westland was provided as an FCL-owned store at Mackenzie, B.C., after a campaign to

sign-up local members, was transferred to Westland. In the ten-month period to the end of the fiscal year at October 31, Westland Co-operatives had sales of $7,143,000, and net savings of $309,000, including patronage refunds from FCL. The number of members served by Westland stood at 7,960.

975. Consumers Co-operative Refineries Limited, Regina, wholly-owned subsidiary of Federated Co-operatives, was greatly occupied with expansion of its refining capacity. In 1973, capacity was increased to 25,000 barrels of crude per day. Work continued in effort to further increase capacity to 28,000 barrels per day during 1974. It was apparent, at the time, that a substantial investment in new facilities would be needed to extend capacity beyond 28,000 barrels per day and to produce low-leaded and non-leaded gasolines that would be required by 1975 model automobiles. Products from the Refinery were being shipped to retail co-operatives in Manitoba, Saskatchewan and some parts of Alberta. To serve the remainder of the Alberta market, and the new

market in British Columbia that resulted from the amalgamation of 1970, products were obtained from other refineries through purchase or exchange arrangements. Transportation costs prohibited service to British Columbia and parts of Alberta from the Regina refinery. However, as inflation and the prevailing 'energy crisis' contributed to higher prices for products obtained from other refiners, CCRL was confronted with need to consider means by which it could more effectively serve the markets in question. Among proposals being considered late in 1973 was the purchase of a refinery owned by Imperial Oil Limited at Calgary. In other areas of activity, the Co-op Refinery completed construction and occupied its new administration building in June.

976. Northern Industrial Chemicals Ltd., incorporated in 1971 as an FCL subsidiary to operate the chemicals complex at Saskatoon first built by Interprovincial Co-operatives in 1963, ceased operations on May 30. On that date, its facilities for producing caustic soda and chlorine were sold to Prince Albert Pulp Mill, and other facilities of the complex, an organic plant, were

transferred to Interprovincial Co-operatives Limited. The organic plant was not being used. Though strong efforts had been put forth, it was not possible to turn the chemical plant into a viable operation due to its indebtness and unfavourable terms of the contract by which it supplied the pulp mill with products.

1973

977. Co-op Vegetable Oils had 1973 sales of $21,500,000, an increase from sales of $16,000,000 in 1972. The 1973 net earnings, at $844,105, were down from $956,000 in 1972. The organization now serving 5,000 farmer-members and employing a staff of 120, announced plans for an expansion program costing $4 to $5 million to be completed in stages in the next 3 to 5 years.

979. Fishing Co-operatives: The minister in charge of Manitoba's Department of Co-operative Development reported that six fishermen's co-operatives were now operating in northern areas of Manitoba, and had paid out to members in cash during the year, more than $77,500. The co-ops served 524 members, most of them Indians and Metis.

978. Dairy Producers Co-operative, formed in 1972, completed a new $2,500,000 milk processing plant at Yorkton. The plant was described as being the most modern of its kind in the Province. In another forward step, the Dairy Producers began manufacturing cheese at Saskatoon. Previously, all cheese sold in Saskatchewan was imported from other provinces of Canada or from other countries.

980. Co-operative Fisheries Limited achieved a small net earning of $13,622 in 1973. A major problem cited by the CFL annual meeting was the high cost of air freight from lakes in remote areas. One fisherman, it was reported, received a net return of $1.56 for a planeload of fish after paying the air freight.

145

1973

1973

981. Co-operative Trust Company of Canada had a highly successful year of operations, with its assets now reaching $122,629,500. Its membership of 457 organizations consisted of 245 credit unions, 59 co-operative organizations, and 69 others, all located in the provinces of Ontario, Manitoba, Saskatchewan, Alberta, and B.C. Growth of the organization and its services made it necessary to expand office facilities, and plans were announced for erection of a six-storey office building at Saskatoon, during 1974.

982. Co-operative Bank Proposed: A committee of representatives from Manitoba Co-operative Credit Society, Saskatchewan Co-operative Credit Society and Federated Co-operatives Limited, announced in late 1973, that steps would be taken to obtain from the federal government, a Charter for a proposed co-operative bank to serve Western Canada. Plans called for the sale of shares to co-operatives and credit unions, and also to the public. Spokesmen explained that the bank was to be a 'merchant' bank serving needs of Western farmers and businessmen through a limited number of branches, and would not actively compete for consumer loan and deposit business. It was further proposed that the co-operative bank be known as "Northland Bank" or "Norbanque", and be based in Winnipeg.

983. Co-operative Superannuation Society, at December 31, 1973, had 5,740 employee members on its roster, and had extended services into Quebec and Nova Scotia. By this time, the Society was directly providing pensions to 79 retired employees of employer members. Management of the Society's investment portfolio was being provided by Co-operative Insurance Services under a program launched on a trial basis in 1972. At a May 2 meeting hosted by the Society at Saskatoon, it was agreed that a study be made of the feasibility of creating a national pension plan for co-operatives through consolidating the various programs being provided by such organizations across Canada.

984. Saskatchewan Co-operative Credit Society was granted incorporation for a subsidiary known as Saskatchewan Co-operative Financial Services Ltd. The subsidiary, incorporated in May, was to provide loans for such purposes as farm improvement and to aid small businesses.

During 1973, assets of SCCS were increased by $67-million, reaching $243,000,000. The Society, which was serving a membership of 250 credit unions and 350 co-operatives, announced plans to build a multi-storey office building at Regina by 1975, to accommodate its expanding needs.

985. Rural Education and Development Association: The Credit Union Federation of Alberta became a member of Rural Education and Development Association, joining with Unifarm, Co-operative Insurance Services, Federated Co-operatives, and Co-operative Implements in support of REDA and its programs.

986. Co-op Section Created In Canada Department of **Agriculture:** The minister in charge of the Canada Department of Agriculture announced in July that a new co-operatives and producer marketing section has been established in that department. The minister explained that "our action is in support of agricultural co-operatives", and that the new department is designed to help co-operative directors and officers solve problems they encounter at the federal, national or international level.

1973

Research and analytical studies were to be an important activity of the department which would also work with co-operatives in developing proposals for new federal programs of direct assistance to co-operatives. Said the Minister: "I have seen what some other countries do for co-operatives, and we have a lot that could and should be done here in Canada to come close to matching their record."

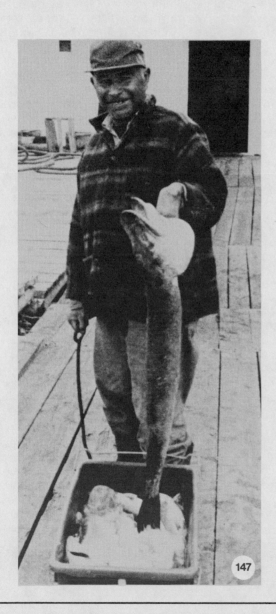

1974

987. Another Troubled Year: In the spring of 1974, seeding was delayed in many parts of the Prairies by a late spring followed by rains, unusually heavy and prolonged for that time of year. Spurred by inflation and world-wide food shortages, grain prices rose to record levels. The year was also made interesting and a time of concern by a number of other developments.:

Rapeseed Marketing: The 1973 controversy as to whether rapeseed should be placed under the Canadian Wheat Board or remain under the open market system, was decided by a vote of rapeseed growers. The wheat pools, National Farmers Union, Unifarm, Saskatchewan Federation of Agriculture, Manitoba Farm Bureau, and other bodies, strongly urged farmers to favor orderly marketing through the Wheat Board. The Winnipeg Commodity Exchange, in a major publicity campaign, argued to the contrary. When the poll was taken, 32,279 rapeseed producers, of the eligible number of 41,142, cast their vote. The result was that 52.6% (16,992) voted in favor of retaining the open market system for rapeseed, while 46.2% (14,894) favored marketing via the Canadian Wheat Board. After noting the narrow margin favoring the open market, the federal minister in charge of the Wheat Board promised to set up a pooling system for marketing rapeseed, for those farmers who desired to use it. The rejection of Wheat Board control of rapeseed marketing was disappointing to all who favored orderly marketing. In retrospect, there was doubt as to whether the result would have been the same if rapeseed prices had not been the highest on record at the same time the vote was taken.

Feed Grains Marketing: On May 22, the federal minister in charge of the Canadian Wheat Board announced a new policy for the marketing of feed grains (barley, oats, feed wheat). The policy, to be effective on August 1, provided that domestic feed grains would be removed from the Wheat Board and turned over to the open market. The effect would be the setting of domestic feed grain prices on the future markets of the Winnipeg Commodity Exchange. The policy, however, provided for feed grain producers to receive for grain sold on the open market, a price equal to the initial price on the export market. The policy also gave assurance that the Wheat Board, which controlled elevator space, would be required to provide space for non-Board grain, and the railways would likewise be required to allocate boxcars for its movement. This policy, which was regarded as depreciating the powers of the Wheat Board, was introduced without providing farmers with an opportunity to express their desires. Canadian Co-operative Wheat Producers, through its Board of Directors, expressed "grave concern" for the new policy, saying it was "imposed on farmers" despite repeated warnings about its effects. Alberta Wheat Pool Budget deplored the policy saying it "will protect livestock feeders in central and eastern Canada from the threat of feed shortages", while eroding the Wheat Board that protects the interests of Western farmers. Following announcement of the policy, an agency of the Saskatchewan Government sent a questionnaire to all Saskatchewan farmers. Of the 41,250 questionnaires returned, 92.9% indicated that farmers desired barley, oats and feed wheat to be handled by the Canadian Wheat Board. In answer to another question, 83.6% disapproved of the marketing of domestic feed grains through the Winnipeg Commodities Exchange. Despite the evidence that farmers, and a strong majority of farm organizations, did not approve the new policy, it was put into effect on August 1.

Winnipeg Commodities Exchange: In late July, and even before the new policy for open market sales of domestic feed grains had come into effect, the Winnipeg Commodities Exchange began trading in feed grains futures.

Canadian Wheat Board: While many spokesmen in Western Canada were expressing fear that forces were at work to undermine the Canadian Wheat Board, that organization was lauded by a study, prepared for the United States' Congress by the U.S. General Accounting Office in Washington. The report declared that the Canadian Wheat Board method of handling grain sales offers a number of advantages over the free market system in the U.S.A. It said, "Canada...has better control over production, delivery and marketing, and can regulate the flow of supplies between domestic and foreign markets, and create a two-price system to insulate the price in Canada from higher world prices. The Canadian system eliminates market fluctuation and speculation and makes it easier to deal with agencies of Communist countries. It also facilitates product research, promotion and development." On the negative side, the report included a comment that the CWB system "produces a potential for inflexibility and inertia because of bureaucracy and political pressures."

Railway Hopper Cars: In January, the three Prairie Wheat Pools, by letter to the minister in charge of the Canadian Wheat

1974

Board, urged that the Canadian Government provide 4,000 more hopper cars for use by railways in moving grain, to augment the 2,000 cars the government had provided in the previous two years. In July, the minister announced that 4,000 more cars would be built. He said 1,600 of the new cars would be constructed of aluminum to be of lighter weight so that they would be used on secondary, main and branch line tracks which, it had been found, could not stand the weight of cars previously built.

Crowsnest Pass Rates: Speaking at Edmonton in October, the federal minister in charge of the Canadian Wheat Board, who also served as Justice Minister, declared that: "As part of a complete overhaul of the railway transportation system we may have to examine the effect of the Crowsnest rates, paticularly as they apply to domestic movement of grain. It is indeed likely that the Crowsnest rate on domestic grain is harmful to western development in livestock in that the Crow rates are discouraging the export of more meat and products of grain. They are also creating serious problems in terms of not only maintaining a deteriorating (railway) system, but in re-building it to a modern, efficient one...The producer would be better off if the benefit of the Crow rate were transferred to him or a fund for many measures which support rural prairies and improvements for grain or agriculture there, for roads, an infra-structure, or for extra trucking costs newly incurred." The remarks were seen as implying an intention by the government to remove the Crowsnest Pass rates, and drew a quick and angry response from the wheat pools and virtually all farm organizations, Palliser Wheat Growers excepted. In addition, Provincial Governments of the Prairie provinces also expressed firm protest.

Rail Line Abandonment: Another issue linked to the railways, came to the fore in 1974—the desire of the railways to abandon many prairie branch lines now mainly used for the movement of grain. This issue too, aroused concern and protest among co-operatives, farm organizations, and prairie governments, es-pecially when coupled with the hint that the Crowsnest rates would be withdrawn. it was seen that whatever advantages were gained by the railways in such a move would be matched by equal disadvantages to farmers and to the rural communities. In December, however, **The Toronto Daily Star** was able to re-port that: "Nearly two-thirds of the railway grain handling track-age on the prairies will be protected against abandonment until

at least the end of the century, according to the minister in charge of the Canadian Wheat Board. He said 12,413 miles of 19,221 miles will be protected to allay fears that the wholesale abandonment of rail lines in Western Canada is about to take place, and 6,283 of the remainder will be protected for at least a year. The report said the minister had noted that 'the grain farmer especially needs a modern, efficient transportation and handling system, and his well-being is fundamental to prosper-ity in the prairies'."

U.S.-Based Grain Companies: Two of the world's largest grain handling companies began active operations in the Prairie Prov-inces during 1974. Cargill Grain Company, a subsidiary of a private Minnesota-based multinational corporation dating back to 1865, Cargill Inc., purchased the country elevators and other assets of National Grain Limited and National Feeds & Livestock Limited. Cargill, said to be the world's largest grain company, had diversified in recent years, owning a salt mine in Louisiana; chemical plants for making paints, plastic coatings and fibre-glass; 55 feed plants in North and South America, Asia and Europe; a fishing fleet in Peru to harvest fish for processing into feeds; vegetable oil and protein plants in Europe and the U.S.A.; a shipping fleet; and railway rolling stock for moving grain and other materials. The second firm, The Continental Grain Com-pany (Canada) Limited, also a subsidiary of a U.S. concern, 90% owned by one individual and with headquarters in New York, was reported to have a vast country elevator system in the U.S.A.; own more than 25 ships, and have under its corporate umbrlla, more than 100 companies. Continental became active in the prairies by offering to buy feed grain and oilseeds directly from farms for delivery to Canadian government elevators in its fleet of hopper-bottom trucks.

Weyburn Inland Terminal: At Weyburn, Saskatchewan, a group of farmers, with at least moral support of Palliser Wheat Growers', announced plans to build an inland terminal large enough to handle grain within a 50-mile radius. It was announc-ed that shares, at $1,000 each, would be offered to farmers, with only 2,000 shares to be sold, and that $1.6 million of the $4.7 million cost of the terminal project was to be raised in this manner. By a later announcement, it was explained that the sale of shares had been delayed until the Saskatchewan Securities Commission had approved a final Prospectus. Meanwhile, the organization, which had become known as Weyburn Inland Ter-minal Ltd., had conducted a campaign for members, and was

1974

said to have sold 500 memberships at $100 each. At the same time, a number of meetings were held at larger towns in Saskatchewan, where spokesmen for the Weyburn Inland Terminal and for Palliser Wheat Growers' sought to arouse support for similar inland terminal projects.

Federal Department of Agriculture: In 1973, by a brief to The Special Committee on Trends in Food Prices, a recommendation had been made by Federated Co-operatives Limited that the federal minister of agriculture encouraged co-operatives to expand activities in the foods marketing and processing fields as a means of helping to control rising consumer food costs. It was recommended that the minister set up a committee of co-operative leaders to assist. Speaking in Ontario during 1974, the fed-

eral Minister of Agriculture appeared to respond to FCL's suggestion when he said: ''I intend to set up a new branch in Agriculture Canada that will deal specifically with co-ops. It will be a 'think-tank'. I want the top men in the industry to find out what kinds of funds co-ops need, and how they can best be used. I have no doubt that taxpayers should be giving more support to co-ops. In the United States and in the United Kingdom, co-ops get the backing they need. Co-ops are fierce watchdogs. They are one of the biggest anti-profiteering groups we've got. It is obvious that co-operatives are a good investment for anyone who eats food.'' The federal Minister of Agriculture, it should be noted, did not have responsibility for the Canadian Wheat Board, although many farm leaders seemed of the opinion that such should be the case.

988. Manitoba Pool Elevators: In May, Manitoba Pool Elevators paid out $1,605,000 to members in cash, bringing the total patronage refund payments to members since it was formed, to $39,900,000.

989. Saskatchewan Wheat Pool, at its 50th Annual Meeting, reported that savings to members in the 1973-74 crop year, were $32-million. The Pool's plans to reduce its number of elevator points by almost one-half was discussed by Delegates. It was proposed that the present elevator system be replaced, in a major, long-term program, by elevators of 'high-throughput' capacity located at more central points. It was noted that the pool had handled about 67.1% of the grain delivered by Saskatchewan farmers in the past year.

990. Alberta Wheat Pool allocated patronage refunds of $10,533,000 to members on business done in the 1973-74 crop year, repaying to members in cash, $7,183,000 of that sum. Since first formed, the AWP had allocated patronage refunds to its members, more than $95.6-million.

Membership now stood at 54,203 farmers. In the 1973-74 crop year, AWP handled about 67.5% of the grain deliveries in Alberta and B.C.

991. CVO Merges With MPE: Members of Manitoba Pool Elevators and of Co-operative Vegetable Oils Limited approved a merger by which MPE became responsible for operation of CVO's vegetable oils plant. CVO, with 5,000 members, handled about 30% of the 1973 Manitoba rapeseed crop. In passing from the scene, Co-operative Vegetable Oils could look back upon its history with much satisfaction, for it had introduced a new crop to the Prairies and pioneered co-operative plants for processing sunflower, rapeseed and other vegetable oils, all of which had helped improve income of the farmer-members served.

992. SWP Rapeseed Crushing: Two moves involving further rapeseed crushing facilities were announced by Saskatchewan Wheat Pool in 1974. At Nipawin, in NE Saskatchewan, the Pool purchased the crushing plant of Agra Industries, and also became involved with Agra in a 50-50 venture for operation of an adjacent rapeseed oil refinery. The Pool also announced plans to build a rapeseed crushing plant able to process 600 tons per day.

993. AWP Rapeseed Crushing: Plans to build a rapeseed crushing plant near Edmonton were announced by the Alberta Wheat Pool. Construction of a plant to process 600 tons per day was expected to begin in early 1975.

1974

994. New Oilseed Co-operative Proposed: The merger between CVO and MPE was in reality part of a larger plan whereby the Manitoba and Saskatchewan Pools would form a new, jointly-owned organization to operate the oilseed crushing plants of the two Pools. By this means, the economies of scale to be achieved would assist the co-operative plants to better compete with large, privately-owned plants.

995. Palliser Wheat Growers Association: The Toronto Daily Star, in a January news report on the annual meeting of Palliser Wheat Growers Association, indicated that the organization now had members in all three Prairie Provinces, with 180 in Alberta, 2,604 in Saskatchewan, and 29 in Manitoba. **The Star** described PWGA as "an outspoken critic of the Canadian Wheat Board and prairie wheat pools...composed of the more wealthy farmers." The report indicated that at PWGA's annual meeting "several speakers contended that the Crowsnest limits on railway charges for moving grain are so low that the railways cannot modernize." The report said resolutions were passed in favor of:

* Removal of maximum grain handling tariffs "to allow free competition to estabish the charges levied against the farmers' grain."

* Provision, by the federal government, of 2,000 more hopper railway cars to carry grain "with the understanding that the cars will be sold to the railways at a time as the rail rates become compensatory.

* An open market for feed grains rather than having the Wheat Board as sole selling agency for shipments from the Prairies to British Columbia or to the East.

* Limiting annual grain carryover to 100 million bushels in commercial storage.

* Having farmers truck their grain at their own expense to central inland terminals.

* Greater storage capacity at West Coast ports and the Port of Churchill, and greater use of unit trains to move grain.

In November, it was reported that PWGA was awarded a grant of $28,500 by the federal Department of Agriculture, to study and promote the growing of utility wheat varieties in Western Canada.

996. United Grain Growers: The 68th Annual Meeting of United Grain Growers was informed that the organization had commissioned a $30,000 study of the potential feasibility of inland grain terminals. Record earnings of $13,300,000 before taxes and patronage dividends were reported. Farmers delivering to UGG elevators in the 1973-74 crop year were allocated patronage dividends of $7.2 million.

THE PECKING ORDER

Licensed Primary Elevators Western Canada at January 1, 1974

	Man.	Sask.	Alta.	B.C.	Total
Saskatchewan Wheat Pool	—	1519	—	—	1519
Alberta Wheat Pool	—	—	828	11	839
United Grain Growers	128	306	320	7	761
Pioneer Grain Co.	11	336	98	—	445
Manitoba Pool Elevators	321	—	—	—	321
Cargill Grain Co.*	28	173	82	1	284
Paterson and Sons Ltd.	39	50	2	—	91
Parish and Helmbecker	4	31	21	—	56
Others	9	3	22	3	37
Total	540	2418	1373	22	4353

* Elevators owned on January 1, 1974 by National Grain are listed as owned by Cargill Grain Co.

Source: Canadian Grain commission special interim report on Grain Elevators in Canada at January 1, 1974.

997. XCAN Grain Limited: In January it was announced that XCAN Grain Limited, by mutual agreement, would be owned by the three Prairie wheat pools as those organizations had acquired the shares of the fourth partner-owner, United Grain Growers. A joint release said: "In spite of the cordial relationship that has existed between the four companies, there has been a growing recognition that because United Grain Growers is a direct competitor with each of the Pools...some of the objectives of XCAN have been difficult to achieve." Other reports noted that XCAN had a record year in the crop year ended at mid-1974; the most successful in its four year history. It had become established in the international trading community to carry out its purpose of selling Canadian grain to which it devoted exclusive attention.

998. Western Co-operative Fertilizers Limited: During the 1973-74 crop year, WCFL supplied about 33.3% of the agricultural fertilizers used in the four Western Provinces. Total volume handled by the fertilizer industry in Western Canada, which had fallen off to 774,000 tons in the 1971-72 crop year, reached a record of 1,346,000 tons in the 1973-74 crop year. With world demand for fertilizer at a high level, and with inflation further contributing, fertilizer prices reached record levels in the U.S.A., other countries, and in Eastern Canada. After studying the situation, a spokesman for WCFL stated that fertilizer prices in Western Canada were the lowest in the world. The three Prairie wheat pools and FCL, the partner-owners of WCFL, had followed a policy of price restraint, making only such increases as were needed to offset higher costs of raw materials, production, transportation and distribution.

999. Canadian Fertilizers Limited: A new co-operative organization was formed by Western Co-operative Fertilizers Limited, United Co-operatives of Ontario, Co-operative Federee de Quebec and CF Industries Inc. (a major U.S. fertilizer co-operative) joined in a venture for production of anhydrous ammonia and urea-based fertilizers, types not produced by WCFL. Plans were laid for construction of a major plant at Medicine Hat, costing in excess of $100-million, and to begin production by late 1976. Canadian Fertilizers Limited, according to agreement, was to be 51% owned by the three Canadian co-operatives, with CF industries being a 49% owner. CF Industries was then the 5th largest distributor of fertilizers in the U.S.A., and held substantial interests in potash mine at Colonsay, Saskatchewan.

1000. Canadian Co-operative Implements Limited: Although CI's sales in the year ended October 31, 1974, reached $41.1-million, the shortages of materials and machinery parts that existed at the time presented difficulties. Additional sales of $8.5-million could have been achieved, it was said, if the shortages had not

prevented delivery of machines. In 1974, CI's Winnipeg factory produced, for the first time, Volvo combines which previously had been built and imported from Sweden. Three new types of farm machines were also introduced by CI. At the year's end, however, an operating loss of $96,597 was recorded.

1001. Federated Co-operatives Limited: In the year ended October 31, 1974, FCL sales were $487-million. Savings available for allocation to member organizations, were $13.6-million. During the year, $7.1-million was returned to retail co-operatives and other members in cash. The membership consisted of 419 retail co-operatives plus Westland Co-operatives and its 19 retailing units; 69 other co-operatives; and 15 non-profit institutions. During 1974, FCL:

* Purchased a newly-built feed plant at Lethbridge, Alberta, and laid plans to replace the feed plant owned at Edmonton.

* Entered into a contract to provide management services to Newell Vegetables Co-op of Brooks, Alberta, a producer-owned growers' co-operative. That organization was experiencing operational difficulties, and the Alberta government proposed that assistance from FCL be sought.

* Took initial steps for expansion of its subsidiary, Consumers'

Co-operative Refineries Limited. The Board of Directors authorized installation of a larger platformer unit needed to produce higher quantities of gasoline, and for production of non-leaded or low-leaded gasolines. Design work was begun in preparation for an eventual expansion of refining capacity from 28,500 barrels of crude per day, to 50,000 or more.

* FCL started construction of a new warehouse in Vancouver and doubled capacity of warehouses in Calgary and Edmonton, warehouses that had been built respectively, in 1966 and 1967. It was also becoming evident that warehouse capacity at Regina, Saskatoon and Winnipeg would soon have to be expanded.

* Announced plans to establish a plant for production of manufactured homes and other small buildings, at or near Saskatoon. Delegates to FCL annual meetings had urged that such a venture be undertaken.

1002. Westland Co-operatives: Since operations began January 1, 1973, Westland Co-operatives had 5 retailing units. In the fiscal year ended October 31, the sales by the organization through these units were $11.6-million. Savings available to members as

patronage refunds, were $379,000. At November 1, 1974, 14 retail co-operatives amalgamated with Westland, bringing the number of retailing units to 19.

1003. Calgary Co-operative Association, Canada's largest retail co-operative and a member of FCL, had sales of $61.5-million, up by 32.7% over 1973. After tax savings of $3.04-million it enabled the association to declare a patronage refund to members of 5.2% of their 1974 purchases.

1004. UFA Co-operative: With record 1974 sales of $63-million, up 33% over 1973, UFA Co-operative was able to allocate patronage refunds of $5.5-million to its members, returning $3.7-million of that amount in cash.

1974

1974

1005. Co-op Credit Society of Manitoba: By the end of its 1974 fiscal year, assets of the CCSM had reached $92.6-million. As a result of efforts by CCSM, the Manitoba Legislature amended provisions respecting credit unions to enable them to serve as depositories of trust funds. CCSM was not as successful, it appears, in efforts to dissuade the government from forming a system of treasury branches to provide banking services. CCSM urged that more use be made of Manitoba's 165 autonomous credit unions, the combined membership of which was said to equal about one-quarter of the Province's total population.

1006. Saskatchewan Co-operative Credit Society: Serving as the central organization for 251 Saskatchewan credit unions, SCCS achieved a net savings of $2.9-million on its 1974 operations. About 350 co-operative associations in Saskatchewan also held membership in the Society to make use of its financial services. Assets of the credit unions exceeded $1-billion for the first time in 1974, and it was said that membership in the credit unions had reached 395,488.

1007. Saskatchewan Co-operative Financial Services: A new organization was established as a wholly-owned subsidiary of Saskatchewan Co-operative Credit Society. Known as Saskatchewan Co-operative Financial Services, its purpose was to make long-term residential mortgage and small business development loans. The first loan was made to the owner of a small welding and electrical business at Muenster, who desired to expand his facilities.

1008. Co-operative Trust Company of Canada: Rapid growth and expansion was noted by the Co-operative Trust Company of Canada during 1974. After-tax net earnings of $728,000 were achieved, from which $552,000 was paid out as dividends to Co-op Trust's 555 member organizations of the four Western provinces— 293 co-operatives and credit unions in Saskatchewan, 94 in Manitoba, 76 in Alberta, 30 in British Columbia; and 61 in Ontario where, in 1974, the Company opened a new office in Toronto.

1009. Northland Bank (Norbanque): The committee which, in 1973, began development of plans for a co-operative bank to be known as Northland Bank or Norbanque, continued to make progress. In early 1974, it was announced that a petition to Parliament for the chartering of a merchant bank to concentrate on providing financial needs of small and medium-sized businesses, would be sponsored by a number of co-operatives and credit unions. It was also explained that the proposed bank, which is to have head offices at Winnipeg, would not actively compete with or otherwise be in conflict with credit unions or credites societies, but would aim to augment services provided by those organizations. It would aim also, "to break down economic disparities between various regions of Canada."

1974

1010. Co-operative Hail Insurance Company: The farmer-owned Co-operative Hail Insurance Company had $64,000,000 worth of insurance in effect during 1974—more than it had ever had since begun in 1947. The company, which insures any type of crop, employs its own adjusters, and operates under a board of directors consisting of 12 active farmers.

1011. Co-operative College of Canada: At September 30, 1974, the Co-operative College of Canada completed its first year of operations under that name. In a message that was reprinted in the annual report, Pierre Elliott Trudeau, Prime Minister of Canada, said:

"It is with great pleasure that I extend greetings and good wishes to the annual meeting of the Co-operative College of Canada in Saskatoon as you celebrate your first year of incorporation as a Canadian Co-operative College.

"The importance of co-operation and co-operative ventures can hardly be over-emphasized today. The need for a new ethic in our society, based on sharing, the need for a new consciousness of the patterns and habits at work in our society and in ourselves, the need to relate beyond specialization and isolation to a more wholistic relationship with nature and with each other—these needs are the concern of the spirit of co-operation.

"I wish you well in your chosen role of education. As we together face the challenges that we see at all levels in society, we will encourage and sustain one another."

1012. General Election of 1974: In the General Election held July 8, 1974, the Liberal Party won a clear majority:

PROVINCE	LIB.	PROG. CONS.	N.D.P.	CREDIT-ISTE	INDEP.	TOTAL	% OF TOTAL SEATS
Ontario	55	25	8			88	33.3%
Quebec	60	3		11		74	28.0
Nova Scotia	2	8	1			11	4.2
New Brunswick	6	3			1	10	3.8
Newfoundland	4	3				7	2.7
P.E.I.	1	3				4	1.5
Manitoba	2	9	2			13	4.9
Saskatchewan	3	8	2			13	4.9
Alberta		19				19	7.2
British Columbia	8	13	2			23	8.7
Yukon		1				1	.4
N.W.T.			1			1	.4
	141	95	16	11	1	264	100.0%

Appendix A

Statistical Data

POPULATION, FARMS AND CULTIVATED ACRES

Prairie Provinces

YEAR	PROVINCE	RURAL POPULATION	URBAN POPULATION	TOTAL POPULATION	FARMS	CULTIVATED ACRES	AV. ACRES PER FARM
1871	Manitoba	24,170	1,058	25,228			
1881	Manitoba	52,015	10,245	62,260		2,384,337	
1891	Manitoba	111,498	41,008	152,506		5,228,272	
1901	Manitoba	184,775	70,436	255,211	32,252	8,843,347	274
	Saskatchewan	77,013	14,266	91,279	13,445	3,833,434	285
	Alberta	54,489	18,533	73,022	9,479	2,735,630	289
	Total	316,277	103,235	419,235	55,176	15,412,411	279
1911	Manitoba	261,029	200,365	461,394	43,631	12,184,304	279
	Saskatchewan	361,037	131,395	492,432	95,013	28,099,207	296
	Alberta	236,633	137,662	374,295	60,559	17,359,333	287
	Total	858,699	469,422	1,328,121	199,203	57,642,844	289
1921	Manitoba	348,502	261,616	610,118	53,252	14,615,844	274
	Saskatchewan	538,552	218,958	757,510	119,451	44,022,907	369
	Alberta	365,550	222,904	588,454	82,954	29,293,053	353
	Total	1,252,604	703,478	1,956,082	255,657	87,931,804	344
1931	Manitoba	384,170	315,969	700,139	54,199	15,131,685	279
	Saskatchewan	630,880	290,905	921,785	136,472	55,673,460	408
	Alberta	453,097	278,508	731,605	97,408	38,977,457	400
	Total	1,468,147	885,382	2,353,529	288,079	109,782,602	381
1936	Manitoba	400,289	310,927	711,216	57,774	15,668,927	271
	Saskatchewan	651,274	280,273	931,547	142,391	56,903,639	400
	Alberta	486,335	286,447	772,782	100,358	40,539,934	404
	Total	1,537,898	877,647	2,415,545	300,523	113,112,500	376
1941	Manitoba	407,871	321,873	729,744	58,024	16,891,322	291
	Saskatchewan	600,846	295,146	895,992	138,713	59,960,927	432
	Alberta	489,583	306,586	796,169	99,732	43,277,295	434
	Total	1,498,300	923,605	2,421,905	296,469	120,129,544	405
1951	Manitoba	336,961	439,580	776,541	52,383	17,730,393	338
	Saskatchewan	579,258	252,470	831,728	112,018	61,663,195	550
	Alberta	489,003	450,498	939,501	84,315	44,459,632	526
	Total	1,405,222	1,142,548	2,547,770	248,716	123,853,220	498

YEAR	PROVINCE	RURAL POPULATION	URBAN POPULATION	TOTAL POPULATION	FARMS	CULTIVATED ACRES	AV. ACRES PER FARM
1956	Manitoba	339,457	510,583	850,040	49,201	17,931,817	364
	Saskatchewan	558,662	322,003	880,666	103,391	62,793,979	607
	Alberta	487,292	635,824	1,123,116	79,424	45,970,395	579
	Total	1,385,411	1,468,410	2,853,821	232,016	126,696,191	546
1961	Manitoba	332,879	588,807	921,686	43,306	18,169,951	420
	Saskatchewan	527,090	398,091	925,181	93,924	64,415,518	687
	Alberta	488,733	843,211	1,331,944	73,212	47,228,653645	
	Total	1,348,702	1,830,109	3,178,811	210,442	129,814,122	617
1966	Manitoba	317,018	646,048	963,066	39,747	19,083,817	480
	Saskatchewan	487,017	468,327	955,344	85,686	65,409,363	763
	Alberta	455,796	1,007,407	1,463,203	69,411	48,982,875	706
	Total	1,259,831	2,121,782	3,381,613	194,844	133,476,055	685
1971	Manitoba	301,800	686,445	988,245	34,981	19,008,259	543
	Saskatchewan	435,610	490,635	926,245	76,970	65,056,875	845
	Alberta	431,625	1,196,250	1,627,875	62,702	49,506,287	790
	Total	1,169,035	2,373,330	3,542,365	174,653	133,571,421	765

Appendix B

Chicago Tribune
Sunday, June 29, 1975

Bribery, short-weighting

Grain exports seed a scandal

By Richard Orr

A NEW Orleans woman tells a newsman: "My husband would wind up in the river, I'd be a widow and my children would be fatherless if he ever tells what he knows."

A New Orleans man, hearing that hired killers are looking for him, reportedly has left his family for their own safety, gone into hiding, and drives his car with a revolver in his lap.

Another New Orleans man reportedly is frightened by rumors that a "contract" is out to disable him by breaking both his kneecaps.

SUCH FEARS and rumors, whether real or imagined, do not involve some gangland dispute. They reflect heightening tensions generated by an intensive federal investigation of an unfolding scandal involving the handling, weighing, and grading of billions of dollars' worth of grain at some of the nation's major grain-exporting ports.

Evidence that has become public thus far reveals a sordid story of corruption that includes alleged bribery, payoffs, grain-theft rings, adulteration and misgrading of grain, short-weighting of cargoes, and falsification of grading certificates and other docu-

Richard Orr is The Tribune's rural affairs editor.

ments. While the investigation has centered on the ports of New Orleans and Houston thus far, it is also being conducted at other East and West Coast ports.

The scandal has serious implications, both for hundreds of thousands of Midwest farmers who produce grain for export and scores of their customers in countries abroad who complain they are not getting the quality and quantity of grain they pay for. It also affects employment of hundreds of thousands of Americans in agriculture-related jobs as well as consumers who depend on American farmers for full food production.

Six European grain company executives were in the United States recently seeking answers to their questions about adulteration and low quality of grain exports from this country. Said Bill Duncan of Ireland, a director of Unilever, Ltd., a conglomerate corporation:

"Our main concern is trying to get what we pay for. You may not realize how important this is to the United States. You and your farmers are losing a major market. A lot of mistrust is building up."

AT STAKE, basically, is the United States' reputation as a reliable supplier of grain and soybeans, vital commodities in this country's foreign exchange.

The agencies trying to unravel the

scandal are the United States Department of Agriculture's Office of Investigations, the Federal Bureau of Investigation, the Internal Revenue Service, and United States attorneys and local law officials in the various port cities. A Senate subcommittee on foreign agriculture policy under Sen. Hubert Humphrey [D., Minn.] has been holding hearings.

The investigation began in September, 1973, according to Department of Agriculture officials, but became public only a few weeks ago. Domestically, one aspect of the inquiry includes the possibility that organized crime may be involved.

Investigators h a v e also traveled abroad to gather evidence in other countries, including Spain and the Soviet Union.

Since last August, 20 individuals and firms have been indicted, including 15 in New Orleans and five in Houston. They include 14 federally licensed grain inspectors and samplers indicted on charges of bribery; a ship cleaning company and its president, and another company and three employes on various charges, including false statements to a grand jur yand fraudulent manpulation of soybean sales. Nine of the indicted have already been convicted.

One of the indicted grain inspectors is the husband of the New Orleans woman mentioned at the start of this story. The two New Orleans men men-

tioned are respectively former and current grain inspectors. Their identities are withheld to protect their safety.

The widening probe was disclosed recently to have expanded to two of the world's largest grain-exporting companies and the American subsidiary of an Italian-owned firm. The two big grain companies are Bunge Corp. and Cook Industries, Inc.

The third firm is Mississippi River Valley Grain Elevator, Inc., owned by Serafino Ferruzzi of Ravenna, Italy. The three firms have denied any wrongdoing.

None of the indicted grain inspectors, samplers, or firms is a federal employe. Grain inspectors are licensed by the Department of Agriculture's Marketing Service, but they work for department-designated, nonfederal agencies. These agencies may be operated by state governments, local boards of trade, or private individuals and organizations.

Under the U.S. Grain Standards Act, original federal inspection and grading of grain in the United States is prohibited. Federal employes do, however, perform appeal inspections and supervise the inspection activities of licensees.

SEN. DICK Clark [D., Ia.], a member of the Senate foreign relations policy subcommittee, has charged there is a "pervasive system" of cash kick-

Continued on following page

The spreading roots of the scandal in

Grain grading

To measure and maintain standards of quality, grains are graded in various grades. Grading also helps determine prices. Starting with the best quality and highest priced grain as No. 1, the grades go down thru No. 2, No. 3, No. 4, No. 5, and sample grade, the lowest.

Department of Agriculture regulations specify precise requirements as to the test weight, moisture content, foreign matter, and kernel damage that can be permitted for each grade. For example, No. 1 corn must have a minimum test weight of 56 pounds per bushel, no more than 14 per cent moisture content, and no more than 2 per cent foreign matter [dust, chaff, bits of corn cobs, etc.] and 1 per cent damaged kernels.

It is the job of federally licensed grain inspectors to determine these various grades as grain comes into elevators or is loaded onto ships for export. The inspector does this by using a device called a probe to gather a uniform sample of a shipment of grain.

Continued from first Perspective page

backs involving inspectors and other employes of major grain exporting firms. He explains some aspects of the scandal this way:

"As I understand the practice, a company owning the grain elevator will pay its operators an annual bonus for grain that they have been able to save by 'shaving' on reported shipments . . . They can tip the scales, mix or blend beyond what is acceptable under U.S. standards.

"They can misrepresent loading so that either the night or day shifts in the elevators are totally confused; or they can bribe the agency and, perhaps, even the federal inspector to misgrade the grain going out of their elevators.

"Regardless of the methods used, the net result is excess stock which is cream off the top."

Both Clark and Humphrey have called on Earl Butz, the secretary of agriculture, to explain why his department "has not followed up on these foreign complaints" of off-quality and off-weight grain shipments.

Humphrey asserts that foreign-buyer complaints against the quality of American grain go back to early 1969 when "serious charges were made by European customers about bribery and fraudulent issuance of inspection certificates."

To such charges Butz replies that the indictments against 14 federally licensed inpectors and samplers comprise only 7 per cent of the 200 licensed inspectors and samplers on duty at the ports. He maintains that the "vast majority of the inspectors and samplers at these ports are hard-working, honest, dependable people," and that the publicity surrounding the investigation should be kept in this perspective.

"We've been taking every action possible for a year and a half, long before Sen. Humphrey saw a headline in it," says Butz. "The U.S. is the world's most dependable source of grain and agricultural products. Our inspections of grain exports, overall, are sound and dependable."

Farm exports account for the production of about one in four crop acres. Without exports, farmers could not earn the income they need to offset continually increasing costs of food production and make a reasonable profit.

GRAINS AND soybeans last year accounted for more than half of the more than $21 billion of America's agricultural exports. Such exports create vital foreign exchange to help pay for the oil, electronic goods, autos, and a wide assortment of other imported consumer items used by domestic consumers.

Agricultural exports also create jobs. The Department of Agriculture estimates that one of every eight farm jobs—more than 475,000—depends on exports of grains and other farm commodities.

In addition, in the nonagricultural segment of the economy 450,000 jobs are dependent on assembling, processing, and distributing agricultural exports.

grain exports

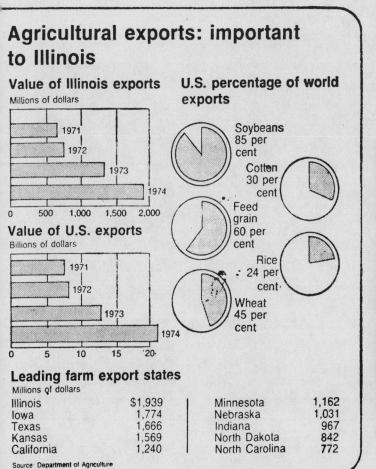

Agricultural exports: important to Illinois

Value of Illinois exports
Millions of dollars

1971
1972
1973
1974

0   500   1,000   1,500   2,000

Value of U.S. exports
Billions of dollars

1971
1972
1973
1974

0   5   10   15   20

U.S. percentage of world exports

Soybeans
85 per
cent

Cotton
30 per
cent

Feed
grain
60 per
cent

Rice
24 per
cent

Wheat
45 per
cent

Leading farm export states
Millions of dollars

Illinois	$1,939	Minnesota	1,162
Iowa	1,774	Nebraska	1,031
Texas	1,666	Indiana	967
Kansas	1,569	North Dakota	842
California	1,240	North Carolina	772

Source: Department of Agriculture

Tribune Graphics

151

INDEX

Index numbers refer to the item numbers.

Grain Growers' Export Company, 189.

Grain Growers' Grain Company, formation, 137; membership on Winnipeg Grain Exchange, 138; expelled from Winnipeg Grain Exchange, 139; reinstated on Winnipeg Grain Exchange, 143; selling agent for Saskatchewan Co-operative Elevator Company on exchange, 185; lease elevators from Manitoba Government, 191; establishment of elevator department, 196; farm supply warehouse, 220.

Grain Growers' Guide, on co-op legislation, 87/169; establishment of paper, 153; on Dominion Retail Merchants Association regarding co-op whole-sale, 213; on Federal Legislation for co-ops, 229; response to World War I, 231; response to War Income Tax, 250.

Grand Territorial Lodge, 99.

Grosilliers, Medart Chauart, 4.

H

Hamiota Co-operative, 223.

Harmona Industrial Association, 101.

Harris, Loyd, 169.

Haslam, J.H., 206.

Hawkes, John, 62/86/99/106.

Hendry, Anthony, 6.

Hind, Henry, 37.

Homestead Act, 59.

Houghman, George, 457.

Hudson's Bay Railway, plans for railway to Hudson's Bay, 71; Ottawa endorsement, 102; construction, 218/352; completion, 373; promote use of route, 679.

I

Immigration, government encouraged, 92; Western Canadian settlement, 107.

Indian Head, 116.

Interprovincial Co-operatives Limited, involvement with Consumer Co-operative Refineries, 448; Jute bag factories, 553/680; flour distribution, 573; food processing, 592; cannery, 612/653;

chemical plant, 620/841; membership 633/779; fertilizer, 637; Co-op tires, 642; pesticide plant, 727; future trends, 911.

Interprovincial Council of Grain Growers, 176.

Interprovincial Honey Sales Co-operative Limited, formation, 652.

J

Jewish Lithuanian Credit Union, 179.

K

Keen, George, response to War Income Tax, 251; on credit unions, 398.

Keenozoe Co-operative Limited, 907.

Kelly, Oliver Hudson, 49.

King, Prime Minister William Lyon Mackenzie, 286.

L

La Caisse Centrale de St. Boniface, incorporation, 607.

La Caisse Populaire d'Albertville, 239.

Lacombe Farmers Association, 125.

Lampman Grain Growers Co-op. 224.

Laurier, Prime Minister Sir Wilfred, reciprocity issue, 103; legislation re co-operative societies, 172; compulsory military services act, 246.

Lebel, Rev. Fr. Albert, 239.

Legislation-Co-operatives; Act Respecting Co-operative Legislation, 87/145/147/148/173. Agricultural Co-operative Associations Act, 288; Alberta Co-operative Associations Act, 209; Alberta Pharmacy Act, 524/815; Co-operative Associations Act, 338/638/639; Co-operative Farm Act, 510; Co-operative Guarantee Act, 539; Federal Co-operative Act, 728/809/892; Incorporation of Co-operative Societies, 167/207; Manitoba Companies Act, 386; Manitoba Registrar of Co-operative Associations, 237; Saskatchewan Co-operative Creameries Act, 249; Saskatchewan Co-operative Marketing Associations Act, 306.

Lemieux, Hon. R., 148.

Liquor, 5.

Liverpool Corn Exchange, 446.

Lower Inventories for Tomorrow (L.I.F.T.) 887.

Louis XIV, King of France, 3/4.

Louisbourg, 7.

M

MacDonald, Prime Minister Sir John A., Canada West, 36; Confederation, 41; National Policy, 72; Territorial Council, 86; Protective Tariff, 98.

MacKenzie, Alexander, 14.

MacKenzie, Prime Minister Alexander, 69.

Manitoba, 69.

Manitoba Central Credit Union, 497.

Manitoba Co-operative Dairy Association, 279.

Manitoba Co-operative Honey Producers, formation, 905; Clover Crest, 436.

Manitoba Co-operative Poultry Marketing Association, 305.

Manitoba Co-operative Services Branch, formation, 580.

Manitoba Co-operative Society, incorporation, 87.

Manitoba Co-operative Wheat Producers, incorporated, 301; charges of mismanagement, 368.

Manitoba Co-operative Wholesale, formation, 331; effects of Depression, 359, petroleum co-ops, 374, grocery wholesaling, 516; dry goods 559; coal mining, 559; bulk petroleum distribution 577; lumber department, 621.

"Manitoba Co-operator", 488.

Manitoba Department of Co-operative Development, formation 930; Co-operative Curriculum Project, 955; fishing co-operatives, 979.

Manitoba Farm Bureau, formation, 805.

Manitoba Federation of Agriculture, (formerly Canadian Chamber of Agriculture, Western Section), 433/521/686.

Manitoba Grain Growers' Association, formation, 124; approval of grain marketing co-ops, 136; publicly owned elevators, 177; Brandon Conference on Buying, 200.

Index numbers refer to the item numbers.

V

Vanguard Co-operative Supply Company, 228.

Vegreville, 215.

Vote, Manitoba women enfranchised, 243; Saskatchewan women enfranchised, 244; Alberta women enfranchised, 245.

W

Walter, L.J., 288.

Wasagaming Foundation, 806.

Western Co-operative College, 713; new facilities, 767.

Western Co-operative Fertilizers Limited, formation, 788; completion, 811.

Western Grain Elevator Association, 935.

"Western Producer", 372.

Westland Co-operatives, formation, 974.

Westminster Conference, 45.

White Paper on Taxation, formation, 882; report, 891.

Wholesale Grocers' Guild, 171.

Winnipeg Co-operative Association, 82.

Winnipeg Co-operative Society, 197.

Winnipeg Co-operative Trading Association, incorporation, 87.

Winnipeg Daily Sun, 82.

Winnipeg Grain Exchange, formation, 90; incorportion, 97; E.A. Partridge, 131; selling agent for Grain Growers' Grain Company, 138; regulations, 166; World War 1, 252; actions by federal government, 267; resumes operations, 275; activity during World War II, 446,

Winnipeg Retail Co-operative, 197.

Wolfe, General George, 7.

Woodsworth, J.S., 389.

World War II, 445.

X

Xcan Grain Limited, formation, 888; foreign wheat markets, 919; flour mill in Venezuela, 937; on grain marketing, 966; relationship with Pools and United Grain Growers' Limited, 997.

Y

Young, Brigham, 57.

Z

Zion's Co-operative Mercantile Institute, 57.

Index Of Photographs And Illustrations